MW00526960

The International Critical Commentary on the Holy Scriptures of the Old and New Testaments.

UNDER THE EDITORSHIP OF

THE REV. SAMUEL ROLLES DRIVER, D.D.,
Regius Professor of Hebrew, Oxford;

THE REV. ALFRED PLUMMER, M.A., D.D.,
Master of University College, Durham;

AND

THE REV. CHARLES AUGUSTUS BRIGGS, D.D.,
Edward Robinson Professor of Biblical Theology, Union Theological Seminary, New York.

THE EPISTLES TO THE PHILIPPIANS AND TO PHILEMON

Rev. MARVIN R. VINCENT, D.D.

THE INTERNATIONAL CRITICAL COMMENTARY

A

CRITICAL AND EXEGETICAL COMMENTARY

ON THE

EPISTLES TO THE PHILIPPIANS AND TO PHILEMON

BY

REV. MARVIN R. VINCENT, D.D.
BALDWIN PROFESSOR OF SACRED LITERATURE IN UNION THEOLOGICAL SEMINARY, NEW YORK

EDINBURGH:
T. & T. CLARK, 38 GEORGE STREET

PRINTED IN THE UNITED KINGDOM BY
PAGE BROS (NORWICH) LTD.,
BOUND BY HUNTER & FOULIS LTD., EDINBURGH
FOR
T. & T. CLARK LTD., EDINBURGH

0 567 05031 9

LATEST IMPRESSION 1985

PREFACE

THE two epistles treated in this volume have always had a peculiar attraction for both readers and expositors. On the Epistle to the Philippians more than a hundred commentaries have been produced, some of them by scholars of the first rank. It would be strange, therefore, if this work did not contain a great deal which has appeared elsewhere; and I am sure that the call for its publication has not arisen from the deficiencies of my predecessors.

I find, nevertheless, some satisfaction in the thought that the knowledge of any subject is promoted, in however small a degree, by the independent and honest treatment of each new expositor, who, by approaching his work from a different direction, seeing his material at a different angle and in the light of the most recent criticism, and shifting the points of emphasis, may reawaken attention to what is already familiar, and thus stimulate inquiry if he does not widen the sphere of knowledge.

The main object in this commentary has been to exhibit St. Paul's thought in these two letters which I am fully convinced are from his pen. To this end all comment — grammatical and lexical as well as exegetical — has been directed, and special care has been given, to the paraphrases with which the several sections are prefaced, and to the illustration of the apostle's nervous and picturesque diction upon which the marks of his personality are so deeply set. The theological bearings of certain passages it is manifestly impossible to overlook; and the student is entitled to demand of the commentator such notice and treatment of these as are consistent with the recognised difference between a commentary and a theological treatise. To such passages I trust that I have brought no dogmatic bias to prevent or to modify the application of strict exegetical principles.

I am conscious of the difficulties which attach, at certain points, to all attempts to place the Philippian letter in its complete and truthful historical setting. These difficulties are inevitable in the present fragmentary and limited state of our knowledge concerning some conditions of the Roman and Philippian churches which are presupposed in the epistle, so that whatever conclusions may be reached by the most conscientious study will awaken question and criticism.

I have had constantly in view the fact that these two letters are familiar and informal productions, and have allowed that fact due weight in the exegesis. Epistolary colloquialisms present serious difficulties to an interpreter who refuses to recognise them, and who insists upon the rigid application of rhetorical, logical, and dogmatic canons to the unstudied and discursive effusions of the writer's heart.

In seeking to avoid the *selva selvaggia* of technical discussion which impairs the value of some most important works of this class, I have not felt bound to go to the opposite extreme of dogmatic conciseness. A brief discussion has sometimes seemed necessary; but, as a rule, I have given my own interpretation with the reasons for it at the beginning of each note, appending a simple statement of different views with the names of those who hold them.

I avail myself of this opportunity to acknowledge gratefully my obligations to previous workers in this field, and not least to some of those from whom I have often had occasion to differ.

MARVIN R. VINCENT.

UNION THEOLOGICAL SEMINARY, NEW YORK.

CONTENTS

THE EPISTLE OF ST. PAUL TO THE PHILIPPIANS

INTRODUCTION

I

MACEDONIA

In the earliest times, Macedonia was included in that vast region called Thrace, which had no definite boundaries, but was regarded as comprising all that part of Europe lying to the north of Greece.

The original seats of the Macedonians were bounded on the west by the chain of Scardus, the northerly continuation of Pindus; on the south by the Cambunian Mountains which formed the northwestern boundary of Thessaly; on the east by Mt. Bermius. The northern boundary cannot be determined. The original Macedonia, therefore, did not reach the sea.

The country included within these boundaries is mountainous; but between the lateral ridges connecting with the main line of Scardus were three wide alluvial basins, two of which were possessed by the original Macedonians. The territory was fertile, affording abundant pasture and cornland. The inhabitants of the mountains and of the plains acknowledged a common ethnical name, though distinguished from each other by local titles. Their language differed from those of the Illyrians, Thracians, and Greeks. The different sections, at first distinct and independent, were finally absorbed into one under the name of Macedonia, having its centre at Ægæ or Edessa, the modern Vodhena, which, according to Phrygian legends, was the site of the gardens of Midas. Edessa was always retained as the royal burying-place, and was regarded as the religious centre of the nation.

Such was the position of the Macedonians in the seventh century B.C. It was changed by a family of exiled Greeks of the Herakleid or Temenid race of Argos (Hdt. viii. 137, 138). According to Herodotus, Perdiccas was the founder of the new Macedonian dynasty; and he gives a list of five successive kings from Perdiccas to Alexander, the son of Amyntas (B.C. 520–500). During the reigns of Amyntas and Alexander, Macedonia became implicated with the affairs of Greece. The Temenid kings extended their dominions on all sides. Among their conquests was Pieria, between Mt. Bermius and the sea, which gave them the command of a part of the coast of the Thermaic Gulf.

Philip, the father of Alexander the Great, ascended the Macedonian throne B.C. 360. He subjugated the Pæonians and Illyrians, recovered Amphipolis, and gained possession of Pydna, Potidæa, and Krenides, into which last-named place he introduced colonists and named it, after himself, Philippi. By the battle of Chæronea (B.C. 338), he became master of all Greece. At his death Macedonia had become a compact empire. Its boundaries had been extended as far as the Propontis, and from the coast of the Propontis to the Ionian Sea, and the Ambracian, Messenian, and Saronic gulfs.

His son Alexander succeeded him B.C. 336. The victory over the Persians at the Granicus in Troas (B.C. 334) was followed by the submission of nearly all Asia Minor. The campaign against the Persians ended in the battles of Issus (B.C. 333) and Arbela (B.C. 331), which decided the fate of the Persian Empire and were followed by the submission of Syria and Phœnicia. Passing into Egypt, he founded Alexandria, and carried his conquests into the far East, where Babylon, Susa, Persepolis, and Pasargadæ fell into his hands. This wonderful campaign closed B.C. 327, by which time his design had become manifest to combine Macedonia, Greece, and the East into one vast empire. The execution of this plan was cut short by his death (B.C. 323). The ultimate bearing of Alexander's conquests upon the diffusion of Christianity is familiar to every student.

After Alexander's death the Macedonian empire fell into the hands of his principal generals, and after a series of wars extending over twenty-two years, it was broken into three great states, — Macedonia, Egypt, and Syria.

Macedonia was first brought into contact with Rome through the Carthaginian victories at Trasimene and Cannæ (B.C. 217, 216). Philip, the son of Demetrius, then king of Macedonia, sent to Hannibal proffering his alliance; and a treaty was concluded a year later. The result of this treaty was the first Macedonian war with Rome, which was terminated by the treaty of Dyrrhachium (B.C. 205). A second war followed, which ended in the annihilation of the Macedonian army at Cynocephalæ (B.C. 197). A peace was concluded which destroyed the political standing of the Macedonians, and by which all the states which had previously been subject to Philip were declared free.

Philip was succeeded by his son Perseus, whose efforts against Eumenes of Pergamus, the ally of the Romans, brought on a third war (B.C. 171). The Macedonians experienced a crushing defeat at Pydna (B.C. 168), by the Roman army under Lucius Æmilius Paullus. The whole country was divided into four districts (Livy, xlv. 29), each of which was to constitute a separate republic; but the citizens of each were forbidden to form any commercial or connubial relations with those of any of the others. Thus perished the empire of Alexander the Great, a hundred and forty-four years after his death. The isolation of Macedonia was secured, while the people were amused with a show of liberty.

Two claimants for the Macedonian throne, both professing to be sons of Perseus, successively attempted to stir the Macedonians to revolt. The Achæans broke with Rome. L. Mummius was sent to Greece B.C. 146, and burned the city of Corinth. By the commission which arrived from Rome soon after, all Greece south of Macedonia and Epirus was formed into a Roman province under the name of Achaia, and Macedonia with Epirus into another province.

Upon the succession of Augustus the provinces were divided between the emperor and the senate (B.C. 27; see Suet. *Augustus*, 47). The provinces which enjoyed absolute peace were assigned to the senate, while the frontier provinces, which required military force, fell to the emperor. Augustus thus strengthened his own military power, under pretence of relieving the senate of the cares and dangers of the empire.

The governors of the senatorial provinces were called proconsuls. Their term of office was one year. They had no military authority, and therefore no power of life or death over the soldiers in their provinces. The full title of governors of the imperial provinces was "Legatus Augusti pro Praetore." They were appointed by the emperor, and their term of office depended upon his pleasure. Their long residence made them familiar with the country and the people. There were fewer temptations to peculation, and the imperial provinces were so much better governed than the senatorial, that the people of the latter sometimes petitioned to be transferred to imperial supervision; especially as the expenses of proconsular administration were paid by the provinces, and the proconsuls were able to practise sundry abuses by which the amounts were increased. Macedonia and Achaia, which originally fell to the senate, were, at their own request, made imperial provinces by Tiberius (Tac. *Ann.* i. 76). By Claudius they were again placed under the senate (Suet. *Claud.* 25).

LITERATURE

BIBLIOGRAPHY OF THE HISTORY OF ALEXANDER

C. MÜLLER: *Fragmenta Historicorum Graecorum*, 1841.

A. SCHÄFER u. H. NISSEN: *Abriss der Quellenkunde der griech. u. röm. Geschichte*, 1885–1889.

FABRICIUS: *Bibliotheca Graeca.*

J. G. DROYSEN: *Die Materialien zur Geschichte Alexanders.*

A. FRÄNKEL: *Die Quellen der Alexandergeschichte*, 1883.

J. KAERST: *Forschungen zur Gesch. d. Alex. d. Gr.*, 1887.

Fragments of lost writers collected by R. GEIER: *Scriptores Historiarum Alex. Mag. aetate suppares*, 1844; and

C. MÜLLER: *Scriptores Rerum Alex. Mag.*, 1846.

FOR THE ROMAN PERIOD

POLYBIUS: covering 220–144 B.C.

DIODORUS SICULUS: Βιβλιοθήκη Ἱστορική, B. xi.–xx., from the second Persian war (B.C. 480) to B.C. 302.

LIVY: B. xxxi.–xlv. (201–167 B.C.).

TEUFFEL: *Gesch. d. röm. Lit.*, 5 Aufl., 1890.

G. HERZBERG: *Gesch. Griechenlands unter der Herrschaft der Römer*, 1886.

W. SCHOEN: *Gesch. Griechenlands von der Entstehung des ätolischen und achäischen Bundes bis auf die Zerstörung Korinths*, 1883.

HISTORY OF ALEXANDER AND HIS SUCCESSORS

J. G. DROYSEN: *Gesch. Alex. d. Gr.*, 1833; *Gesch. des Hellenismus*, 1836, 1843. Comes down to B.C. 220. The two works in a 2d ed. under the title *Gesch. d. Hellenismus*, 1877, 1878.

B. NIESE: *Gesch. d. griech. u. maked. Staaten seit der Schlacht bei Chaeronea.* Pt. i. to B.C. 281. Good bibliography. 1893.

THIRLWALL: *Hist. Greece*, to B.C. 146. GROTE: to B.C. 301. CURTIUS: to B.C. 338.

G. FINDLAY: *Hist. Greece*, 1877. B. G. NIEBUHR: *Lectures on Anc. Hist.*; trans. by Schmitz; 1852.

E. A. FREEMAN: *Alex. G. and Greece during the Maced. Period*; review of Niebuhr. *Alex. G.*; review of Grote. *Historical Essays*, 2d ser.

ROMAN PROVINCIAL ADMINISTRATION

J. MARQUARDT: *Römische Staatsverwaltung*, 2 Aufl., 1881.

W. T. ARNOLD: *The Roman System of Provincial Administration to the Accession of Constantine the Great*, 1879.

TH. MOMMSEN: *The Provinces of the Roman Empire*; trans. by Dickson, 1886.

INSCRIPTIONS

"*Corpus*" *of Gk. and Rom. Insc., Berlin Akad.*; supplemented by the Collection of LE BAS-WADDINGTON, *Voyage Archéologique en Grèce et en Asie Mineure*, 1847.

Later and more complete Berlin Collection, 1877–1883.

A. J. LETRONNE: *Recueil des Inscr. Grecques et Latines de l'Egypte*, 1842.

Collection of Ancient Greek Inscr. in Brit. Mus., 1874.

E. L. HICKS: *A Manual of Greek Historical Inscr.*, 1882.

COINS

J. H. ECKHEL: *Doctrina Numorum Veterum*, 1792–1798.

MIONNET: *Description de Médailles Antiques Grecques et Romaines*, 1806.

B. V. HEAD: *Historia Numorum*, 1887.

II

PHILIPPI

The district occupied by Philippi was originally called Krenides, 'Little Fountains' (Strabo, 331; Appian, *Bell. Civ.* iv. 105), from the numerous springs which arose in the mountains on the north, and ran into the neighboring marsh.

According to Appian (*Bell. Civ.* iv. 105), Krenides was also known as Datos or Daton. This statement has been too hastily set down as an error, largely on the authority of Leake (*N. Greece*, iii. 223. See Lightf., *Philip.*, p. 47; Rawlinson, *Herodotus*, on ix. 75). It appears that Daton was a Thasian town near the Strymonic Gulf, and was the centre of the continental possessions of the Thasians. According to Strabo (vii. frag. 36), Neapolis was a dependency of Daton. The name of the town passed into a proverb, as a place endowed with all good things. The probability is that the first Thasian colony of Daton originally extended up to the plain of Krenides, and included it in its territory, but had fallen into the hands of the northern barbarians. About 360 B.C. the Thasians, aided by the banished Athenian orator Callistratus, with some Athenian adventurers, founded a new colony at Krenides under the old name. The year 360, which followed the arrival of Callistratus at Thasos, is noted by Diod. Sic. (xvi. 3) as the date of the occupation of the mines of Krenides by the Thasians. It is an interesting fact that the coins struck by the Thasians on the occasion of reviving the mines of Krenides, and which bore the head of the Thasian Hercules, the tripod (the symbol of foundation) and the legend ΘΑΣΙΩΝ ΗΠΕΙΡΟ, were preserved by the city of Philippi with only a change of inscription (see Heuzey and Daumet, *Mission Archéologique de Macédoine*, p. 60 ff. Comp. Curtius, *Hist. Greece*, Trans. v. 53).

The site was between the rivers Strymon and Nestus, and answered, geographically, to the basin of the Angites (Hdt. vii. 113), which issued from the right bank of the Strymon, and formed, two leagues from the sea, the lake Kerkinitis. The basin might rather be described as a plain, now known as the plain of Drama, and framed on every side by mountains. The vast masses of Pangæus separated it from the sea; but at one point the range was depressed, affording easy access to the gulf where now the Turkish harbor of Kavala, the ancient Neapolis, opens, opposite to the island of Thasos.

Thrace contained rich deposits of gold. Golden particles from Hæmus were borne down by the waters of the Hebrus, and the Pæonian laborers, according to Strabo (vii. frag. 35), turned them up with their ploughshares. But the treasures of Pangæus and of the mountains adjoining Krenides surpassed all others in richness. Gold-mining was the principal industry of the region for a long series of years; and from the time that the treasures of the mountains were first brought to light by the Phœnicians, they played an important part in the history of the northern kingdoms. The feverish greed for gain did not promote the advance of civilisation; agricultural and commercial interests suffered, and the rapacity of foreign invaders was stimulated.

The Thasians, at the instigation of Callistratus, in the year before the accession of Philip of Macedon, penetrated into the interior to the plain of the Angites, and revived Krenides as a centre of mining operations. But the assaults of the Thracians upon the new colony soon compelled it to seek the assistance of Philip. He drove back the Thracians, annexed to Macedonia all the country as far as the Nestus, and built a fortress which became the centre of the mining district. He also gave the place his own name, Philippi. The plural form of the name seems to indicate that the new town, at the time when it fell into his hands, was composed of several distinct groups of dwellings defended by detached works for the protection of the miners, and not by a common and continuous enceinte. A fort on the hill which commanded the defile was a necessity. Under the protection of this work it was sufficient to bar the defile by a temporary wall in order to allow an important group of dwellings to be erected at the foot of the rocks. Philip improved the region, drying up the marshes and laying out roads, and Theophrastus (*Causae Plantarum*, v. 14) relates that by these works the climate was perceptibly modified.

The gold-mining industry yielded to Philip an annual revenue of a thousand talents, — a treasure which furnished him with the means of establishing and maintaining a navy, and which was quite as potent as his army in securing the future triumphs of Macedonia. "The gold of Krenides spread itself over Greece, preceding the phalanx like an advance-guard, and opening more gates than the battering-rams and catapults" (Heuzey).

On the mines, see Curtius, *Hist. Greece*, v. 52; Appian, *Bell. Civ.*, iv. 106; Boeckh, *Public Economy of Athens;* Heuzey and Daumet, *Mission Archéologique*. See especially their interesting description of the rock formations of Philippi, and the comparison with the auriferous rocks of California (p. 55 ff.). On mining under the Romans, Marquardt, *Röm. Staatsverwaltung*, Bd. ii. 245, 252–258.

The Romans became masters of this region upon the defeat of the Republican forces under Brutus and Cassius by Octavianus and Antony (B.C. 42). Philippi was the scene of the final conflict. The Republicans occupied two hills facing the town to the south-east, while the triumviral army was posted in the open plain. Two battles were fought: the first indecisive, resulting in the death of Cassius; the second, twenty days later, which decided the fate of the republic.

The sojourn of Octavianus at Philippi revealed to him its importance both as a military position and as a source of revenue. After his victory, and in commemoration of it, he made Philippi a military colony, and bestowed upon it the *jus Italicum*. The inscription COHOR. PRAE. PHIL. found on little copper coins of Philippi goes to show that this colony was originally composed of a division of veterans belonging to the prætorian cohorts of the triumvirate. It bore the name COLONIA JULIA AUGUSTA VICTRIX PHILIPPENSIUM. The colony was not a mere town with its outskirts, but a great department, with boroughs and secondary towns, of which Philippi was the administrative centre. The Romans succeeded the Macedonians in the working of the mines, but never made them as profitable as the Macedonians had done.

Communities in the Roman provinces were either *municipia* (free towns) or *coloniae* (colonies). The colony represented transplanted citizenship, while the *municipium* was engrafted upon the state. A provincial town became a *municipium* when its inhabitants received the Roman franchise, and a constitution from a Roman governor or commissioner. At the time of the Republic, and among the Italian cities, the *municipia* were the more important; but in the imperial period the colonies outranked them. Extraordinary privileges were mostly, if not exclusively, confined to the colonies. The principal of these privileges was the *jus Italicum*, which was a grant to the community, not to individuals, and consisted in the right of proprietorship according to the Roman civil status. This right involved the acquisition of ownership by long use or prescription (*usucapio*); the right of transferring ownership by a fictitious suit (*in jure cessio*); the right of the purchase or transfer of property (*mancipatio*), and the right of civil action or lawsuit (*vindicatio*). As, according to Roman law, landed property in Italy was exempt from taxation, the *jus Italicum* conferred the same immunity upon provincial land. The right was never given except to a colony; but all colonies did not possess it, and when they did not, the colonists were subjected to both a poll-tax and a land-tax.

A colony was a miniature Rome. The colonists proceeded to their destination under their standards, and marked out with the plough the limits of the new city. The land was divided into sections of two hundred acres, which were subdivided into lots (*sortes*), and in military colonies these were apportioned according to rank. Even in the form and appearance of the city the mother-city was imitated. The coinage bore Roman inscriptions. The colonies were free from any intrusion by the governor of the province. Their affairs were regulated by their own magistrates called *Duumviri*, who delighted to style themselves *Praetores* (στρατηγοί). The officers of Philippi are referred to by Luke under this title (Acts xvi. 20–38).

On colonies see Marquardt, *Röm. Staatsverwaltung*, Bd. i. 360 ff.; Savigny, *Gesch. des röm. Rechts*; 'Coloni,' in *Philological Museum*, ii. 117; Walther, *Gesch. des röm. Rechts*; Arnold, *Roman Provincial Administration*. Good summaries in Conybeare and Howson's *Life and Epistles of St. Paul*, ch. ix., and Lewin, *Life and Eps. of St. P.*, ch. xi.

The name Philippi was long preserved in the village of Filibedjik or Filibat, but has now disappeared. The only inhabited place near the enceinte of Philippi is the village of Ratchka, half hidden in a ravine of the mountain a little on one side of the ancient acropolis. In the higher town, which represents the ancient Macedonian city, an enclosure of rough stones preserves traces of the Hellenic wall. The whole plain at the foot of the mountains is covered with ruins. The circular outline of the theatre on the steep slope of the acropolis facing Pangæus may still be seen. The neighboring rocks are covered with numerous pious inscriptions, and with images of the deities venerated by the colonists, together with the names of their worshippers. At the foot of these rocks are vestiges of a temple of Silvanus, one of the deities most revered by the Romans of the imperial period, as the guardian of plantations, as one of the household gods, and as the protector of the empire and of the emperor. His worship extended everywhere over the provinces. Two large statues of this deity have been discovered, one of which appears to have been the image worshipped in the sanctuary of the temple; also tablets containing lists of offerings for the construction and decoration of the temple, and of the names of the members of the sacred college. Among these names are some which are familiar to the readers of the Acts and Pauline epistles; as Crescens, Secundus, Trophimus, Pudens, etc. In the lower town is found a ruin known by the Turks as *Dérékler* or 'the columns,' consisting of a portion of a wall and four massive columns, and which cannot be identified. It is supposed to have been a public bath. Lewin (*Life and Eps. etc.*, i. 211) says, without any authority for the statement, that this was the forum where the apostles were scourged.

See the *Mission Archéologique de Macédoine* by Heuzey and Daumet, one of the most interesting and important of modern contributions to the study of the history and antiquities of Macedonia. The expedition was undertaken in 1861 under the auspices of Napoleon III.

III

PAUL IN MACEDONIA

Philip and Alexander, Æmilius, Mummius, and Octavianus had thus prepared the way for Paul. According to the account in Acts xvi., Paul, at Alexandria Troas, saw in a vision a Macedonian man who said to him, "Come over to Macedonia and help us."

Professor Ramsay (*St. Paul, the Traveller and the Roman Citizen*, p. 201) says that Paul did not infer the Macedonian origin of the man in the dream from his words, but recognised him as a Macedonian by sight; and since the Macedonians dressed like Greeks, it follows that the man in the vision was personally known to him. Professor R. also holds with Renan (*St. Paul*, ch. v.) that Luke was a Macedonian. I do not know the grounds of his statement that it has been generally recognised that Luke must have had some connection with Philippi. In our ignorance of Luke's antecedents the possibility of his having been a Macedonian cannot be denied.

Paul, therefore, embarked at Troas with Luke, Timothy, and Silvanus (Acts xv. 49, xvi. 1, 3. Comp. Acts xvi. 8, 10), and landing at Neapolis, proceeded over Mt. Pangæus, about eight miles, to Philippi, by a branch of the great *Via Egnatia*.

See Renan's beautiful description of the route (*St. Paul*, ch. vi.). Cousinéry (*Voyage dans la Macédoine*) and Tafel (*De Via Militari Romanorum*

Egnatia) have endeavored unsuccessfully to identify the site of Neapolis with Eski Kavala, fifteen miles S.W. of Kavala.

With the arrival of Paul at Neapolis the gospel first entered Europe. Yet the apostle was not consciously entering a new continent. The distinction between Europe and Asia did not exist for him. Asia, in the New Testament, denotes the Roman province of that name, and the word Europe does not occur. To St. Paul these later divisions represented only sections of the one Roman world.

In Acts xvi. 12, Philippi is described as ἥτις ἐστὶν πρώτη τῆς μερίδος Μακεδονίας πόλις κολωνία. There is probably an error in the text. To the epithet πρώτη explained as denoting the political rank of Philippi, it is objected that Thessalonica was the general capital, and that πρώτη, though common as an honorary title of cities in Asia, was not so used in Greece or Macedonia. Again, if μερὶς be explained as denoting one of the four districts into which Macedonia was divided by Æmilius, it may be replied that that division was made more than two hundred years before Paul's arrival, and continued for only twenty-two years to the time when the country was formed into a single province; so that the fourfold division had long been abandoned and was perhaps forgotten. Moreover, if this division had survived, the centre of this district would have been Amphipolis and not Philippi.

Even stronger are the objections against taking πρώτη to mean the first city which Paul reached in his Macedonian tour (so Erasm., Beng., Olsh., Lightf., and others). Philippi was not the first city of Macedonia at which Paul arrived. It cannot be shown that Neapolis was at this time regarded as a Thracian town (Lightf., *Phil.*, p. 50. See contr. Hort, *N. T. Notes on Select Readings*, ad loc.). Μερίδος, on this interpretation, is apparently superfluous; for Philippi was, in that case, regarded not as the first city of that district, but of all Macedonia. Neither ἥτις nor ἐστὶν suit this meaning, since both are used for characterising, and ἦν would probably have been chosen to mark a mere stage of the apostle's journey. Moreover, πρῶτος by itself never has the local sense. If there is no error in the text, πρώτη, I think, must denote rank; though, even if it were proved that Luke was a Macedonian, I should not be disposed to accept Professor Ramsay's view that Luke exaggerated the dignity of Philippi from pride in his own city (*St. Paul the Traveller*, etc., p. 206). Μερὶς, which does not mean 'province' (ἐπαρχία), may indicate some subdivision, not recognised in the formal political arrangement, of which Philippi was the centre; and πρώτη may mark an emphasis on its colonial rank as possessing the *jus Italicum* (note the emphatic position of κολωνία); so that Philippi is designated as the most considerable colonial city of this part of Macedonia, πόλις κολωνία being taken together. In this designation lies the motive expressed by ἥτις ἐστὶν, 'seeing it is,' — that the prominence of the city led Paul to choose it as the starting-point of his missionary work.

See Wendt's *Meyer on Acts* xvi. 12; Ramsay, *The Church in the Roman Empire*, p. 156 f.; O. Holtzmann, *Neutestamentliche Zeitgeschichte*, p. 104; Lightf., *Phil.*, p. 50.

The events of St. Paul's Macedonian ministry are related in Acts xvi., xvii. Imprisoned at Philippi, and then expelled by the magistrates, he went to Thessalonica, and thence to Berœa, from both which places he was driven by the fanatical opposition of the Jews. From Berœa he went to Athens.

The narrative in Acts is sketchy and full of movement, dwelling only upon salient points, and furnishing no definite information as to the length of the apostle's stay in Philippi. Slight hints like ἡμέρας τινάς (xvi. 12), and ἐπὶ πολλὰς ἡμέρας (xvi. 18), and the fact that some time must have been required to form a circle of "brethren" (xvi. 40), and to develop those strong and affectionate relations which appear in the Philippian letter, seem to indicate a longer stay than might be inferred from the surface of the narrative.

See Clemen, *Die Chronologie der paulinischen Briefe*, s. 192; Klöpper, *Komm. Einleit.*, S. 3.

From the dropping of the first person plural at Acts xvi. 40, it has been inferred that Luke remained behind in Philippi. About five years later the apostle again visited Macedonia, and having gone thence to Corinth, was about to return to Syria by sea, when a plot against his life determined him to return to Macedonia (Acts xix. 21, xx. 1–3; 2 Cor. i. 15, 17, ii. 13, vii. 5). The last meeting with his Philippian converts is noted (Acts xx. 6), after which he departed for Troas. This is our last notice of the Philippians until the time of the Roman imprisonment.

IV

PAUL AT ROME

After the shipwreck at Malta, Paul arrived at Rome in the spring of 56 A.D., during the reign of Nero (54–68). Burrhus, the prætorian prefect, a rough but kindly disposed soldier, extended to him every liberty which the law allowed; permitting him to occupy a lodging of his own under the charge of a prætorian soldier (Acts xxviii. 16), and allowing his friends and other visitors free access to him (Acts xxviii. 30).

I follow the chronology of Harnack, *Die Chronol. d. altchr. Lit. bis Eusebius*, Bd. i. S. 233. See also O. Holtzmann, *Neutest. Zeitgesch.* S. 132; and Prof. A. McGiffert, *Amer. Journ. Theol.* Jan. 1897, p. 147. Against these see Schürer, *Gesch. d. jüd. Volkes*, 2 Aufl. i. S. 483 ff. (Clarks' Trans. Divis. i. Vol. ii. p. 182), and Professor Ramsay, *Expositor*, May, 1896, p. 338, and April, 1897, p. 245 ff.

The church at Rome had been for some time in existence before the apostle's arrival, although we are ignorant of the circumstances of its foundation. In Acts xxviii. 15 its existence is assumed, and the company which meets Paul at Appii Forum has the character of a deputation. Nor is it likely that the church was insignificant either in numbers or influence, since the important letter to it, with its numerous salutations, was composed three or four years before his arrival at Rome.

His influence quickly made itself felt in the prætorian guard, and among his visitors from the city; and the brethren of the Roman church were stimulated to greater boldness and zeal in the proclamation of the gospel (Phil. i. 12–14). His presence and activity also stirred up certain hostile elements in the church itself; men who made the preaching of the gospel a means of promoting their own partisan interests, and of venting their envy and spite against the apostle. See on ch. i. 15, 16.

Paul's long detention before his trial was nothing unusual, as is shown by Josephus' account of some Jewish priests sent by Felix to Rome, who were not released for three years (Jos. *Vita*, 3). The delay may have been caused by the non-arrival of his prosecutors, and possibly by the loss in the shipwreck of the official record of the proceedings forwarded by Festus; although there was a law of Claudius which permitted the discharge of a prisoner if the prosecutors did not appear within a certain time (Di. Cass. lx. 28). The pressure of judicial business also was enormous: a long time might have been required for bringing witnesses from Syria and Proconsular Asia after the arrival of the prosecutors; and a vacation occurred during the winter months when judicial proceedings were suspended (Suet. *Aug.* 32; *Claud.* 23; *Galba*, 14).

See Wieseler, *Chron.*, and Geib, *Gesch. d. römischen Criminalprocess.*

V

EPISTLE TO THE PHILIPPIANS: WHERE AND WHEN COMPOSED

That the Philippian letter was written from Rome is now generally conceded. The view of Paulus (1799), Böttger (1837), Rilliet (1841), Thiersch (1879), placing its composition at Cæsarea, has been mostly abandoned, and even those who assign Colossians, Ephesians, and Philemon to Cæsarea, hold that Philippians was written at Rome. The environment of the apostle as indicated by the letter itself, the different groups of persons which it includes, the number and complexity of the relations, and the different and influential party tendencies do not suit the narrow limits of a provincial city; while the prætorian guard and the saints of Cæsar's household clearly point to Rome. Paul's expectation of a speedy decision of his case (ii. 23) agrees better with Rome. In i. 25, 27, ii. 24, he expresses the hope of returning to Philippi in the event of his liberation, while in Cæsarea he would still have been directing his thought to Rome.

The date of composition as related to that of the three Asiatic letters cannot be determined with certainty. The majority of critics assign the epistle to the later period of Paul's imprisonment, and place it last of the four (Mey., Weiss, Alf., Ellic., Kl., Godet, Lips., Holtzn., Jül.).

The reasons assigned for this opinion are the following: 1. The evidence assumed to be furnished by the epistle that a long period of imprisonment has elapsed (i. 12 ff.). 2. The abandonment of the apostle by his more intimate companions (ii. 20), and the absence of salutations from Luke and Aristarchus. 3. The time required for journeys in the communications between Rome and

Philippi implied in the letter. 4. A spirit of depression assumed to be manifest in the epistle, indicating a later stage of confinement and increased severity of treatment. 5. The expectation expressed of a speedy release.

Lightfoot's ingenious discussion (*Comm.* p. 30 ff.) does little more than to show the futility of these reasons. No decisive evidence of a long imprisonment is furnished by i. 12 ff. All the results detailed in i. 13–17 might easily have come to pass in a few months after the apostle's arrival, especially since he was in constant contact with the prætorian soldiers, the residents of the city had free access to him, and the church in Rome had been founded some years before. Our ignorance of the movements of his companions forbids any positive conclusions from the allusions in the letter. The statement in ii. 20, 21, is quite inexplicable (see note). The names of Luke and Aristarchus, which occur in Colossians and Philemon, are wanting in Ephesians, together with that of Timothy, and an argument from silence is in any case precarious. The tone of depression ascribed to the epistle is a pure fancy. The letter is preëminently joyful and hopeful. If the date assigned to St. Paul's arrival in Rome is correct, the events which are assumed to have increased the rigor of the apostle's treatment and thus to have depressed his spirits — the death of Burrhus, the accession of Tigellinus as prætorian prefect, and Nero's marriage to Poppæa — are too late. Poppæa's influence over Nero did not begin until 58 (Tac. *Ann.* xiii. 45, 46), and the marriage was not celebrated until 62 (Tac. *Ann.* xiv. 60). Burrhus died and was succeeded by Tigellinus in 62 (Tac. *Ann.* xiv. 51). The expectation of a speedy release is also expressed in the letter to Philemon.

As to the time necessary for sending a message to Philippi announcing Paul's imprisonment, for Epaphroditus' journey to Rome with the contribution, for the message to Philippi concerning Epaphroditus' sickness, and for the message to Rome announcing that the Philippians had received this report, — the distance between Rome and Philippi was only seven hundred miles, and even with the imperfect means of travelling, all the four journeys could have been accomplished in four months. Lightfoot's attempt to reduce the four journeys to two is founded on the assumption that Aristarchus left Paul at Myra and proceeded to Thessalonica, thus carrying the news of the apostle's removal to Rome. But for this there is not a particle of evidence.

On the other hand, Lightfoot's constructive argument for the earlier date of the letter is anything but conclusive, and is, I venture to think, illogical in method, although it has the weighty indorsement of Dr. Hort. Lightfoot urges that in style and tone this epistle more resembles the earlier letters than do the epistles to the Ephesians and Colossians; that it represents the transition from the conflict with Pharisaic Judaism to that with the new type of error which was emerging in the Asiatic churches. But granting the striking parallels between Romans and Philippians, and granting that Ephesians and Colossians exhibit an advanced stage of development in the churches both on the side of heresy and of Christian knowledge, surely it by no means follows that the order of composition corresponds with the stages of development. The special circumstances in the case of each church must be taken into the account. I cannot see the force of Farrar's statement (*Paul*, ii. p. 419) that the Philippian epistle, if it had been written later than the Asiatic epistles, must have borne traces of the controversy with the incipient gnosticism of the Colossian church. Why? — "The incipient gnosticism of the Colossian church" had not reached Philippi. As Professor Ramsay observes, "It was not in Paul's way to send to Philippi an elaborate treatise against a subtle, speculative heresy which had never affected that church." And, in any case, it is not easy to construct, on the data furnished by these epistles, a scale of church development so accurately graded as to furnish a satisfactory basis of reasoning in a case like this. Philippians, it is true, presents some striking parallels with Romans; but parallels with Romans may be pointed out in both Ephesians and Colossians (see v. Soden, *Hand-Comm. Koloss.*, *Einl.* iv.); and it would not be difficult to make out a case for a development in the Philippian church quite as advanced as that represented in Ephesians, though possibly on different lines.

Nothing in the epistle compels us to place it later than the others, and nothing prevents our placing it earlier; but it must be admitted that positive evidence for the earlier date is lacking. It may be remarked that the Philippians would follow the apostle's movements as closely as possible. It is not impossible that the news of his departure for Rome might have reached them from Asia before his arrival, especially as the voyage was so long. In that case their gift would probably have reached him comparatively early. The tone of the letter, so far as it relates to himself, seems to indicate fresh impressions rather than those received after a long and tedious confinement.

VI

OCCASION OF THE EPISTLE

The immediate occasion of the epistle was a contribution of money brought by Epaphroditus from the members of the Philippian church (ii. 25, iv. 18). They had sent him similar tokens of their affection on former occasions (iv. 15, 16; comp. 2 Cor. xi. 9); but an opportunity of repeating their gifts had been long wanting (iv. 10). Whether from the hardships of the journey, or from over-exertion in forwarding Paul's work in Rome, Epaphroditus became dangerously sick (ii. 27, 30). On his recovery he was troubled lest the Philippians should be anxious about him, and was eager to return in order to relieve their fears, besides suffering, no doubt, from the homesickness peculiar to an invalid in a foreign land (ii. 26). Paul therefore sent him back, and sent by him this letter (ii. 25, 28), containing not only thanks for the gift (iv. 10–18), but also information about his own condition, his success in preaching the gospel, and other matters of special interest to the Philippians; besides such exhortations and admonitions as the condition of the church as reported by Epaphroditus seemed to demand.

VII

CRITICAL QUESTIONS

The external evidence for the authenticity and genuineness of the epistle is substantially the same as for the principal epistles. It appeared in Marcion's Canon, and Hippolytus (*Haeres.* v. 143, x. 318) says that the Sethians, an Ophite sect of the second century, interpreted Phil. ii. 6, 7, to explain their doctrines. The excerpts from the Valentinian Theodotus preserved by Clement of Alexandria contain two references to Phil. ii. 7 (35, 43). The letter of Polycarp to the Philippians appeals to the epistle or epistles of Paul to the Philippian church (c. iii. See note on Phil. iii. 1). A few passages which have the appearance of reminiscences of the Philippian letter occur in Clement (*Ad Cor.* xvi., xlvii.); Ignatius (*Rom.* ii.; *Philad.* viii.); The Epistle to Diognetus, 5, and Theophilus of Antioch (*Ad Autolycum*). The Muratorian Canon places it among the letters of Paul. It is included in the Syriac (Peshitto) and Old-Latin versions. At the close of the second century it is in use by Irenæus, Tertullian, and Clement of Alexandria.

See Iren. iv. 18, 4; Clem. Alex. *Paedag.* i. 524; *Strom.* iv. 12, 19, 94; Tert. *De Resur.* 23; *Cont. Marc.* v. 20; *De Praescr.* 26.

It is cited in the letter from the churches of Lyons and Vienne to the brethren in Asia and Phrygia (A.D. 177, Euseb. *H. E.* v. 1, 2). Origen and Eusebius admit and use it as a work of Paul. From the time of Irenæus and Clement of Alexandria its authenticity and genuineness were generally recognised.

The epistle was first assailed by Baur (*Paulus*, 1845; *Th. J.*, 1849, 1852), followed by several representatives of the Tübingen school, — Schwegler (*Nachap. Zeital.*, 1846), Planck (*Th. J.*, 1847), Köstlin (*Th. J.*, 1850), Volkmar (*Th. J.*, 1856, 1857), Bruno Bauer (*Christus und die Cäsaren*, 1877). The grounds of attack were: lack of originality and imitation of other epistles; traces of gnostic ideas; the antedating of the offices of Bishop and Deacon; and the disagreement of the statements concerning justification by faith with Paul's statements elsewhere. The epistle was a product of the second century, intended to reconcile the two parties then struggling in the church. These parties were symbolically represented by Euodia and Syntyche (iv. 2). Clement of Rome was a myth, founded upon the conversion of Flavius Clemens, the kinsman of Domitian. The writer of the Clementine Homilies, in order to represent Clement as the disciple of Peter, represents him as the kinsman of Tiberius. The Pauline writer of Philippians, accepting this fiction, and anxious to conciliate the Petrine faction, represents this fictitious disciple of Peter as the fellow-laborer of Paul (iv. 3).

These objections are mainly imaginary. On the antedating of the episcopate see Excursus on i. 1. The identification of Clement with Flavius Clemens is absurd. The assumed imitation of other epistles amounts only to an occasional relationship in expression, the absence of which would be remarkable, and which does not imply dependence. Baur asserted that in ii. 5–8 the writer had in view the gnostic Sophia, the last of the æons, which, in the attempt to grasp the knowledge of the absolute One, fell from the πλήρωμα into κένωμα or emptiness. The ambition of the æon was contrasted with the self-emptying of the eternal Christ. Volkmar explained Euodia ('right path') as a synonym for orthodoxy, and Syntyche ('partner') as designating the Gentile church. Such vagaries are their own refutation.

The assault was renewed after an interval by Hitzig (*Zur Krit. paulin. Br.*, 1870); Kneucker (*Die Anfänge d. röm. Christenthums*, 1881); Hinsch (*Zw. Th.*, 1873); Hoekstra (*Th. J.*, 1875); Biedermann (*Christl. Dogmatik*, ii. 1885); and especially by Holsten, in a vigorous and searching critique (*Jp. Th.*, 1875, 1876).

The objections of this group of critics turned mainly on alleged divergencies in style and matter from the acknowledged Pauline epistles. The principal points are the following:

1. The sharp contrast between the divine and the human form of existence (ii. 6–11) is unpauline. In 1 Cor. xv. 47–49, Paul conceives Christ in his preëxistence as ἄνθρωπος ἐπουράνιος, 'a heavenly man,'—an ideal man (see Excursus on ii. 6–11). According to the Epistle to the Philippians, Christ's manhood begins with his incarnation, while his preincarnate state is described as ἐν μορφῇ θεοῦ ὑπάρχων. In other words, according to 1 Corinthians, the preincarnate Christ would be only an ideal man. According to Philippians, the preincarnate Christ would belong to an order of beings higher than the heavenly humanity.

The error lies in the misinterpretation of ἐπουράνιος. It is true that Phil. ii. 6 presents a notion of the preincarnate Christ superior to that of a mere heavenly man; but ἐπουράνιος in 1 Corinthians does not refer to the preincarnate Christ, but to the risen and glorified Christ. According to Corinthians, while the first man, Adam, is of earthly origin (ἐκ γῆς, χοϊκός), the second man, Christ, is of heavenly derivation (ἐξ οὐρανοῦ), and is in heaven with his glorified body in which he will appear at his second coming. Ὁ ἐπουράνιος is he who is in heaven, not as the heavenly archetype existing ideally in the mind of God, but as exalted to heaven (Eph. iv. 8;

Phil. ii. 9). This appears from the term ἐπουράνιοι applied to risen and glorified Christians (comp. Phil. iii. 20, 21). The question which Paul is answering in 1 Cor. xv. 35 ff., is, "With what kind of a body do they come?" and the question is answered by showing the relation of the resurrection-body, not to that of the preincarnate Christ, but to that of the risen and glorified Christ. Hence there is no contradiction between the ἐν μορφῇ θεοῦ ὑπάρχων by which Paul represents the preincarnate glory of Christ, and the ἐπούρανιος by which he represents Christ risen and glorified. In Corinthians Paul is not contemplating the mode of Christ's preëxistence at all, but the mode of his existence as the risen and glorified Saviour, in which all true believers shall share.

2. Divergences from the Pauline theology in the conception of Jewish law and the doctrine of justification (iii. 4–11). Such are: the assumption that Paul is blameless as touching the righteousness that is in the law; the antithesis of δικαιοσύνη ἡ ἐκ νόμου and δικαιοσύνη ἡ ἐκ θεοῦ; the representation of justification by faith as δικαιοσύνη ἐπὶ τῇ πίστει; the connecting of objective and subjective righteousness; the putting of communion with Christ's resurrection before communion with his death.

Some of these objections are treated in the notes on iii. 4–11. The words, "as touching the righteousness which is of the law, blameless" (iii. 6), have their parallel in Gal. i. 14; and, in any case, are used of merely legal righteousness, and are to be read in the light of Paul's conception of righteousness in vs. 9. The doctrine of justification by faith is not treated otherwise than in Romans, except that the appropriation of Christ by the act of faith and the union of the life with Christ are combined in one conception and are not considered separately as in Romans.

3. Indifference to the objective truth of his gospel (i. 15–18). The same parties who, in Gal. i. 6, 7; 2 Cor. xi. 4, are said to preach another Jesus and another gospel, are declared to be preaching Christ, instead of being anathematised as in Gal. i. 8, 9.

But the parties are not the same (see notes on i. 15, 16). The words concerning the Judaisers in ch. iii. 2 have the indignant flavor of Galatians and 2 Corinthians, and exhibit no indifference to the objective truth.

4. Paul expresses uncertainty concerning his resurrection (iii.

11), which is inconsistent with the assurance that he displays elsewhere (Rom. v. 17, 18, 21, viii. 38, 39; 2 Cor. v. 1 ff.). But the words εἴ πως are an expression of humility and self-distrust, not of doubt. He elsewhere urges the necessity of caution and watchfulness against a possible lapse from the faith (ii. 12; 1 Cor. x. 12; Gal. iii. 3, v. 4), and he takes the same caution to himself (see note on iii. 11). He displays no uncertainty as to the objective basis of salvation, and the fellowship of suffering with Christ as the subjective condition of sharing his glory agrees with Rom. viii. 17.

5. Self-glorification on the part of Paul in setting himself before his readers as a type of the righteousness of the law, and afterwards of justification by faith (iii. 4–17). This requires no answer. Where he speaks of his advantages as a legally righteous Jew, he describes them as a trusting in the flesh (vs. 4), while as a Christian he expressly disclaims confidence in the flesh (vs. 3, 7–12).

6. Contradictory expressions as to his expectations for the future. On the one hand, he looks for a speedy release (i. 25, ii. 24); on the other, he contemplates martyrdom (ii. 17). But he says nothing but what is compatible with the alternations of hope and fear which are natural to a prisoner; and circumstances might have awakened his hopes at one time, and clouded them at another.

7. The words concerning the gift of the Philippians (iv. 10–19) contradict 1 Thess. ii. 9. There is no contradiction. The latter passage confirms the statement of iv. 15, that the Thessalonians were not among the Macedonians who contributed to Paul while in Corinth. Holsten's assertion that Paul's way of thanking the Philippians is thankless, is nonsense. Nothing can be more delicate, more hearty, and more manly than his expression of gratitude.

8. Differences in style from the acknowledged Pauline letters. Holsten collects these, and classifies them as non-pauline, unpauline, and anti-pauline.

It would seem self-evident that any writer whose mind is alive and whose thoughts do not move always in the same round, will use in one book or letter words and phrases which he does not use in another. The difference in subject or mood may be sufficient to account for this. The mere counting of unique words in any single epistle amounts to little or nothing. To forty-three hapaxlegomena in Ephesians, there are above a hundred in Romans, and more than two hundred in 1 Corinthians. In Ephesians the special treatment of the unity of the Christian body accounts for a group of words with σύν not found in the other epistles.

But Pauline words abound in this epistle. For a very full table, see *Speaker's Commentary on Phil.*, supplementary note at the close of the Introduction, "On the Pauline Diction of this Epistle." For parallels with Romans, see Lightf. *Comm.* p. 43.

Schürer (cit. by Godet) says: "All the reasons advanced in this sphere against the authenticity, have weight only with him who makes the Apostle Paul, that most living and mobile spirit the world has ever seen, a man of habit and routine, who behoved to write each of his letters like all the others, to repeat in the following ones what he had said in the preceding, and to say it again always in the same way and in the same terms."

The authenticity and genuineness of the epistle are defended by Lünemann (*Pauli ad Phil. Ep. contra Baurium defendit*, 1847); B. Brückner (*Ep. ad Phil. Paulo auctori vindicata contra Baurium*, 1848); Ernesti (*Stud. u. Krit.*, 1848, 1851); Grimm (*Zw. Th.*, 1873); Hilgenfeld (*Zw. Th.*, 1873, 1875, 1877, 1884); Schenkel (*Bibellex.* iv. 534, *Christusbild der Apostel*); Weizsäcker (*Jd. Th.*, 1876; *Apost. Zeital.*); A. Harnack (*ZKG.* ii., 1878); Mangold (*Der Römerbrief*, 1884, and Bleek's *Einl. in d. N. T.*, 1886); Pfleiderer (*Urchristenthum; Paulinismus*); Davidson (*Introd. to the Study of the N. T.*); Lipsius (*Hand-Comm.* ii., *Einl. z. Phil.*); Godet (*Introd. au Nouv. Test.*, pt. i., 1893); B. Weiss (*Lehrb. d. Einl. in d. N. T.*, 1889); Jülicher (*Einl. in d. N. T.*, 1894); Klöpper (*Paulus an die Philipper*, 1893).

H. J. Holtzmann (*Einl. in d. N. T.* 3 Aufl., 1892) says: "It is the testament of the apostle which we have before us, and he wrote it at Rome." It is accepted by Reuss and Renan.

For the history of the controversy, see the Introds. of Holtzmann and Weiss, and Lips. in the *Hand-Comm.*, Bd. ii. See also Knowling (*The Witness of the Epistles*, p. 6 ff.) and Theo. Zahn (*Die Briefe des Paulus seit fünfzig Jahren im Feuer der Kritik, ZWL.*, 1889).

VIII

INTEGRITY

To any one reading this epistle as a familiar letter of Paul to a greatly beloved church, intended to inform them concerning his own circumstances, to thank them for their generous care for him, and to give them such counsel as his knowledge of their condition might suggest, its informal and unsystematic character, and its abrupt transitions from one theme to another, will appear entirely natural. Modern criticism, however, refuses to be satisfied with this view of the case, and has discovered, as it thinks, substantial reasons for challenging the integrity of the letter.

The principal stumbling-block is at iii. 2, where, after being about to close the letter, as is claimed (vs. 1), the apostle begins afresh, and proceeds to the discussion of most important matters, and then returns thanks for the contribution, which the letter conveyed to Philippi by Epaphroditus could not have omitted. This, it is asserted, forms an abrupt and harsh transition, since the point at which he proposed to close is really the middle of the epistle. Holtzmann remarks that "the rush of all the tides of criticism upon this passage raises the suspicion of a hidden rock."

Stephan Lemoyne (*Varia Sacra*), Heinrichs (in Koppe's *N. T.*, 1803), Paulus (*Heidelb. Jhrb.*, 1812), Hausrath (*N. T. Zeitgesch.* iii. 2 Aufl., 1873–1877; *Der Apostel Paulus*, 2 Aufl., 1872), Weisse (*Beitr. z. Kritik d. paulin. Br.*, 1867), — all assumed two letters. The last four assumed that iii. 1–iv. 20 was addressed to a narrower circle of readers, — perhaps the superintendents of the church. Hausrath held that the first letter was written after Paul's first hearing before the imperial tribunal, and the second some weeks later, after his receipt of the gift. Schrader (*Der Apostel Paulus*) regarded iii. 1–iv. 9 as an interpolation; while Ewald (*Sendschr. des Ap. Paulus*, 1857), Schenkel (*Bibellex.*), and Reuss (*Gesch. d. heil. Schr. N. T.*, 1874) held the portion from iii. 1 to be a later addition, prompted by fresh information received by Paul. Völter (*Th. J.*, 1892) holds that there were two letters, — a genuine and a spurious one. The former consisted of i. 1, 2 (exc. ἐπισκ. καὶ διακ.), 3–7, 12–26, ii. 17–30, iv. 10–20, 21, and perhaps 23; the latter of i. 8–11, 27–30, ii. 1–16, iii. 1–iv. 9. Lünemann, Ewald, Schenkel, Hilgenfeld, and Mangold hold that iii. 1 implies former and lost Philippian letters; and the question thus becomes complicated with the interpretation of the passages in *Polyc. ad Phil.*, iii., xiii. (see note on iii. 1).

The theory of two letters rests mainly on the assumption that τὸ λοιπόν in iii. 1 indicates an intention to close the letter. But while τὸ λοιπόν may mean 'finally,' it also means 'for the rest'; 'as to what remains,' as 1 Thess. iv. 1; 2 Thess. iii. 1. The phrase is common with Paul where he loosely attaches, even in the middle of an epistle, a new subject to that which he has been discussing. In 1 Thess. iv. two entire chapters follow τὸ λοιπόν in vs. 1. If Paul had meant to close the letter at iii. 1, he would surely have expressed his thanks for the Philippians' gift before reaching that point. Τὸ λοιπόν means there 'as to what remains,' and is an introduction to what follows, not the close of what precedes.

The abrupt transition and apparent lack of connection accord, as has been remarked, with the unsystematic, informal, familiar character of the whole letter. If the Judaistic and Libertine influences as a germ of discord demanded such an utterance as iii. 2 ff., the transition was not easy to make in a familiar letter to those with whom the apostle's relations were so intimate and affectionate. The want of connection, however, is rather apparent than real, since the divisions likely to be created by these dangerous influences would militate against that unity and concord which the apostle urges in the former part of the letter. Without specifying and pressing some such definite points, the earlier exhortations might have appeared abstract and vague.

There seem to be, therefore, no sufficient grounds for disputing the integrity of the epistle. If the partition theory is admitted, the attempt to fix the dividing lines must be regarded as hopeless in the face of the differences between critics.

See R. A. Lipsius (*Hand-Comm. Einl. z. Phil.*), Holtzmann (*Einl. N. T.*), Klöpper (*Komm. Einl.*), Lightfoot (*Phil.* p. 69).

IX

CONTENTS AND GENERAL CHARACTER

The opening salutation is of unusual length, consisting of the first eleven verses, and containing thanks to God for the Philippians' former Christian fellowship with the apostle, and their coöperation in promoting the gospel, expressions of confidence in the completion of the good work begun in them by God, and prayer for their spiritual growth.

From vs. 12 to vs. 26 St. Paul describes his own condition as a prisoner, the progress of the gospel, the work of his opposers, the increased zeal and boldness of the Christians in Rome, and expresses his own feelings in view of the alternative of his speedy death or of his continuing to live and labor for the church.

With vs. 27 he begins an exhortation to Christian unity and courage which extends to the fourth verse of ch. ii., where he introduces the example of Jesus Christ as an exhibition of the humility and self-abnegation which are essential to the maintenance of their fellowship. A few words of exhortation follow; and ch. ii. closes with an expression of the hope of his speedy release, his intention of sending Timothy to Macedonia, and the announcement of the sickness, recovery, and return of Epaphroditus.

Chapter iii. opens with an exhortation to joy, after which he proceeds to warn the church against the possible attempts of the Judaisers to influence its members, characterises them in severe terms, and contrasts their religious attitude and teachings with those of the true household of faith; the true circumcision with the false; the power of faith with the inefficiency of works and ordinances; and adduces in illustration a comparison of his own early education, aims, and religious attainments with his present position and hopes as a Christian. He follows this with an exhortation to steadfastness, a lament over those who had yielded to the influence of the Epicurean Libertines, and had thus fallen into sensuality and worldliness, and a contrast of such with the citizen of heaven, who minds not earthly things, but confidently awaits the appearing of the Lord Jesus as Saviour.

Chapter iv. begins with a repetition of the exhortation to steadfastness. Two prominent women of the church are urged to reconcile their differences, and a former fellow-laborer of the apostle is entreated to aid them in this. Then follow exhortations to forbearance, trustfulness, prayer, and giving of thanks, to the cultivation of all holy and gracious thoughts and dispositions, and to the imitation of his own Christian example as they had seen it in the days of their former intercourse. To all is added the promise of the comfort of God's peace.

With iv. 10 begins the acknowledgment of the gift received from the church, accompanied with hearty commendations of their habitual thoughtfulness and generous care for himself, and an expression of his assurance that such a spirit and such ministry will redound to their spiritual growth.

The closing salutations are general. No names are mentioned. The epistle ends with the benediction, "The grace of the Lord Jesus Christ be with your spirit."

The pervading tone of the letter is imparted by Paul's strong personal attachment to the church, in which respect it resembles the first Thessalonian epistle. It is entirely devoid of official stateliness. The official title is dropped from the opening salutation, and the apostle greets the church as their friend and fellow-servant of Jesus Christ. The character of the epistle is almost wholly commendatory, in strong contrast with the epistle to the Galatians and with portions of the two Corinthian letters. While 2 Corinthians is tumultuous, often stern, sometimes almost menacing, this letter flows on to the end in a steady stream of thankful joy. It breathes the spirit of unimpaired confidence. It somewhat resembles Ephesians in the freedom with which the apostle abandons himself to those spontaneous impulses of thought which lead away from the direct line of his subject into the profound depths of some divine counsel, or bear his soul upward in impassioned prayer. It exhibits "none of the sensitiveness about the behavior of his converts to himself which appears in Galatians and 2 Corinthians; none of the earnestness about points of difference, none of the consciousness of the precarious basis of his authority in the existing state of the two churches" (Jowett). There is the assumption throughout of frank understanding and Christian friendship.

The epistle is also marked by the absence of formulated doctrinal statement. It exhibits the substance and heart of the gospel rather than its relation to any specific form of doctrinal error. The doctrinal points elaborated in other epistles are here matters of allusion rather than of discussion. Between the apostle and his readers there is assumed a community of faith in the truths to which he so confidently appeals for the enforcement of all that is pure, lovely, and of good report, and a knowledge of those truths which renders formal instruction unnecessary.

Where points of doctrine are touched, it is invariably with a view to their practical application. The ethical character of the epistle is very pronounced. Even the splendid passage, ii. 5–11, is introduced, not for the purpose of formulating the doctrine of Christ's preëxistence and of defining the nature of his humanity as related to his preincarnate condition, but in order to enforce the practical exhortation to humility. Thus, too, the doctrine of justification by faith as treated in ch. iii. lacks none of the essential elements of the discussion in Romans; yet it gains in practical force and attractiveness by being intertwined with the doctrine of mystical union with Christ. It is this which makes that passage, brief as it is, so valuable for the study of the real Pauline doctrine of justification, affording as it does no room for that scholastic and mechanical interpretation according to which justification is resolved into a forensic adjustment effected by a legal fiction of imputed righteousness.

Yet the attitude of the epistle towards doctrinal error is neither hesitating nor compromising. Its dealing with the Judaisers in ch. iii. reminds us that the writer is still the Paul of the Galatian and second Corinthian letters. None the less it bears witness to the discriminating quality of a ripe charity, to the sound wisdom of Christian love which knows how to draw the line between weakness and perverseness; between the occasional lapses of Christian immaturity and the wicked obstinacy of an estranged heart; between the mistakes of an untutored conscience and the selfish persistence of unholy desire.

But while the character of the epistle is ethical rather than doctrinal or controversial, it gives no countenance to the tendency to resolve the gospel into a mere code of morals. The moral inspiration which it represents has its impelling centre in a person and a life, and not in a code. The personal Christ is its very heart. It exhibits Christ *in* Paul rather than *before* him. Christ is not a subject of controversy; he is not simply a pattern of conduct. He is the sum of Paul's life. Paul's ideal is to be found in him. His death is not a sorrowful reminiscence; it has been shared by the apostle in his own death to sin. The view of the resurrection, which this letter in common with that to the Romans presents, is a standing rebuke to the superficial conception and the loose grasp which the church too often brings to that truth. The resurrection of the Lord is to Paul a present, informing energy and not only a memory and a hope. He would know the power of the resurrection now and here as well as hereafter. He not only lives according to Christ's life, he lives it. Christ loves, obeys, suffers, sympathises, toils, and hopes in him. Under the power of this life his own natural affection is transfigured. He knows not men after the flesh, but loves and longs for them in the heart of Jesus Christ.

With the exhibition of these facts goes the corresponding emphasis of the apostle's personality. The letter is more distinctively personal than any of the epistles to the churches except 2 Corinthians. In this lies largely its peculiar fascination. But the personality is accentuated on a different side. Its sensitive, indignant, self-vindicatory aspect, so marked in the Corinthian letter, is completely in the background here. The Paul of the Philippian letter is not the man whose apostolic credentials have been challenged, and whose personal motives have been impugned; not the vindicator of himself and of his ministry against the pretensions of false apostles; not the missionary who is reluctantly constrained in his own defence to unfold the record of his labors and sufferings. He is the disciple who counts all things but loss for the excellency of the knowledge of Christ Jesus his Lord; for whom to live is Christ, and to die is to be with Christ. What a blending of the restfulness of faith with the tenseness of aspiration! What an upreach of desire! With an experience behind him unique in its depth and richness and variety, with the memory of personal vision of Christ and of ravishment into the third heaven, with a profound knowledge of the mysteries of divine truth won through heart-shaking moral crises, in solitary meditation and in the vast experience of his missionary career, — his attainment is only a point for a larger outlook, an impulse to more vigorous striving. In Christ he is in a sphere of infinite possibilities, and he counts not himself to have apprehended, but stretches forward under the perpetual stress of his heavenward calling.

TEXT

THE epistle presents no textual questions of importance. The authority for the sources is Tischendorf's 8th ed. *Crit. Maj.* I have also used the 4th ed. of Scrivener's *Introduction to the Criticism of the N. T.*, ed. Miller, and in some places have noted the readings of Weiss in his recent *Textkritische Untersuchungen und Textherstellung*, 1896.

The text followed is that of Westcott and Hort with two or three exceptions.

The following manuscripts are referred to:

PRIMARY UNCIALS

ℵ *Cod. Sinaiticus*: 4th century. Discovered by Tischendorf in the convent of St. Catherine on Mt. Sinai, in 1859. Now at St. Petersburg. Contains both epistles complete. Correctors: $ℵ^a$, nearly contemporary; $ℵ^b$, 6th century; $ℵ^c$, beginning of 7th century, treated by two correctors, — $ℵ^{ca}$ $ℵ^{cb}$.

A. *Cod. Alexandrinus*: 5th century. British Museum. Contains both epistles entire.

B. *Cod. Vaticanus*: 4th century. Vatican Library. Contains both epistles entire. Correctors: B^2, nearly the same date; B^3, 10th or 11th century.

C. *Cod. Ephraem*: 5th century. Palimpsest. National Library, Paris. Very defective. Wanting from τοῦτο οὖν (Eph. iv. 17) to καὶ τί αἱρήσομαι (Phil i. 22), and from μειν (Βενιαμειν) (Phil. iii. 5) to the end. Correctors: C^2, 6th century; C^3, 9th century.

D. *Cod. Claromontanus*: 6th century. Græco-Latin. National Library, Paris. Contains both epistles entire. Corrector: D^b, close of 6th century.

F. *Cod. Augiensis*: 9th century. Græco-Latin. Library of Trinity College, Cambridge. Philippians entire; Philemon wanting in the Greek from πεποιθὼς (vs. 21) to the end.

G. *Cod. Boernerianus*: 9th century. Græco-Latin. Dresden. Wanting Greek and Latin, Philem. 21–25.

An asterisk added to the title of a MS., as D*, signifies a correction made by the original scribe.

SECONDARY UNCIALS

K. *Cod. Mosquensis:* 9th century. Moscow. Contains both epistles entire.

L. *Cod. Angelicus:* 9th century. Angelican Library of Augustinian monks at Rome. Wanting from ἐξουσίαν (Heb. xiii. 10) to the end of Philemon.

P. *Cod. Porphyrianus:* beginning of 9th century. Palimpsest. St. Petersburg. Both epistles entire, but many words illegible.

MINUSCULES

17. National Library, Paris: 9th or 10th century. Both epistles entire.
31. British Museum: 11th century. Both epistles entire.
37. Library of Town Council of Leicester: 15th century. Both epistles entire. See Miller's *Scrivener*, vol. i. 202.
47. Bodleian Library: 11th century. Both epistles entire.
67. Vienna: 11th century. Both epistles entire.
80. Vatican: 11th century. Philippians entire; Philemon mutilated.
137. Paris: 13th or 14th century. Both epistles entire.

VERSIONS

Latin:

Vetus Latina (Lat. Vet.).
Vulgate (Vulg.).

Egyptian:

Coptic, Memphitic, or Bohairic (Cop.).
Sahidic (Sah.).
Bashmuric (Basm.).

Syriac:

Peshitto (Pesh.).
Harclean (Harcl.).
Syr.^{sch} (Schaaf's ed. of Peshitto).
Syr.^{utr} (Peshitto and Harclean versions).
Syr.^{p} (Harclean).

Other versions:

Armenian (Arm.).
Gothic (Goth.).
Ethiopic (Æth.).

COMMENTARIES

PATRISTIC

Chrysostom, Theodoret, Œcumenius, Theophylact, Theodore of Mopsuestia.

Chrysostom's commentary is in the form of fifteen homilies. It is not regarded as one of his best, but it illustrates his peculiarities as an expositor: his honest effort to discover and interpret his author's meaning; his sound grammatical and historical treatment; his avoidance of forced and fanciful allegorical interpretations; his felicitousness in illustration, fluency of style, dramatic power, and general knowledge of Scripture. Migne's *Patrologia*, Paris, 1863; Trans. *Library of the Fathers*, Oxford, 1843; Schaff's *Nicene and Post-Nicene Fathers*.

Theodoret: simple and literal, mingling the expository and apologetic. Migne.

The commentaries of Theodore of Mopsuestia remain only in a few Greek fragments and a Latin version. They are valuable as a protest against the vicious allegorical method of the Alexandrian school. Theodore is distinguished by close adherence to the text, attention to grammatical points and textual variations, — by his exegetical instinct and his effort to adhere to the line of his author's thought. *Theodore of Mopsuestia's Commentary on the Minor Epistles of St. Paul: The Latin Version with the Greek Fragments. Ed. from the MSS., with Notes and an Introduction*, by H. B. Swete, Cambridge University Press.

EARLIER COMMENTARIES

Among these may be named those of Erasmus, Bucer, Zwingli, Beza, Calvin, Calixtus, Daillé, Musculus or Meusslin, Velasquez,

Le Clerc, Hyperius, Vorstius, Grotius, Crocius, Aretius, Piscator, Estius, a Lapide, Breithaupt, am Ende, Rheinwald, Matthies, van Hengel, Hoelemann, Bengel, Rilliet.

JOHN CALVIN is marked by solid learning, contempt for exegetical tricks, independence, thoroughness, terseness, and precision of language.

JOHN ALBERT BENGEL: *Gnomon Novi Testamenti.* Ed. of Steudel, 1855. Translations by Fausset, Edinburgh, and Lewis and Vincent, Philadelphia, 1860. While most of his critical work is obsolete, he remains distinguished for keen spiritual insight, terse and pithy diction, and suggestive exposition of the force and bearing of individual words. Always mentioned with respect by modern commentators.

A. RILLIET: *Commentaire sur l'Épitre de l'Apôtre Paul aux Philippiens.* 1841. With illustrative essays. Learned,— not controversial or dogmatic,— interesting, Scriptural, clear in statement. Issued before the attacks of the Tübingen school.

MODERN COMMENTARIES

HENRY ALFORD: *Greek Testament*, 1849–1861 and later. Largely a digest of German exegesis which he was the first to introduce to the scholars of the established church in England. He is judicial rather than original, sometimes too much given to balancing opinions after the earlier German method; but in his treatment of this epistle, his judgments show considerable independence and decisiveness, and the commentary contains matter which is still valuable.

W. M. L. DE WETTE: *Kurzgefasstes exegetisches Handbuch zum Neuen Testament. Kurze Erklärung der Briefe an die Kolosser, an Philemon, an die Epheser und Philipper.* 1836–1848. Wide and accurate scholarship; sound exegetical tact,— independent, acute, concise.

H. A. W. MEYER: *Kritisch exegetisches Handbuch über die Briefe an die Philipper, Kolosser, und an Philemon*, 5 Aufl. A. H. Franke, 1886. New ed. in preparation. This volume of the *Kommentar über das Neue Testament* was prepared by Dr. Meyer's own hand. Meyer stands in the very front rank of exegetes. Great learning; remarkable exegetical insight; devout, fair, independent, clear and forcible in statement; strong historic sense. He leans somewhat towards excessive literalism, and is not a good authority on text. The American edition, 1885, 4th Germ., contains the notes of President T. Dwight of Yale University. These are discriminating and helpful. Dr. Dwight has a rare faculty of putting into a clear and simple form the factors of a complicated exegetical discussion.

C. J. ELLICOTT: *A Critical and Grammatical Commentary on St. Paul's Epistles to the Philippians, Colossians, and Philemon.* 5th ed. Ripe exegetical judgment; careful discrimination of grammatical niceties; remarkable power of stating fine distinctions and shades of meaning; great accuracy. His commentary is still most valuable.

J. B. LIGHTFOOT: *St. Paul's Epistle to the Philippians. Revised Text with Introduction, Notes, and Dissertations.* 1st ed. 1868; 12th ed. 1896, a reprint of the revised and slightly altered 4th ed. of 1885. Has long held a very high rank among commentaries on this epistle. The lamented author's large and varied learning appears especially in the essays and excursuses which so delightfully exhibit the historical setting of the letter. In point of exegesis, the commentary, while always suggestive, is not equal to some others.

B. WEISS: *Der Philipperbrief ausgesetzt und die Geschichte seiner Auslegung kritisch dargestellt.* 1859. A most thorough piece of work. It leaves no point untouched, and treats every point with ample learning, conscientious painstaking, independence, and positiveness. It is valuable in studying the history of the exegesis.

ALBERT KLÖPPER: *Der Brief des Apostel Paulus an die Philipper.* 1893. A commentary which must be reckoned with. Carefully and conscientiously done, with adequate scholarship. Needlessly elaborated; too diffuse; but the reader who has the patience to make his way through the mazes of an involved style will commonly be rewarded for his pains. His critical tendencies are radical, but he accepts and defends the authenticity of the epistle.

JOSEPH AGAR BEET: *A Commentary on St. Paul's Epistles to the Ephesians, Philippians, and Colossians, and to Philemon.* 1891. With a good scholarly basis. It can hardly be called a popular commentary, but does not meet the demands of a full critical commentary. In the attempt to condense, some things are passed over with mere statement which deserve more careful notice.

J. RAWSON LUMBY: *The Epistle of Paul to the Philippians.* Schaff's *Popular Commentary*, 1882. Bright, interesting, and suggestive.

KARL BRAUNE: *Die Briefe Sti Pauli an die Epheser, Kolosser, Philipper, theologisch-homiletisch bearbeitet.* Lange's *Bibelwerk*, 1867. Trans. with additions by H. B. Hackett, Schaff's *Lange*, 1870. The value of Lange's *Bibelwerk* is impaired by an accumulation of doctrinal, ethical, homiletical, and practical material. The quality of Dr. Hackett's work is always good, and his additions are valuable.

R. A. LIPSIUS: *Briefe an die Galater, Römer, Philipper. Hand-Commentar zum Neuen Testament, von Holtzmann, Lipsius, Schmiedel, und von Soden.* Bd. ii. Abth. 2, 2 Aufl., 1892. In striking contrast with most earlier German commentaries in which conflicting opinions are elaborately discussed; terse and condensed; learned, acute, penetrating, and clear. Introduction valuable. Represents the radical German school of N. T. criticism.

H. VON SODEN: *Der Brief des Apostels Paulus an die Philipper.* 1889. A charming homiletical exposition.

JOHN EADIE: *A Commentary on the Greek Text of the Epistle of Paul to the Philippians.* 2d ed. 1884. A full and useful commentary; too much of the homiletic element.

ABBREVIATIONS

ECCLESIASTICAL WRITERS

Ambrost.	Ambrosiaster.
Ans.	Anselm.
Aug.	Augustine.
Chr.	Chrysostom.
Clem. Alex.	Clement of Alexandria.
Clem. Rom.	Clement of Rome.
Cyr. Alex.	Cyril of Alexandria.
Euseb.	Eusebius.
Greg. Nys.	Gregory of Nyssa.
Hil.	Hilary.
Hippol.	Hippolytus.
Ign.	Ignatius.
Jer.	Jerome.
Joh. Dam.	John of Damascus.
Jos.	Josephus.
Just. M.	Justin Martyr.
Œc.	Œcumenius.
Polyc.	Polycarp.
Tert.	Tertullian.
Thdrt.	Theodoret.
Theo. Mop.	Theodore of Mopsuestia.
Theoph.	Theophylact.

CLASSICAL WRITERS

Æs.	Æschylus.
App.	Appian.
Aristid.	Aristides.
Aristoph.	Aristophanes.
Aristot.	Aristotle.
Athen.	Athenæus.
Corp. I. Lat.	*Corpus Inscriptionum Latinarum.*
Corp. I. Gr.	*Corpus Inscriptionum Graecarum.*
Dem.	Demosthenes.
Diod. Sic.	Diodorus Siculus.
Dion. H.	Dionysius of Halicarnassus.
Eur.	Euripides.
Hdt.	Herodotus.
Hom.	Homer.
Juv.	Juvenal.
Ov.	Ovid.
Petron.	Petronius.
Pind.	Pindar.
Plut.	Plutarch.
Polyb.	Polybius.
Q. Curt.	Quintus Curtius.
Soph.	Sophocles.
Suet.	Suetonius.
Tac.	Tacitus.
Ter.	Terentius.
Thuc.	Thucydides.
Xen.	Xenophon.

COMMENTATORS AND WRITERS ON N. T.

Alf.	Alford.
am E.	am Ende.
Aq.	Aquila.
B. Crus.	Baumgarten Crusius.

Beng.	Bengel.
Bl.	Bleek.
Calov.	Calovius.
Calv.	Calvin.
Con. H.	Conybeare and Howson.
Croc.	Crocius.
De W.	De Wette.
Dw.	Dwight.
Ead.	Eadie.
Ellic.	Ellicott.
Erasm.	Erasmus.
Ew.	Ewald.
Grot.	Grotius.
Heinr.	Heinrichs.
Hack.	Hackett.
Hofn.	Hofmann.
Holtzn.	Holtzmann.
Holst.	Holsten.
Hoel.	Hoelemann.
Jül.	Jülicher.
Kl.	Klöpper.
Lips.	Lipsius.
Lightf.	Lightfoot.
Lum.	Lumby.
Luth.	Luther.
Mey.	Meyer.
Matth.	Matthies.
Mich.	Michaelis.
Nedr.	Neander.
Pfl.	Pfleiderer.
Pisc.	Piscator.
Rhw.	Rheinwald.
Ril.	Rilliet.
Rosenm.	Rosenmüller.
Str.	Storr.
Symm.	Symmachus.
v. Fl.	von Flatt.
van Heng.	van Hengel.
van Oos.	van Oosterzee.
v. Sod.	von Soden.
Weizs.	Weizsäcker.
Westc.	Westcott.
Wetst.	Wetstein.
Wiesel.	Wieseler.
Wies.	Wiesinger.
W. St.	Vincent: *Word Studies in the N. T.*

GRAMMARIANS AND LEXICOGRAPHERS

Burt.	Burton: *N. T. Moods and Tenses.*
Crem.	Cremer: *Biblico-Theological Lexicon of N. T. Greek.*
Herz.	Herzog: *Real-Encyclopädie für protestantische Theologie und Kirche.*
Hesych.	Hesychius: *Lexicon.*
Suid.	Suidas: *Lexicon.*
Thay.	Thayer: *Greek-English Lexicon of the N. T.*
Win.	Winer: *Grammar of N. T. Greek.* 8th ed. of Eng. Transl. by Moulton. *Grammatik des neutestamentlichen Sprachidioms,* 8 Aufl., von P. W. Schmiedel. 1 Theil, 1894.

TEXTUAL

WH.	Westcott and Hort: *The New Testament in the Original Greek.*
Tisch.	Tischendorf: *Novum Testamentum Graece. Editio Octava Critica Major.*
R.V.	Revised Version of 1881.
A.V.	Authorized Version.
TR	*Textus Receptus.*

PERIODICALS

Zw. Th.	*Zeitschrift für wissenschaftliche Theologie.*
Th. LZ.	*Theologische Literaturzeitung.*
Th. J.	*Theologische Jahrbücher.*
Th. T.	*Theologisch Tijdschrift.*
Jp. Th.	*Jahrbücher für protestant. Theologie.*
Stud. u. Krit.	*Studien und Kritiken.*
Jd. Th.	*Jahrbücher für deutsche Theologie.*
Heidelb. Jhrb.	*Heidelberg Jahrbücher.*
ZKG.	*Zeitschrift für Kirchengeschichte.*
ZWL.	*Luthardt's Zeitschrift für kirchl. wissenschaft und kirchl. Leben.*

OTHER ABBREVIATIONS

Apocr.	Apocrypha.
Art.	Article.
Bib. Gk.	Biblical Greek.
Bib.	Bible.
Class.	Classics or Classical.
Comp.	Compare.
Const.	Construe.
LXX	Septuagint Version.
Sap.	Wisdom of Solomon.
Sir.	Wisdom of Sirach.
=	Equivalent to.

TO THE PHILIPPIANS

I. 1–11. THE PROLOGUE

The Prologue contains:

An Address and Greeting (1–2);
A Thanksgiving (3–5);
A Commendation and Prayer (6–11).

Paul and Timothy, bondservants of Jesus Christ, send greeting to the members and officers of the church at Philippi. Grace and peace to you from God our father and the Lord Jesus Christ.

All my remembrance of you is mingled with thanksgiving to God. On every occasion of my prayers I joyfully make my petition for you all, giving thanks for your coöperation in promoting the gospel from the time it was first preached among you until the present, and with confidence that God will perfect the good work which he has begun in you and will show it completed in the day when Christ shall appear. And my confidence in you is justified by my personal affection for you, by your sympathy with me in my imprisonment, and by the aid which you give me in the defence and establishment of the gospel; thus showing yourselves to be sharers in the grace which enables me to preach Christ and to suffer for his sake.

God is my witness how I long after you all with a Christly affection. I pray that you may abound in intelligent and discriminating love: that in your inquiries into truth and duty you may approve that which is supremely good: that you may be sincere and blameless in view of the day when Christ shall appear: and that you may be filled with the fruit of righteousness which shall redound to the glory and praise of God.

The character of the whole Epistle is reflected in this introduction. It is unofficial, affectionate, familiar, unlike the opening of the Galatian Epistle, and more nearly resembling the introductions to the two Thessalonian letters. At the same time it is solemn and deeply earnest.

Address and Greeting

1. Παῦλος καὶ Τιμόθεος: So in the introductions of 2 Cor., Col., and Philem., and of 1 and 2 Thess. where the name of Silvanus is added. Timothy was well known to the Philippian Church as Paul's intimate friend and companion. He was with Paul at Rome. He had been his companion in his first visit to Macedonia (Acts xvi. 1, 3, 10, 13). He had visited Macedonia later (Acts xix. 22, xx. 1, 4); and Paul was proposing to send him again as his representative to the Philippian Church (Phil. ii. 19–23). His name, however, in this letter, is associated with Paul's only in the salutation, although the omission of Paul's apostolic title is not due to his naming Timothy with himself. (Comp. 2 Cor. i. 1; Col. i. 1.) That Timothy acted as amanuensis is possible, but is not indicated by anything in this letter. The omission of the title "apostle" (comp. Introductions to 1 and 2 Cor., Rom., and Gal.) accords with the familiar and unofficial character of the letter, and also with the fact that his apostolic claims were not challenged by a Judaising party in Philippi as they were in Galatia and Corinth.

Δοῦλοι Χριστοῦ Ἰησοῦ: Δοῦλος occurs in Paul's introductory salutations only here and in Rom. and Tit. The phrase 'bondservants of Jesus Christ' exhibits the general conception under which 'apostle' is classed. Jerome observes: "Ambo servi, non ambo apostoli. Omnis enim apostolus servus, non omnis autem servus apostolus." The servile element does not enter into Paul's use of the expression. It carries for him the thoughts of cheerful and willing service which, in his view, is inseparable from true freedom (Rom. vi. 18, 22); of dependence upon Christ; of ownership by Christ (1 Cor. iii. 23, vii. 22); and of identification with Christ in his assuming the form of a bondservant (Phil. ii. 7). The term may be slightly colored with a reference to his special calling, as is διάκονος in 1 Cor. iii. 5; 2 Cor. iii. 6; Eph. iii. 7. He would thus announce himself as not acting in his own name, but as the agent of another. (Comp. Gal. i. 10; Rom. i. 1; Col. iv. 12.) The phrase עֶבֶד יְהוָֹה, LXX δοῦλος θεοῦ or κυρίου, is often applied to the O.T. prophets in a body. (See Amos iii. 7; Jer. vii. 25; Ezra ix. 11; Dan. ix. 6.) Also to Moses, Jos. i. 2 (ὁ θεράπων); to Joshua, Jud. ii. 8 (δοῦλος); to David, Ps. xxxvi. (xxxv.), title, lxxviii. (lxxvii.) 70, lxxxix. (lxxxviii.) 4, 21 (δοῦλος). It is found in the introductory greetings of Rom., Tit., Jas., Jude, 2 Pet., "showing," as Professor Sanday justly remarks, "that as the apostolic age progressed, the assumption of the title became established on a broad basis. But it is noticeable how quietly St. Paul steps into the place of the prophets and leaders of the Old Covenant, and how quietly he substitutes the name of his own Master in a connection hitherto reserved for that of Jehovah" (*Comm. on Rom.*, i. 1).

The MS. readings of the Pauline introductions vary between Ἰησοῦς Χριστὸς and Χριστὸς Ἰησοῦς. For a table of the variations see Sanday's note on Rom. i. 1.

From this it appears that ἸΧ is peculiar to the earlier group of introductions, and ΧἸ to the later; 1 and 2 Cor. and Rom. being doubtful. The change seems to point to the increasing use of Χριστὸς as a proper name instead of a title. Nevertheless, in the bodies of the Epistles both designations occur; in Rom., Gal., Eph., Col., and the Pastorals, almost equally, while ΧἸ predominates in 1 and 2 Cor. and Phil., and ἸΧ predominates decidedly only in the Thessalonian Epistles.

πᾶσιν τοῖς ἁγίοις: It will be observed that the letter is addressed to all the individual Christians in Philippi, though the superintendents and ministers are named immediately after. See farther in Excursus on Bishops and Deacons. Ἅγιος, which is rare in classical Greek, in the LXX is the standard word for "holy." Both the LXX and N.T. writers bring it out of the background in which it was left by classical writers. Its fundamental idea is *setting apart*. Thus, in class., "devoted to the gods." Occasionally in a bad sense, "devoted to destruction"; "accursed"; but not in Biblical Greek. In O.T., "set apart to God," as priests (Lev. xxi. 6, 7); the tithe of the land (Lev. xxvii. 30); the holy place in the house of God (1 K. viii. 10; comp. Heb. ix. 2); the most holy place (Ex. xxvi. 33; comp. Heb. ix. 3); the Israelites, as separated from other nations and consecrated to God (Ex. xix. 6; Lev. xx. 26; Deut. vii. 6; Dan. vii. 22; 2 Esdras viii. 28). This idea is transferred to the N.T. and applied to Christians (Acts ix. 13, 32, 41; Rom. i. 7; 1 Cor. vi. 1, 2; 1 Pet. ii. 9). Ideally ἅγιος implies personal holiness; moral purity. See Lev. xi. 44, xix. 2; 1 Cor. vii. 34; 1 Pet. i. 16. Of John the Baptist (Mk. vi. 20); of Christ (Acts iii. 14); of God (1 Sam. vi. 20; Jn. xvii. 11; 1 Pet. i. 15); of God's law (Rom. vii. 12); of the Spirit of God (Acts ii. 33, 38; Rom. v. 5; etc.). Paul uses it here as a common designation of Christians belonging to the Philippian community. It does not imply actual holiness, but holiness as appropriate to those addressed and obligatory upon them, as persons set apart and consecrated. In this sense it does not occur in the Gospels (except, possibly, Mt. xxvii. 52) or in the Epistles of Pet. and John. It is rare in Acts. It appears in the opening salutations of all Paul's letters to Churches except Gal. and 1 and 2 Thess. It is applied to Jewish Christians (1 Cor. xvi. 1, 15; 2 Cor. viii. 4, ix. 1, 12; Rom. xv. 25, 26, 31). Chrys. remarks: "It was likely that the Jews too would call themselves 'saints' from the first oracle, when they were called 'a holy and peculiar people' (Ex. ix. 6; Deut. vii. 6). For this reason he added 'that are in Christ Jesus.' For these alone are holy, and those henceforward profane." Similarly Theoph. (See Delitzsch, Art. "Heiligkeit Gottes" in Herz. *Rl. Enc.*)

ἐν Χριστῷ Ἰησοῦ: Connect with τοῖς ἁγίοις. This, and the kindred formulas ἐν Χριστῷ, ἐν Ἰησοῦ, ἐν Κυρίῳ, ἐν αὐτῷ, are common Pauline expressions to denote the most intimate communion of the Christian with the living Christ. Ἐν Χριστῷ Ἰησοῦ occurs 48 times, ἐν Χριστῷ 34, ἐν Κυρίῳ 50. These phrases are not found in the Synoptic Gospels, though their equivalent appears in John in the frequent ἐν ἐμοί. The conception is that of a sphere or environment or element in which a Christian lives, as a bird in the air, a fish in the water, or the roots of a tree in the soil. Christ glorified, Christ as πνεῦμα (2 Cor. iii. 17), is the normal life-element of the believer. He "puts on" Christ as a garment (Gal. iii. 27). In Christ alone he truly lives, and his powers attain their full range and efficiency. The order is invariably ἐν Χριστῷ Ἰησοῦ.

The formula is elaborately and ably discussed by G. A. Deissmann in his monograph *Die neutestamentliche Formel 'in Christo Jesu,'* Marburg, 1892. He carefully traces the use of ἐν with the personal singular through the Classics, the LXX and the N.T., and concludes that the phrase is original with Paul. His discussion as to whether a material conception is at the bottom of it, or whether it is a purely rhetorical mode of speech is not important.

συν ἐπισκόποις καὶ διακόνοις:

B[3] DK read συνεπισκοποις, "to the fellow-bishops." So Chrys., Theoph.

Render: 'with the superintendents and ministers,' and notice that the mention of these officials is appended to the more special salutation to the members of the Church. See Excursus at the end of this chapter.

2. χάρις ὑμῖν καὶ εἰρήνη ἀπὸ Θεοῦ πατρὸς ἡμῶν καὶ κυρίου Ἰησοῦ Χριστοῦ: So in Rom., 1 and 2 Cor., Gal., and Eph. Col. omits καὶ κυρ. ΊΧ. 1 Thess. has χάρις ὑμῖν καὶ εἰρήνη. 2 Thess. omits ἡμῶν after πατρὸς. 1 and 2 Tim. add ἔλεος to χάρις and εἰρήνη and have Χτοῦ Ἰησοῦ τοῦ κυρίου ἡμῶν. Tit.: χάρις καὶ εἰρήνη ἀπὸ θεοῦ πατρὸς καὶ Χτοῦ Ἰησοῦ τοῦ σωτῆρος ἡμῶν. Notice the combination of the Greek and Hebrew forms of salutation. Χάρις is primarily that which gives joy or pleasure (χαρά, χαίρειν). Its higher, Christian meaning is based on the emphasis of *freeness* in a gift or favor. It is the free, spontaneous, absolute lovingkindness of God towards men. Hence it often stands in contrast with the ideas of debt, law, works, sin. Sometimes the cause is put for the effect; so that it means the *state* of grace into which God's freely-bestowed favor brings Christians (Rom. v. 2; Gal. v. 4), and consequently the capacity or ability due to that gracious state (Eph. iv. 7). It is this free favor of God, with all that follows it, that Paul in his salutation desires for his readers. Εἰρήνη is not tranquillity or repose, save as these are conceived as resulting from the cessation of hostility between God and man. Reconciliation is always at the basis of the Pauline conception of peace. Similarly Ps. xxix. 11, lxxxv. 8; Is. liii. 5. These terms, therefore, are not to be regarded as mere equivalents of the ordinary forms of salutation. They link themselves with these, and it is also true that Paul does not use them with any distinct dogmatic purpose; but it is inconceivable that he should have employed them without some consciousness of the peculiar sense which attaches to them throughout his letters. Thus Weiss justly says that "the fact that these terms connect themselves with the ordinary Greek and Hebrew greetings does not exclude the employment of 'grace' in its specifically Christian and Pauline sense in which it denotes the unmerited divine operation of love, which is the source and principle of all Christian salvation. Similarly, 'peace' is not to be understood primarily in the technical sense of Rom. v. 1, as the first-fruit of justification; but we may be sure that, in Paul's mind, the whole state of tranquillity and general well-being which was implied in 'peace' attached itself at the root to the fact of reconciliation with God."

The fact that God and Christ appear on an equality in the salutation cannot be adduced as a positive proof of the divine nature of Christ, though it falls in with Paul's words in ch. ii., and may be allowed to point to that doctrine which he elsewhere asserts. We cannot be too careful to distinguish between ideas which unconsciously underlie particular expressions, and the same ideas used with a definite and conscious dogmatic purpose. This Epistle especially has suffered from the overlooking of this distinction.

The Thanksgiving

3. Εὐχαριστῶ τῷ θεῷ μου ἐπὶ πάσῃ τῇ μνείᾳ ὑμῶν, πάντοτε ἐν πάσῃ δεήσει μου, ὑπὲρ πάντων ὑμῶν μετὰ χαρᾶς τὴν δέησιν ποιούμενος:

ευχαριστω τω θεω μου ℵ ABDKLP, Vulg., Syr.utr, Cop., Basm.
εγω μεν ευχαριστω τω κυριω ημων D* FG.

Render: 'I thank my God in all my remembrance of you; always, in every supplication of mine, making my supplication for you all with joy.' Thus πάντοτε ἐν πάσῃ δεήσει μου is attached to the following words, and ὑπὲρ πάντων ὑμῶν belongs, not to ἐν πάσῃ δεήσει μου, but to τὴν δέησιν ποιούμενος.

This is the most natural and simple arrangement of the words (so Weiss, Kl., Lips., Weizs.). Lightf. makes a single clause of πάντοτε . . . ὑμῶν and attaches it to the foregoing words; and makes **μετὰ χαρᾶς . . . ποιούμενος** a separate explanatory clause defining the character of **πάσῃ δεήσει**. He joins πάντοτε with εὐχαριστῶ. Ellic. connects ὑπὲρ πάντων ὑμῶν with δεήσει μου, as Mey.

Comp. 1 Thess. i. 2; Rom. i. 9, 10; Eph. i. 16; Col. i. 4; Philem. 4.

τῷ θεῷ μου: For μου with the sense of personal relationship, see Acts xxvii. 23; Rom. i. 8; Philem. 4.

ἐπὶ πάσῃ τῇ μνείᾳ ὑμῶν: The local sense of ἐπὶ runs into the temporal, and blends with it (Jelf, *Gr.* 634, 2). Render 'in,' and comp. ii. 17. The sense is similar if not identical where ἐπὶ occurs with the genitive in 1 Thess. i. 2; Eph. i. 16; Philem. 4. But see Ellic. here. Not 'upon every remembrance' as A.V., which is precluded by the article with μνείᾳ, but 'in all my remembrance'; my remembrance of you as a whole is mingled with thanksgiving. Μνεία is not 'mention' (as Kl.), a meaning which it has only when joined with ποιεῖσθαι, as Rom. i. 9; Eph. i. 16; 1 Thess. i. 2. To make ὑμῶν the subjective genitive, 'your thought of me,' with an allusion to their gift, is against usage, and would require a definite mention of the object of remembrance. Harnack, *Th. LZ.*, 1889, p. 419, wrongly renders "for every mode of your remembrance," adding "whereby, in the very beginning of the letter, the Philippians' gift is thought of with tenderness." The thought is quite unsuitable that Paul is moved to remembrance only by the exhibition of their care for him.

4. πάντοτε ἐν πάσῃ δεήσει: Πάσῃ δεήσει defines πάντοτε, as πάντοτε marks the occasions of εὐχαριστῶ. On every occasion of his praying he makes request for them. Δέησις is petitionary prayer; 'supplication.' Paul alone joins it with προσευχῇ, which is the more general term for prayer. (See Phil. iv. 6; Eph. vi. 18; 1 Tim. ii. 1.) Προσευχὴ is limited to prayer to God, while δέησις may be addressed to man. (See Trench, *N. T. Syn.* li.; Schmidt, *Synon.* 7, 4; Ellic. on 1 Tim. ii. 2; Eph. vi. 18.) Τὴν δέησιν defines the more general πάσῃ δεήσει, and is in turn defined by ὑπὲρ πάντων ὑμῶν.

μετὰ χαρᾶς: The petitions are accompanied with joy, the cause of which is indicated in vs. 5–7.

5. ἐπὶ τῇ κοινωνίᾳ ὑμῶν: Connect with εὐχαριστῶ, not with τὴν δέησιν ποιούμενος. For, 1. εὐχαριστῶ would thus be left without an object. 2. The 'fellowship' is not the subject of Paul's prayer, but of his thanksgiving. 3. Εὐχαριστεῖν and similar verbs are used by Paul with ἐπὶ, as 1 Cor. i. 4; 2 Cor. ix. 15; but ἐπὶ never occurs with δέησιν ποιούμενος or δεῖσθαι to mark their cause or ground. Neither should ἐπὶ τῇ κοινωνίᾳ be connected with μετὰ χαρᾶς which would require τῆς before ἐπὶ.

κοινωνία: 'Fellowship' (κοινὸς, 'common'). A relation between individuals which involves common and mutual interest and participation in a common object. The word occurs often in Paul and in John's epistles. Occasionally of the particular form which the spirit of fellowship assumes, as the giving of alms (Rom. xv. 26; Heb. xiii. 16), but always with an emphasis upon the principle of Christian fellowship which underlies the gift. Here it means sympathetic participation in labor and suffering.

τῇ κοιν. ὑμῶν: 'your fellowship.' 'Not fellowship with you' (objective genitive); for when Paul uses the objective genitive with κοινωνία, it is to express fellowship with a divine and not a human person (1 Cor. i. 9; 2 Cor. xiii. 13; Phil. ii. 1). Moreover, when κοινωνία is used of fellowship *with* (*una cum*) human persons, the relation is indicated by μετὰ (1 John i. 3, 7). Comp. πρὸς, 2 Cor. vi. 14. Hence ὑμῶν here is subjective. No defining word indicates their fellowship with him. The meaning is their fellowship with each other in the cause of the gospel. If the reference had been particularly to their fellowship with Paul, μετ' ἐμοῦ would probably have been added.

εἰς τὸ εὐαγγέλιον: Describes the character and object of the fellowship. For κοινωνία with εἰς, see Rom. xv. 26; 2 Cor. ix. 13; and comp. ἐκοινώνησεν εἰς, Phil. iv. 15. The meaning is not 'contribution,' though the thought of their gifts may have been distinctly present to the apostle's mind (so Ellic. and Lightf.); nor 'participation' in the gospel as sharers of its blessings; but 'your close association in the furtherance of the gospel.'

ἀπὸ τῆς πρώτης ἡμέρας:

WH. and Weiss retain της with ℵ ABP 37. Tisch. omits with DFGKL.

'The first day' is the day when they received the gospel. (See Acts xvi. 13; Col. i. 6.) Connect with τῇ κοινωνίᾳ ὑμῶν, not with πεποιθὼς.

ἄχρι τοῦ νῦν: As Rom. viii. 22. Only in Paul.

The Commendation and Prayer

6. πεποιθὼς: 'being confident.' Appended to εὐχαριστῶ and parallel with ποιούμενος.

αὐτὸ τοῦτο: Not governed by πεποιθὼς, but appended to it as specially marking the content and compass of the action (Ellic.). It prepares the way for the matter introduced by ὅτι. (Comp. Eph. vi. 22; Col. iv. 8.) Not 'for this very reason' (Mey.), *i.e.* by reason of your past coöperation, but referring to what follows.

ὁ ἐναρξάμενος: 'He'—God—is the source of Paul's confidence, not only for himself, but for his converts; God, whom he thanks in all his remembrance of them. For the omission of θεὸς, comp. Rom. viii. 11; Gal. i. 6, ii. 8, iii. 5, v. 8; 1 Thess. v. 24. That ἐναρξάμενος contains a sacrificial metaphor, the beginning of the gospel-work among the Philippians being conceived as the inauguration of a sacrifice (Lightf.), is not probable. The word is used in that sense mostly in poetry, and the conception, in any case, is far-fetched. Lightf. compares ii. 17, but that can hardly be said to be in point. Ἐνάρχεσθαι occurs three times in the N.T. (2 Cor. viii. 6; Gal. iii. 3), only in Paul, and always with ἐπιτελεῖν.

ἐν ὑμῖν: 'In you'; in your hearts. Not 'among you.' (Comp. ii. 13.)

ἔργον ἀγαθὸν: Comp. ii. 13. The work begun in their reception of the gospel, and developed in their activity and close fellowship for its promotion. The thought is taken up again in vs. 7.

ἐπιτελέσει: 'Complete,' 'consummate.' For the thought, comp. 1 Cor. i. 8; 1 Thess. v. 24; 2 Thess. iii. 3. The sense is pregnant; will carry it on toward completion, and finally complete.

ἄχρι ἡμέρας Ἰησοῦ Χριστοῦ: 'Day of Jesus Christ' is the second coming or *parousia* of the Lord. The phrase is varied in Paul's epistles: ἡ ἡμέρα, absolutely (1 Thess. v. 4; 1 Cor. iii. 13; Rom. xiii. 12); ἡ ἡμέρα ἐκείνη (2 Thess. i. 10); ἡμέρα Χριστοῦ (Phil. i. 10, ii. 16); ἡμέρα κυρίου or τοῦ κυρίου (1 Cor. v. 5; 1 Thess. v. 2; 2 Thess. ii. 2); ἡμέρα τοῦ κυρίου ἡμῶν Ἰησοῦ (Χτοῦ) (1 Cor. i. 8; 2 Cor. i. 14). It refers to a definite point of time when the Lord will appear, and Paul expects this appearance soon. Attempts to evade this by referring his expressions to the day of death, or to the advance toward perfection after death until the final judgment, are forced and shaped by dogmatic preconceptions of the nature of inspiration. (See Jowett, "On the Belief of the Coming of Christ in the Apostolical Age," in *The Epistles of St. Paul to the Thessalonians*, etc.).

7. καθώς ἐστιν δίκαιον ἐμοὶ τοῦτο φρονεῖν ὑπὲρ πάντων ὑμῶν: 'Even as it is right for me to be thus minded on behalf of you all.'

Καθώς is a nearer definition of πεποιθὼς, stating its ground in the affectionate relation between Paul and his readers. For a similar usage, see Gal. iii. 6. I am confident, *even as* it is right for me to have such confidence. Comp. also iii. 17; Rom. i. 28; 1 Cor. i. 6; Eph. i. 4.

δίκαιον: in the general moral sense, as iv. 8; Acts iv. 19; Eph. vi. 1; Col. iv. 1; referring, as in classical usage, to the conception of what is normal, yet having at its foundation, not the natural relation of man to man, but the moral relation of man to God. The classical construction of the clause would be δίκαιον ἐμὲ τοῦτο φρονεῖν, or δίκαιος εἰμὶ τοῦτο φρ. (See Win. lxvi.)

φρονεῖν: 'To be minded'; not as A.V., 'to think.' The word denotes rather a general disposition of the mind than a specific act of thought directed at a given point. Comp. iii. 15, 19, iv. 2; Rom. viii. 5, xi. 20; 1 Cor. xiii. 11; Gal. v. 10; Matt. xvi. 23; and see on iii. 15. Comp. also φρόνημα (Rom. viii. 6, 7, 27). Mey. defines 'the ethical Christian quality.' Similarly, in class. Greek, φρονεῖν often occurs with εὖ, καλῶς, ὀρθῶς, κακῶς: τά τινος φρονεῖν is to be of one's party or on his side. (See Schmidt, *Synon.* 147, 7, 8.) The reference of φρονεῖν here is to πεποιθὼς, not to the 'supplication' (vs. 4), which the sense of φρονεῖν does not admit.

ὑπὲρ παντῶν ὑμῶν: Ὑπὲρ is stronger than περὶ, 'concerning.' Const. with φρονεῖν, as iv. 10. 'All,' collectively. The reference of this frequently recurring 'all' to Paul's deprecation of divisions in the church is far-fetched.

διὰ τὸ ἔχειν με ἐν τῇ καρδίᾳ ὑμᾶς: 'Because I have you in my heart.' Not, 'because you have me,' which is forbidden by the position of the words, and by the following verse (Win. xliv.). It is right for me so to think, because I have a personal affection for you (comp. 2 Cor. vii. 3), as those who are my partakers in grace and my co-laborers in the work of the gospel. This is not to be understood as if Paul's natural affection for his readers made it right for him to expect that the work begun in them would be completed, but the expectation *was* justified by his love for them *in Christ.* He knew no man after the flesh (2 Cor. v. 16); he loved them 'in the heart of Jesus Christ' (vs. 8), and the reason for his love was also the fundamental reason for his confidence in the completion of the work of God in them.

ἔν τε τοῖς δεσμοῖς μου, etc.: Not to be taken with the preceding sentence, so as to read 'I have you in my heart both in my bonds,' etc. (so Mey., De W., Alf., Beet, Weizs.), but to be attached to the following συνκοινωνούς . . . ὄντας (so Lips., Lightf., Dw., Weiss, Ellic., Kl., Ead., WH., R.V.), 'I have you in my heart as being (ὄντας) partakers with me in grace both in my bonds and in the defence,' etc. The development of the thought as related to κοινωνία (vs. 4) and the repetition of ὑμᾶς, which is more easily accounted for if the new clause begins with ἔν τε τοῖς δεσμοῖς, make this connection the more probable one. The apostle is confident because of his love for them in Christ, and he cherishes them in his heart because of the evidence furnished by them that in his sufferings and in the defence of the gospel they are united with him in the closest Christian fellowship.

καὶ ἐν τῇ ἀπολογίᾳ καὶ βεβαιώσει τοῦ εὐαγγελίου:

εν repeated before τη απολογια with ℵ BD^bc EKLP. Probably omitted (as in ADFG) because it was wanting before βεβαιωσει, the transcriber overlooking that βεβ. was included with ἀπολ. under one article.

Ἀπολογία occurs in the sense of defence against a judicial accusation (Acts xxv. 16; 2 Tim. iv. 16). As a defence against private persons (1 Cor. ix. 3; 2 Cor. vii. 11). In a loose sense, including both these (Phil. i. 16; 1 Pet. iii. 15). Here it may include Paul's defence before the Roman authorities, but it must not be limited to that. It includes all his efforts, wherever put forth, to defend the gospel.

Βεβαίωσις occurs only here and Heb. vi. 16. It is closely allied but not synonymous with ἀπολογία, and does not form a hendiadys with it—'defence for confirmation.' Notice the binding of the two words under the same article. The defence was made for establishment or confirmation, and resulted in it. For the kindred verb βεβαιοῦν, see 1 Cor. i. 6, 8; 2 Cor. i. 21.

συνκοινωνούς μου τῆς χάριτος: Συνκοινωνὸς occurs in the N.T. with both persons (1 Cor. ix. 23) and things (Rom. xi. 17). Render 'partakers with me of grace,' not as A.V. 'partakers of my grace.' Against this is the order of the pronouns, and the fact that when Paul speaks of the grace peculiar to himself he never says μοῦ ἡ χάρις or ἡ χάρις μου, but ἡ χάρις ἡ δοθεῖσα μοι (Gal. ii. 9; 1 Cor. iii. 10; Rom. xii. 3, xv. 15); or ἡ χάρις αὐτοῦ ἡ εἰς ἐμὲ (1 Cor. xv. 10). Moreover, the grace is characterised by 'in my bonds,' etc. For a similar construction of a noun with a double genitive, of the person and of the thing, see i. 25, ii. 30. The article with χάριτος characterises the absolute grace of God in its peculiar applications to his trials and theirs, and in its manifestations in their sympathy and effort. Grace prompted them to alleviate his imprisonment, to coöperate with him in defending and propagating the gospel, and to suffer for its sake.

8. μάρτυς γάρ μου ὁ θεός:

The reading μοι for μου, Vulg. *mihi*, has little support.

A strong adjuration thrown in as a spontaneous expression of feeling, like "God knows." (Comp. Rom. i. 9; 2 Cor. i. 23; 1 Thess. ii. 5, 10.) Chrys. says it is an expression of his inability to express his feeling, 'I cannot express how I long.' Similarly, Aretius, "No necessity compels him to this appeal, yet the greatness of his love does not satisfy itself without betaking itself to God's tribunal."

Some of the earlier interpreters explained the words as an attestation of Paul's love made with a view of heightening that of his readers; as a formal oath in verification of his teaching; as a protection against slanderers and against suspicion. Klöpper thinks that they were aimed at certain persons in the church who were not in full sympathy with him and did not wholly trust his assurances. All these explanations are forced. The general statement, 'I have you in my heart,' is carried out by the stronger expression.

ὡς ἐπιποθῶ πάντας ὑμᾶς ἐν σπλάγχνοις Χριστοῦ Ἰησοῦ:

ὡς: 'how,' as Rom. i. 9; 1 Thess. ii. 10. Not 'that.' (See Thay. *Lex. sub voce*, i. 6.)

ἐπιποθῶ: Mostly in Paul. The only exceptions are Jas. iv. 5; 1 Pet. ii. 2. Ἐπὶ denotes the direction, not the intensity of the emotion, as Lightf. and Kl.

σπλάγχνοις: Σπλάγχνα are the nobler entrails—the heart, liver, and lungs, as distinguished from the intestines (τὰ ἔντερα), and regarded collectively as the seat of the feelings, the affections and passions, especially anxiety and anger. 'Heart' is used similarly by us. A like usage appears in Hebrew, though the nobler organs are not selected for the metaphorical usage. Thus מֵעִים, 'bowels,' 'womb,' 'stomach,' and קֶרֶב, 'bowels,' 'belly,' 'womb,' are both used for the heart as the seat of feeling. The plural of רֶחֶם, 'the womb,' רַחֲמִים, is rendered in the LXX by *οἰκτιρμοί*, Ps. xxv. (xxiv.) 6, xl. (xxxix.) 12; by ἔλεος, Is. xlvii. 6; by *σπλάγχνα*, Prov. xii. 10. The word occurs occasionally in the singular, *σπλάγχνον*, in the tragedians. (See Æsch. *Eum.* 240; Soph. *Aj.* 995; Eur. *Orest.* 1201, *Hippol.* 118.) For N.T. usage, see ii. 1; 2 Cor. vi. 12, vii. 15; Col. iii. 12; Philem. 7, 12, 20.

Χριστοῦ Ἰησοῦ: Paul's feeling is not his mere natural affection, but an affection so informed with Christ that it is practically Christ's own love. Christ loves them in him. Thus Beng., "In Paulo non Paulus vivit sed Jesus Christus; quare Paulus non in Pauli, sed Jesu Christi movetur visceribus."

9. *καὶ τοῦτο προσεύχομαι*: With reference to *δέησιν* in vs. 4.

Καὶ not connecting *τοῦτο προσ.* with *ἐπιποθῶ*, so as to read 'how I long and how I pray' (so Ril.). This would weaken, if not destroy the force of vs. 8. A new topic is introduced by *καὶ*.

Τοῦτο points to what follows, calling attention to the subject of the prayer. 'This which follows is what I pray.'

ἵνα ἡ ἀγάπη ὑμῶν ἔτι μᾶλλον καὶ μᾶλλον περισσεύῃ: 'That your love may abound yet more and more.'

Ἵνα marks the purport of the prayer. For *προσεύχ. ἵνα*, see 1 Cor. xiv. 13.

There is abundant evidence that *ἵνα* has, in many cases, lost its telic sense and has come to express result or purport. See, for example, 1 Thess. v. 4; 1 Cor. vii. 29, and the sensible remarks of Canon Evans on the latter passage in the *Speaker's Com.* The examples are drawn out and classified by Burton, *Syntax of the Moods and Tenses of N. T. Greek*, 191–223. See also Simcox, *Language of the N.T.*, p. 176 ff.

ἡ ἀγάπη ὑμῶν: Your mutual love; not your love for me, save as I am one of the common brotherhood.

ἔτι μᾶλλον καὶ μᾶλλον περισσεύῃ: Comp. 1 Thess. iv. 9, 10. Notice the accumulation of comparative phrases so common with Paul, as vs. 23; 2 Cor. iv. 17; Eph. iii. 20.

For *περισσευῃ*, BD 37 read *περισσευσῃ*; so Weiss, and WH. marg. K* P *περισσευει*. FG *περισσευοι*.

Love, like other Christian graces, grows. (Comp. iii. 13.) Notice the progressive present, 'may continue to abound.' Chrys. remarks: "For this is a good of which there is no satiety."

ἐν ἐπιγνώσει καὶ πάσῃ αἰσθήσει: 'in knowledge and in all discernment.' Ἐπίγνωσις and the kindred verb *ἐπιγινώσκειν* are favorite words with Paul. Ἐπὶ has the force of addition; knowledge superadded; advanced knowledge, rather than (as Thay. and Kl.) direction toward; application to that which is known. (See Sanday on Rom. i. 28, and Evans on 1 Cor. xiii. 12.) Thus it signifies here developed knowledge of truth, with more especial reference to the practical knowledge which informs Christian love as to the right circumstances, aims, ways, and means. (See Col. i. 9, 10.) The difference between the simple and the compound word is illustrated in 1 Cor. xiii. 12; Rom. i. 21, 28. Ἐπίγνωσις is always applied in the N.T. to the knowledge of things ethical and divine. In all the four epistles of the captivity it is one of the subjects of the apostle's opening prayer for his readers. It is constructed mostly with a genitive of the object, as ἁμαρτίας, ἀληθείας, and occurs absolutely only in Rom. x. 2.

αἰσθήσει: Only here in N.T. Comp. αἰσθητήρια (Heb. v. 14). In LXX, Prov. i. 4, 7, 22, iii. 20, v. 2; Sir. xxii. 19; Jud. xvi. 17. Primarily of sensuous, but also of spiritual perception. It is the faculty of spiritual discernment of the bearings of each particular circumstance or case which may emerge in experience. It is more specific than ἐπίγνωσις with the practical applications of which it deals. Πάσῃ is added because this discernment operates in manifold ways, according to the various relations of the subject to the facts of experience. Ἐν, which belongs to both nouns, follows the standing usage, περισσεύειν ἐν. (See Rom. xv. 13; 2 Cor. iii. 9, viii. 7.) Paul prays for the abounding of love in these two aspects, advanced knowledge and right spiritual discernment; an intelligent and discriminating love; love which, however ardent and sincere, shall not be a mere unregulated impulse. Even natural love has a quick perception, an intuitive knowledge; but without the regulative principle of the spiritual reason, it is not secure against partial seeing and misconception, and results which do not answer to the purity of its motives. Ἐπίγνωσις is the general regulator and guide. Αἴσθησις applies ἐπίγνωσις to the finer details of the individual life, and fulfils itself in the various phases of Christian tact.

10. εἰς τὸ δοκιμάζειν ὑμᾶς τὰ διαφέροντα: 'That you may put to the proof the things that differ.'

Εἰς governing the infin. with τὸ is frequent in Paul. (See Rom. i. 11, iii. 26, viii. 29; Eph. i. 12.)

Δοκιμάζειν in class. Gk. of assaying metals. (Comp. LXX, Prov. viii. 10, xvii. 3; Sir. ii. 5; also 1 Cor. iii. 13; 1 Pet. i. 7.) In class. the technical word for testing money (Plato, *Tim.* 65, c.). Δοκιμάζειν and πυροῦσθαι occur together (Jer. ix. 7; Ps. xii. (xi.) 6, lxvi. (lxv.) 10). Generally, 'to prove,' 'examine,' as 1 Cor. xi. 28; Gal. vi. 4; 1 Thess. v. 21. 'To accept' that which is proved to be good. This and the more general sense appear together in 1 Cor. xvi. 3; 2 Cor. viii. 22; 1 Thess. ii. 4.

τὰ διαφέροντα: Διαφέρειν, in class. and N.T., means both 'to excel' (Matt. vi. 26, x. 31, xii. 12; Luke xii. 7, 24), and 'to differ' (1 Cor. xv. 41; Gal. iv. 1, ii. 6).

Expositors are divided between two renderings. 1. 'To put to the proof the things that differ,' and so discriminate between them (so Alf., Ead., Lips., Kl., De W., Weiss, Hack.). 2. 'To approve the things that are excellent' (so Ellic., Mey., Beet, Lightf., Vulg., R.V., but with 1 in marg.). The difference is not really essential, since, in any case, the result contemplated is the approval of what is good. But 1 agrees better with what precedes, especially with *αἴσθησις*. Paul is emphasising the necessity of wisdom and discrimination in love. This necessity arises from circumstances which present moral problems, and develop differences of view, and give room for casuistry. The discrimination of love applies tests, and makes distinctions impossible to the untrained moral sense. Therefore the Romans are urged to be 'transformed by the renewing of their mind,' in order that they may prove (*δοκιμάζειν*) the good and acceptable and perfect will of God (Rom. xii. 2). Paul illustrates this discrimination in the matter of eating meat offered to idols (1 Cor. viii., x. 19–33). In that case love abounds, not only in knowledge, but in perception of a delicate distinction between an act which is right in itself, and wrong in the light of the obligation to the weak conscience. The *αἴσθησις* of love is the only sure guide in questions which turn upon things morally indifferent. Thus the whole thought is as follows: 'May your love increase and abound in ripe knowledge and perceptive power, that you may apply the right tests and reach the right decisions in things which present moral differences.' (Comp. Eph. v. 10; 1 Thess. v. 21; Heb. v. 14.)

The majority of the Greek fathers explained the differences as those between believers and unbelievers, heretics or errorists, or between true and false doctrine; many of the moderns of the difference between right and wrong. (See Klöpper on this pass.)

ἵνα ἦτε εἰλικρινεῖς καὶ ἀπρόσκοποι:

There is good ancient authority for *ειλικ.*, both with and without the aspirate. (See WH. *N. T. Append.* sub 'breathings.') The word only here and 2 Pet. iii. 1. The kindred noun *εἰλικρίνεια* in 1 Cor. v. 8; 2 Cor. i. 12, ii. 17. The meaning is 'pure,' 'sincere.'

None of the etymologies are satisfactory. The usual one is *εἵλη*, 'tested by the sunlight,' but *εἵλη* means the *heat* of the sun.

Lightf. suggests a probable(?) derivation from *εἴλη*, 'a troop'; others, from *εἴλω* or *ἴλλω*, 'to turn round,'—hence 'judged by turning round,' or 'sifted by revolution.'

ἀπρόσκοποι: Either (1) 'not causing others to stumble' (Lips., Mey., Ead.), or (2) 'not stumbling' (Alf., Ellic., Kl., Weiss, Lightf.). For 1, see 1 Cor. x. 32; and comp. Rom. xiv. 13; 2 Cor. vi. 3; for 2, Acts xxiv. 16. The former meaning is clearly preferable, as related to what precedes. The discernment of love is especially demanded in adjusting a Christian's true relations to his brethren. Lightf.'s reason for adopting 2 is that the question is solely that of the fitness of the Philippians to appear before the tribunal of Christ, and that therefore any reference to their influence upon others would be out of place. How influence upon others can be left out of the question of such fitness, it is not easy to see. Certainly, if we are to believe Christ himself, the awards of the day of Christ will be determined quite as much by the individual's relations to his fellow-men as by his personal righteousness, if the two can be separated, as they cannot be. Christ's thought on that point is unmistakably expressed in Matt. xxv. 40; and Paul furnishes his own interpretation of ἀπρόσκοποι in Rom. xiv. 13; 1 Cor. x. 32; 2 Cor. vi. 3; and especially 1 Cor. viii. 13.

εἰς ἡμέραν Χριστοῦ:

εἰς, not 'till,' as A.V., but 'for,' 'against,' as those who are preparing for it. For this sense of εἰς, comp. ii. 16; Eph. iv. 30; 2 Tim. i. 12.

11. πεπληρωμένοι καρπὸν δικαιοσύνης: 'being filled with the fruit of righteousness.' Πεπλ. agrees with the subject of ἦτε in vs. 10, and defines εἰλικρινεῖς and ἀπρόσκοποι more fully. Καρπὸν is the accus. of the remote object, as Col. i. 9; 2 Thess. i. 11. (Comp. LXX, Ex. xxxi. 3.) Paul elsewhere uses πληροῦν with the genit. or dat. (See Rom. i. 29, xv. 13, 14; 2 Cor. vii. 4.)

The reading of TR καρπων . . . των is feebly supported.

Καρπὸς in its moral and religious sense occurs in vs. 22, iv. 17; Rom. i. 13, vi. 21, 22, xv. 28; Gal. v. 22, nearly always of a good result. The phrase 'fruit of righteousness' is from the O.T. (See Prov. xi. 30; Amos vi. 13. Comp. Jas. iii. 18.) The genit. δικαιοσύνης is not appositional, 'fruit which consists in righteousness,' but, as Gal. v. 22; Eph. v. 9; Jas. iii. 18, 'the fruit which righteousness produces.'

Δικαιοσύνη, not in Paul's more technical sense of 'righteousness by faith,' but moral rightness; righteousness of life; though, as Mey. justly observes, it is a moral condition which is the moral consequence, because the necessary vital expression of the righteousness of faith. (Comp. Rom. vii. 4; Col. i. 10.) "The technical and the moral conceptions of righteousness may be dogmatically distinguished, but not in fact, since the latter cannot exist without the former" (Weiss). This appears from the next clause — τὸν διὰ Ἰησοῦ Χριστοῦ. Notice the defining force of τὸν.

Righteousness without Christ cannot be fruitful (Jn. xv. 5, 8, 16).

εἰς δόξαν καὶ ἔπαινον θεοῦ: Construe with the whole preceding sentence, and not with καρπὸν only.

Δόξα is not used in N.T. in the classical sense of 'notion' or 'opinion.' In the sense of 'reputation' (Jn. xii. 43; Rom. ii. 7,

10). As 'brightness' or 'splendor' (Acts xxii. 11; Rom. ix. 4; 1 Cor. xv. 40). 'The glory of God' expresses the sum total of the divine perfections. It is prominent in the redemptive revelation (Is. lx. 1; Rom. v. 2, vi. 4). It expresses the form in which God reveals himself in the economy of salvation (Rom. ix. 23; Eph. i. 12; 1 Tim. i. 11). It is the means by which the redemptive work is carried on; in calling (2 Pet. 1, 3); in raising up Christ and believers with him (Rom. vi. 4); in imparting strength to believers (Eph. iii. 16; Col. i. 11). It is the goal of Christian hope (Rom. v. 2, viii. 18, 21; Tit. ii. 13). It is the redemptive aspect of the phrase which gives the key to its meaning here. The love of God's children, abounding in discriminating knowledge, their being filled with the fruit of righteousness, redounds to (εἰς) his glory as a redeeming God. It honors him in respect of that which is preëminently his glory. Every holy character is a testimony to the divine character and efficiency of the work of redemption.

ἔπαινον: The homage rendered to God as a God of 'glory.' (See Eph. i. 6, 12, 14; 1 Pet. i. 7.)

The apostle now enters upon the subject-matter of the letter. From vs. 12 to vs. 26 he treats of—

1. The state of the gospel in Rome.
   (*a*) Its advancement through his imprisonment (12–14).
   (*b*) The different kinds of preachers (15–17).
2. His own condition and hopes (18–26).

12–14. *Though you may have feared that the cause of the gospel is suffering by reason of my imprisonment, I wish to assure you that it has rather been promoted thereby. My imprisonment has become known as being for Christ's sake, not only to the whole band of the prætorian troops, but also to the rest of Rome; and the majority of the Christian brethren have had their faith in God strengthened by my example, and their boldness in preaching the gospel increased.*

12. γινώσκειν δὲ ὑμᾶς βούλομαι: 'now I would have you know.' This phrase does not occur elsewhere in N.T., but Paul uses several similar expressions in order to call special attention to what he is about to say. Thus, θέλω δὲ ὑμᾶς εἰδέναι (1 Cor. xi. 3; Col. ii. 1); οὐ θέλω (ομεν) ὑμᾶς ἀγνοεῖν (1 Cor. x. 1; Rom. i. 13; 1 Thess. iv. 13); γνωρίζω (ομεν) ὑμῖν (1 Cor. xv. 1; 2 Cor. viii. 1; Gal. i. 11).

τὰ κατ' ἐμὲ: 'The things pertaining to me'; my experience as a prisoner. (Comp. Eph. vi. 21; Col. iv. 7.) Not 'that which has been undertaken *against* me,' which would require ἐμοῦ.

μᾶλλον: Not 'more' (quantitatively), but 'rather.' Though you feared that my circumstances might injure the cause of the gospel, they have *rather* promoted it. The comparative is often used without mention of the standard of comparison. (See ii. 28; Rom. xv. 15; 1 Cor. vii. 38, xii. 31; 2 Cor. vii. 7, 13, etc.; Win. xxxv. 4.)

προκοπὴν: Only here, vs. 25, and 1 Tim. iv. 15. A word of later Greek, occurring in Plut., Jos., and Philo. (See Wetst.) In LXX, see Sir. li. 17; 2 Macc. viii. 8. The figure in the word is uncertain, but is supposed to be that of pioneers *cutting* a way *before* an army, and so *furthering* its march. The opposite is expressed by ἐγκόπτειν, 'to cut into,' 'to throw obstacles in the way of,' and so 'to hinder' (Gal. v. 7; 1 Thess. ii. 18; 1 Pet. iii. 7).

εὐαγγελίου: Originally 'a present given in return for good news.' (See Hom. *Od.* xiv. 152; Aristoph. *Knights*, 647; 2 Sam. iv. 10, xviii. 22.) In class. Gk. it meant, in the plu., 'a sacrifice for good tidings'; hence the phrase εὐαγγελία θύειν (Aristoph. *Knights*, 656; Xen. *Hell.* i. 6, 37, iv. 3, 14). Later, 'the good news' itself, as 2 Sam. xviii. 20, 25, 27; 2 Kings vii. 9. Hence 'the joyful tidings of Messiah's kingdom — the gospel.' In the N.T., never in the sense of a book.

εἰς . . . ἐλήλυθεν: Not elsewhere in Paul. (See Sap. xv. 5.) 'Has redounded to'; 'fallen out unto.'

13. ὥστε τοὺς δεσμούς μου φανεροὺς ἐν Χριστῷ:

Ὥστε with the accus. w. inf., as 1 Cor. 1, 7. With an explanatory force, the explanation being regarded as a result of the notion of προκοπὴν. (See Jelf, *Gram.* 863, obs. 7.) Render: 'so that my bonds became manifest in Christ'; not 'my bonds in Christ,' against which is the position of the words. Moreover, the force of the statement lies in the fact that his imprisonment has become a matter of notoriety as being *for Christ.* His confinement as a Christian would excite attention and inquiry. (Comp. Ign. *Smyr.* xi. δεδεμένος θεοπρεπεστάτοις δεσμοῖς πάντας ἀσπάζομαι: "A prisoner in bonds which are divine ornaments, I salute all men.") Jerome says: "Vincula mea manifesta fierent in Christo. Non solum non obsunt sed etiam profuerunt, dum manifestatur me non pro aliquo crimine, sed pro Christo omnia sustinere."

ἐν ὅλῳ τῷ πραιτωρίῳ:

'In (or throughout) the whole prætorian guard.' The prætorians formed the imperial guard. They were ten thousand in number, picked men, originally of Italian birth, but drawn later from Macedonia, Noricum, and Spain. They were originally instituted by Augustus, who stationed three of their cohorts in Rome, and dispersed the others in the adjacent towns. Tiberius concentrated them all at Rome in a permanent and strongly fortified camp. Vitellius increased their number to sixteen thousand. They were distinguished by special privileges and by double pay. Their original term of service was twelve years, afterwards increased to sixteen. On retiring, each soldier received a bounty amounting to nearly nine hundred dollars. Paul was committed to the charge of these troops, the soldiers relieving each other in mounting guard over him in his private lodging. (See note at the end of this chapter.)

καὶ τοῖς λοιποῖς πᾶσιν: (Comp. 2 Cor. xiii. 2.) 'All the rest,' as distinguished from the prætorians. Not as A.V., 'in all other places' (so Chrys., Thdrt., Calv.). His imprisonment as a Christian became known beyond the limits of the guard, in the city at large. Immediately upon his arrival he addressed the chief of the Jews (Acts xxviii. 17), and later a larger number (vs. 23), and for two years received all that came to him (vs. 30).

14. *καὶ τοὺς πλείονας τῶν ἀδελφῶν ἐν κυρίῳ πεποιθότας τοῖς δεσμοῖς μου*: 'And the majority of the brethren having confidence in the Lord by reason of my bonds.'

τοὺς πλείονας: Not as A.V. 'many,' but 'the greater number.' (Comp. 1 Cor. x. 5.)

Differences as to the connection of the words. 1. *ἐν κυρίῳ*: (*a*) with *ἀδελφῶν*, 'brethren in the Lord' (Alf., Kl., Dw., Weiss., De W., Weizs. [Trans.]); (*b*) with *πεποιθότας τοῖς δεσμοῖς*, 'relying on my bonds in the Lord.' According to this, *ἐν κυρίῳ* is the modal definition of *πεπ. τ. δεσμ.* The ground of confidence is *τοῖς δεσμ.*, not *ἐν κυρ.*, which marks the nature and sphere of the confidence (so Mey., Lightf., Ellic., Lips., Ead.). 2. *πεποιθότας*: (*a*) with *τοῖς δεσμοῖς*, as that in which confidence is reposed (Mey., Kl., Ead., Lightf., Alf., Lips.); (*b*) with *ἐν κυρίῳ*, as the ground of confidence (Beet, Hack.).

As to 1 (*a*), *ἀδελφοὶ ἐν κυρίῳ* does not occur elsewhere. None of the passages cited by Kl. and others, such as 1 Cor. iv. 17; Col. iv. 7; Philem. 16, are in point, since in none of them does the preposition depend directly on *ἀδελφὸς*. Moreover, the addition of *ἐν κ.* would seem superfluous. 1 (*b*) is grammatically defensible. (See Gal. v. 10; 2 Thess. iii. 4.) But the sense is forced, if it can be called sense. What is meant by 'having confidence in,' or 'trusting in my bonds'? 2 (*b*) is a legitimate construction. (See Jer. xxxi. 7, LXX, *Eng. Bib.* xlviii. 7; Phil. ii. 24; and the analogous constructions, Phil. iii. 3, 4.) It is true that in such cases *πεποιθ.* usually precedes; but the change of position is for the sake of emphasis, as Phil. iii. 3. *Ἐν κυρίῳ* is the ground of *πεποιθ.*, and *τοῖς δεσμ.* is instrumental. The sense is thus simple and consistent. By Paul's bonds the brethren have had their confidence in the Lord strengthened. He has already said that his bonds have become manifest in Christ. The testimony borne by his imprisonment has been distinctly that of

Christ's prisoner, and has therefore encouraged confidence in Christ.

περισσοτέρως τολμᾶν ἀφόβως τὸν λόγον τοῦ θεοῦ λαλεῖν: 'are more abundantly bold to speak the word of God without fear.' For περισσοτέρως, comp. 2 Cor. i. 12, ii. 4; Gal. i. 14. It belongs with τολμᾶν, not with ἀφόβως.

Τολμᾶν is to carry into action the feeling of resolute confidence expressed by θαρσεῖν. (See 2 Cor. x. 2, and *W. St.* ad loc.)

τὸν λόγον τοῦ θεοῦ: The message of God; the gospel. Very frequent in N.T. Once in the sense of 'the declared purpose of God' (Rom. ix. 6). Not elsewhere in Paul with λαλεῖν. For the phrase τὸν λόγ. λαλ. or τὸν λόγ. θε. λαλ., see Acts iv. 31, xiii. 46, xiv. 25.

Paul's boldness and patience in his captivity have stirred up the courage and zeal of the Roman Christians, and probably have awakened shame in some recreant disciples. Chrys. remarks that their courage had not failed before, but had grown by the apostle's bonds.

15–17. *But all those who preach Christ are not actuated by equally pure motives. While some are moved by love and by sympathy with me as a defender of the gospel, others, in a spirit of envy, contention, and partisanship, proclaim Christ insincerely, seeking to add to the affliction of my captivity.*

15. τινὲς μὲν καὶ διὰ φθόνον καὶ ἔριν: 'some indeed preach Christ even of envy and strife.' These words are independent of the preceding clause, and introduce a new feature of the condition of the gospel in Rome. The words τὸν λόγ. τ. θε. λαλ. open to the apostle the general subject of the preaching of the gospel in the metropolis. Much wearisome discussion has arisen on the question whether Paul includes those who preach Christ of envy and strife in the πλείονας of vs. 14, or treats them as a distinct class. It seems apparent on its face that the motives of envy and strife which attach to the τινὲς μὲν cannot be reconciled with the ἐν κυρίῳ πεποιθ., nor with the sympathetic consciousness that Paul is set for the defence of the gospel. (See Weiss' novel effort to reconcile these.) Moreover, the καὶ has its familiar contrasting force, and introduces another and a different class, and not the same class with the addition of a subordinate and baser motive. Thus the τινὲς μὲν are set over against the πλείονας.

But who are meant by these τινὲς μὲν? Some of the Fathers, as Chrys., Œc., Theoph., explained of unbelievers who proclaimed Christianity in order to awaken the hatred of Paul's enemies; others, as Grot., of Jews, who brought the gospel and its evidences into controversy in order to injure or refute it. Since Beng. the view has prevailed that they were Judaising Christians (so Lightf., Lips., Dw., Mey., Beet, Ellic., Lum., Nedr., Weizs.). But this view does not seem reconcilable with Paul's words concerning the Judaisers in this very epistle (iii. 2), and in the Galatian and Second Corinthian letters. Nowhere in his epistles does Paul speak of the Judaisers as preachers of Christ unless it be "another Jesus" (2 Cor. xi. 4). Although they accepted Jesus as the Messiah, in their preaching he was thrown into the background behind the claims of the law. Paul found worse enemies among these Christians than among the heathen; yet here he virtually sanctions their preaching, and rejoices in it. To say that they are shown to have been Judaising Christians because they preached Christ of envy and strife, is to argue in a circle. The attempt to solve the difficulty by assuming that the form of Judaistic opposition was milder in Rome than in the East (Mey., Dw., Pfl. *Paulinismus*, pp. 42, 332) seems like a desperate resource. To say that a conciliation of the Jewish-Christian element in Rome is implied in Paul's recognition of the value of the old covenant relation (Rom. iii. 1 f., ix. 4, x. 2); in his charity towards a narrow conscientiousness (xiv. 3–23); in his expressions of love and sympathy for his own race (ix. 1–3, x. 1, xi. 1, 13); and in his warning of the Gentiles against self-elation (xi. 17–24) — is a piece of special pleading. Paul shows equal respect for narrow conscientiousness in 1 Cor., and he never fails to treat the law and the covenants with respect; while his love and sympathy for his own race appear everywhere. Weiss (*Einl. i. d. N. T.* § 26) remarks on this passage: "This is generally supposed to refer to Judaistic teachers in Rome, whose appearance is made an argument for the still strongly Jewish-Christian character of the Roman church. But the way in which Paul unreservedly gives expression to his joy respecting this accession of preaching, makes it quite inconceivable that these personal opponents should have preached a gospel in any way differing from that which he preached."

While therefore the τινὲς μὲν, etc., may include individual Judaisers, they are not to be limited to these. I incline rather to regard them as Pauline Christians who were personally jealous of the apostle, and who sought to undermine his influence. It may be, as Weiss suggests, that as the Roman church before Paul's arrival had no definite leadership, it was easy for ambitious and smaller men to obtain a certain prominence which they found menaced by the presence and influence of the apostle. Comp. the state of things in the Corinthian church (1 Cor. iii. 3, 4).

διὰ φθόνον καὶ ἔριν: Directed at Paul personally. Διὰ, 'on account of,' marking the motive. (Comp. Mt. xxvii. 18; Eph. ii. 4; Rom. xiii. 5.)

εὐδοκίαν: A purely Biblical word. As related to one's self, it means 'contentment,' 'satisfaction' (Sir. xxix. 23; 2 Thess. i. 11; on which, see Bornemann, *Comm.* ad loc.). As related to others, it means 'good-will,' 'benevolence.' Of God's good-will to men (Lk. x. 21; Eph. i. 5, 9; Phil. ii. 13). The meaning 'desire' (so Lightf. for Sir. xi. 7, and Rom. x. 1 [see comm. on this pass.], and Thay. *Lex.* for Rom. x. 1) cannot be supported. (See Sanday on Rom. x. 1.) For εὐδοκεῖν, see 1 Cor. x. 5; 2 Cor. xii. 10; 1 Thess. ii. 12. Here 'good-will' towards Paul and the cause of the gospel.

τὸν Χριστὸν κηρύσσουσιν:

Κηρύσσειν, orig. 'to perform the duty of a herald' (κήρυξ), is the standard N.T. word for the proclamation of the gospel. Not often in any other sense. Of the preaching of John the Baptist (Mt. iii. 1; Mk. i. 4; Acts x. 37); of preaching the claims of the Mosaic law (Acts xv. 21; Gal. v. 11). Chiefly, perhaps wholly, confined to the primary announcement of the gospel, and not including continuous instruction or teaching of believers, which is expressed by διδάσκειν. (See both in Mt. iv. 23, ix. 35, xi. 1.) Yet in passages like 1 Cor. i. 23, ix. 27, xv. 11, the distinction between missionary and church preaching cannot be clearly inferred. For the phrase κηρύσσειν Χτὸν or τὸν Χτὸν, Χτὸν Ἰησοῦν, Ἰ. Χτὸν, see Acts viii. 5; 1 Cor. i. 23, xv. 12; 2 Cor. i. 19, iv. 5.

τον before χτον omitted by ℵ[ca] BFG.

16. The TR reverses the order of vs. 16, 17 (so D[bc] KL., Syr.[p], and several Fathers). The change seems to have been made in order to conform to the order of the parties in vs. 15. The words in the correct order of our text exhibit a cross-reference (*chiasmus*), the first specification of vs. 16 referring to the second of vs. 15. Render: 'They that are of love (preach Christ) because they know that I am set for the defence of the gospel; and they that are of faction (preach Christ) not purely, because they think to add affliction to my bonds.'

Οἱ μὲν ἐξ ἀγάπης and οἱ δε ἐξ ἐριθίας (vs. 17) are generic descriptions, and the subjects of καταγγέλλουσιν.

Others, as Lightf., Kl., Alf., Ead., R.V., take οἱ μέν, οἱ δε as the subjects, and ἐξ ἀγ., ἐξ ἐριθ. as qualifying καταγγ. Thus the rendering would be: 'The one preach Christ of love, because they know, etc., and the other class preach Christ of faction because they think,' etc. According to this construction, however, ἐξ ἀγ. and ἐξ ἐριθ. are substantially repetitions of διὰ εὐδοκ. and διὰ φθόν. καὶ ἔρ. Lightf.'s objection to the other construction, that thus τὸν Χτὸν καταγγ. is made too emphatic, is without force. The emphasis is intended in connection with οὐχ ἁγνῶς.

For the expressions οἱ ἐξ ἀγάπης and οἱ ἐξ ἐριθίας, comp. Jn. xviii. 37; Rom. ii. 8; Gal. iii. 7.

Εἰδότες and οἰόμενοι (vs. 17) have a causal force; 'since they know,' 'since they think.'

ἀπολογίαν: See on vs. 7. The meaning as there. Not as Chrys., Theoph., Œc., the 'account' of his ministry which Paul was to render to God.

κεῖμαι: As Luke ii. 34; 1 Thess. iii. 3; 1 Tim. i. 9. Orig. 'to be laid'; 'to lie.' Hence 'to be appointed or destined.'

17. ἐριθίας: Not from ἔρις, but ἔριθος, 'a hired servant.' Hence ἐριθία is, primarily, 'labor for hire' (see Tob. ii. 11), and is applied to those who serve in official positions for their own selfish purposes, and, to that end, promote party-spirit or faction. Render, 'faction.'

καταγγέλλουσιν: Substantially the same as κηρύσσουσιν, though among the compounds of ἀγγέλλειν it signifies 'to proclaim with authority,' with the additional idea of celebrating or commending. Only in Paul and Acts.

οὐχ ἁγνῶς: 'Not purely' or with unmixed motives, summing up all that is included in διὰ φθόν. καὶ ἔρ., δι' ἐριθ., and οἰόμ. θλῖψιν ἐγ.

The οὐχ ἁγνῶς and τὸν Χτὸν are suggestively in juxtaposition. (See on iv. 8.)

οἰόμενοι: Only here in Paul, and only twice besides in N.T. (See LXX, Job xi. 2; 1 Macc. v. 61; 2 Macc. v. 21, vii. 24.) It denotes, in class. Gk., a belief or judgment based principally upon one's own feelings, or the peculiar relations of outward circumstances to himself. In its radical sense it implies the supposition of something future and doubtful. In Attic Gk., an opinion with a collateral notion of wrong judgment or conceit (so in the citations from LXX, above). The *knowledge* of Paul's mission by his friends (εἰδότες) is offset by the malicious *imagining* (οἰόμενοι) of his enemies.

θλῖψιν ἐγείρειν: 'to raise up affliction.'

TR επιφερειν with DKL.

The phrase is unique in N.T., but a similar usage is found in LXX; Prov. x. 12, xv. 1, xvii. 11; Sir. xxxiii. 7. The meaning is not that they deliberately set themselves to aggravate Paul's sufferings, but that their malice was gratified by the annoyance which their efforts to promote their own partisan ends caused him.

18–26. *What then comes of this insincere preaching and of this malice towards me? Only this, that whether Christ is preached in pretext or in truth, he is preached, and in that I rejoice. Yes, and I will continue to rejoice; for I know that this train of afflictions will turn out for my salvation in answer to your prayer and through that which the Spirit of Christ shall supply to me. And thus will be fulfilled my earnest expectation and my hope that I shall be put to shame in nothing; but that, as with all boldness*

I shall continue to preach and to suffer for Christ's sake, Christ will be magnified in this afflicted body of mine, whether I live or die. For as to life, life to me is Christ. As to death, it is gain. Now, if to continue to live means fruitful labor, I have nothing to say as to my own preference. I am strongly appealed to from both sides. If I should consult only my own desire, I should wish to go and be with Christ, for that is by far the better thing. But, on the other hand, I am assured that, for your sake, it is more necessary that I should continue to live; and therefore I know that I shall remain with you, that I may promote your advancement and your joy in your faith; so that, in Christ Jesus, your joy in me may abound through my being present with you again.

18. τί γάρ: To be followed by the interrogation-point. Interjectional, and called out by what immediately precedes. (Comp. Rom. iii. 3.) They think to raise up affliction for me in my chains. What then? Suppose this is so. (Comp. Eng. 'for why.') For γάρ in interrogations suggested by what precedes, see Mt. xxvii. 23; Rom. iv. 3, xi. 34; 1 Cor. ii. 16, xi. 22. (See Win. liii., lxiv.)

πλὴν ὅτι: 'only that.'

TR omits οτι, as DKL. B reads οτι without πλην.

What does it signify? Only that, in any event, Christ is preached. He leaves the annoying side of the case to take care of itself, and passes on to the encouraging aspect. For πλήν, comp. iii. 16, iv. 14; 1 Cor. xi. 11; Eph. v. 33. Πλὴν with ὅτι only Acts xx. 23. (See Blass, *Gramm.* § 77, 13.)

παντὶ τρόπῳ: 'in every way' of preaching the gospel.

εἴτε προφάσει εἴτε ἀληθείᾳ: Expanding and defining παντὶ τρόπῳ.

προφάσει: Using the name of Christ as a cover or mask for personal and selfish ends. For the word, comp. 1 Thess. ii. 5. Used absolutely, Mk. xii. 40; Lk. xx. 47.

Χριστὸς καταγγέλλεται: Christianity thrives even through insincere preaching. The enemies of the truth proclaim it by their opposition. The words imply Paul's confidence in the power of the mere proclamation of Christ as a fact.

Mey. thinks that the interrogation-point should be placed after καταγγ. instead of τί γάρ. In that case the rendering would be: 'What else takes place save that Christ is preached?' But though τί γάρ as an independent question occurs only twice, Paul often uses τί οὖν in that way. There is no instance in his letters of πλὴν ὅτι = τί ἀλλὸ ὅτι. He uses πλὴν elsewhere in the sense given above. The construction of καὶ ἐν τούτῳ χαίρω is simpler and more natural if united with πλὴν . . . καταγγέλλεται than if taken as an answer to a question, τί . . . καταγγ.; (See Dw.)

ἐν τούτῳ: In the fact that Christ is preached, though with different motives.

χαίρω: Joy is a frequent theme in this letter. Beng. says: "The sum of the epistle is, 'I rejoice, do ye rejoice.'" (See i. 25, ii. 2, 17, 18, 28, 29, iii. 1, iv. 1, 4, 10.)

ἀλλὰ καὶ χαιρήσομαι: Punctuate with a period or colon after *χαίρω*, thus connecting *οἶδα γὰρ* with *ἀλλὰ καὶ χαιρήσομαι* (so WH., Tisch.), 'I rejoice. Nay but I will also continue to rejoice, since I know,' etc. His thought passes from the present to the future joy, which is assured by their prayer and by the supply of the Spirit of Christ.

19. *οἶδα γὰρ ὅτι τοῦτο μοι ἀποβήσεται εἰς σωτηρίαν*: 'for I know that this shall turn out to my salvation.'

γαρ with WH. Tisch. B 37, 61, 116, Sah., read *δε*.

Οἶδα as distinguished from *γινώσκειν* is the knowledge of intuition or satisfied conviction, or absolute knowledge. So often, by John, of Christ (iii. 11, v. 32, vi. 6, 61, 64, vii. 29, viii. 14, xiii. 1, 11). So Paul, of God (2 Cor. xi. 11, xii. 2). In Jn. xxi. 17 the two verbs appear together. *Οἶδα* is often used by Paul in appealing to what his readers know well, or ought, or might naturally be expected, to know (Rom. ii. 2, vii. 14; 1 Cor. vi. 2; Gal. iv. 13; 1 Thess. i. 5; etc.).

τοῦτο: In a general sense, explained by *τὰ κατ' ἐμὲ* (vs. 12). This whole train of afflictions which has attended my preaching of the gospel.

So Lightf., Kl., De W., Lum., Hack., and the patristic interpreters. But Mey., Ellic., Dw., Lips., Weiss, Ead., Alf., Beet, refer to the *τούτῳ* of vs. 18. It seems unlikely, however, that Paul should have said 'I know that the fact that in every way Christ is preached will turn out to my salvation.' Kl. justly remarks that, on this supposition, Paul would have been more likely to express his expectation of a favorable result which would offset the fears or wishes of those who looked for an evil result, than of a result which would redound to his own advantage.

ἀποβήσεται εἰς: 'Shall turn out to'; 'effectively go to.' The formula *ἀποβαίνειν εἰς* is not used elsewhere by Paul, and only in one other pass. in N.T. (Lk. xxi. 13). In LXX, Job xiii. 16 (cited here), xv. 31; Ex. ii. 4.

σωτηρίαν: Not his release from prison, since the result will be the same whether he lives or dies (vs. 20). Nor 'will be salutary for me' (Mey.), since Paul habitually uses *σωτηρία* in its Messianic connection. Nor does it mean 'salvation from eternal destruction' (Weiss, Kl.). The key to the meaning is found in vs. 28, ii. 12; Rom. i. 16; and especially 2 Thess. ii. 13. It is used here in its widest N.T. sense; not merely of future salvation, but of the whole saving and sanctifying work of Christ in the believer.

διὰ τῆς ὑμῶν δεήσεως καὶ ἐπιχορηγίας τοῦ πνεύματος Ἰησοῦ Χριστοῦ: 'through your supplication and the supply of the Spirit of Jesus Christ.' *Δέησις ὑμῶν* and *ἐπιχορηγία τ. πν.* 'IX are thus two distinct instruments of ἀποβήσεται, and therefore are not both included under the one article τῆς.

Lightf., Alf., Lips., Weiss, make τῆς cover both nouns, rendering 'through your supplication and supply of the Spirit,' etc.; *i.e.* the supply of the Spirit which you furnish through your supplication. This construction would, further, seem to involve the uniting of ὑμῶν with both nouns. So, distinctly, Weiss, Alf., Lips., and apparently Lightf. It is claimed that if two distinct instruments were intended, τῆς would be repeated. But: 1. The absence of a second article does not necessitate the inclusion of both nouns under τῆς, since each has its own defining genitive, and therefore the second article may be dispensed with (Win. xix. 5 *b*). 2. Even if the two were included under the one article, that would not be decisive as to the union of ὑμῶν with both. If the genitive τοῦ πνεύματος is subjective (see below), there are two personal agents — you, in your supplication, and the Spirit with its supply — coöperating for the same end. Nor, if ὑμῶν is taken with δεήσεως only, is the idea excluded that the supply of the Spirit is in answer to the prayer of the Philippians.

διὰ τῆς ὑμῶν δεήσεως: Paul makes mention of the Philippians in his own supplications (vs. 4). Here he assumes that their fellowship with him in furtherance of the gospel (vs. 5), and their partaking with him of grace (vs. 7), will call out their supplications for him. Comp. 1 Thess. v. 25; 2 Thess. iii. 1 f.; 2 Cor. i. 11; Rom. xv. 30–32; Philem. 22. Also Ign. *Philad.* v. ἀλλ' ἡ προσευχὴ ὑμῶν με ἀπαρτίσει, 'But your prayer will make me perfect.'

ἐπιχορηγίας: Only here and Eph. iv. 16. Lightf.'s explanation of ἐπι, *bountiful* supply, is unwarranted. The force of ἐπι is directive. Comp. ἐπιχορηγῶν (Gal. iii. 5), where the idea of bountifulness resides in the verb. (See Col. ii. 19; 2 Cor. ix. 10.) In 2 Pet. i. 11, πλουσίως is added to ἐπιχορηγηθήσεται.

τοῦ πνεύματος Ἰησοῦ Χριστοῦ: The genitive is subjective, 'the supply which the Spirit of Jesus Christ affords'; not appositional, 'the supply which is the Spirit,' etc. Lightf.'s combination of the two — the Spirit at once the giver and the gift — is contrary to N.T. usage. The exact phrase, πν. 'ΙΧ, occurs only here. Πνεῦμα Χριστοῦ is found Rom. viii. 9; 1 Pet. i. 11. The Holy Spirit is called the Spirit of Christ (Rom. viii. 9; Gal. iv. 6), not as proceeding from Christ (Thdrt.), since the impartation of the Holy Spirit is habitually ascribed by Paul to the Father. (See 1 Cor. vi. 19; Eph. i. 17; Gal. iii. 5; 1 Thess. iv. 8.) In Jn. iii. 34 Christ is represented as dispensing the Spirit. The Spirit of Jesus Christ here is the Spirit of God which animated Jesus in his human life, and which, in the risen Christ, is the life-principle of believers (1 Cor. xv. 45; comp. Rom. viii. 9–11). Christ is fully endowed with the Spirit (Mk. i. 10; Jn. i. 32); he sends the Spirit from the Father to the disciples, and he is the burden of the Spirit's testimony (Jn. xv. 26, xvi. 7, 9, 10, 15). The Paraclete is given in answer to Christ's prayer (Jn. xiv. 16). Christ identifies his own coming and presence with that of the Spirit

(Jn. xiv. 17, 18). Paul identifies him personally with the Spirit (2 Cor. iii. 17). The Spirit which Christ has is possessed also by members of his body (Rom. viii. 9; Gal. iv. 6). In Rom. viii. 9, 10, Paul uses πνεῦμα θεοῦ, πνεῦμα Χριστοῦ, and Χριστὸς as convertible terms.

20. κατὰ τὴν ἀποκαραδοκίαν καὶ ἐλπίδα μου: Connect with ἀποβήσεται (vs. 19). This shall turn out to my salvation as I am expecting and hoping.

ἀποκαραδοκίαν: Only here and Rom. viii. 19. A picturesque word: ἀπὸ, 'away'; κάρα, 'the head'; δοκεῖν (Ion.), 'to watch.' Watching something with the head turned away from other objects; hence *intent* watching. So Chrys. ἡ μεγάλη καὶ ἐπιτεταμένη προσδοκία. Seldom in patristic Greek. Καραδοκεῖν occurs in class. Gk. (Hdt. vii. 163; Xen. *Mem.* iii. 5, 6; Aristoph. *Knights*, 663, etc.), but not the compound ἀποκαρ., which, however, is found in later Gk., as Polybius and Plutarch. Lightf.'s ref. to Josephus, *B. J.* iii. 7, 26, is felicitous. See also Philo, *De Jos.* 527 D.

Others, however, give ἀπο a local sense — the place from which (Ellic., Ead.); others an intensive sense, 'to wait to the end; wait it out' (Mey. on Rom. viii. 19. See also Crem. and Thay. *Lexs.*).

ἐλπίδα: The inward attitude, while ἀποκαρ. represents the outward attitude. Ἐλπὶς sometimes in N.T. as the *object* of hope: the thing hoped for. (See Gal. v. 5; Col. i. 5; Heb. vi. 18; Tit. ii. 13.) This can hardly be the meaning here.

ὅτι: 'that'; not 'because.' It denotes the object of the hope, supplying the specific definition of the more general εἰς σωτηρίαν (vs. 19).

ἐν οὐδενὶ, 'in nothing': in no point or respect. Not 'by no one,' since no persons are brought forward in what follows.

αἰσχυνθήσομαι: 'shall I be put to shame.' Rare in N.T., and only twice in Paul. Frequent in LXX, as Ps. xxxv. (xxxiv.) 4, 26; lxx. (lxix.) 2. (Comp. 2 Cor. x. 8.) He will not be brought into disgrace by the frustration of his efforts and the disappointment of his hopes. He will not be shown to be a deluded enthusiast, a fanatic, a preacher of a fancied and impossible good. On the contrary, —

μεγαλυνθήσεται Χριστὸς ἐν τῷ σώματί μου:

Μεγαλυνθήσεται = 'shall be glorified'; lit. 'enlarged.' Often in LXX for הִגְדִּיל. (See 2 Sam. vii. 26; 1 Chron. xvii. 24; Ps. xxxiv. [xxxiii.] 3, xxxv. [xxxiv.] 27.)

ἐν τῷ σώματί μου: Instead of the simple ἐμοί; because the question of bodily life or death was imminent. In his afflicted, imprisoned body Christ will be magnified. (Comp. 2 Cor. iv. 10; Gal. vi. 17.)

The force of this positive and general statement, 'Christ shall be magnified in my body,' is heightened by three incidental clauses, which are to the following effect: 1. Christ will be magnified, though Paul shall refuse to modify his preaching and shall continue to proclaim the gospel with all boldness. 2. Christ's being magnified in spite of opposition will be nothing new. It has always been so. 3. The result will be the same whether Paul shall live or die.

ἐν πάσῃ παρρησίᾳ: in contrast with *αἰσχυνθήσομαι*, as 1 Jn. ii. 28; LXX, Prov. xiii. 5. The primary meaning of *παρρησία* is 'free and bold speaking'; speaking out every word (*πᾶν, ῥῆμα*). The verb *παρρησιάζεσθαι* always in N.T. in connection with speaking. The dominant idea of *παρρησία* is boldness, confidence. (See 2 Cor. iii. 12, vii. 4; Eph. vi. 19; 1 Thess. ii. 2; Philem. 8; and Lightf. on Col. ii. 15.) It is opposed to fear (Jn. vii. 13), and to ambiguity or reserve (Jn. xi. 14). The idea of publicity sometimes attaches to it, but as secondary (Jn. vii. 4). *Πάσῃ*, the direct opposite of *οὐδενὶ*; every way in which boldness can manifest itself. (Comp. Eph. vi. 18.) Christ will be magnified in his bold and uncompromising preaching of the unpalatable truth.

ὡς πάντοτε καὶ νῦν: 'As always, so now.' *Καὶ* in the apodosis answers to *ὡς* in the protasis. (See Mt. vi. 10; Jn. vi. 57; Gal. i. 9; 1 Jn. ii. 18; Win. liii. 5.) It is the testimony of history that Christ has always been magnified in spite of opposition. As Paul's imprisonment has, up to this time, ministered to the progress of the gospel (vs. 12), he is no less confident of the same result now that his fate is hanging in the balance.

εἴτε διὰ ζωῆς εἴτε διὰ θανάτου: "Inimicis suis insultat, quod ei nocere non valeant. Si enim eum occiderint, martyrio coronabitur. Si servaverint ad Christum annunciandum, plurimum facient fructum" (Jer.).

The last words lead him to speak of his own feelings respecting the possible issue of his trial.

21. *ἐμοὶ γὰρ τὸ ζῆν Χριστὸς*: 'For to me to live is Christ.' For Paul life is summed up in Christ. Christ is its inspiration, its aim, its end. To trust, love, obey, preach, follow, suffer, — all things are with and in Christ. So Theoph. *καινήν τινα ζωὴν ζῶ, καὶ ὁ Χριστὸς μοί ἐστι τὰ πάντα, καὶ πνοὴ, καὶ ζωὴ, καὶ φῶς*: "A kind of new life I live, and Christ is all things to me, both breath and life and light." See further on *ἐν αὐτῷ* (ch. iii. 9), and comp. iii. 7–10, 20, 21; Rom. vi. 11; Gal. ii. 20; 2 Cor. v. 15; Col. iii. 3. Also Ign. Eph. iii., 'IX *τὸ ἀδιάκριτον ἡμῶν ζῆν*, 'our inseparable life'; and Mag. 1, 'IX *τοῦ διὰ παντὸς ἡμῶν ζῆν*, 'our never-failing life.' *Τὸ ζῆν* is the continuous present. In the three other passages of Paul in which it occurs (vs. 22; Rom. viii. 12; 2 Cor. i. 8), it denotes the process, not the principle, of life.

τὸ ἀποθανεῖν κέρδος: 'to die is gain'; because it will introduce him to complete union with Christ, unhampered by limitations of the flesh. His gain will therefore magnify Christ. (See Rom. viii. 17.) This is in striking contrast with the Stoic apathy which, in proud resignation, leaves all to fate. (See a beautiful passage in Pfleiderer, *Paulinismus*, 2 Aufl. p. 219.)

22. εἰ δὲ τὸ ζῆν ἐν σαρκί, τοῦτό μοι καρπὸς ἔργου, . . . καὶ τί αἱρήσομαι οὐ γνωρίζω:

B reads αιρησωμαι.

Render: 'But if living in the flesh — (if) this is fruit of toil to me, then what I shall choose I do not declare.'

The protasis is thus εἰ δὲ τὸ ζῆν . . . ἔργου. The apodosis is καὶ τί αἱρήσομαι, etc. The subject of the protasis, τὸ ζῆν ἐν σαρκί, is resumed by τοῦτο, which brings out the contrast of καρπὸς ἔργου with the subjective personal κέρδος (vs. 21). The apodosis is introduced by καὶ 'then.' (So Chrys., Œc., Mey., Ellic., Dw., De W., Alf., Lum., Kl., Lips., Ead.) Several other arrangements have been advocated, the principal one of which is to take εἰ δὲ τὸ ζῆν ἐν σαρκί as protasis, and τοῦτο . . . ἔργου as apodosis, making καὶ merely connective: 'But if living in the flesh (be my lot), this is fruit of toil to me, and what I shall choose I do not declare.' (So Weiss and Beet.) Lightf. suggests an arrangement in which he has been anticipated by Rilliet, — to take εἰ as implying an interrogation (as Rom. ix. 22; Acts xxiii. 9), and to regard the apodosis as suppressed: 'But what if my living in the flesh is to bear fruit? In fact what to choose I know not.' The rendering adopted seems to me to satisfy most of the conditions, though neither of those proposed is entirely free from objection. On the one hand, the awkward ellipsis required by the second appears quite inadmissible. On the other hand, the καὶ introducing the apodosis after a conditional protasis with εἰ is of doubtful authority, though I think that Jas. iv. 15, with the reading ζήσομεν καὶ ποιήσομεν, is a fair case in point, not to mention 2 Cor. ii. 2, which is perhaps a little more doubtful. Some weight also should be allowed to the LXX passages, Ex. xxxiii. 22; Lev. xiv. 34, xxiii. 10, xxv. 2; Josh. iii. 8, viii. 24. Though not strictly analogous, these imply a sort of condition in the protasis. The exact construction is certainly found in Gk. poetry (see Hom. *Il.* v. 897; *Od.* xiv. 112). Δὲ is also used in the same way (Hom. *Il.* i. 135, xii. 246; *Od.* xii. 54). In Apoc. iii. 20, καὶ in the apodosis after ἐάν is retained by Tisch. and stands in marg. in WH. (See Blass, § 77, 6.) The use of εἰ as explained by Lightf., though legitimate, leaves some awkwardness attaching to καί. (See Win. lxiv. 7.)

Εἰ is not conditional or problematical (Beet), but syllogistic. (Comp. Rom. v. 17.) It assumes that fruitfulness will follow his continuance in life. Τοῦτο is not redundant, but resumptive and emphatic, calling attention to remaining in life. It was just *this*, in contrast with dying, which was to mean fruit of toil.

καρπὸς ἔργου: fruit which follows toil and issues from it.

τί αἱρήσομαι. Τί for πότερον. (Comp. Mt. ix. 5, xxi. 31; Lk. vii. 42, xxii. 27; and see Win. xxv. 1.) The future αἱρήσομαι takes the place of the deliberative subjunctive (Win. xli. 4 *b*).

οὐ γνωρίζω: 'I do not declare.' Most modern commentators render 'I do not perceive' or 'know.' The meaning 'to make known,' 'point out,' 'declare,' is extremely rare in class. One case occurs (Æsch. *Prom.* 487). In the sense of 'to become known' (passive) it is found in Plato and Aristotle (see Stallbaum on *Phaedrus*, 262 B); but the prevailing sense is 'to become acquainted with,' 'to gain knowledge of.' In the N.T. the sense, without exception, is 'to make known' or 'declare.' This is also the prevailing sense in LXX, though there are a few instances of the other meaning, as Job xxxiv. 25. See, on the other hand, 1 Sam. vi. 2, x. 8, xiv. 12; Dan. ii. 6, 10, v. 7; Ps. xvi. (xv.) 11; cit. Acts ii. 28. For Paul's usage, see iv. 6; 1 Cor. xii. 3, xv. 1; Gal. i. 11. No sufficient reason can be urged for departing from universal N.T. usage. Paul says 'to die is gain; but if the case is put to me that it is for your interest that I should continue to live, then I have nothing to say about my personal choice.' Possibly he felt that under the strong pressure of his desire to depart, he might be tempted to express himself too strongly in favor of his own wish. As it is, he will leave the matter in the hands of his Master. "Marvellous!" says Chrys. "How great was his philosophy! How hath he both cast out the desire of the present life, and yet thrown no reproach upon it."

23. *συνέχομαι δε ἐκ τῶν δύο*:

The TR *γαρ* for *δε* is very slenderly supported.

Δὲ introduces an explanation, and at the same time separates it from that which is to be explained. (See Jn. iii. 19, vi. 39; 1 Cor. i. 12.) It may be rendered 'now.' I do not declare my preference. Now the reason is that I am in a strait, etc. Συνέχομαι is used by Paul only here and 2 Cor. v. 14. (See Lk. xii. 50; Acts xviii. 5; LXX; Job iii. 24, vii. 11, x. 1, xxxi. 23.) The figure is that of one who is in a narrow road between two walls. I am *held together*, so that I cannot move to the one or the other side. (Comp. Ign. *Rom.* vi.) The pressure comes *from* (ἐκ) both sides, from '*the* two' (τῶν δύο) considerations just mentioned, departing and abiding in the flesh.

τὴν ἐπιθυμίαν ἔχων: 'having the desire.' Τὴν has the force of a possessive pronoun, 'my' desire. 'Επιθυμία is used in N.T. in both a good and a bad sense. (Comp. Lk. xxii. 15 and Mk. iv. 19; Rom. i. 24, vii. 7; Gal. v. 16; 1 Jn. ii. 16.)

εἰς τὸ ἀναλῦσαι: Lit. 'to break up'; 'unloose'; 'undo.' It is used of loosing a ship from its moorings, of breaking camp, and of death. Paul uses ἀνάλυσις of his own death (2 Tim. iv. 6). If he employs the verb here with any consciousness of its figurative meaning, the figure is probably that of breaking camp. Paul's circumstances would more naturally suggest the military than the nautical metaphor; and, singularly enough, nautical expressions and metaphors are very rare in his writings. The idea of striking the tent and breaking camp falls in with 2 Cor. v. 1. For the construction with εἰς, comp. Rom. i. 11, iii. 26, xii. 2; 1 Thess. iii. 10; Heb. xi. 3.

σὺν Χριστῷ εἶναι: Beng. says: "To depart was sometimes desired by the saints (of the O.T.), but to be with Christ is peculiar to the New Testament." Paul assumes that, on departing this life, he will immediately be with the Lord. (Comp. 2 Cor. v. 6–8; Acts vii. 59.) On the other hand, Paul elsewhere treats death as a sleep from which believers will awake at the appearing of the Lord (1 Cor. xv. 51, 52; 1 Thess. iv. 14, 16).

The passage does not lend itself to controversies on the condition of the dead in Christ. It is not probable that the dogmatic consciousness enters at all into this utterance of the apostle. Discussions like those of Weiss and Klöpper as to the agreement or disagreement of the words here with those of Cor. and Thess. are beside the mark, as is the assumption that Paul's views on this subject had undergone a change which is indicated in this passage. Lightf. is quite safe in the remark that the one mode of representation must be qualified by the other. Weiss (*Bibl. Theol.* § 101) justly says that "if the more particular dealing with eschatological proceedings is reserved in the four principal epistles, to a yet greater extent is this the case in the epistles of the captivity, without its being possible to show any essential change in the position on these points." In this familiar epistle, in this passage, written under strong emotion, Paul throws out, almost incidentally, the thought that death implies, for him, immediate presence with Christ. If it be asserted that death introduces believers into a condition of preparation for perfect glorification, that supposition is not excluded by either these words or those in Cor. and Thess. In 2 Cor. v. 8 the intimation is the same as in this passage. In any case we are warranted in the belief that the essential element of future bliss, whether in an intermediate or in a fully glorified state, will be the presence of Christ. These words do not exclude the idea of an intermediate state, nor do the words in 1 Cor. exclude the idea of being with Christ.

πολλῷ γὰρ μᾶλλον κρεῖσσον: 'for it is very far better.'

DF[gr] G read ποσω for πολλω.

γαρ with ℵ[a] ABC 17, 31, 47, 67, WH. Tisch. Omitted by ℵ* DFGKLP, Vulg., Goth., Syr.[utr], Basm., Arm., Æth.

Notice the heaping up of comparatives according to Paul's habit. (Comp. Rom. viii. 37; 2 Cor. vii. 13, iv. 17; Eph. iii. 20.) Render, 'very far better.'

24. τὸ δε ἐπιμένειν τῇ σαρκὶ:

For επιμενειν B reads επιμειναι.

BDFGKL add εν with σαρκι. ἐπιμένειν ἐν occurs only in Paul (1 Cor. xvi. 8).

Observe the change of construction from τὴν ἐπιθυμίαν ἔχων. Render, 'to abide by the flesh.' Not precisely the same as τὸ ζῆν ἐν σαρκί (vs. 22), which was a little more abstract, expressing life in general, while this refers specifically to his own staying by the flesh. (Comp. Rom. vi. 1.)

ἀναγκαιότερον: The comparative is slightly illogical. The strong emotion which shaped the comparative πολλῷ μᾶλλον κρεῖσσον carries on that form, by its own momentum, to the succeeding adjective. The point of comparison is not definitely conceived. Living is the more necessary under the present circumstances. (Comp. Seneca, *Ep.* 98: "Vitae suae adjici nihil desiderat sua causa, sed eorum quibus utilis est." Also a striking passage *Ep.* 104). Two practical errors are suggested by these words,—the subsiding of all interest in the future world, and the undue longing for it which strikes at patient submission to the will of God. There is also to be noted the higher grade of self-abnegation exhibited by Paul, not in the casting aside of earthly pleasures and honors, which really possessed little attraction for him, but in the subjugation of the higher longing to enjoy the perfect vision of Christ.

25. καὶ τοῦτο πεποιθὼς οἶδα: 'And being confident of this I know.' Construe τοῦτο with πεποιθὼς, not with οἶδα, as Lightf., who takes πεπ. adverbially with οἶδα, 'I confidently know,' citing Rom. xiv. 14; Eph. v. 5. But these are hardly in point. (Comp. vs. 6.) Οἶδα is not prophetic. It merely expresses personal conviction.

μενῶ καὶ παραμενῶ:

TR συμπαραμενω with DEKLP and some Fathers.

For similar word-plays, see Rom. i. 20, v. 19; 2 Cor. iv. 8, v. 4; 2 Thess. iii. 11; Acts viii. 30. Μενῶ is absolute, 'to abide in life': παραμενῶ is relative, 'to abide with some one.' Παραμενῶ in a manner defines the simple verb. The value of his remaining in life lies chiefly in his being with his brethren and promoting their spiritual welfare. Paul uses μένειν in the sense of continuing to live, only here and 1 Cor. xv. 6.

εἰς τὴν ὑμῶν προκοπὴν καὶ χαρὰν τῆς πίστεως: 'for your progress and joy in the faith.' For προκοπὴν, see on vs. 12. The genitives τῆς πίστεως and ὑμῶν to be taken with both nouns. (Comp. i. 20, and see Win. xix.) For the phrase 'joy of faith,' comp. χαρὰ ἐν τῷ πιστεύειν (Rom. xv. 13). Progressiveness and joyfulness alike characterise faith.

Kl. and Weiss take πίστεως with χαρὰν only.

26. ἵνα τὸ καύχημα ὑμῶν περισσεύῃ: 'that your glorying may abound.' Ἵνα marks the ultimate aim of μενῶ καὶ παραμενῶ, and the clause defines more specifically the general statement εἰς τὴν ὑμ. προκ., etc. Καύχημα is the *matter* or *ground* of glorying, not the *act* of glorying, which would be καύχησις, as Rom. iii. 27; 2 Cor. i. 12. (Comp. Rom. iv. 2; 1 Cor. ix. 15; Gal. vi. 4.)

Ὑμῶν is subjective: Not 'my ground of glorying in you,' but 'your ground of glorying.'

ἐν Χριστῷ Ἰησοῦ: With περισσεύῃ, not with καύχημα. (Comp. i. 9; Rom. iii. 7; Col. ii. 7.) Christ is the element or sphere in which the abounding develops. Christ is always needed to control, no less than to promote, overflow. The abundant glorying does not take place in the sphere of human ambition, like that of the Jew in his law and his nationality, — the 'boasting according to the flesh' (2 Cor. xi. 18); 'in men' (1 Cor. iii. 21); 'in appearance' (2 Cor. v. 12).

ἐν ἐμοὶ: The immediate occasion of the glorying would be Paul. The ground of boasting would attach specially to him as the representative of the cause which was the great matter of glorying. Ἐν ἐμοὶ is a special cause or ground within the sphere designated by ἐν Χ'Ι.

διὰ τῆς ἐμῆς παρουσίας πάλιν πρὸς ὑμᾶς: Connect with ἐν ἐμοὶ as a special instance. The ground of glorying is first, and comprehensively, in Christ; then in Paul as representing Christ; then in Paul's personal presence again with them. Παρουσίας, in its ordinary sense, as ii. 12; 1 Cor. xvi. 17, etc. There is a slight emphasis on the word as contrasted with letters or messages. How far Paul's confidence in his liberation and future personal intercourse with the Philippians was justified, it is impossible to determine without more knowledge concerning the latter portion of his career.

He now proceeds to give his readers some practical exhortations. Until he can personally minister to their faith, he must content himself with writing to them. Their standard of Christian consistency and efficiency must not be regulated by his personal presence or absence.

27–30. *Only, under any circumstances, — whether I shall come to you, as I hope to do, or remain absent, as I may be compelled to do, — I exhort you to bear yourselves as becomes members of a Christian community, in your steadfastness, unity, and active exertion on behalf of the gospel, and in your courage in the face of your adversaries; which will demonstrate the hopelessness of their efforts and their doom to destruction, and will be God's own evidence to you of your own salvation. For the privilege conferred upon you of suffering for Christ will show that you are one with him, and partakers of that same grace which has enabled me to contend for his cause, and of that same conflict which you saw me undergo, and which you now hear of my still waging in my Roman prison.*

27. μόνον ἀξίως τοῦ εὐαγγελίου τοῦ Χριστοῦ πολιτεύεσθε: 'only let your manner of life be worthy of the gospel of Christ.' For a similar usage of μόνον see 1 Cor. vii. 39; Gal. ii. 10; 2 Thess. ii. 7. Not as though he would say: 'Look to your own conduct and God will take care of me'; nor as though he intended to state the only condition on which he would come to them; but, 'whether I come or not, I have only to say,' etc. Only on this condition can he successfully minister to their furtherance and joy of faith if he shall come to them, and only thus can these be maintained if he shall not come.

πολιτεύεσθε: Lit. 'be citizens'; 'exercise your citizenship.' The verb occurs in N.T. only here and Acts xxiii. 1. In LXX, see 2 Macc. vi. 1, xi 25. For the kindred noun πολίτευμα see ch. iii. 20. Paul's usual word for Christian conduct is περιπατεῖν, 'to walk' (Rom. vi. 4, viii. 4; 1 Cor. iii. 3), with ἀξίως, Eph. iv. 1; Col. i. 10. The primary reference is to their membership in the church at Philippi; and the word is selected as pointing to their *mutual* duties as members of a local Christian commonwealth; probably not without an underlying thought of the universal Christian commonwealth embracing all the saints in earth and heaven. (Comp. iii. 20, and Clem. Rom. *ad Cor.* iii., xxi., liv.) Clement develops the idea of individual obligation to a spiritual polity by comparison with the obligations due to secular states, in lv. See also Polyc. *ad Phil.* v. The word would naturally suggest itself to Paul, contemplating from the metropolitan centre the grandeur of the Roman state, and would appeal to the Philippians as citizens of a Roman 'colonia' which aimed to reproduce, on a smaller scale, the features of the parent commonwealth. (See Introd. II.) Here, as elsewhere in Paul's letters, may be detected the influence of Stoicism upon his mode of thought. Stoic philosophy had leavened the moral vocabulary of the civilised world. Its language was fruitful in moral terms and images and furnished appropriate forms of expression for certain great Christian ideas. A favorite Stoic conception was that of a world-wide state. (See Lightf.'s essay on "St. Paul and Seneca," *Comm.* p. 270 ff.)

ἀξίως τοῦ εὐαγγελίου τοῦ Χριστοῦ: 'in a manner worthy of the gospel of Christ.' Τοῦ Χτοῦ is the objective genitive, — the gospel which proclaims Christ. This is Paul's more usual formula. (See 1 Cor. ix. 12; 2 Cor. ii. 12; Gal. i. 7; 1 Thess. iii. 2.) We find also εὐαγγ. τοῦ υἱοῦ αὐτοῦ (Rom. i. 9); τοῦ κυρίου ἡμῶν Ἰησοῦ (2 Thess. i. 8); τῆς δόξης τοῦ Χριστοῦ (2 Cor. iv. 4).

ἵνα εἴτε ἐλθὼν καὶ ἰδὼν ὑμᾶς εἴτε ἀπὼν ἀκούω τὰ περὶ ὑμῶν.

ℵ[a] ACDFGKL read ακουσω.

The construction is rhetorically inexact. Ἵνα goes with ἀκούω, and εἴτε ἐλθ. κ. ἰδ. ὑμ. and εἴτε ἀπ. are appositional with the personal subject of ἀκούω. Ἀκούω, which in regular construction would be ἀκούων followed by γνῶ or some similar verb, takes the finite form from the suggestion of the personal subject in ἀπών. The construction is moulded by the thought of absence, which is last and most prominent in the writer's mind. The verb which would have been used on the supposition of his seeing them is dropped, and that which implies his absence is alone expressed. Τὰ περὶ ὑμῶν, as ii. 19, 20; Col. iv. 8; comp. τὰ κατ' ἐμὲ (ch. i. 12): 'the things concerning you'; 'your state' (R.V.). Render the whole: 'That whether I come and see you or remain absent, I may hear of your state.'

ὅτι στήκετε, etc.: Explaining the details of their 'state.' Στήκειν mostly in Paul, and always signifying *firm* standing, acquiring that meaning, however, from the context. In Mk. iii. 31, xi. 25, it means simply 'to stand.'

ἐν ἑνὶ πνεύματι: 'in one spirit.' (Comp. Eph. iv. 4, and see Clem. *ad Cor.* xlvi.) Πνεῦμα here is not the Holy Spirit (as Weiss), but that disposition which is communicated in Christ to believers, filling their souls, and generating their holy qualities and works. In the possession of this they are πνευματικοί, — they are joined to the Lord and are one spirit with him (1 Cor. vi. 17. See 2 Cor. xii. 18; Lk. i. 17; Jn. vi. 63; Acts vi. 10). The character, manifestations, or results of this disposition are often defined by qualifying genitives; as, the spirit of meekness, faith, power, wisdom. (See Rom. viii. 2, 15; 1 Cor. iv. 21; 2 Cor. iv. 13; Gal. vi. 1; Eph. i. 17; 2 Tim. i. 7.) At the same time it is to be carefully observed that these combinations are not mere periphrases for a faculty or disposition of man. The energy of the Holy Spirit is always assumed as behind and animating the disposition in its various manifestations. (See *W. St.* on Rom. viii. 4.)

μιᾷ ψυχῇ: 'with one mind.' (Comp. ch. ii. 2, 20.) Ψυχή is the mind as the seat of sensation and desire. It is that part of the individual, personal life which receives its impressions on the one hand from the πνεῦμα, the higher divine life-principle, and on the other hand from the outer world. There are cases where the meanings of ψυχὴ and πνεῦμα approach very nearly, if indeed they are not practically synonymous. (See Lk. i. 46, 47; Jn. xi. 33, comp. xii. 27; Mt. xi. 29; 1 Cor. xvi. 18.) But there must, nevertheless, be recognised a general distinction between two sides of the one immaterial nature which stands in contrast with the body. Πνεῦμα expresses the conception of that nature more generally, being used both of the earthly and of the non-earthly spirit; while ψυχὴ designates it on the side of the creature. Πνεῦμα, and not ψυχή, is the point of contact with the regenerating forces of the Holy Spirit, — the point from which the whole personality is moved Godward. Ψυχὴ must not be restricted to the principle of animal life; nor must it be distinguished from πνεῦμα as being alone subject to the dominion of sin, since πνεῦμα also is described as being subject to such dominion. See 2 Cor. vii. 1; Eph. iv. 23; 1 Cor. vii. 34; 1 Thess. v. 23, which imply that the πνεῦμα needs sanctification. Ψυχὴ is never, like πνεῦμα, used of God. (See *W. St.* on Rom. xi. 3.) Here μιᾷ ψυχῇ is not to be construed with στήκετε, but only with συναθλοῦντες.

συναθλοῦντες τῇ πίστει τοῦ εὐαγγελίου: 'striving together for the faith of the gospel.' Συναθ. only here and iv. 3. The simple verb ἀθλεῖν occurs in 2 Tim. ii. 5, where it signifies 'to contend in the games'; but in class. it is used also of contending in battle (Hdt. vii. 212; Hom. *Il.* vii. 453, xv. 30); of conflicts of cities (Plat. *Tim.* xix. C). The compounded σὺν does not mean with Paul (so Mey.), but in fellowship with each other. Mey. appeals to vs. 30, but there the apostle's conflict is introduced as a new point. Others refer to iv. 3, but there μοί is written. Lightf., after Erasm., renders 'in concert with the faith,' faith being personified. He cites 1 Cor. xiii. 6; 2 Tim. i. 8; 3 Jn. 8. The first is fairly in point, but the two others are too much in dispute to be decisive.

τῇ πίστει: Dat. of interest. The trustful and assured acceptance of Jesus Christ as the Saviour from sin and the bestower of eternal life, is the clear sense of πίστις in the majority of N.T. passages. At the same time, there is an evident tendency of the subjective conception to become objective. The subjective principle of the new life is sometimes regarded objectively as a power. It is the sender or proclaimer of a message (Gal. iii. 2; Rom. x. 16. See Sieffert on Gal. iii. 2, and Bornemann on 1 Thess. ii. 13). It is something to be contended for (Jude 3). It is a precious gift to be obtained (2 Pet. i. 1). It is something to be held fast (1 Tim. i. 19). Hence, though not equivalent to *doctrina fidei* (so Lightf. here and on Gal. iii. 23, and Sanday on Rom. i. 5), its meaning may go beyond that of the subjective energy to that of the faith as a rule of life (so Gal. iii. 23; 1 Tim. i. 19, iv. 1; and here). Thus Kl. explains πίστις here as "the new regimen of those who are Christ's; the objectively new, obligatory way of life." The phrase πίστις τοῦ εὐαγγελίου occurs nowhere else in N.T. According to the common analogy of genitives with πίστις, εὐαγγελίου would be the objective genitive, 'faith in the gospel'; but according to the meaning of πίστις given above, it will be rather 'the faith which belongs to the gospel,' the rule of life which distinctively characterises it.

28. πτυρόμενοι: 'startled,' 'affrighted.' Used of a frightened horse.

ἐν μηδενὶ: As 2 Cor. vi. 3, vii. 9; Jas. i. 4.

τῶν ἀντικειμένων: 'your adversaries.' (See Lk. xiii. 17, xxi. 15; 1 Cor. xvi. 9; 2 Thess. ii. 4.) Of all kinds, Jewish and Pagan. Paul's sufferings at Philippi had been caused by Gentiles.

ἥτις: 'seeing it is.' 'It,' *i.e.* your unterrified attitude. The relative, with an explanatory force (as Eph. iii. 13; Col. iii. 5; Heb. x. 35), takes its gender from the predicate ἔνδειξις (Win. xxiv. 3), but agrees logically with μὴ πτυρόμενοι, etc.

αὐτοῖς: whether they recognise the token or not.

ἔνδειξις: 'an evidence,' 'a proof.' R.V., 'evident token.' The word is not common in N.T. (See Rom. iii. 25, 26; 2 Cor. viii. 24.)

Comp. ἔνδειγμα: 2 Thess. i. 5. The verb ἐνδείκνυσθαι almost entirely confined to Paul. Lit., 'a pointing out.' Used in Attic law of a writ of indictment.

ἀπωλείας: 'destruction' or 'waste' in general (as Mk. xiv. 4; Acts viii. 20); but specially and principally as here, the destruction which consists in the loss of eternal life. The meaning is determined by the contrary σωτηρίας. The undaunted bearing of the Philippians in the face of opposition and persecution will be a token of destruction to their adversaries. It will show that their persecutors are powerless to thwart God's work; that their resistance is working out their own spiritual ruin; that they are fighting against God, which can mean only destruction.

ὑμῶν δε σωτηρίας: 'but of your salvation.'

υμων, as ℵ ABC² P 17, 31, 47, Arm., Syr.P.
υμιν in DKL Vulg., Cop., Basm., Goth., Æth.

Future and eternal salvation as contrasted with ἀπωλείας.

καὶ τοῦτο ἀπὸ θεοῦ: 'and that from God.'

Καὶ has an ascensive force; not only a token, but a token from God.

Τοῦτο refers to the whole preceding statement; viz. that an evidence of their enemies' destruction and of their own salvation is furnished in their brave bearing. Not merely to ἀπωλείας and σωτηρίας, nor merely to ἔνδειξις (as Weiss). "It is not the token alone that is from God, but the token and what it points to" (Ead.).

29. ὅτι: 'because,' justifies the preceding statement, but with special reference to σωτηρία. The evidence that your courage is a divine token of salvation lies in the fact that God has graciously bestowed on you, along with faith in Christ, the privilege of suffering with him. For faith implies oneness with Christ, and therefore fellowship with his sufferings (Rom. viii. 17; 2 Thess. i. 5; 2 Tim. ii. 12; Phil. iii. 10). That you suffer with Christ proves your union with him, and your union with Christ insures your salvation.

Ὑμῖν has an emphatic position corresponding with that of ὑμῶν in vs. 28.

ἐχαρίσθη: 'it hath been granted'; freely bestowed as a gracious gift. The word is significant as opening the conception of suffering from the Christian point of view. God rewards and indorses believers with the gift of suffering. In Paul's bonds the Philippians are partakers with him of *grace* (vs. 7. Comp. Acts v. 41). The aorist points to the original bestowment of the gift. (See Mt. v. 11; Mk. x. 38, 39.)

τὸ ὑπὲρ Χριστοῦ: 'on behalf of Christ.' Τὸ belongs to *πάσχειν*, but the connection is broken by *οὐ μόνον . . . πιστεύειν*, after which *τὸ* is repeated. With the whole passage, comp. 2 Thess. i. 4–10.

30. *ἔχοντες*: 'you having,' or 'so that you have.' Characterising *ὅτι ὑμῖν ἐχαρ. . . . πάσχειν* by the concrete case of their share in his own conflict. The participle agrees with *ὑμεῖς*, the logical subject of the entire clause. (Comp. similar construction in Eph. iii. 17, iv. 2; 2 Cor. i. 7; Col. ii. 2.) Not with *στήκετε* (vs. 27), making *ἥτις . . . πάσχειν* a parenthesis, which would be clumsy.

ἀγῶνα: 'conflict.' (Comp. *συναθλοῦντες* [vs. 27] and Col. ii. 1; 1 Thess. ii. 2; 1 Tim. vi. 12; Heb. xii. 1.) The word applied originally to a contest in the arena, but used also of any struggle, outward or inward. For the latter see Col. ii. 1, and comp. Col. iv. 12. The reference here is to his experience in his first visit to Philippi, and to his latest experience in Rome. Their conflict is the same (*τὸν αὐτὸν*). They too have suffered persecutions, and for the same reason, and from the same adversaries.

εἴδετε: 'ye saw,' when I was with you at Philippi (Acts xvi. 19; 1 Thess. ii. 2). They saw him scourged and imprisoned.

νῦν ἀκούετε: 'you now hear,' as you read this letter, and listen to the account of Epaphroditus.

ἐν ἐμοί: in my person.

EXCURSUS

BISHOPS AND DEACONS (PHIL. I. 1)

It is evident that these words are related to the large and complicated question of primitive church polity. Do they denote official titles, or do they merely designate functions? What is their relation to the *πρεσβύτεροι* of the Acts and Pastoral Epistles? Were the offices of bishop and presbyter originally the same, and the names synonymous; or, was there an original distinction? Were the *ἐπίσκοποι* the direct successors of the apostles, distinct from the *πρεσβύτεροι* and higher; or, was the episcopate a development from the presbyterate, formed by gradual elevation, and, finally, appropriating to itself the title which was originally common to both, so that the New Testament knows only two orders — presbyters and deacons? What light is thrown on the question by the use of the terms here?

To deal adequately with these questions, and with the voluminous discussion which they have called out, is manifestly impossible within the limits of an excursus, and the result of the most elaborate discussion cannot be decisive, owing to the imperfection of the sources at our disposal.

The theory of the original identity of bishops and presbyters has been a subject of controversy from a very early date. It was opposed to the Roman theory that bishops were the only successors of the apostles, and had from the beginning the divine commission to rule the church. This latter theory was issued as a dogma by the Council of Trent, and the opposite view was declared heretical. The Roman dogma was rejected by the Calvinists and Lutherans. About the middle of the seventeenth century the battle over this question raged between the Anglican church on the one hand, and the English Puritans and the French Reformers on the other. Dissatisfaction with the Roman view developed as the discussion gradually shifted from a dogmatic to a historical basis. The present century has been prolific in attempts to solve the problem. Passing by those of Baur, Kist, Rothe, and Ritschl, the three most significant discussions from 1868 to 1883 were those of Lightfoot in his essay on "The Christian Ministry" in his *Commentary on Philippians;* Hatch, in the Bampton Lectures for 1880 (*The Organisation of the Early Christian Church*), and Harnack's translation and development of Hatch's work (*E. Hatch: Die Gesellschaftsverfassung der christlichen Kirchen im Alterthum, übers. von A. Harnack,* 1883). Harnack's views were further expounded in his *Lehre der zwölf Apostel,* 1884; his Review of Loening's *Gemeindeverfassung* in *Th. LZ.*, 1889, No. 17; in Gebhardt and Harnack's *Texte und Untersuchungen*, Bd. ii. Heft 1, 5, and in his *Dogmengeschichte.*

Among the most important of the later discussions are: Lechler, *Das apostolische und das nachapostolische Zeitalter*, 3 Aufl., 1885; Kühl, *Die Gemeindeverfassung in der Pastoralbriefen*, 1885; E. Loening, *Die Gemeindeverfassung des Urchristenthums*, 1889; F. Loofs, *Die urchristliche Gemeindeverfassung, Stud. u. Krit.*, 1890, Heft 4; Weizsäcker, *Das apostolische Zeitalter der christlichen Kirche*, 2 Aufl., 1892; Rud. Sohm, *Kirchenrecht*, Bd. i., 1892; Jean Réville, *Les Origines de l'Épiscopat*, 1894. Harnack is reviewed by Professor Sanday in *The Expositor*, 3d ser. vol. v. This and the succeeding volume contain an interesting group of papers by J. Rendel Harris, J. Macpherson, C. Gore, W. Milligan, G. Salmon, G. A. Simcox, and Professor Harnack.

The Pauline epistles, omitting for the present the Pastorals, exhibit church polity in a rudimentary and fluid state in which official designations are not sharply defined, and the offices themselves have not taken permanent and definite shape. The forms of polity are simple, founded upon local conditions, and not uniform over the entire area of the church. The official designations, so far as they have arisen, are the natural and familiar expressions of particular functions. The terms often overlap or are confused, and a term in use in one part of the church does not appear in another part. An apostle, a bishop, a teacher, a deacon, are alike "servants." An overseer will be likely to be a presbyter, chosen on account of his age and experience. The overseers may be called προϊστάμενοι, ἡγούμενοι, or κυβερνήσεις. The assistants of an overseer may be known as διάκονοι or ἀντιλήμψεις.

In short, we find within this circle an entire lack of uniformity in the terms applied to church officials, and a marked vagueness in their use. The terms do not wholly explain themselves. Most of them are capable of a functional meaning; and in most, if not all, cases of their occurrence, they may be explained as indicating the peculiar function of an official instead of his official title. This is the case in Acts xx. 28, which is so often cited as decisive of the original identity of presbyter and bishop. Ἐπίσκοπος occurs but once in these epistles (Phil. i. 1); διάκονος but once in an official sense (Phil. i. 1); προϊστάμενοι in Rom. xii. 8; 1 Thess. v. 12, both times functionally. In 1 Cor. xii. 28, we have, besides apostles, prophets, and teachers, δυνάμεις, ἀντιλήμψεις, and κυβερνήσεις, which are abstract terms. Ἐπίσκοπος, διάκονος, προϊστάμενος, however they may be explained in any particular case, denote functions. Ἐπίσκοπος is an overseer; διάκονος a servant; προϊστάμενος one who stands in front. Διακονία is applied to religious and churchly ministries of all kinds. In Eph. iv. 11, 12, Paul says that Christ gave apostles, prophets, evangelists, pastors, and teachers to the work of διακονία for the perfecting of the saints. Paul and Apollos, Timothy and the secular ruler, are alike διάκονοι (1 Cor. iii. 5; 1 Thess. iii. 2; Rom. xiii. 4).

This unsettled state of the nomenclature corresponds with the fact that the primitive church was not a homogeneous body throughout Christendom. While the Jewish-Christian church assumed the connection of all local congregations with the mother-church at Jerusalem, there was no similar bond among the Gentile churches. Paul's *ideal* was one body — the church, as the body of Christ, embracing all Christians of every nationality and social condition. He aspired to found a world-wide society, united neither by national tradition nor by common rites, but by a common faith and a common inspiration (1 Cor. x. 16, xii. 27; Rom. xii. 5; Eph. ii. 14–22). He speaks of "the church of God" (1 Cor. x. 32), and of "the church" (1 Cor. xii. 28). He labored to hold the provincial churches together by his letters and messengers (1 Cor. xvi. 19; 2 Cor. i. 1). The boldness of his ideal, and his profound faith in the truth which he proclaimed, are all the more striking when the heterogeneous character of his churches is considered. (See a fine passage in Réville, *Les Origines de l'Épiscopat*, p. 115.) But the Gentile churches were united mainly through their relation to him, and all the churches were not within the sphere of his personal authority and work. Hence a collective Christendom was, as Holtzmann observes, "a genuine, *ideal* whole, identical with the body of the Lord, but not an actual fact" (*Pastoralbriefe*, p. 193). The primitive Pauline church consisted of a number of little fraternities, composed largely of the poor and of the lower orders of society, holding their meetings in the private houses of some of their members.

These communities were self-governing. The recognition of those who ministered to the congregations depended on the free choice of their members. At Corinth the household of Stephanas is commended by Paul to the church as being the earliest converts in Achaia, and as having voluntarily assumed the work of ministry to the saints (1 Cor. xvi. 15, 16). They were not regularly appointed to office. The church is exhorted to render obedience to them, and also to every one who shall coöperate with them in their ministry. (See Pfleiderer, *Paulinismus*, 2 Aufl. p. 244.) Phœbe is not a deaconess, but a servant of the congregation, a patroness (προστάτις) of Paul and of others (Rom. xvi. 1, 2). The congregation exercises discipline and gives judgment (1 Cor. v. 3–5; 2 Cor. ii. 6, 7, vii. 11, 12; Gal. vi. 1). In 1 Cor. vi. 1, Paul recommends to the church to settle their differences by arbitration. The alternative is litigation before heathen tribunals. There is, in short, no hint of any one ecclesiastical office endowed with independent authority. "Paul," to quote the words of Réville (p. 99), "is a sower of ideas, not a methodical administrator; a despiser of ecclesiastical forms and of ritualism; a mighty idealist filled with Christian enthusiasm, and who knew no other church government than that of Christ himself inspiring his disciples with the knowledge of what they ought to say and do."

It is thus evident that within the circle of the generally acknowledged Pauline epistles there is no trace of formally constituted church officers, except, apparently, in the Philippian epistle where bishops and deacons are addressed. Of this presently. Certain functions, however, are distinctly recognised by Paul as of divine institution in the church; and to these, necessarily, pertained a degree of prominence and influence in the congregation.

The measure of this prominence and influence cannot be discussed here. Harnack (on Loening, *Th. LZ.*, 1889) thinks that the pneumatic functions carried with them a "despotic" authority. (See Loening, *Gemeindeverfassung*, ch. ii.; Loofs, *Stud. u. Krit.*, 1890, p. 622.)

Apostles, prophets, and teachers are declared by Paul to have been set by God in the church, and to these are added δυνάμεις, ἰάματα, ἀντιλήμψεις, κυβερνήσεις, γένη γλωσσῶν (1 Cor. xii. 28; comp. Eph. iv. 11, 12; and see Réville, p. 124 f.).

I do not agree with Réville that the προϊστάμενοι of 1 Thess. v. 12 (comp. Rom. xii. 8) are to be regarded as charismatically endowed.

These do not represent offices resting on the appointment of the church. Their warrant is a special divine endowment or χάρισμα. Apostles, prophets, teachers, do not signify three official grades in the church. The same man could be both a prophet and a teacher. Whatever authority they possessed depended upon the church's conviction that their charisma was of divine origin.

In Paul's two lists in 1 Cor. and Eph. of those who have been divinely commissioned in the church, neither ἐπίσκοποι, πρεσβύτεροι, nor διάκονοι appear. Nor do they appear anywhere in the acknowledged epistles of Paul with the exception of the greeting to the bishops and deacons in the Philippian letter. But in the Ignatian epistles (100–118 A.D.) we find a clear recognition of three orders of ministry, — bishops, presbyters, and deacons, — without which it is asserted that a church is not duly constituted (*Trall.* iii.). This ministry is the centre of church order. The bishop is distinguished from the presbyter as representing a higher order. He is to be regarded as the Lord himself (*Eph.* vi.); to be obeyed as Christ and as God (*Trall.* ii.; *Mag.* iii.). Nothing is to be done without his consent (*Polyc.* iv.). He is to be followed as Jesus followed the Father (*Smyr.* viii.). The presbyters are to preside after the likeness of the council of the apostles (*Mag.* vi.). Obedience is to be rendered to them as to the apostles of Jesus Christ (*Trall.* ii.). The deacons are to be respected as Jesus Christ (*Trall.* iii.). In short, we have in these epistles the strongly marked beginnings of the monarchical episcopacy.

See Lightf. *Ignatius*, vol. i. p. 389 ff.

Somewhat earlier, in the Epistle of Clement to the Corinthians (about 96 A.D.), we find a greater variety of names applied to church functionaries. Besides ἐπίσκοποι, πρεσβύτεροι, and διάκονοι, occur the titles ἡγούμενοι, προηγούμενοι, πρεσβύτεροι καθεσταμένοι, and ἐλλόγιμοι ἄνδρες. But it is also distinctly asserted (xlii., xliv.) that the apostles appointed bishops and deacons to succeed them because they knew through Christ that strife would arise over the name of the bishop's office (ἐπισκοπή). It is to be noticed that presbyters are not mentioned.

Assuming the Philippian letter to have been written in 61 or 62 A.D., we have less than forty years to the time of Clement's epistle, and less than sixty to the time of the Ignatian letters. A great development has taken place in those years from the rudimentary conditions of church polity which we have been considering. This change did not come at a leap. Its elements must have been long in solution in the fluid and more democratic polity of the earlier time. The important and difficult question is the process by which the earlier and crude forms of polity developed into that system which is more than foreshadowed in Clement, sharply defined in Ignatius, and an accepted fact in Irenæus, Tertullian, and Cyprian.

Here a difficulty arises as to our sources. Ἐπίσκοποι and

διάκονοι appear in Phil.; ἐπίσκοποι, πρεσβύτεροι, and διάκονοι in the Pastoral Epistles; ἐπίσκοποι and πρεσβύτεροι in the Acts and 1 Pet.; πρεσβύτεροι in Jas., 1 Pet., 2 and 3 Jn., and the Apocalypse. Harnack places the Pastorals in the middle of the second century; Holtzmann, in its former half. The modern radical criticism of the Acts pushes its date forward into the second century (so Harnack) besides impugning its reliability on various grounds.

See Weizsäcker, *Apost. ZA.* 84 ff., 167 ff., 199 ff.; J. Jüngst, *Die Quellen der Apostelgeschichte*, 1895; C. Clemen, *Die Chronologie der paulinischen Briefe*, 1893.

The point to be observed is, that if the later date of the Pastorals be accepted, they must be held to represent an advanced stage in the development toward the episcopal polity. Only let it be noted that Harnack's date brings us within the circle of the Ignatian polity, and warrants us in expecting a far more precise use of terms in the three epistles than we actually find. There is a great distance between the episcopate of the Pastorals and that of the Ignatian epistles. (See Réville, p. 304.)

If, on the other hand, the Pastorals be accepted as late products of Paul's hand, and the Acts as composed within the first century, we have in these, along with the Epistle to the Philippians and the Catholic epistles, traces of the transition from the looser to the better defined polity. We have evidence of the existence of πρεσβύτεροι and ἐπίσκοποι in the church contemporary with Paul, without our being compelled to admit either that the ἐπίσκοπος was a regularly ordained ecclesiastical officer, or that πρεσβύτεροι and ἐπίσκοποι are synonymous. We have simply what we have reason to expect; namely, that the three titles, ἐπίσκοποι, πρεσβύτεροι, and διάκονοι, fall within the period of unsettled polity and loose nomenclature. The fact that all these names may represent functions without designating official titles accords with this view. The process of crystallisation is going on. These different designations emerge here and there in the church as local developments, just as the terms προϊστάμενοι and ἡγούμενοι. It may be admitted that one term might, on occasion, have been loosely used for another; but the recognised and habitual identification of ἐπίσκοποι and πρεσβύτεροι is precluded by the very assumption that these functions had assumed the character of regularly constituted church offices or orders of the ministry. If such had been the case, such looseness and confusion in the use of the names of formally appointed and recognised church officers is inconceivable. I think that the indications of the nature of church polity furnished by the Pastorals are far fewer and less definite than is often assumed, and much too scanty to warrant the positive inferences based upon them as to the later date and the non-Pauline authorship of the letters. Harnack's admission that older documents have been used in the composition of the Pastorals is an important concession, which makes against the theory of their testimony to a later stage of ecclesiastical polity.

According to our view of the case, therefore, the mention of bishops and deacons in the Philippian letter furnishes no exception to the statement that, within the circle of the acknowledged Pauline letters, there is no evidence of regularly constituted church officers representing distinct orders in the ministry. While the greeting to bishops and deacons is unique, it does not imply a polity differing substantially from that exhibited in 1 Cor. and 1 Thess. It will be observed that the greeting is first to the church, and that the letter is addressed to the whole church. The special mention of the bishops and deacons by way of appendage is explained by the fact that the letter was called out by the pecuniary contribution of the Philippian church to Paul, of the collection and sending of which these functionaries would naturally have charge. It will also be noticed that the address assumes several ἐπίσκοποι, showing that the right of administration is possessed by no single one.

At the same time, I think it must be granted with Harnack (*Expositor*, 3d ser. vol. v. p. 330) that while there cannot yet be any reference to an ecclesiastical authority over the church, the greeting of the Philippian letter implies a development of polity, in that the ministry has become divided into a higher and a lower ministry, and that its functionaries have obtained special designations, so that the name διάκονος has received a narrower signification, and designates a lower grade of ministry. The church at Philippi, at the time when Paul wrote this letter, had been in existence for ten years, and was the oldest Pauline church in Europe. It would not have been strange if its polity had become somewhat matured and more sharply defined, especially since it had suffered less distraction than other churches from conflicts with the Jews.

The Didache or Teaching of the Twelve Apostles is most important in its bearing on this subject. This brief church manual or directory, composed, probably in Syria, about 100 A.D., is a valuable contribution to the literature of the period between the destruction of Jerusalem (A.D. 70) and the middle of the second century, the least-known period of church history. Its special value consists in marking the transition-period from the apostolic to the later church polity, in which the spiritual functions pass over from the apostles, prophets, and teachers to the local officers — the bishops and deacons. On the one side it is linked with the apostolic polity. The principal offices are still the charismatic offices. The apostle, who is to be received as the Lord (xi. 4), is a travelling missionary, and is not to remain for more than two days in a place (xi. 5). The prophet speaks by divine inspiration, and is not to be tried or proved, as if for appointment to his office (xi. 7). The prophets are the chief priests (xiii. 3). Comp. the emphasis on prophecy in 1 Cor. xii. 28, xiv. 1–37. Presbyters are not mentioned, though it does not follow from this that they did not exist in some of the Syro-Palestinian churches. (See Réville, p. 259.) But bishops and deacons are distinctly recognised. They are local officers. They are elected to office (xv. 1), and on occasion they are to perform the ministry of the prophets and teachers (xv. 1); that is to say, the distinctively spiritual functions of the prophets may be discharged by them when the prophet is not present (xiii.).

The testimony of the Didache, therefore, does not bear out the original prominence which is claimed for the bishop. He is a secondary officer. He falls into the background behind the apostles, prophets, and teachers. The testimony, further, goes to show that spiritual functions did not originally attach to the offices of bishop and deacon. The evidence prior to the Didache that bishops or presbyters exercised such functions is very slight. The principal point insisted on is the laying on of hands (1 Tim. iv. 14 [see especially Loening, p. 75 ff.]) and the allusions to the gift of teaching or preaching as a qualification of presbyters or bishops (1 Tim. iii. 2, v. 17; Tit. 1. 9). As to ordination, it will be observed that the charisma described as imparted to Timothy is given through the medium of prophecy (διὰ προφητείας). As to teaching or preaching, 1 Tim. v. 17 shows that even if this function was occasionally exercised by presbyters or bishops, it did not pertain to the office as such. "The elders who rule well" are to be accounted worthy of double honor, *especially* those who labor in word and teaching, which clearly implies that there were elders who did not labor in word and teaching.

In the Didache the spiritual functions belong, as in 1 Cor., to the prophets and teachers. The prophet is to discharge them when he is present. The prophet alone is allowed the free use of extemporary prayer (x. 7). In other respects the teacher is on the same footing with him. In the absence of the prophet or teacher, his ministry may be assumed by the bishops and deacons (xiii., xv. 1). In other words, the evidence of the Didache is to the effect that, as the special supernatural endowments subside, as the visits of the prophets become less frequent, the ministrations of worship devolve more and more upon the subordinate and local officers.

This view is carried out by Harnack in his discussion of the *Apostolical Ordinances or Canons* (*Tt. u. Unt.* ii. 5). One portion of this formed a considerable part of the Didache. Two more parts, dating from forty to eighty years later than the Didache, mention the church officers in the following order:

bishop, presbyter, reader, deacon. The bishop is the shepherd of the flock. The presbyters, two in number, form the council of the bishop, oversee church discipline, and take part with the bishop in the celebration of the Eucharist. The deacon has charge of the church charities, and keeps an eye upon disorderly members. The reader discharges the duties of an evangelist. He is a preacher or expounder, succeeding the evangelist, who belonged originally to the class of charismatically endowed teachers (comp. Eph. iv. 11) ; thus showing how formally appointed officials gradually succeeded to the functions of those who were supernaturally endowed by the Spirit.

The office of the ἐπίσκοπος thus acquired a different character when it assumed the teaching function. This does not yet appear in Clement. The function is described as λειτουργεῖν and προσφέρειν τὰ δῶρα (xliv.), yet the position is different from that of the Pauline period. With the passing away of the apostles, the authority of the bishop has increased. Its recognition no longer depends so exclusively on the approval of the members. Clement proclaims the apostolic origin and authority of the office, and at least suggests its life-long tenure (xliv.), a theory, as Harnack justly says, which has the appearance of being devised to meet an emergency; while some remnant of the earlier democratic sentiment is apparent in the ejection of the church authorities which was the occasion of Clement's letter.

The bishop's office, therefore, was originally not spiritual but administrative. He had a local function in a particular community. The question as to the precise nature and range of this function cannot be answered decisively; but some modern critics have, I think, narrowed it too much. Hatch, following in the track of Renan, Foucart, Lüders, Heinrici, and Weingarten, derives the term ἐπίσκοπος from the financial officers in the heathen municipalities or in the confraternities or guilds which were so common in the Roman Empire (see note on τῇ κατ' οἶκον σου ἐκκλησίᾳ [Philem. 2]), and regards the original ἐπίσκοπος as simply a financial officer.

Sanday justly remarks that the evidence, on this theory, is rather better for ἐπιμελητής than for ἐπίσκοπος (*Expositor*, 3d ser. v. p. 98). See also on this point, Réville, *Les Origines de l'Épiscopat*, p. 153 f. The subject of the relations of the Christian official nomenclature to that of the heathen guilds is ably discussed by Loening, *Gemeindeverfassung*, pp. 12, 20, 64. See also Sohm, *Kirchenrecht*, p. 87, and Salmon, *Expositor*, 3d ser. vi. p. 18 ff.

In favor of this view it is also urged that the earliest authorities concur in demanding that bishops should be free from covetousness. Thus the Didache requires that bishops and deacons shall be ἀφιλαργύρους (xv. 1). So in 1 Tim. iii. 3, a bishop must be ἀφιλάργυρος, and a deacon (vs. 8) μὴ αἰσχροκερδῆς. It is also claimed that Tit. i. 7 is to the same effect, the bishop being described as θεοῦ οἰκονόμος. It is assumed, in short, that such expressions were determined by the special temptations which attached to the financial function of the bishop.

It seems to me quite possible to lay undue stress upon these indications. Without denying that the episcopal function included, and was possibly largely concerned with the financial interests of the church, it could not have been confined to these. It must have extended to the social relations of the community, to inspection of the performance of social duties, to guardianship of those rules and traditions which were the charter of the infant organisation, and to representation of the community in its relations with other Christian churches or with the outside world. It can hardly be supposed that, in associations distinctively moral and religious, one who bore the title of overseer should have been concerned only with the material side of church life. (See Réville, p. 306 ff.).

Sohm, whose *Kirchenrecht* is among the very latest and strongest contributions to this discussion, holds that, though the original character of the bishop's office was administrative, the teaching function attached itself naturally to his duty of receiving and administering the offerings of the congregation presented at the celebration of the Eucharist. He claims that the episcopal office grew, primarily, out of this celebration, and that the bishop's distribution of the offerings to the poor involved a cure of souls and the consequent necessity of teaching. See also Réville, pp. 178, 309.

But though it cannot be shown that the Christian title ἐπίσκοπος was formally imitated from the Pagan official, we are not thereby compelled to deny entirely the influence of the Pagan nomenclature in determining it. No doubt its adoption came about, in both cases, in the same natural way; that is to say, just as *senatus*, and γερουσία, and πρεσβύτερος passed into official designations through the natural association of authority with age, so ἐπίσκοπος would be almost inevitably the designation of an overseer. The term was not furnished by the gospel tradition; it did not come from the Jewish synagogue, and it does not appear in Paul's lists of those whom God has set in the church. The process of natural selection, however, would be helped by the familiar employment of the title in the clubs or guilds to designate functions analogous to those of the ecclesiastical administrator. (See the interesting remarks of Réville, p. 160 f.) The title can hardly, I think, be traced to the Old Testament. The usage there is predominantly functional. There are but two passages in the LXX where ἐπίσκοπος has any connection with religious worship (Num. iv. 16; 2 K. xi. 18). It is applied to God (Job xx. 29), as it is applied to Christ in the New Testament (1 Pet. ii. 25). It is used of officers in the army, and of overseers of workmen. The prevailing meaning of ἐπισκοπὴ is "visitation," for punishment, inquisition, or numbering. In any case, little light can be thrown on the question by the derivation of the word, until we clearly understand the functions of the Christian officials.

Into the complicated question of the origin of the presbyterate it is not necessary to enter. It may be remarked that modern critical opinion has largely abandoned the view maintained by Rothe, Baur, Lightfoot, Hatch, and others, that the original Christian church polity was an imitation of that of the synagogue. This is largely due to the investigations of Schürer into the Jewish church constitution.

See *Geschichte des jüdischen Volkes im Zeitalter Jesu Christi*, 2 Aufl. Bd. ii., 1866, Eng. trans., 2d divis. vol. ii. p. 56 ff.; *Die Gemeindeverfassung der Juden in Rom in der Kaiserzeit*, 1879.

The secular and religious authorities of the Jewish communities, at least in purely Jewish localities, are shown by Schürer to have been the same (comp. Hatch, Lect. iii.),—a fact which is against the probability that the polity was directly transferred to the body of Christian believers. The prerogatives of the Jewish elders have nothing corresponding with them in extent in the Christian community. Functions which emerge later in the Jewish-Christian communities of Palestine do not exist in the first Palestinian-Christian society. At the most, as Weizsäcker observes, it could only be a question of borrowing a current name. The use of *συναγωγή* for a Christian assembly occurs but once in the New Testament, and that by James, whose strong Jewish affinities are familiar. The regular designation of the Christian assembly was *ἐκκλησία*. The Christian society regarded itself as the inaugurator, not of a new worship, not of an ecclesiastical organisation, but of a new society representing the beginnings of the kingdom of God on earth, the institutions of which would soon be definitely and permanently established by the return of the Son of Man in his glory. Such a society would not be satisfied with forming a separate synagogue merely, nor would the mere reading and exposition of the law and the prophets interpret their fresh Christian sentiment.

See Holtzmann, *Pastoralbriefe*, p. 217.

However they originated, in the Acts and the Pastoral Epistles presbyters appear as a factor of church government, forming a collective body in the congregation. Whatever may have been their original functions, in these documents the office of teaching pertains to both them and the bishops. (See 1 Tim. iii. 2, v. 17; Tit. i. 9.) It is at this point that the tendency to confound and identify the two distinct offices reveals itself. It would be strange if the two were synonymous, and that two names should be given to the same functions. Yet Hatch (Lect. ii. p. 39, note) declares that this identity is so well established that it has been practically removed from the list of disputed questions. Such certainly is not the testimony of later critical discussion in which this question bears a prominent part. The reasons which make against the identity, moreover, are not trifling. Acts xx. 17, 28, which is so often urged as conclusive, proves absolutely nothing, or rather favors the opposite conclusion. Either it may be said that the word ἐπισκόπους is not titular, but expresses function, describing the body of presbyters generally as "overseers" of the flock of God; or that the ἐπίσκοποι regarded as officers are represented as belonging to the class of presbyters and appointed from their number, which does not imply the identification of the official titles.

Bishops and deacons are habitually associated, while no mention of presbyters occurs along with them. It is a begging of the question to affirm that presbyters are not mentioned because they are identical with bishops. It cannot be proved for instance that there were not presbyters at Philippi when Paul wrote to that church; and the probability is that if they had held a rank identical with that of the bishops or equal with it, notice of them would not have been omitted.

Turning to the Pastoral Epistles, in 1 Tim. iii. 1–13, we find the qualifications of bishops and deacons described, with no mention of presbyters. These are referred to in 1 Tim. v. 17–19, but in an entirely different connection, — as worthy of a double maintenance, and not to be accused except on the testimony of two or three witnesses. In the Epistle of Clement (xlii.) the apostles are declared to have appointed bishops and deacons, not presbyters. Passing on to a later date (140?), the *Shepherd* of Hermas distinguishes bishops and deacons from presbyters (3 Vis. v. 1; Sim. ix. 27, 2. Comp. 2 Vis. iv. 2 f; 3 Vis. i. 8, ix. 7; Mand. xi. 12).

The testimony of Clement's letter to the Corinthians is of special importance. It was written on behalf of the Roman church, rebuking the church at Corinth for ejecting its rulers from office. (See Lightf. *Clem.* i. p. 82.) The passages in point are in chs. i., iii., xxi., xlii., xliv., xlvii., liv., lvii.

At first sight it appears as if Clement uses ἐπίσκοπος and πρεσβύτερος as synonymous terms (see especially xliv., liv., lvii.); but in chs. i., xxi. the ἡγούμενοι and προηγούμενοι, by whom the bishops are meant, are placed side by side with πρεσβύτεροι as distinct, πρεσβύτεροι in both cases being contrasted with the young. In short, a more careful examination of the epistle goes to show that if the bishops are apparently designated as presbyters, it is because they have been chosen from the body of presbyters, and have retained that name even when they have ceased to hold office. For this reason the deceased bishops are called presbyters (xliv.). As the presbyters are not designated by Clement among those appointed by the apostles as their successors, it appears that "presbyter" signifies, not an office, but a class or estate. The presbyters are church members of long standing, who have approved themselves by their good works and pure character. The leaders of the church are to be sought among these; but "the aged" as such are not described as office-bearers regularly appointed, but merely as a body of persons distinguished by ripe wisdom and approved character. Thus the exhortation "Submit yourselves to the presbyters" (lvii.) tallies with the same expression in 1 Pet. v. 5, where the younger are bidden to be subject unto the elder. "The office-bearers belong to the πρεσβύτεροι, but the πρεσβύτεροι as such are not office-bearers. The bishops are reckoned as πρεσβύτεροι, not because the presbyter as such is a bishop, but because the bishop as such is a presbyter" (Sohm). The "appointed presbyters" (πρεσβύτεροι καθεσταμένοι [liv.]) are not the πρεσβύτεροι collectively, but a smaller circle within the πρεσβύτεροι. It is the bishops who are appointed (xlii., xliv.), and who count with the "aged" from whose ranks they proceed. They are summoned to a specific official activity as ἐπίσκοποι.

A linguistic usage of the second century which appears in Irenæus goes to confirm this view,—the use of πρεσβύτερος to denote the authorities for the tradition, the survivors of the preceding generation (Iren. *Haer.* ii. 22, 5, iv. 27, 1, 2, 30, 14, 32, 1, v. 5, 1, 33, 3, 36, 1). (See Weizs., *Ap. ZA.* p. 618.) The bishops would therefore be called πρεσβύτεροι (*Haer.* iii. 2, 1, 3, 1), in so far as they successively vouched for the tradition, and thus reached back into the preceding age.

The qualifications which distinguish a presbyter are indicated at the close of Clement's epistle in the description of the three commissioners from the Roman church who are the bearers of the letter. They are "old, members of the Roman church from youth, distinguished by their blameless life, believing, and sober" (lxiii.). No official title is given them.

To the same effect is the testimony of the Pastoral Epistles. 1 Tim. iii. treats of the officers of the church, but only of bishops and deacons, concluding with the statement that this is the direction concerning the ordering of the church as the house of God (vs. 14, 15). The offices are exhausted in the description of bishops and deacons. Nothing is said of presbyters until ch. v., where Timothy's relations to individual members of the church are prescribed (v. 1); and in Tit. ii. 2 ff. these church members are classified as old men (πρεσβύτας), old women, younger men, and servants. Similarly, in 1 Pet. v. 1, the apostle describes himself as a "fellow-elder" (συνπρεσβύτερος); and the church is divided into elders who feed the flock of God, and the younger (νεώτεροι) who are to be subject to the elders. In 1 Tim. v. 17

mention is made of "elders who rule well" (οἱ καλῶς προεστῶτες πρεσβύτεροι). Assuming that elders had an official position identical with that of bishops, a distinction between two classes of bishops would be implied, — those who rule well and those who do not. Whereas the distinction is obviously between old and honored church members collectively considered, forming the presbyterial body, and certain of their number who are worthy to be appointed as overseers. All of the presbyters do not fulfil equally well the duty of ruling. All are not alike worthy to be chosen as overseers. Only those are to be accounted worthy of double honor who have approved themselves as presbyters to be worthy of the position of ἐπίσκοποι. The following statement in vs. 19 refers to the rights of the presbyters generally. The presbyters as such are not invested with office. There is no formal act which constitutes an elder or a well-ruling elder. The bishops are reckoned among the elders, but the elders as such are not officers.

Thus are explained the allusions to "appointed" elders. Titus (Tit. i. 5) is enjoined to appoint elders in the Cretan churches, men who shall be blameless, husbands of one wife, having believing children who are free from scandal. Then follows, "*For* the *bishop* (τὸν ἐπίσκοπον) must be blameless," etc. The qualifications of the elders are thus fixed by those of the bishop; and the injunction is to appoint elders to the position of overseers, for the overseers must have the qualifications of approved presbyters. Similarly the ordination of presbyters, in Acts xiv. 23, is to be understood as setting apart elders to the position of superintendents.

The ecclesiastical eldership is, therefore, not identical with the episcopate, though in the unsettled state of ecclesiastical nomenclature, the names might, on occasion, be interchanged, and though, in the later stage of ecclesiastical development, the assumption of the teaching function by both classes, through the gradual subsidence of charismatic endowments, tends to confuse them. The presbyterate denotes an honorable and influential estate in the church on the ground of age, duration of church membership, and approved character. Only bishops are "appointed." There is no appointment to the presbyterate.

The special office of deacon occurs in the Pastorals, and nowhere else in the writings attributed to Paul; for the deacons in Phil. i. 1 do not stand for an ecclesiastical office, although, as has been already observed, they mark an advance towards it. They appear as regular church officers in Clement and in the Didache, and Clement asserts their apostolic appointment. The testimony does not bear out the older view of the origin of the diaconate in the appointment of the seven (Acts vi. 1–6). The terms διάκονος and διακονία are common expressions of service, either to Christ or to others. Paul habitually uses them in this way, applying them to his own ministry and to that of his associates. Διακονία is applied to the service of the apostles (Acts i. 25, vi. 4), and διάκονοι is used of the ministers of Satan in 2 Cor. xi. 15. The appointment of the seven grew out of a special emergency, and was made for a particular service; and the resemblances are not close between the duties and qualifications of deacons as detailed in 1 Tim. and those of the seven. The word διάκονος does not occur at all in the Acts; and when Paul and Barnabas brought the contribution for the poor saints to Jerusalem, they handed it over to the elders.

Our evidence on this question is, at best, incomplete. Loening does not put the case too strongly when he describes the sources from which alone our knowledge can be drawn as *lückenhaft*. Such as the evidence is, however, it seems to be fatal alike to the Roman and to the Presbyterian theory of an apostolic norm of church polity. There can be no doubt that discussions of this subject have too often been unduly influenced by ecclesiastical preconceptions, and conclusions reached in which the wish was father to the thought. To be able successfully to vindicate for any system of ecclesiastical polity an apostolic origin and sanction is to put into the hands of its representatives a tremendous lever. Investigation of this subject, if it is to lead to the truth, must be conducted on purely historical grounds apart from all dogmatic or ecclesiastical prepossessions. In the conduct of such investigations we shall do well to heed the caution conveyed in the words of Réville. "The prolonged and minute analysis of the smallest texts, in which one thinks to find an echo of the first Christian ecclesiastical organisation, tends to a forcing of the meaning and to an exaggeration of the value of each trace that we discover; because we cannot be satisfied without reconstructing a complete organism, in which all the parts are logically related and mutually adjusted like the wheels of a perfect machine. Not only is the mechanism not complete, but, properly speaking, there is yet no regular mechanism. The organisation of these humble communities which were still unnoticed by the great world, or noticed only to be despised, was not the result of sage legislative labor. . . . The functions, the dignities, the spiritual magistracies of primitive Christianity emerge little by little by organic growth" (*Les Origines de l'Épiscopat*, p. 330).

The forms of church polity were gradual evolutions from primitive, simple, crude modes of organisation shaped by existing conditions. Official titles were naturally suggested by official functions. The church was not one body, but only an aggregate of local communities; and the features of organisation and government in any single community and the official titles which their administrators bore were not the same in other communities.

Nothing is clearer than the absence of any uniform system of ecclesiastical nomenclature in the church of the Pauline period. We see at first a loose, democratic organisation, in which leadership depends upon spiritual endowment and its recognition by the spiritual community. The early enthusiasm gradually passes away. The apostle, prophet, and teacher recede, formal election takes the place of general recognition of the gifts of prophecy or tongues; the spiritual functions pass from the charismatic leaders to the administrative functionaries; gradually the official polity crystallises as the church grows stronger and its intercourse with the outside world and among its several branches extends. The tendency observable in the history of all organisations towards the concentration of authority in fewer hands develops; and by the time the first half of the second century is reached, the episcopal polity has defined itself in the Ignatian letters, and the tide is setting towards the monarchical episcopacy.

Note on πραιτωρίῳ (I. 13)

It is impossible to determine with certainty the place of Paul's confinement in Rome. The explanations of πραιτώριον (*prætorium*) are the following:

1. The prætorian camp at the Porta Viminalis (Kl., Lips., Mey., Weiss, Hack.).
2. The whole prætorian camp whether within or without the city (Ellic.).
3. The prætorian barracks attached to the Neronian palace (Alf., Con. H., Weizs. [*Ap. Zeit.*], O. Holtzmann [*Neutestamentliche Zeitgeschichte*], Merivale [*Hist. Rom. under the Emp.*]).
4. The prætorian guard (Lightf., Lewin, De W., Beet, Mangold [Bleek's *Einl.*]).

I do not think that Lightf.'s note (*Comm.* p. 99) has ever been successfully answered or his conclusion shaken. He has shown that there is no sufficient authority for applying the term 'prætorium' to the imperial residence on the Palatine; and his view on this point is confirmed by Mommsen (*Römisches Staatsrecht*, 3 Aufl. ii. p. 807). After stating that the word was used to denote the headquarters of the emperor, Mommsen goes on to argue against Hirschfeld's assertion that the imperial palace itself was regarded as a camp. "Against this," he says, "are both tradition and theory. When the emperor was absent from Rome he was 'in praetorio,' and so Juvenal (iv. 34) rightly calls Domitian's Albanum a camp. But the palace in the city is never called so; for such a designation would be against the existence of the Augustan principate, and Augustus' tendency to conceal military domination."

Livy, xxvi. 15, xxx. 5; Tac. *Hist.* i. 20, ii. 11, iv. 46; Suet. *Nero*, 9; Pliny, *N. H.* xxv. 2, 6, with the testimony furnished by inscriptions, are decisive for the use of 'prætorium' to denote the prætorian guard.

So Marquardt (*Römische Staatsverwaltung*, ii. pp. 460, 464), and Mommsen

(*Röm. Staatsr.* ii. 865, 3 Aufl.), who says of the prætorian troops: "Their collective designation was *praetorium*, as appears in the expressions *praefectus in praetorio, mittere ex praetorio, decedere in praetorio.* The name of the emperor was not usually added, though Vespasian speaks of the soldiers who have served *in praetorio meo* (Corp. I. Lat. p. 583)."

Professor Ramsay (*St. Paul, the Traveller and the Roman Citizen*, p. 357) says that 'prætorium' means "the whole body of persons connected with the sitting in judgment — the supreme imperial court; doubtless in this case the prefect or both prefects of the prætorian guard, representing the emperor in his capacity as the fountain of justice, together with the assessors and high officers of the court." For this explanation he cites the authority of Mommsen, but without giving any references. I must confess that this definition of 'prætorium' is new to me, and I am unable to reconcile it with Mommsen's statements. Mommsen says (*Röm. Staatsr.* ii. p. 959) that the first emperors, for the most part, personally conducted the imperial court. On p. 972 he says: "From the penal sentences of the provincial governors, the appeal, about the middle of the third century, lay to the prætorian prefects; and, as accused persons from the provinces, sent to Rome for judgment, were, in the earlier period, committed to the prætorian prefects as guards (here he cites the case of St. Paul), so, *in the third century*, the judgment of such persons passed over to them."

The unquestionable fact that 'prætorium' was used to denote the prætorian guard makes it unnecessary to assume that the apostle in this passage refers to any place, and furnishes a simple explanation and one entirely consistent with the narrative in Acts xxviii. Paul was permitted to reside in his private lodging under the custody of a prætorian soldier. As the soldiers would naturally relieve each other in this duty, it would not be very long before Paul could say, as he does here, that the entire body of the prætorians had become aware that the imprisonment was for Christ's sake. This explanation, moreover, agrees with καὶ τοῖς λοιποῖς πᾶσιν, which, on the other interpretations, is exceedingly awkward.

II. 1–4. EXHORTATION TO UNANIMITY, LOVE, AND HUMILITY

If therefore there is any power of exhortation in your experience as Christians; if your mutual love affords you any consolation; if you are in true fellowship with the Spirit of God; if there are any tender mercies and compassions in your hearts — I beseech you to complete my joy by your unanimity and your love to each other. Do not act from a spirit of faction or vainglory, but each of you account his brother as better than himself, and study his interests in preference to your own.

1. *εἴ τις οὖν παράκλησις ἐν Χριστῷ*: 'if there be any exhortation in Christ.'

The particular connection of *οὖν* is clearly with i. 27, *ἥτις . . . ἐν ἐμοί* being a digression, though not parenthetical. The main element of *πολιτεύεσθε* is brave standing for the gospel in a spirit of concord. It is this which is taken up and expanded in the opening of this chapter. 'I have exhorted you to stand fast in one spirit; to strive with one mind for the faith of the gospel, unterrified by your adversaries. *Therefore* complete my joy by being of one accord and avoiding faction and vainglory.' Out of this appeal grows, logically, the exhortation to humility, without which such unanimity cannot be maintained. The exhortation opens in the form of an adjuration. The rapid succession and variety of the appeals and the repetition of *εἴ τις* are peculiarly impressive. Says Chrys.: *πῶς λιπαρῶς, σφοδρῶς, μετὰ συμπαθείας πολλῆς*! "How earnestly, how vehemently, with how much sympathy!"

This earnestness was largely due to the fact that Paul was disturbed by reports of internal dissensions in the Philippian church. This is indicated not only by his words here, but by his moving appeal to the example of Christ; his admonition to do all things without murmurings and disputings (vs. 14); his entreaty of Euodia and Syntyche (iv. 2); his exhortation to moderation or forbearance (iv. 5); and his reference to the peace of God (iv. 7).

The appeal is upon four grounds. The first and third set forth objective principles of Christian life; the second and fourth, subjective principles. The appeal is not to what was demanded by the readers' personal relations to Paul. So Chrys. "If ye wish to give me any comfort in my trials, and encouragement in Christ; if you have sympathy with me in my sufferings," etc. So the Gk. Fathers generally. It is the Christian experience of the Philippians that is appealed to. 'I exhort you by those feelings of which, as Christians, you are conscious.'

παράκλησις ἐν Χριστῷ: If the fact of your being in Christ has any power to exhort you to brotherly concord. (Comp. 1 Cor. xii. 12–27; Eph. iv. 15, 16.)

Παράκλησις from *παρακαλεῖν*, 'to call to one's side' for help, counsel, etc. Thus *παράκλητος*, 'an advocate,' is one who is called in to plead another's cause. With this primary sense are associated the ideas of entreaty, exhortation, and consolation. In the sense of 'entreaty,' the noun appears in N.T. only in 2 Cor. viii. 4, but the verb is common. (See Mt. viii. 34, xiv. 36; Mk. i. 40, etc.) As 'consolation' or 'comfort,' the noun, Lk. ii. 25, vi. 24; 2 Cor. i. 3, vii. 4; the verb, 2 Cor. i. 4, 6, vii. 6. As 'exhortation' or 'counsel,' the noun, Acts xiii. 15; Rom. xii. 8; Heb. xiii. 22; the verb, Acts ii. 40, xi. 23; Rom. xii. 8; Tit. ii. 15. The last sense is the usual one in Paul.

παραμύθιον: 'persuasion.' Only here, but the earlier form παραμυθία, 1 Cor. xiv. 3. Class. 'address,' 'exhortation' (Plat. *Leg.* vi. 773 E, ix. 880 A); 'assuagement' or 'abatement' (Soph. *Elec.* 130; Plat. *Euthyd.* 272 B). Hence 'consolation' (Plat. *Repub.* 329 E). See παρακαλεῖν and παραμυθεῖσθαι together, 1 Thess. ii. 11. Here, the form which παράκλησις assumes — a friendly, mild persuasion, "not pædagogic or judicial" (Kl.). Paul means, therefore, 'if love has any persuasive power to move you to concord.'

κοινωνία πνεύματος: 'fellowship of the Spirit.' (Comp. Rom. xv. 30.) For κοινωνία, see on i. 5. The exact phrase only here, and κοιν. with πν. only 2 Cor. xiii. 13.

Πνεῦμα is the Holy Spirit. The meaning is 'fellowship with the Holy Spirit,' not 'fellowship of spirits among themselves.' The genitive is the genitive of that of which one partakes. So habitually by Paul (1 Cor. i. 9, x. 16; 2 Cor. viii. 4, xiii. 13; Eph. iii. 9; Phil. iii. 10). Not 'the fellowship which the Spirit imparts,' which would be grammatical, but contrary to N.T. usage. Hence Paul means, 'if you are partakers of the Holy Spirit and his gifts and influences.'

εἴ τις σπλάγχνα καὶ οἰκτιρμοί: 'if any tender mercies and compassions.'

τις σπλαγχνα with ℵ ABCDFGKLP and nearly all the verss. is overwhelmingly supported agt. τινα in a few minusc., Clem., Chrys., Thdrt., Theoph. But the attested reading is a manifest solecism, — either a transcriber's error, or a hasty repetition of τις.

For σπλάγχνα, see on i. 8, and comp. Philem. 7, 12, 20. The exact phrase σπλ. καὶ οἰκ. only here, but see Jas. v. 11; Col. iii. 12.

Σπλάγχνα is the organ or seat of compassionate emotion: οἰκτιρμοί are the emotions themselves. (See Schmidt, *Synon.* 143, 4.)

2. πληρώσατέ μου τὴν χαρὰν: 'fulfil' or 'fill ye up my joy.'

Πληρ., in its original sense, 'to make full'; the joy regarded as a measure to be filled. (Comp. Jn. iii. 29, xv. 11, xvii. 13; 2 Cor. x. 6.)

Μου before τὴν χαρὰν implies no special emphasis. (See Col. iv. 18; Philem. 20; and often elsewhere.) (Win. xxii.)

ἵνα: not 'in order that,' but to be taken with 'I bid' or 'exhort,' which is implied in the imperat. πληρώσατε, and indicating the purport of the bidding. (See on i. 9.)

Mey. maintains the telic sense, and Lightf. renders 'so as to,' but refers to i. 9, where he explains ἵνα as signifying purport.

τὸ αὐτὸ φρονῆτε: 'be of the same mind.' (Comp. Rom. xii. 16, xv. 5; 2 Cor. xiii. 11; Phil. iv. 2.) For φρονῆτε, see on i. 7. This more general expression is defined by the following two, not three, separate clauses.

τὴν αὐτὴν ἀγάπην ἔχοντες: 'having the same love.' Mutual love, and the one love of God in all. (See Col. i. 4; 1 Thess. iii. 12; 2 Thess. i. 3; 1 Jn. iv. 12–16.)

σύνψυχοι τὸ ἓν φρονοῦντες: 'with harmony of soul cherishing the one sentiment.' This second participial clause points back to τὸ αὐτὸ φρονῆτε, and is illustrated by σύνψυχοι, which marks the common disposition under the influence of which unanimity of sentiment is to be attained. So Mey., Alf., Ellic., Weiss, Beet.

Others, as WH., Kl., Lightf., De W., Lips., Weizs., take σύνψ. and τὸ ἓν φρον. as separate predicates. The attempted distinctions between τὸ αὐτὸ and τὸ ἓν are hypercritical. Thus, τὸ ἕν, agreement of mind and will; τὸ αὐτὸ, agreement in doctrine (Calov., Am E., Rosenm.); τὸ αὐτὸ, unanimity in general; τὸ ἕν, the one concrete object of their striving (Weiss). The two are practically synonymous. Wetstein cites λέγοντες ἓν καὶ ταὐτὸ (Polyb. v. 441), and ἓν καὶ ταὐτὸ φρονοῦντες (Aristid. *Concord. Rhodior.* 569). This is the only occurrence of σύνψυχος in Bib. Gk. (Comp. ἰσόψυχος, vs. 20.)

For το εν φρον. ℵ* AC 17, Vulg., Goth., read το αυτο φρον., a mechanical conformation to το αυτο φρονητε.

The same exhortation to concord is now put negatively, showing what the requirement excludes.

3. μηδὲν κατ' ἐριθίαν μηδὲ κατὰ κενοδοξίαν: 'being in nothing factiously or vaingloriously minded.' (Comp. Ign. *Philad.* i., viii.) Supply φρονοῦντες from vs. 2, which is better than ποιοῦντες or πράσσοντες (A.V.; R.V.), since the thought is on the line of moral disposition rather than of doing. For the suppression of the verb, comp. Gal. v. 13; 2 Cor. ix. 6; Mt. xxvi. 5.

ἐριθίαν: see on i. 17.

κατὰ: 'by way of'; marking the rule or principle according to which something is done. (See Jn. ii. 6; Rom. ii. 2, xi. 21; Win. xlix.)

κενοδοξίαν: 'vainglory.' Only here in N.T., but comp. LXX; Sap. xiv. 14; 4 Macc. ii. 15, viii. 18; and κενοδοξῶν (4 Macc. v. 9); also κενόδοξοι (Gal. v. 26). Primarily, 'vain opinion,' 'error,' as Ign. *Magn.* xi., ἄγκιστρα τῆς κενοδοξίας. (See on δόξα, i. 11.) A vain conceit of possessing a rightful claim to honor. Suidas defines, 'any vain thinking about one's self.' It implies a contrast with the state of mind which seeks the true glory of God, as ch. i. 26. Its object is vain and fleshly — something which imparts only a superficial glitter in the eyes of the worldly-minded. In Gal. v. 26, κενόδοξοι is further defined by ἀλλήλους προκαλούμενοι, ἀλλήλοις φθονοῦντες. The temptation to this fault would arise, on the Jewish side, from the conceit of an exclusive divine call, privilege, and prerogative, and an exaggerated estimate of circumcision and the law (Rom. iii. 1, ix. 4). Against these the Philippians are warned in ch. iii. On the Gentile side the temptation would lie in the conceit of a profound gnosis, and in their self-esteem growing out of their call and the rejection of the Jews. Paul deals with this in Rom. xi. 20–25. They might also be tempted by the fancy of their own superior culture and breadth of view to despise the scruples of weak brethren. (See Rom. xiv.; 1 Cor. viii.)

τῇ ταπεινοφροσύνῃ: 'in lowliness of mind.' In class. Gk. ταπεινὸς usually implies meanness of condition; lowness of rank; abjectness. At best the classical conception is only modesty, absence of assumption, an element of worldly wisdom, and in no sense opposed to self-righteousness. The word ταπεινοφροσύνη is an outgrowth of the gospel. It does not appear before the Christian era. The virtue itself is founded in a correct estimate of actual littleness conjoined with a sense of sinfulness. It regards man not only with reference to God, but also with reference to his fellow-men, as here. The article τῇ probably denotes the virtue considered abstractly or generically. (Comp. Rom. xii. 10 ff.) It may, however, be used possessively, '*your* lowliness' (Lightf.), or as indicating the *due* lowliness which should influence each (Ellic.).

ἀλλήλους ἡγούμενοι ὑπερέχοντας ἑαυτῶν: 'each counting other better than himself.' (Comp. Rom. xii. 10.) Ἡγεῖσθαι implies a more conscious, a surer judgment, resting on more careful weighing of the facts, than νομίζειν. (See Schmidt, *Synon.* 105, 4; 70, 1, 3, 7.)

Ὑπερέχειν with genit. not elsewhere in Paul. (Comp. iv. 7; Rom. xiii. 1.)

B reads τους with υπερεχοντας. DFG υπερεχοντες.

4. ἕκαστοι σκοποῦντες — ἕκαστοι:

1st εκαστοι, as ABFG 17, Vulg.; ℵ CDKLP, Goth., Cop., Arm., Syr.[utr], read εκαστος, WH. marg. 2d εκαστοι, as ℵ ABC[vi] D[gr] P 17, 31, 47, Cop.; KL, Goth., Syr.[utr], Arm., read εκαστος.

For σκοπουντες L with a few Fath. reads σκοπειτε.

σκοποῦντες: 'looking.' For this use of the participle instead of the imperative, comp. Rom. xii. 9; Heb. xiii. 5. It forms an expansion of the previous words. Σκοπεῖν is 'to look attentively'; to fix the attention upon a thing with an interest in it. (See Rom. xvi. 17; 2 Cor. iv. 18; Gal. vi. 1; Phil. iii. 17.) Hence, often, 'to aim at.' (Comp. σκοπὸν, iii. 14.) Schmidt defines: "to direct one's attention upon a thing, either in order to obtain it, or because one has a peculiar interest in it, or a duty to fulfil towards it. Also to have an eye to with a view of forming a right judgment" (*Synon.* 11, 12).

ἀλλὰ καὶ: Καὶ, 'also,' is inserted because Paul would not have it understood that one is to pay no attention to his own affairs.

ℵ* AC 17 join 2d εκαστοι with τουτ. φρον. following. The previous sentence would therefore end with ετερων.

Humility is urged because it is necessary to concord, as κενοδοξία is fatal to concord. For the supreme example and illustration of this virtue, the readers are now pointed to Jesus Christ. (Comp. Rom. xv. 3; 2 Cor. viii. 9; 1 Pet. ii. 21, and the striking parallel in Clem. *ad Cor.* xvi.)

5–8. *Cherish the disposition which dwelt in Christ Jesus. For he, though he existed from eternity in a state of equality with God, did not regard that divine condition of being as one might regard a prize to be eagerly grasped, but laid it aside, and took the form of a bondservant, having been made in the likeness of men: and having been thus found in fashion as a man, he humbled himself by becoming obedient to God even so far as to suffer death, yea, the ignominious death of the cross.*

On the whole passage, see note at the end of this chapter.

5. τοῦτο φρονεῖτε ἐν ὑμῖν ὃ καὶ ἐν Χριστῷ Ἰησοῦ: 'have this mind in you which was also in Christ Jesus.'

ℵ[c] DFGKLP, Goth., Syr.[p], insert γαρ after τουτο; ℵ* ABC 17, 37, Cop., Arm., Æth., omit γαρ; φρονειτε with ℵ ABC* DFG 67**, Vulg., Syr.[utr]; C[3] KLP, Cop., Arm., Goth., read φρονεισθω.

ἐν ὑμῖν: 'in you'; not 'among you,' which is precluded by the following ἐν Χ'Ι. (Comp. Mt. iii. 9, ix. 3, 21.) Ἐν ὑμῖν with the active φρονεῖτε presents no difficulty if it is remembered that φρονεῖν signifies the general mental attitude or disposition. (See on i. 7.)

ἐν Χ'Ι: There was a slight difference of opinion as to whether that which is commended to imitation is Christ's ταπεινοφροσύνη (so the Gk. Fathers), or his self-denying zeal for the salvation of others (Aug. Ans.). It is both combined. They are represented respectively by ἐταπείνωσεν (vs. 8) and ἐκένωσεν (vs. 7). So Beng., "qui non sua quaesiverit sed se ipsum demiserit."

6. ὃς: Refers to Christ as the subject. It is the subject of both classes of statements which follow, — those predicated of Christ's preincarnate state and of his human condition. The immediate context defines the specific reference in each case.

ἐν μορφῇ θεοῦ: 'in the form of God.' 'Form' is an inadequate rendering of μορφή, but our language affords no better word. By 'form' is commonly understood 'shape,' 'sensible appearance.' So of Christ's human form (Mk. xvi. 12). But the word in this sense cannot be applied to God. Μορφή here means that expression of being which is identified with the essential nature and character of God, and which reveals it. This expression of God cannot be conceived by us, though it may be conceived and apprehended by pure spiritual intelligences.

ὑπάρχων: 'subsisting' or 'though he subsisted.' Originally 'to begin,' 'make a beginning'; thence 'to come forth'; 'be at hand'; 'be in existence.' It is sometimes claimed that ὑπάρχειν, as distinguished from εἶναι, implies a reference to an antecedent condition. Thus R.V. marg. 'being *originally*.' Suidas, = προεῖναι. That it does so in some cases is true. (See Thuc. iv. 18, vi. 86; Hdt. ii. 15; Dem. iii. 15, v. 13.) Comp. the meaning 'to be taken for granted' (Plat. *Symp.* 198 D; *Tim.* 30 C). On the other hand, it sometimes denotes a present as related to a future condition. (See Hdt. vii. 144; Thuc. ii. 64; and the meaning 'to be in store' [Æs. *Ag.* 961].) The most that can be said is that the word is very often used with a relative meaning; while, at the same time, it often occurs simply as 'to be.' (See Schmidt, *Synon.* 81, 7.)

οὐχ ἁρπαγμὸν ἡγήσατο τὸ εἶναι ἴσα θεῷ: 'counted it not a prize to be on an equality with God.'

Ἁρπαγμὸν is here equivalent to ἅρπαγμα, the more regular form for the object of the action, — the thing seized, — while substantives in μος have usually an active sense. There are, however, exceptions to this. Thus θεσμός and χρησμός are neither of them used actively. Φραγμός, 'a fencing in,' is also used like φράγμα, 'a fence.' Ἁγιασμός is both 'the act of consecration' and 'sanctification.' (Comp. ὀνειδισμός, σωφρονισμός, and ἱλασμός.) There is only one example of ἁρπαγμός in any class. author (Plut. *Moral.* p. 12 A) where the meaning is apparently active. It occurs in two passages of Cyr. Alex., *De Adorat.* i. 25, and *Cont. Jul.* vi., both in a passive sense, and in Euseb. *Comm. in Luc.* vi., also passive. Max. Conf. *Schol. in Lib. de divin. nom.* 57 D, explains οὐχ ἁρπ. ἡγ. by οὐκ ἀπηξίωσεν ὡς ἄνθρωπος ὑπακοῦσαι. It should also be observed that *rapina*, by which ἁρπαγμὸν is rendered in the Lat. trans. of Origen and Theo. Mops., is used both actively and passively, the latter in poetry and late Latin. In this condition of the evidence it is certainly straining a point, to say the least, to insist on making the rendering of the passage turn on the active meaning of ἁρπαγμὸν, as Mey. Ἅρπαγμα is often used with ἡγεῖσθαι, as ἁρπαγμὸν here, in the sense of 'to clutch greedily.'

ἡγήσατο: See on vs. 3. Weiss suggests that the phrase ἁρπ. ἡγ. may have been chosen with reference to ἡγούμενοι of vs. 3, in order to emphasise the disposition from which Christ's self-humiliation proceeded.

τὸ εἶναι ἴσα θεῷ: Εἶναι, 'to exist'; not as the abstract substantive verb 'to be.' Ἴσα is adverbial, 'in a manner of equality.' (Comp. Thuc. iii. 14; Eurip. *Orest.* 882; and other examples in Win. xxvii.) (See LXX; Job v. 14; Sap. vii. 3.) The phrase therefore does not mean 'to be equal with God,' but 'existence in the way of equality with God' (Mey., Ellic., Weiss, De W., Kl.).

Others, as Lightf., take ἴσα predicatively, and εἶναι as 'to be.'

7. ἀλλὰ ἑαυτὸν ἐκένωσεν: 'but emptied himself.' For the verb, comp. Rom. iv. 14; 1 Cor. i. 17, ix. 15; 2 Cor. ix. 3; LXX; Jer. xiv. 2, xv. 9. Not used or intended here in a metaphysical sense to define the limitations of Christ's incarnate state, but as a strong and graphic expression of the completeness of his self-renunciation. It includes all the details of humiliation which follow, and is defined by these. Further definition belongs to speculative theology. On Baur's attempt to show traces of Gnostic teaching in these words, see Introd. vi.

μορφὴν δούλου λαβών: 'having taken the form of a bondservant.' Characterising ἑαυ. ἐκ. generally. The participle is explanatory, 'by taking.' (Comp. Eph. i. 9; and see Burt. 145, and Win. xlv.) Μορφὴν, as in vs. 6, an expression or manifestation essentially characteristic of the subject. Christ assumed that form of being which completely answered to and characteristically expressed the being of a bondservant. Only μορφὴ δούλου must not be taken as implying a slave-condition, but a condition of service as contrasted with the condition of equality with God.

Some, as Mey., Ellic., supply θεοῦ, 'servant of God.' But this limits the phrase unduly. He was not servant of God only, but of men also. (Comp. Mt. xx. 27, 28; Mk. x. 44, 45; Lk. xii. 37; Jn. xiii. 1–5, 13–17.)

ἐν ὁμοιώματι ἀνθρώπων γενόμενος: 'having become (been made) in the likeness of men.' Defining μορ. δού. λαβ. more specifically. Ὁμοιώματι does not imply the reality of Christ's humanity as μορφὴ θε. implied the reality of his deity. The former fact is stated in ἐν μορ. δού. As that phrase expressed the inmost reality of Christ's servantship, — the fact that he really became the servant of men, — so ἐν ὁμ. ἀνθ. expresses the fact that his mode of manifestation *resembled* what men are. This leaves room for the other side of his nature, the divine, in the likeness of which he did not appear. His likeness to men was real, but it did not express his whole self. The totality of his being could not appear to men, for that would involve the μορ. θε. The apostle views him solely as he could appear to men. All that was possible was a real and complete *likeness* to humanity. (Comp. Rom. v. 14, vi. 5, viii. 3.) "To affirm likeness is at once to assert similarity and to deny sameness" (Dickson, *Baird Lect.*, 1883).

γενόμενος: Contrasted with ὑπάρχων. He entered into a new state. (Comp. Jn. i. 14; Gal. iv. 4; 1 Tim. iii. 16.) For the phrase γενόμενος ἐν, see Lk. xxii. 44; Acts xxii. 17; Rom. xvi. 7; 2 Cor. iii. 7.

καὶ σχήματι εὑρεθεὶς ὡς ἄνθρωπος: 'and being found in fashion as a man.' Σχῆμα is the outward *fashion* which appeals to the senses. The 'form of a bondservant' expresses the fact that the manifestation as a servant corresponded to the real fact that Christ came as a servant of men. In ἐν ὁμ. ἀνθ. the thought is still linked with that of his essential nature, which rendered an absolute identity with men impossible. In σχῆμ. εὑρ. the thought is confined to the outward guise as it appealed to human observation. Σχῆμα denotes something changeable as well as external. It is an accident of being. (See 1 Cor. vii. 31.) The compounds of μορφὴ and σχῆμα bring out the difference between the inward and the outward. Thus συμμόρφους, Rom. viii. 29; συμμορφιζόμενος, Phil. iii. 10; μεταμορφούμεθα (οὖσθε), 2 Cor. iii. 18; Rom. xii. 2; μορφωθῇ, Gal. iv. 19; — all of an inner, spiritual process, while συσχηματίζεσθαι (Rom. xii. 2; 1 Pet. i. 14) marks a process affecting that which is outward. See the two together in Phil. iii. 21. See Lightf.'s note on the synonyms μορφὴ and σχῆμα (*Comm.* p. 127).

Mey. and De W. take καὶ σχ. . . . ἀνθ. with the preceding clause: 'becoming in the likeness of men and (so) found in fashion,' etc. This is plausible, but it makes the next sentence very abrupt, and breaks the progression. Εὑρεθεὶς introduces a new portion of the history. The laying aside of the form of God — the self-emptying — consisted in his taking the form of a servant and becoming in the likeness of men. In this condition he is *found.* In this new guise he first becomes apprehensible to human perception; and on this stage, where he is seen by men, other acts of humiliation follow. (Comp. Is. liii. 2.)

Εὑρεθεὶς is not a Hebraism, nor does it stand for εἶναι. Εἶναι expresses the quality of a person or thing in itself; εὑρ. the quality as it is discovered and recognised. (Comp. Mt. i. 18; Lk. xvii. 18; Acts v. 39; Rom. vii. 10; 2 Cor. xi. 12; and see Win. lxv.)

ὡς: not *what* he was recognised to be, which would have been expressed by ἄνθρωπος alone; but *as*, keeping up the idea of semblance expressed in ὁμοιώματι.

8. ἐταπείνωσεν ἑαυτὸν: 'he humbled himself.' The emphasis is on the act, not on the subject. Not synonymous with ἐκένωσεν. (Comp. 2. Cor xi. 7; Phil. iv. 12.)

The more general ἐταπείνωσεν is now specifically defined. γενόμενος ὑπήκοος: 'becoming obedient or subject.' He became as a man; in that condition he humbled himself; his humiliation appeared in his subjection. Γενόμ., with an explanatory force, 'by becoming.' Understand θεῷ. (Comp. Mt. xxvi. 39; Rom. v. 19; Heb. v. 8.)

μέχρι θανάτου: 'even unto death.' To the extent of death. (Comp. Heb. xii. 4; 2 Tim. ii. 9.)

θανάτου δὲ σταυροῦ: 'yea, death of the cross.'

Δὲ introduces another and more striking detail of the humiliation, and leads on to a climax: 'death, yea, the most ignominious of deaths.' For this force of δὲ, comp. Rom. iii. 22, ix. 20.

σταυροῦ: ℵ adds *του*. The close of the description leaves the reader at the very lowest point of Christ's humiliation, death as a malefactor; the mode of death to which a curse was attached in the Mosaic law. (See Deut. xxi. 23; Gal. iii. 13; Heb. xii. 2.) Paul, as a Roman citizen, was exempt from this disgrace.

The result of this humiliation was the highest exaltation.

9–11. *On this account God exalted him above all creatures, and bestowed on him the name which is above every name; that in the name of Jesus all beings in heaven, earth, and hades, should bow the knee and acknowledge him as Lord, and by this confession glorify God the Father.*

9. *διὸ καὶ ὁ θεὸς αὐτὸν ὑπερύψωσεν*: 'wherefore also God highly exalted him.'

διὸ: 'in consequence of which.' (Comp. Heb. ii. 9, xii. 2.) The idea of Christ's receiving his exaltation as a reward was repugnant to the Reformed theologians. Calvin attempts to evade it by explaining *διὸ* as *quo facto*, which is utterly untenable. At the same time, it is not necessary to insist on the idea of recompense, since *διὸ* may express simply consequence; and exaltation is the logical result of humility in the N.T. economy (Mt. xxiii. 12; Lk. xiv. 11, xviii. 14). As Mey. remarks, "Christ's saying in Mt. xxiii. 12 was gloriously fulfilled in his own case." "Die Erniedrigung ist nur die noch nicht eingetretene Herrlichkeit," says Schmidt (Art. "Stand, doppelter Christi," Herz. *Rl. Enc.*). For *διὸ καὶ* introducing a result, see Lk. i. 35; Acts x. 29. The consequence corresponding to the humiliation is expressed by *καὶ*.

Different explanations of *καὶ* are given, however. Lightf. and Kl. maintain the sense of reciprocation, — 'God, on his part'; Ellic., contrast of the exaltation with the previous humiliation.

ὑπερύψωσεν: Only here in N.T. In LXX; Ps. xcvii. (xcvi.) 9; Dan. iv. 34. Not in class. Gk. Paul is fond of *ὑπὲρ* in compounds, and the compounds with *ὑπὲρ* are nearly all in his writings. (See Ellic. on Eph. iii. 20.) Its force here is not 'more than before,' nor 'above his previous state of humiliation,' but 'in superlative measure.' This exaltation took place through Christ's ascension (Rom. i. 3, 4, viii. 34; Eph. iv. 9, 10; Col. iii. 1). But the exaltation is viewed, not in respect of its mode, but as a state of transcendent glory, including his sitting at God's right hand (Rom. viii. 34; Col. iii. 1); his lordship over the living and the dead (Rom. xiv. 9); and his reign in glory (1 Cor. xv. 25).

καὶ ἐχαρίσατο αὐτῷ τὸ ὄνομα τὸ ὑπὲρ πᾶν ὄνομα: 'and gave unto him the name which is above every name.'

ἐχαρίσατο: See on i. 29. Christ obtained as a gift what he renounced as a prize. (See Eph. i. 21; Heb. i. 4.)

τὸ ὄνομα: Possibly with a reference to the practice of giving a new name to persons at important crises in their lives. (See Gen. xvii. 5, xxxii. 28; Apoc. ii. 17, iii. 12.) The name conferred is JESUS CHRIST, combining the human name, which points to the conquest won in the flesh, and the Messianic name, 'the Anointed of God.' The two factors of the name are successively taken up in vs. 10, 11.

There is a great variety of explanations on this point: Κύριος (Kl., Lips., Weiss), Ἰησοῦς (Ellic., Ead.), Ἰησοῦς Χριστὸς (De W., Mey.), Υἱὸς (Thdrt., Pelag., Aug.), Θεὸς (Theoph., Œc.). Lightf. holds that ὄνομα means 'title' or 'dignity,' and must be taken in the same sense in both verses. (See on next vs.)

The reading το ονομα is acc. to ℵ ABC 17. το is omitted by DFGKLP.

10. ἵνα: Denotes the purpose of the exaltation.

ἐν τῷ ὀνόματι Ἰησοῦ: '*In* the name of Jesus'; not '*at* the name.' Ὄνομα with τοῦ κυρ. ἡμ. ἸΧ, or τ. κυρ. Ι., or κυρ. Ἰ., or αὐτοῦ (Cht.), occurs ten times in Paul. In none of these cases is the word a mere title of address. Paul follows the Hebrew usage, in which the name is used for everything which the name covers, so that the name is equivalent to the person himself. (So Mt. vi. 9, x. 41.) To baptize into the name of the Father, Son, and Holy Spirit is to put the subject of baptism symbolically into connection and communion with all that those names represent. He who believes on the name of the Lord believes on the Lord himself. Hence, to bow the knee in the name of Jesus is to pay adoration in that sphere of authority, grace, and glory for which the name stands; as being consciously within the kingdom of which he is Lord, as recognising the rightfulness of the titles 'Jesus,' 'Saviour,' 'Lord,' and as loyally accepting the obligations which those titles imply.

πᾶν γόνυ κάμψῃ: Comp. Is. xlv. 23; Rom. xiv. 11. The meaning can only be that Christ is presented as the object of worship; his claim to that honor being fixed by the previous declarations. Before his incarnation he was on an equality with God. After his incarnation he was exalted to God's right hand as Messianic sovereign.

ἐπουρανίων καὶ ἐπιγείων καὶ καταχθονίων: The whole body of created intelligent beings in all departments of the universe. (See Rom. viii. 21; 1 Cor. xv. 24; Eph. i. 20–22; Heb. ii. 8; Apoc. v. 13; and comp. Ign. *Trall.* ix.; Polyc. *Phil.* ii.) Ἐπουράνιοι are heavenly beings, angels, archangels, etc. (Eph. i. 21, iii. 10; Heb. i. 4–6; 1 Pet. iii. 23); Ἐπίγειοι, beings on earth (1 Cor. xv. 40).

καταχθονίων: Only here in Bib. and Apocr. In class. of the infernal gods. Chr., Œc., Theoph., and the mediæval expositors explain of the demons, citing Lk. iv. 34; Jas. ii. 19. These, however, are not regarded by Paul as in Hades. (See Eph. ii. 2, vi. 12.) Rather the departed in Hades. Nothing definite as to Christ's descent into Hades can be inferred from this.

Lightf. regards all the genitives as neuter, urging that the whole creation is intended, and that the limitation to intelligent beings detracts from the universality of the homage. This, however, seems to be over-subtilising.

11. ἐξομολογήσηται: 'should confess.' The LXX, Is. xlv. 23, has ὀμεῖται, 'shall swear,' for which the seventh-century correctors of ℵ read ἐξομολογήσεται.

WH., Treg., R.T., Weiss. (*Txtk. Unt.*), read εξομολογησηται with ℵ B; Tisch. εξομολογησεται, with ACDFGKLP. It is possible that εται may have been altered to ηται by transcribers in order to conform it to κάμψῃ.

Lightf. renders 'confess with thanksgiving.' He says that the secondary sense of ἐξομολ., 'to offer thanks,' has almost entirely supplanted its primary meaning, 'to declare openly.' But out of eleven instances in the N.T., four are used of confessing sins, one of Christ's confession of his servants before the Father, and one of Judas' 'agreeing' or 'engaging' with the chief priests. He says, further, that 'confess with thanksgiving' is the meaning in Is. xlv. 23. But the reading there is ὀμεῖται.

Κύριος does not necessarily imply divinity. It is used in LXX of Abraham (Gen. xviii. 12; comp. 1 Pet. iii. 6); of Joseph (Gen. xlii. 10, 33); of Elkanah (1 Sam. i. 8). In the Pauline writings the master of slaves is styled both δεσπότης (1 Tim. vi. 1, 2; Tit. ii. 9), and κύριος (Eph. vi. 9; Col. iv. 1). Often in N.T. in the general sense of 'master,' or in address, 'sir.' Of God, Mt. i. 20, 22, 24, ii. 15; Acts xi. 16. Ὁ κύριος is used by Mt. of Christ only once (xxi. 3) until after the resurrection (xxviii. 16). In the other gospels much oftener. In the progress of Christian thought in the N.T. the meaning develops towards a specific designation of the divine Saviour, as may be seen in the expressions 'Jesus Christ our Lord,' 'Jesus our Lord,' etc. Von Soden remarks: "God gave him the name Jesus Christ. It was necessary that his human, Messianic character should be developed before men would confess that Jesus is Lord. What God as Jehovah in the old Covenant has determined and prepared, Christ shall now carry out."

εἰς δόξαν θεοῦ πατρός: 'to the glory of God the Father.' (Comp. Jn. xii. 28, xiii. 31, 32, xiv. 13, xvii. 1.) The words are dependent upon ἐξομολ., not on ὅτι. It is *the confession* that is to be to the glory of God the Father, not the fact that Christ is Lord. (See Rom. xv. 7–9; Eph. i. 6, 11, 12; 2 Cor. i. 20.) "Everywhere where the Son is glorified the Father is glorified. Where the Son is dishonored the Father is dishonored" (Chr.). (See Lk. x. 16; Jn. v. 23.)

Some practical exhortations are now drawn from the divine example just portrayed, especially from the spirit of subjection exhibited by the incarnate Lord.

12–18. *Wherefore, my beloved brethren, even as you have always manifested a spirit of obedience, so now, not as though I were present, but much more in my absence, carry out your own salvation with conscientious caution and self-distrust, because you are appointed to carry out God's good pleasure; and it is for this that God energises your will and stimulates you to work. That you may thus carry the divine will into effect, perform all its dictates without murmuring or criticising, that so you may show yourselves blameless and guileless, true children of God in the midst of an ungodly society, in which you are to appear, holding forth the gospel as luminaries in a dark world. Thus I shall have good reason to boast when Christ shall appear, that my labors for you have not been in vain. Yes, even if, along with the offering of your faith to God, my own blood is to be poured out like a libation at a sacrifice, I rejoice in this, because my death will only promote the working out of your salvation; and this will be a cause of joy to you no less than to me.*

12. ὥστε: 'so that'; 'so then.' The point of connection through ὥστε with the preceding passage is ὑπήκοος in vs. 8. As Christ obtained exaltation and heavenly glory through perfect obedience to God, therefore do you, with like subjection to him, carry out your own salvation. The spirit of obedience is to be shown in their godly fear, in the avoidance of murmuring and skeptical criticism, and in their holy lives and their bold proclamation of the gospel in the midst of ungodly men. For a similar use of ὥστε, comp. iv. 1; Rom. vii. 12; 1 Cor. xiv. 39, xv. 58.

ὑπηκούσατε: Ὑπακούειν is, properly, to obey as the result of listening or hearkening (ἀκούειν). Πειθαρχεῖν, which is much less frequent, is the only word which expresses the conception of obedience absolutely — as to authority (ἀρχή). (See Acts v. 29, 32, xxvii. 21; Tit. iii. 1.) The question whether θεῷ or μοὶ is to be supplied is quite superfluous, since ὑπηκ. is used absolutely. Ye have always shown a spirit of obedience, whether to God or to me as his apostle.

μὴ ὡς ἐν τῇ παρουσίᾳ μου μόνον: 'not as in my presence only.' Connect with κατεργάζεσθε, not with πάντ. ὑπηκ., which would require οὐ instead of μὴ (see Win. lv, and Burt. 479), and would imply that the readers, left to themselves, had been more obedient than when Paul was with them.

ὡς: Introduced because Paul could not give an admonition for the time when he would be present. It points to an inward motive by which the readers are not to suffer themselves to be influenced. (Comp. Rom. ix. 32; 2 Cor. ii. 17; Philem. 14.) They are not to work out their salvation *as if* they were doing it in Paul's presence merely, neglecting it in his absence.

ὡς omitted by Lat., Vet., Vulg., Syr.p, Cop., Arm., Æth., B, 17. WH. bracket.

μόνον: with ἐν τῇ παρ. μου, on which the emphasis lies. For its position after the emphatic word, comp. Rom. iv. 16, 23; 1 Thess. i. 5.

νῦν: Now that you are deprived of my personal presence.

ἀπουσίᾳ: Only here in Gk. Bib., and not common anywhere.

μετὰ φόβου καὶ τρόμου τὴν ἑαυτῶν σωτηρίαν κατεργάζεσθε: 'carry out your own salvation with fear and trembling.' (Comp. Heb. xii. 28.)

Φόβος and τρόμος often occur together in LXX. (See Gen. ix. 2; Ex. xv. 16; Is. xix. 16.) In N.T. see 1 Cor. ii. 3; 2 Cor. vii. 15; Eph. vi. 5. Φόβος is godly fear, growing out of recognition of weakness and of the power of temptation; filial dread of offending God. (See Acts ix. 31; Rom. iii. 18; 2 Cor. vii. 1; 1 Pet. i. 17, iii. 15.) Chr. justly observes that καὶ τρόμου only strengthens the μετ. φόβ. Paul would say: 'The work is great. Failure is possible. Do not be over confident.' "It is necessary to fear and tremble in each one's working out of his own salvation, lest he be tripped up (ὑποσκελισθεὶς) and fail of this" (Œc.).

τὴν ἑαυτ. σωτ. κατεργ.: Κατεργάζεσθαι is 'to accomplish'; 'achieve'; 'carry out or through.' So Beng., "usque ad metam"; Calov., "ad finem perducere"; Grot., "peragere." (See Rom. iv. 15, v. 3; 2 Cor. v. 5; Jas. i. 3; Eph. vi. 13; and comp. especially 2 Cor. vii. 10.) There is no contradiction implied of the truth that salvation is the gift of God's grace (Eph. ii. 8). That grace itself engenders moral faculties and stimulates moral exertions. *Because* grace is given, man must work. The gift of grace is exhibited in making man a co-worker with God (1 Cor. iii. 9); the salvation bestowed by grace is to be carried out by man with the aid of grace (Rom. vi. 8–19; 2 Cor. vi. 1). What this carrying out includes and requires is seen in Phil. iii. 10, iv. 1–7; Eph. iv. 13–16, 22 ff.; Col. ii. 6, 7. For these things the believer is constantly strengthened by the Spirit. The possibility of success appears in Paul's prayer (Eph. iii. 16–20). (See a good passage in Pfleiderer, *Paulinismus*, p. 234.)

ἑαυτῶν: 'your own'; not = ἀλλήλων, 'one another's,' as some earlier expositors, against which is the emphatic position of ἑαυτ., though the rendering would be grammatically justifiable. (See Mt. xvi. 7, xxi. 38; Eph. iv. 32.) Ἑαυτῶν is emphatic as related to the following θεὸς. *God* is working in you; do *your* part as co-workers with God.

13. θεὸς γάρ ἐστιν ὁ ἐνεργῶν ἐν ὑμῖν καὶ τὸ θέλειν καὶ τὸ ἐνεργεῖν ὑπὲρ τῆς εὐδοκίας: 'for it is God that worketh in you both the willing and the working for his good pleasure.' The reason for the exhortation κατεργ. is that it is *God's* own work which they have to do. It is *God's* good pleasure which they are to fulfil, as did their great example, Jesus Christ; and it is God who, to that end, is energising their will and their working. (See 2 Cor. v. 18.) This is a serious task, to be performed in no self-reliant spirit, but with reverent caution and dependence on God.

Γάρ does not introduce the reason for the fear and trembling especially, but only as these are attached to κατεργ. It gives the reason for the entire clause, κατεργ. . . . τρόμου.

ὁ ἐνεργῶν: Ἐνεργεῖν is 'to put forth power'; and the kindred ἐνέργεια (always in N.T. of superhuman power) is 'power in exercise.' Paul invariably uses the active, ἐνεργεῖν, of the working of God or of Satan, and the middle, ἐνεργεῖσθαι, in other cases, as Rom. vii. 5; Gal. v. 6. Never the passive. The verb carries the idea of effectual working, as here; and the result is often specified. (See Rom. vii. 5; Gal. ii. 8, iii. 5; Eph. i. 11 ff.) On the different words for 'power' in N.T., see *W. St.* on Jn. i. 12.

ἐν ὑμῖν: '*in* you,' as 1 Cor. xii. 6; 2 Cor. iv. 12; Eph. ii. 2; Col. i. 29. Not '*among* you.'

τὸ θέλειν: As between θέλειν and βούλεσθαι, the general distinction is that θέλ. expresses a determination or definite resolution of the will; while βούλ. expresses an inclination, disposition, or wish. The two words are, however, often interchanged in N.T. when no distinction is emphasised. (Comp. Mk. xv. 15 and Lk. xxiii. 20; Acts xxvii. 43 and Mt. xxvii. 17; Jn. xviii. 39 and Mt. xiv. 5; Mk. vi. 48 and Acts xix. 30.) (See *W. St.* on Mt. i. 19.) Here θέλειν, of a definite purpose or determination.

τὸ ἐνεργεῖν: The inward working in the soul, producing the determination which is directed at the κατεργ. (Comp. 1 Cor. xii. 6; Gal. iii. 5; Eph. iii. 20.) The two substantive-infinitives are used rather than nouns because active energy is emphasised; and the two καί's point to the fact that *both* — the willing and the working alike — are of God. God so works upon the moral nature that it not only intellectually and theoretically approves what is good (Rom. vii. 14–23), but appropriates God's will as its own. The willing wrought by God unfolds into all the positive and determinate movements of the human will to carry God's will into effect.

ὑπὲρ τῆς εὐδοκίας: 'for the sake of his good pleasure.' Different connections have been proposed for this clause. That with the succeeding verse, 'for good will's sake do all things,' etc., may be summarily dismissed. The majority of interpreters rightly connect it with ὁ ἐνεργῶν: 'it is God who works in you the willing and the working in order that he may carry out his good pleasure.' Paul's thought is this: Carry out your own salvation with holy fear, and especially for the reason that it is God's good pleasure that you should achieve that result; and therefore he energises your will and your activity in order that you may fulfil his good pleasure in your completed salvation.

εὐδοκίας: See on i. 15. Not mere arbitrary preference, as if Paul meant that God thus works because it suits him to do so. Nor, as Weiss, the pleasure which he has in working. Rather that his good pleasure is bound up with his fatherly love and benevolence which find their satisfaction in his children's accomplished salvation. Hence ὑπὲρ is not = κατὰ, as if εὐδοκία were the norm or standard of God's working (however true that may be abstractly), but expresses "the interested cause of the action" (Ellic.), as Jn. xi. 4; Rom. xv. 8.

Certain elements of the σωτ. κατεργ.

14. πάντα ποιεῖτε χωρὶς γογγυσμῶν καὶ διαλογισμῶν: 'do all things without murmurings and questionings.'

πάντα: Everything that may fall to them to do. (Comp. 1 Cor. x. 31.)

γογγυσμῶν: Not elsewhere in Paul. (See Jn. v. 12; Acts vi. 1; 1 Pet. iv. 9; LXX; Ex. xvi. 7, 8, 9, 12; Num. xvii. 5, 10.) Murmuring against the dictates of God's will is meant. (See 1 Cor. x. 10.)

διαλογισμῶν: Skeptical questionings or criticisms. (Comp. 1 Tim. ii. 8.) Usually by Paul in the sense of 'disputatious reasoning.' (See Rom. i. 21, xiv. 1; 1 Cor. iii. 20.) So LXX; Ps. lvi. 5 (lv. 6), xciv. (xciii.) 11; Is. lix. 7. The verb διαλογίζεσθαι, always to 'reason' or 'discuss,' either with another or in one's own mind.

Mey., De W., Lips., Ellic., Ead., render 'doubtings.' Œc., Theoph., Ans., 'hesitation' whether to perform God's commands. So De W. and Mey. Weiss, 'hesitation' with reference to things which are to be done or suffered for the sake of salvation. Others, 'doubts' about future reward, or the divine promises.

15. ἵνα γένησθε ἄμεμπτοι καὶ ἀκέραιοι: 'that ye may become blameless and guileless.'

For γενησθε ADFG, Vet., Lat., Vulg., read ητε.

γένησθε: 'become,' in the process of σωτ. κατεργ.

ἄμεμπτοι: Before both God and men.

ἀκέραιοι: lit. 'unmixed,' 'unadulterated,' describing the inward condition. (Comp. Mt. x. 16; Rom. xvi. 9.)

τέκνα θεοῦ ἄμωμα: 'children of God without blemish.'

Both τέκνον and υἱός signify a relation based upon parentage. It is usually said that τέκνον emphasises the natural relationship, while υἱός marks the legal or ethical status (Thay. *Lex.* sub **τέκνον**, and Sanday on Rom. viii. 14. Comp. Westcott, *Eps. of John*, p. 121); but this distinction must not be too closely pressed. In LXX both **τέκνα** and υἱός are applied ethically to the people of Israel as God's peculiarly beloved people; so **τέκνα** (Is. xxx. 1; Sap. xvi. 21); or so by implication as inhabitants of his favored seat (Joel ii. 23; Zech. ix. 13, comp. Mt. xxiii. 37); υἱός (Is. xliii. 6; Deut. xiv. 1; Sap. ix. 7, xii. 19, etc.). In the ethical sense, in which the distinctive character is indicated by its source, we find **τέκνα** ἀδικίας (Hos. x. 9), σοφίας (Mt. xi. 19), ὑπακοῆς (1 Pet. i. 14), φωτὸς (Eph. v. 8), ὀργῆς (Eph. ii. 3). Similarly υἱοὶ, according to the Hebrew use of בֵּן, בְּנֵי to mark characteristic quality as conditioned by origin. Thus υἱοὶ τῶν ἀνθρώπων, indicating changeableness, Num. xxiii. 19; indicating people accursed, 1 Sam. xxvi. 19; υἱ. τοῦ αἰῶνος τούτου, φωτὸς, Lk. xvi. 8; ἀπειθίας, Eph. ii. 2; διαβόλου, Acts xiii. 10; γεέννης, Mt. xiii. 15. It is true that John never uses υἱός to describe the relation of Christians to God (Apoc. xxi. 7 is a quotation); but both the ethical relation and the relation of conferred privilege, as well as that of birth, attach to **τέκνα**. See Jn. i. 12, where believers receive ἐξουσία or conferred right to become **τέκνα** θεοῦ, on the ground of faith. Believers are **τέκνα** in virtue of the gift of divine love (1 Jn. iii. 1). The **τέκνα** θεοῦ are manifest as such by their righteous deeds and their brotherly love (1 Jn. iii. 10). On the other hand, those who have the true filial disposition are described as 'begotten' or 'born' of God (γεγεννημένοι), Jn. i. 13, iii. 3, 7; 1 Jn. iii. 9, iv. 7, v. 1, 4, 18. It is also true that Paul often regards the Christian relation, from the legal point of view, as adoption. He alone uses υἱοθεσία (Rom. viii. 15, 23; Gal. iv. 5; Eph. i. 5). But in Rom. viii. 14, 17, we have both υἱοὶ and **τέκνα**. They who are led by the Spirit are υἱοὶ; the Spirit witnesses that they are **τέκνα**. Both these are ethical. In vs. 21 the legal aspect appears in τὴν ἐλευθερίαν . . . τ. τέκ. τ. θε. (Comp. Eph. v. 1; Rom. ix. 8.)

ἄμωμα: 'without blemish.'

αμωμα as א ABC, 17. DFGKLP read αμωμητα.

αμωμητος never in LXX. The citn. is from Deut. xxxii. 5, and αμωμητα is probably due to μωμητα there.

For ἄμωμα comp. Eph. i. 4, v. 27; Col. i. 22; ἀμώμητος, 'that cannot be blamed,' only in 2 Pet. iii. 14.

μέσον γενεᾶς σκολιᾶς καὶ διεστραμμένης: 'in the midst of a crooked and perverse generation.' (See Deut. xxxii. 5, and comp. Mt. xii. 39, xvii. 17.)

Μέσον (TR ἐν μέσῳ) is adverbial, with the force of a preposition (Win. liv.).

σκολίας: 'indocile,' 'froward.' Only here in Paul. (See Acts ii. 40; 1 Pet. ii. 18; LXX; Ps. lxxviii. [lxxvii.] 8; Prov. ii. 15, etc.)

διεστραμμένης: 'twisted' or 'distorted.' Only here in Paul. It denotes an abnormal moral condition. Σκολιὸς is the result of διαστρέφειν. Comp. στρεβλοῦν (2 Pet. iii. 16), 'to twist or dislocate on the rack.'

ἐν οἷς φαίνεσθε ὡς φωστῆρες ἐν κόσμῳ: 'among whom ye are seen (appear) as luminaries in the world.'

οἷς: For the plural after γενεᾶς comp. Acts xv. 36; 2 Pet. iii. 1; Gal. iv. 19; and see Blass, *Gramm.* p. 163.

φαίνεσθε: Not 'shine,' which would be φαίνετε. (Comp. Mt. ii. 7, xxiv. 27; Jas. iv. 14.) The word is indicative, not imperative. For the thought, comp. Mt. v. 14, 16; Eph. v. 8; 1 Thess. v. 5.

φωστῆρες: Only here and Apoc. xxi. 11. In LXX of the heavenly bodies, as Gen. i. 14, 16.

ἐν κόσμῳ: With φωστῆρες: luminaries in a dark world (Ellic., Mey., Kl., Lips.).

Lightf., De W., and Weiss connect with φαίνεσθε. Lightf.'s interpretation turns on his explanation of κόσμος, which, he says, has in the N.T. a sense so dominantly ethical that it cannot well be used here of the physical as distinguished from the moral world. An examination of the number of instances in which κόσμος occurs in a physical sense will show that this view is groundless. If taken with φαίνεσθε, ἐν κόσμῳ would be merely an unmeaning expansion of ἐν οἷς; while with φωστῆρες we have a definite image. For the omission of the article with κόσμῳ see Win. xix. 1 *a*.

16. λόγον ζωῆς ἐπέχοντες: 'holding forth the word of life.'

λόγον ζωῆς: the gospel: a word which has life in itself, and which leads to life. The phrase not elsewhere in Paul. (Comp. Jn. vi. 68; Acts v. 20; 1 Jn. i. 1.) By ζωὴ is not to be understood Christ himself, nor the eternal life, but the life which the Christian possesses through faith in Christ, and leads in fellowship with Christ (Rom. vi. 13, viii. 6, 10). The genitive is the genitive of contents: not, 'the word *concerning* life,' but the word 'which has in itself a principle as well as a message of life'; or, as Mey., "the divinely efficacious vehicle of the spirit of life." (Comp. Jn. vi. 68.) Life and light appear in correlation in Jn. i. 4; Eph. ii. 1; and especially since heathenism is regarded as a state alike of death and of darkness (Eph. ii. 1; Col. ii. 13). Ζωὴ is the correlative of salvation. With quickening from the death of sin the believer enters upon 'newness of life' (Rom. vi. 4, 11). This life, as to its quality, is that which shall be lived with the exalted Christ. Now it is hidden with Christ, because the exalted Christ is still hidden (Col. iii. 3; comp. Col. i. 5). But it will be manifested in glory when Christ, who is our life, shall be manifested (Col. iii. 4). Then will come the change into 'the likeness of the body of his glory' (Phil. iii. 21), and "mortality" will be "swallowed up of life" (2 Cor. v. 4).

ἐπέχοντες: 'holding forth.' In Paul only here and 1 Tim. iv. 16. In LXX only in the sense of 'apply,' as Job xviii. 2, xxx. 26; or 'forbear'; 'refrain,' as 1 K. xxii. 6, 15. Lit. 'to hold upon' or 'apply.' So 'to fix the attention' (Lk. xiv. 7; Acts iii. 5, xix. 22). In the sense of 'to hold out' or 'present' it occurs only in class.

'Holding forth,' as Ellic., Alf., Ead., Lightf.; 'holding fast' (Luth., Beng., De W.); 'having in possession' (Kl., Lips., Mey., Weiss). Lightf. regards ἐν οἷς . . . κόσμῳ as parenthetical, and connects λόγ. ζω. ἐπέχ. with ἵνα γέν. . . . διεστραμ. (vs. 15). He finds an incongruity in the images φαίν. and ἐπεχ. Surely this is hypercritical. 'Ye appear holding forth the word as a light.' It is common to personify a luminary as a light-bearer. Paul was not always so consistent in his metaphors as this criticism would imply. See for inst. 2 Cor. iii. 2, 3, and Lightf. on 1 Thess. v. 4, *Notes on Eps. of St. P. from unpublished Commentaries.* (See Mey.'s citn. from *Test. xii. Patr.*)

εἰς καύχημα ἐμοὶ: 'for a matter of glorying unto me.' For καύχημα see on i. 26. Their success in working out their own salvation and proclaiming the gospel to others will be a cause of boasting to Paul. (Comp. 2 Cor. i. 14; 1 Thess. ii. 19.) Εἰς καύχ. ἐμ. belongs to the whole passage ἵνα γεν. . . . ἐπέχ.; not merely to λόγ. ζω. ἐπέχ.

εἰς ἡμέραν Χριστοῦ: 'against the day of Christ.' (See on i. 10, and comp. Gal. iii. 23; Eph. iv. 30.) The day is the point with reference to which the boasting is reserved. Not '*until* the day,' etc. The glorying is put in relation to the decisions and awards of the *parousia*, as 2 Cor. i. 14.

Ὅτι may be taken as explicative either of the nature of the glorying ('that'), or of its ground ('because').

εἰς κενὸν: 'in vain'; '*to* no purpose.' See for the phrase, 2 Cor. vi. 1; Gal. ii. 2; 1 Thess. iii. 5. LXX, εἰς κενὸν, τὸ κεν., κενὰ, Lev. xxvi. 20; Job ii. 9, xx. 18, xxxix. 16; Is. xxix. 8; Jer. vi. 29. 'In vain' is the dominant thought here, as is shown by the repetition.

ἔδραμον: Metaphor of the stadium, as Gal. ii. 2. (Comp. Acts xx. 24; 1 Cor. ix. 24; 2 Tim. iv. 7.) The aorist is used from the point of view of the day of Christ.

ἐκοπίασα: Κοπιᾶν, lit. 'to labor to weariness'; κόπος, 'exhausting toil.' (See 1 Cor. xv. 10; Gal. iv. 11; Col. i. 29; 1 Thess. ii. 9, iii. 5.)

Lightf. thinks that ἐκοπίασα is a continuation of the metaphor in ἔδραμον, —'labor such as is bestowed in training for the race.' In his note on Ign. *Polyc.* vi. he says that κοπιᾶν is used especially of such training, and cites 1 Cor. ix. 24–27; Col. i. 29; 1 Tim. iv. 10. I do not find any evidence of this special sense of the verb either in classical or N.T. Greek. Certainly in the athletic contests the wearisome labor was not confined to the preparation.

Paul does not shrink from these labors. He will rejoice even in his martyrdom, since he believes that it will promote the work of salvation among his Philippian brethren. The assumption that vs. 16 implies his conviction that he will be alive at the *parousia*, and that vs. 17 is an admission of the contrary possibility, is entirely gratuitous.

17. ἀλλὰ εἰ καὶ: 'but if even.' The feebly supported reading καὶ εἰ, which does not appear elsewhere in Paul, would introduce an improbable supposition. Καὶ refers to the whole clause σπένδ. . . . πίστ., putting the case as possible (Win. liii.).

σπένδομαι ἐπὶ τῇ θυσίᾳ καὶ λειτουργίᾳ τῆς πίστεως ὑμῶν: 'I am poured out (as a libation) in addition to the sacrifice and service of your faith.'

Ἐπὶ may mean 'at,' 'upon,' or 'in addition to.' Better the last (Ellic., De W., Weiss, Kl., Lips.). 'At' (Mey.) would give an active meaning to θυσία. 'Upon' is precluded by λειτουργία.

θυσίᾳ: Not the act of sacrificing, but the thing sacrificed. So always in N.T. (See Lk. xiii. 1; Acts vii. 41; Rom. xii. 1; 1 Cor. x. 18; Eph. v. 2.)

λειτουργίᾳ: 'ministry' or 'service.' (See Lk. i. 23; 2 Cor. ix. 12; Heb. viii. 6, ix. 21.) From an old adjective λεῖτος or λέϊτος, found only in this compound, 'belonging to the people,' and ἔργον, 'work.' Hence, originally, 'service of the state in a public office.' In LXX the verb λειτουργεῖν, of the performance of priestly functions (Neh. x. 36); λειτουργεῖν and λειτουργὸς, of service rendered to men (1 K. i. 4, xix. 21; 2 K. iv. 43, vi. 15). In N.T., of sacerdotal ministry (Acts xiii. 2; Heb. x. 11; Lk. i. 23; Heb. ix. 21; Rom. xiii. 6, xv. 16; Heb. viii. 2). Also of human, non-official ministry (Rom. xv. 27; 2 Cor. ix. 12; Phil. ii. 25, 30). In the general sense of 'servants of God' (λειτουργοὺς αὐτοῦ), Heb. i. 7. Here metaphorically in the priestly sense. Θυσ. and λειτ. have the article in common, and form one conception (not a hendiadys), a sacrifice ministered.

τῆς πίστεως ὑμῶν: The objective genitive common to θυσ. and λειτ.; a sacrifice which consists of your faith; a ministry which offers faith as a sacrifice.

According to Paul's metaphor, therefore, the Philippians as priests offer their faith to God in the midst of an ungodly generation who had already shed Paul's blood at Philippi, had imprisoned him at Rome, and would probably put him to death. If they should do this, Paul's blood would be the libation which would be added to the Philippians' offering.

This explanation, in which Lightf. stands almost alone among modern expositors, is preferable because it accords better with the course of thought from vs. 12, in which the Philippians are the agents, and distinctly corresponds with Rom. xii. 2, where the Romans are exhorted to present their bodies as a sacrifice (θυσίαν), which is further described as λατρεία, 'a service rendered to God.' See note on λατρεύοντες (iii. 3). In iv. 8, the gift of the Philippians is described as a sacrifice to God. The other and favorite interpretation makes Paul the priest, the Philippians' faith the sacrifice, and Paul's apostolic activity the ministry offering the sacrifice. Then the blood of the priest is poured out upon the sacrifice which he is offering. This explanation is urged principally upon the ground of Rom. xv. 16, 17, where Paul represents himself as λειτουργὸς, ministering the gospel in sacrifice, and presenting the Gentiles as an offering to God. But in that passage Paul is specially exhibiting his apostolic office as a priestly service of offering ordained by Christ, who was himself made a minister that the Gentiles might glorify God for his mercy (vs. 8). That is the only instance of the figure, and in view of the great variety of Paul's metaphors cannot be regarded as decisive.

The fact that Paul is writing from Rome and to a Gentile church seems to indicate that the metaphor is cast in the mould of heathen rather than of Jewish sacrificial usage. Comp. 2 Cor. ii. 14, where the picture of a Roman triumph is suggested, with the clouds of incense rising from the altars.

χαίρω καὶ συνχαίρω πᾶσιν ὑμῖν: 'I joy and rejoice with you all.' Comp. *μενῶ καὶ παραμενῶ* (i. 25). The natural connection is with *εἰ καὶ σπένδομαι* as the subject of congratulation, not in itself, but as a means of promoting their salvation — that cause of boasting which he desires to have in them. Thus his joy will be fulfilled in them (vs. 2).

συνχαίρω: 'I rejoice with.' This is the natural and appropriate meaning in every N.T. passage in which the word occurs. The rendering 'congratulate' (Lightf., Mey.) is admissible in Lk. i. 58, xv. 6, 9, but the other is equally good. 'Congratulate' does not suit vs. 18.

'Rejoice with' is the rendering of the Gk. Fathers, Luth., Calv., De W., Wies., Weiss, Weizs., Lips., von Sod. Mey.'s objection, repeated by Lightf., that the apostle would thus summon his readers to a joy which, according to vs. 17, they already possessed, requires no notice beyond a reminder of the informal and familiar style of the epistle.

Paul therefore says: Even if I should be poured out as a libation in addition to the sacrifice of faith which you are offering to God, I rejoice, and rejoice with you, because such a result will promote your salvation, and that will be a cause of joy to us both alike. (Comp. Eph. iii. 13.)

18. *τὸ δὲ αὐτὸ καὶ ὑμεῖς χαίρετε καὶ συνχαίρετέ μοι*: 'for the same reason do ye also joy and rejoice with me.'

τὸ δὲ αὐτὸ: 'for the same reason'; to wit, the advancement of the work of your salvation. For the grammatical construction, see Win. xxxii. 4 *a*; and comp. Rom. vi. 10. The verbs *χαίρ.* and *συνχαίρ.* acquire a *quasi*-transitive force.

Rill., Weiss, Lightf., Weizs., R.V., render 'in the same manner.'

χαίρετε καὶ συνχαίρετέ μοι: Comp. the striking figure of the Romans forming a chorus and singing a sacrificial hymn round the martyr Ignatius. (Ign. *Rom.* ii.; see also *Trall.* i.)

He hopes soon to send Timothy to them.

19–24. *But, though the worst may come to the worst, yet I hope for such a favorable issue in my case as will enable me to dispense* *with the services of Timothy here and to send him to you, in order that I may be comforted by hearing of your condition. For besides him I have no one likeminded with myself who will care for you with the same fatherly care. For they all are occupied with their own interests, not with the things of Jesus Christ. But Timothy you yourselves have proved; for you know with what filial devotion he served me in the work of promoting the gospel. I hope therefore to send him shortly, as soon as I shall have learned something definite about my own case, but I trust in the Lord that I shall soon be with you in person.*

19. ἐλπίζω δὲ: The δὲ, 'but,' offsets the possibility at which he has hinted in σπένδομαι, and which he knows is disturbing the minds of his faithful friends at Philippi. Mey.'s statement that there is an immediate change from a presentiment of death to a confidence of being preserved in life and liberated, is too strong. The εἰ καὶ σπένδομαι, etc., on its face, at least, merely contemplates a possibility. The words rather revert to i. 25.

Lightf. and Lips. connect with vs. 12: 'I urged you to work out your salvation in my absence, *but* I do not mean to leave you without personal superintendence, and therefore I propose to send Timothy. The connection, however, seems too remote and labored. According to Weiss the δὲ offsets the joy to which he has exhorted them with the means which he proposes to employ to obtain joyful news from them.

ἐν κυρίῳ Ἰησοῦ: The sphere or element in which his hope moves. (Comp. i. 8, 14, iii. 1; Rom. ix. 1, xiv. 14; 1 Cor. i. 31, vii. 39, etc.)

ἵνα κἀγὼ εὐψυχῶ: 'that I also may be of good heart.'

κἀγὼ: 'I *also*,' by the tidings which I shall hear from you, as you by the accounts of me.

εὐψυχῶ: Not elsewhere in Bib. Gk. Εὔψυχος, -ως, -ία, in LXX; 1 Macc. ix. 14; 2 Macc. vii. 20, xiv. 18.

20. οὐδένα γὰρ ἔχω ἰσόψυχον: 'for I have no one likeminded.'

γὰρ: reason for sending Timothy.

ἰσόψυχον: Only here in N.T. (See LXX, Ps. lv. [liv.] 13 [14].) Supply μοὶ, not Τιμοθέῳ. Timothy was to be sent to minister to them in Paul's stead. Moreover, the quality of Timothy's care for them is just that which marks Paul's care — γνησίως, 'naturally,' 'by birth-relation,' and therefore 'truly' or 'genuinely'; with such a care as springs from a *natural*, parental relation. In other words, there is no one who will care for them in a fatherly way as Paul does. (See 1 Cor. iv. 15; 1 Thess. ii. 11; Philem. 10; 1 Tim. i. 2; Tit. i. 4.) Timothy would have such a feeling for the Philippian Christians, since he was associated with Paul in founding their church. For γνήσιος, see iv. 3; 2 Cor. viii. 8; 1 Tim. i. 2; Tit. i. 4.

Lightf., Lips., Weiss, and others refer ἰσόψυχον to Timothy.

21. οἱ πάντες γὰρ τὰ ἑαυτῶν ζητοῦσιν, οὐ τὰ Χριστοῦ Ἰησοῦ: 'for they all seek their own, not the things of Christ Jesus.'

οἱ πάντες: Collective; the whole number in a body. (See Acts xix. 7; Rom. xi. 32; 1 Cor. x. 17; Eph. iv. 13.) The statement is very sweeping, especially in view of the high commendation of Epaphroditus which follows. The common explanations are that all who were likeminded with himself, as Luke, were absent at the time of his writing; or that those about him were interested in promoting party interests, Gentile or Jewish-Christian. The Fathers attempted various explanations, — as that no one was willing to sacrifice his own quiet and security by undertaking the journey to Macedonia; that they were unwilling to sacrifice their own honor and profit to the welfare of the church; or that the words were used only in comparison with Timothy's exceptional zeal and fidelity. None of these help the case. Augustine and Anselm held to the full severity of the charge, maintaining that all the apostle's companions were mercenary. Without more information a satisfactory explanation seems impossible.

22. τὴν δοκιμὴν: 'the proof' or 'approvedness.' Used only by Paul, and meaning both 'the process of trial' (2 Cor. viii. 2) and 'the result of trial,' as here, Rom. v. 4; 2 Cor. ii. 9, ix. 13. You know that he has approved himself to you.

γινώσκετε: Not imperat., for they had known Timothy in Philippi (Acts xvi., xvii.).

ὡς πατρὶ τέκνον σὺν ἐμοὶ ἐδούλευσεν: 'as a child a father so he served with me.' Paul began the sentence as if he were going to write, 'Timothy served me as a child serves a father'; but he was checked by the thought that both himself and Timothy were alike servants of Jesus Christ (i. 1), and also by that of his intimate and affectionate relations with Timothy. Accordingly he wrote '*with* me' instead of 'me.'

εἰς τὸ εὐαγγέλιον: As i. 5.

23. οὖν: Resuming vs. 19; he being thus qualified.

ὡς ἂν ἀφίδω: Whenever he shall have definite reports to send them concerning his own fate. The ἀπὸ implies looking away from the present circumstances to what is going to happen, which will decide the question of his sending Timothy.

24. πέποιθα δὲ ἐν κυρίῳ: See on i. 14; and with Paul's language here comp. 1 Cor. iv. 17, 19.

ὅτι καὶ αὐτὸς ταχέως ἐλεύσομαι: Expectation of speedy release. (Comp. i. 25.)

ℵ* ACP with several minusc. add προς υμας to ελευσομαι.

How soon Timothy or Paul himself may be able to visit them is uncertain, but he is sending them a messenger at once.

25–30. *Meanwhile, whether Timothy and I come to you or not, I send you a messenger at once — my brother and fellow-worker and fellow-soldier Epaphroditus, who came as the bearer of your gift to me. I thought it necessary to send him because he was really homesick, longing to see you, since he feared that you would be distressed by the report of his sickness. And very sick he was, so much so that it seemed as though he would die. But God was merciful to both him and me, and restored him and spared me the additional sorrow of his death. I send him therefore in order that his return to you may restore your cheerfulness, and that the sorrow of my captivity may be mitigated by your joy. Joyfully receive him therefore in the Lord. Such as he are to be honored; for he wellnigh died through his zeal for the work of Christ, hazarding his life in order that he might render to me that sacrificial service of love which, if it had been possible, you would gladly have performed in your own persons.*

25. ἀναγκαῖον: Comp. 2 Cor. ix. 5. Emphatic as contrasted with the possible visits of Timothy and of himself. I *hope* to send Timothy and to come in person, but I think it *necessary* to send Epaphroditus at once.

ἡγησάμην: See on vs. 6. If this is the epistolary aorist, as is probable, it points to Epaphroditus as the bearer of the letter. (See Introd. v.)

Ἐπαφρόδιτον: Mentioned only in this letter. Examples of the name are common in both Greek and Latin inscriptions. (See Wetst.) It is not probable that Ἐπαφρᾶς (Col. i. 7, iv. 12) is a contraction of Ἐπαφρόδιτος. (See Thay. *Lex.* sub Ἐπαφρᾶς.) Win. xvi. says "probable"; Schmiedel, *Rev. of Win.* xvi. 9, "possible." (See Lightf. *Introd.* and *Comm.* ad loc.) Even if the names can be shown to be the same, it is unlikely that the persons were the same. Eadie justly remarks that it is scarcely supposable that the Asiatic Epaphras, a pastor at Colossæ and a native of that city, could be Epaphroditus, a messenger delegated to Paul with a special gift from the distant European church of Philippi, and by him sent back to it with lofty eulogy, and as having a special interest in its affairs and members. From two allusions in Suetonius (*Nero*, 49; *Domitian*, 14), a tradition arose that Epaphroditus was Nero's secretary.

ἀδελφὸν, συνεργὸν, συνστρατιώτην: 'a brother,' as a Christian; 'a fellow-worker,' in the cause of the gospel; 'a fellow-soldier,' in the conflict with the adversaries of the faith. (Comp. Rom. xvi. 3, 9; Philem. 2; Phil. i. 28, 30; 2 Tim. ii. 3.)

ὑμῶν δὲ ἀπόστολον καὶ λειτουργὸν τῆς χρείας μου: 'your messenger and minister to my need.'

ὑμῶν: With both ἀπόστ. and λειτ. A messenger from you and ministering on your behalf.

ἀπόστολον: Not in the official sense, but a messenger sent on a special commission. So 2 Cor. viii. 23.

λειτουργὸν: See on vs. 17, and comp. vs. 30. The explanation 'sacrificial minister' (Mey., Lightf.), regarding the gift of the Philippians as an offering to God, is favored by iv. 18. Westcott, on Heb. i. 7, observes that the word seems always to retain something of its original force, as expressing a public, social service. (See Rom. xv. 27; 2 Cor. ix. 12.)

26. ἐπειδὴ ἐπιποθῶν ἦν πάντας ὑμᾶς: 'Since he was longing after you all.' Giving the reason for vs. 25. The participle with the substantive verb indicates a continued state. For ἐπιποθεῖν, see on i. 8.

ℵ* ACD add ιδειν after υμας. WH. bracket ιδειν.

ἀδημονῶν: Also with ἦν. Only here in Paul. (See Mt. xxvi. 37; Mk. xiv. 33.) In LXX only in second-century revisions (Symm. Eccl. vii. 17; Ps. cxvi. 11 [cxv. 2], lxi. 2 [lx. 3]; Aq. Job xviii. 20). The etymology is uncertain. Commonly from ἀ, δῆμος, 'away from home.' (See Lightf. ad loc.)

27. καὶ γὰρ ἠσθένησεν: '*and* (you were correctly informed about him) *for* he *was* sick.'

παραπλήσιον θανάτῳ: Παραπ. not elsewhere in Bib. The adv. παραπλησίως, Heb. ii. 14. Here adverbially. Not precisely 'nigh unto death,' but 'in a way nearly resembling death.'

ℵ* ACDFGKL read θανατω; so Tisch., R.T., Weiss, *Txtk. Unt.* ℵ^c BP, 31, 80, θανατου; so WH.

λύπην ἐπὶ λύπην: 'sorrow upon sorrow,' or 'after' sorrow, as we say 'wave upon wave,' ἐπὶ having a sense of motion. (See LXX; Ezek. vii. 26; Is. xxviii. 10, 13; Ps. lxix. [lxviii.] 27.) Not the sorrow for Epaphroditus' death following upon the sorrow for his sickness, but the sorrow for Epaphroditus' death following that of Paul's imprisonment.

Weiss prefers the former explanation, for the singular reason that i. 12–24, ii. 16–18, do not indicate sorrow on Paul's part for his captivity. (See Mey.'s ingenious note.)

28. σπουδαιοτέρως: 'with the greater despatch.' (Comp. Lk. vii. 4; Tit. iii. 13.) More hastily than I would have done otherwise. For the comparative without statement of the standard of comparison, see on μᾶλλον (i. 12).

The older commentators render 'studiosius,' 'sollicitius.' So A.V., 'carefully'; R.V., 'diligently'; Lightf., 'with increased eagerness'; Ellic., 'more diligently.' Our rendering as Thay. *Lex.*, Ead., Lips., Hack., Weiss, Weizs., Mey., v. Sod.

ἔπεμψα: 'I send.' Epistolary aorist.

ἵνα ἰδόντες αὐτὸν πάλιν χαρῆτε: 'that when ye see him ye may rejoice again.' Construe πάλιν with χαρῆτε, not with ἰδόντες (as R.V.). Paul's habit is to place πάλιν before the verb which it qualifies. The Philippians' joy had been clouded by Epaphroditus' sickness. They would rejoice *again* when he should arrive.

ἀλυπότερος: 'the less sorrowful.' The sorrow of captivity still remains. The word only here.

29. οὖν: Since I sent him that you might rejoice, 'therefore' receive him with joy.

πασῆς χαρᾶς: Every kind of joy. (Comp. i. 20; Eph. vi. 18; 1 Pet. ii. 1.)

τοὺς τοιούτους: The article marks Epaphroditus as belonging to the class designated by τοιούτ. (Comp. Mk. ix. 37; Rom. xvi. 18; 2 Cor. xi. 13, xii. 3; Gal. v. 23, vi. 1; and see Win. xviii. 4.)

ἐντίμους ἔχετε: The only occurrence of the phrase in N.T. In class. usually ἐντίμως ἔχ.

30. ἔργον Χριστοῦ: All his exertions in forwarding Paul's work in Rome, and the risk and hardship of the journey thither.

Χριστου, BFG, 80, Tisch., Weiss.
του Χριστου, DEKL, Vulg., Goth., Syr.[sch], four Lat. verss. (d, e, f, g).
For Χριστου, ℵ AP, 17, 31, 47, Cop., Syr.[p], Arm., Æth., WH., read κυριου.
το εργον without addn. C.

Lightf. reads διὰ τὸ ἔργον on the sole authority of C, and says it must be the correct reading. He cites Acts xv. 38; Ign. *Eph.* xiv., *Rom.* iii., and the analogy of ἡ ὁδός, τὸ θέλημα, and τὸ ὄνομα for the absolute use of τὸ ἔργον. But while τὸ ἔργον is used absolutely in these cases, it is too much to assert, in the face of such strong MS. authority, that Χτοῦ, τοῦ Χτοῦ, or κυρίου are mere "insertions to explain τὸ ἔργον." Κυρίου might be substituted for Χτοῦ in order to assimilate to 1 Cor. xv. 58, xvi. 10; and ΧΥ or ΚΥ might easily be overlooked and omitted in transcription, as by C.

μέχρι θανάτου ἤγγισεν: 'he came nigh unto death.' (Comp. LXX; Ps. cvii. [cvi.] 18, lxxxviii. 3 [lxxxvii. 4]; Job xxxiii. 22.)

παραβολευσάμενος: Only here. A gambler's word, from παράβολος, 'venturesome,' 'reckless.' He gambled with his life; recklessly hazarded it. (Comp. Rom. xvi. 4.) A most generous and appreciative recognition of Epaphroditus' services. The voluntary visitors of the sick, who, in the ancient church, formed a kind of brotherhood under the supervision of the bishop, were styled 'Parabolani.' The graphic description of these in Kingsley's *Hypatia* is familiar. The word might have been suggested to Paul by seeing the soldiers throwing dice. Comp. κυβία, 'dicing' (Eph. iv. 14).

TR with CKLP and several Fath. reads παραβουλευσαμενος, 'having consulted amiss.'

ἵνα ἀναπληρώσῃ τὸ ὑμῶν ὑστέρημα τῆς πρὸς με λειτουργίας: 'that he might supply that which was lacking in your service toward me.' (Comp. 1 Cor. xvi. 17; 2 Cor. ix. 12.)

ἀναπληρώσῃ: Not synonymous with the simple verb *πληροῦν*, 'to fill up a total vacancy,' but denoting the making up of what is lacking to perfect fulness; the filling up of a partial void. So Erasm.: "Accessione implere quod plenitudini perfectae deerat." For double compounds of the verb, see 2 Cor. ix. 12, xi. 9; Col. i. 24.

ὑμῶν: Genitive of the subject, with *ὑστέρημα*, not with *λειτουργίας*: 'the lack which was yours.'

λειτουργίας: See on vs. 17. It describes the service as the act of the Philippian community, and as a sacrificial act. So far from implying a censure in *τὸ ὑμῶν ὑστέρημα*, that clause is a most delicate, courteous, and sympathetic tribute to both Epaphroditus and the Philippians. The gift to Paul was the gift of the church as a body. It was a sacrificial offering of love. What was lacking, and what would have been grateful to Paul and to the church alike, was the church's presentation of this offering in person. This was impossible, and Paul represents Epaphroditus as supplying this lack by his affectionate and zealous ministry. He thus, in this single sentence, recognises the devotion of Epaphroditus and the good-will of the Philippians, and expresses the pleasure which he himself would have had in their personal presence and ministry. Withal there is a touch of tender sympathy for Epaphroditus. It would have been a great thing if you could, as a body, have offered this sacrifice of love here in my prison; and poor Epaphroditus made himself sick unto death in his efforts to supply this want.

πρός με: Πρός combines with the sense of direction that of relation with, intercourse. (Comp. Mt. xiii. 56; Mk. ix. 16; Jn. i. 1; Acts iii. 25, xxviii. 25; 1 Thess. iv. 12; Col. iv. 5; Heb. ix. 20.) Their gift to Paul was a sacrificial offering to God, in which the spirits of Paul and of the Philippians communed.

EXCURSUS ON VS. 6–11

Much of the difficulty which appears to attach to this passage arises from the assumption that in it Paul is aiming to formulate a statement of the character of Christ's mode of existence before and during his incarnation. This is inconsistent with the informal and familiar tone of the letter, and with the obviously practical character of this passage, the principal object of which is to enforce the duty of humility. As the supreme illustration of this virtue, the apostle adduces the example of Jesus Christ in his voluntary renunciation of his preincarnate majesty, and his identification with the conditions of humanity. The points of the illustration are thrown out in rapid succession, merely stated and not elaborated, and are all brought to bear upon the exhortation, "Look not every one at his own things, but every one also on the things of others." Paul does, indeed, rise here above the level of epistolary colloquialism; but the impulse to the higher flight is emotional rather than philosophical.

I think that Lightfoot has fallen into the error just mentioned in his excursus on the synonyms σχῆμα and μορφὴ (*Commentary*, p. 127 ff.). Prior to the philosophical period of Greek literature, the predominant sense of μορφὴ was "shape" or "figure." Schmidt (*Synon.* 182, 4) says it is distinguished from εἶδος and ἰδέα as the outward appearance of a thing considered in and for itself, and partially contrasted with the inner and spiritual being. It includes the coloring and the whole outward appearance — the body itself with no reference to other than outward peculiarities. This sense is retained to some extent in philosophical usage. Both Plato and Aristotle employ μορφὴ with this meaning (Plat. *Repub.* ii. 381 C; *Phaedr.* 271 A; Arist. *Hist. An.* i. 1, 7, ii. 10, 1, 2).

But the word has also a far wider meaning in Plato and Aristotle. Both apply it to immaterial things, and it is especially from Aristotle's usage that Lightfoot draws the meaning *specific character* for μορφή. That Aristotle uses it in this sense may be granted, though there are three things to be said on that point without entering into discussion: (1) That Aristotle, as has been said already, uses the word in the external and earlier sense also. (2) That his more abstract conception of μορφὴ is not uniform throughout, being more purely intellectual in his logic than in his physics. And (3) that even in his most abstract and immaterial conception of "form" the abstract is brought into concrete realisation. His doctrine is familiar that sensible objects consist of matter and form; matter being simply the potentiality of becoming, while form makes this potentiality actual, so that matter is not intelligible without form, though the form is not necessarily external or material.

I do not, however, believe that Paul's use of the term was derived from this source, or applied in the sense of "specific character." The starting-point of his conception lay nearer to the anthropomorphic than to the philosophic: not necessarily that he definitely conceived God as invested with a human form, but that he conceived of the essential personality of God as externalising itself and expressing itself in some mode apprehensible by pure spiritual intelligences if not apprehensible by the human mind. But it seems probable that Paul's mind touched the conception of "the form of God" very slightly and incidentally, and only on its outskirts, and that the application of the term μορφὴ to God was principally a reflection of its application to a bondservant. Christ's *humiliation* was the dominant thought in Paul's mind, and the μορφὴ of a bondservant therefore came first in the order of thought. The idea of some embodiment of the divine personality was not altogether absent from his mind, but μορφὴ θεοῦ was chiefly a rhetorical antithesis to μορφὴ δούλου.

Still, there is evidence that Paul uses μορφὴ with a recognition of a peculiar relation of the word to the essential and permanent nature of that which is expressed or embodied, so that μορφὴ is purposely selected instead of σχῆμα, which signifies merely the outward and transient configuration without regard to that which is behind it. This has been clearly shown by Lightfoot in his examination of the compounds into which the two words severally enter. (See Rom. xii. 2; 2 Cor. iii. 18, xi. 13–15; Phil. iii. 21.) It is possible that in illustrating this legitimate distinction, Lightfoot, in one or two instances, may have refined too much. His remarks on μεταμορφοῦσθαι in Mt. xvii. 2; Mk. ix. 2, are just, since a compound of σχῆμα, denoting merely a change in the outward aspect of Christ's person and garments, would not have expressed the fact that this change acquired its real character and meaning from the divineness which was essential in Christ's personality. A foreshadowing or prophecy of his real "form" — the proper expression of his essential being — comes out in the transfiguration. He passes for the moment into the form prophetic of his revelation in the glory which he had with the Father before the world was.

The case is more doubtful in Mk. xvi. 12, where it is said that Jesus, after his resurrection, appeared ἐν ἑτέρᾳ μορφῇ. It is possible that μορφὴ may have been selected with conscious recognition of the fact that, though the accidents of figure, face, and pierced hands and feet were the same as before, yet the indefinable change which had passed upon Jesus prefigured his transition to the conditions of his heavenly life; but it is quite as probable that the writer used μορφὴ in its earlier sense of "shape."

However that may be, I cannot accept Lightfoot's explanation of μόρφωσις in Rom. ii. 20 as signifying an *aiming after* or *affecting* the true μορφὴ of knowledge and truth. There was actually a truthful embodiment of knowledge and truth in the law. The law was "holy and just and good," and Paul habitually recognised in it the impress of the divine character and will. It was this fact which aggravated the culpability of the Jew, to whom had been committed the oracles of God (Rom. iii. 2).

Thus it is quite legitimate to define μορφὴ in this passage as that "form," whatever it be, which carries in itself and expresses or embodies the essential nature of the being to whom it belongs. (See note on vs. 6.)

Μορφὴ, however, applied to God, is not to be identified with δόξα, as by Weiss (*Bib. Theol.* § 103 *c, d,* Clarks' Trans.). Weiss reaches this conclusion by a very circuitous and inconclusive process. He says: "The identification of the μορφὴ θεοῦ with the δόξα depends on this; that here also the δόξα, which the perfected attain to and which belongs to the glorified body of Christ (Phil. iii. 21), belongs originally to God, who is called (Eph. i. 17) the πατὴρ τῆς δόξης, and therefore, on that account, it belongs to the Son of his love in his original heavenly existence." Δόξα is the manifestation, the "unfolded fulness," of the divine attributes and perfections, while μορφὴ θεοῦ is the immediate, proper, and personal investiture of the divine essence. Δόξα attaches to Deity; μορφὴ is identified with the inmost being of Deity. Δόξα is and must be included in μορφὴ θεοῦ, but δόξα is not μορφὴ. Indeed, the difference may be roughly represented by the English words "glory" and "form." Glory may belong to one in virtue of birth, natural endowment, achievement, and the possession of great qualities; but it does not belong to him in the immediate and intimate sense that his form does.

A study of the usage, both in the Old and in the New Testament, will confirm this distinction. In the Old Testament כָּבוֹד applied to God occurs often in connection with theophanies, where, if anywhere, we might expect the peculiar sense of μορφὴ to appear.[1] The passage which seems most to favor this view is Ex. xxxiii. 18–23, xxxiv. 5–7. But it will be observed that in answer to Moses' prayer that God will show him his *glory*, God promises to reveal his *goodness*, and to proclaim his *name*, with the reservation, however, which is put anthropomorphically, that Moses cannot bear that revelation in its fulness, and that therefore it will be tempered for him. In the sequel the Lord descends and proclaims "the Lord God, merciful, gracious, longsuffering, and abundant in goodness and truth." This was what Moses desired, not, like Semele, to behold Deity clothed in outward splendor, but to behold the true glory of God as revealed in his moral attributes.

The phrase "glory of the Lord" (כְּבוֹד יהוה) is used of the voice and fire on Sinai (Ex. xxiv. 17; Deut. v. 24); of the splendor which, on different occasions, filled the tabernacle and the temple (Ex. xl. 34; Num. xiv. 10, xv. 19, 42, xx. 6; 2 Chron. v. 14, vii. 1, 2, 3; Ezek. x. 4, xliii. 4, 5, xliv. 4). It appears as a bow in the cloud (Ezek. i. 28); as the glory which the prophet saw by Chebar (Ezek. iii. 23; comp. i. 4–28); in the fire which consumes the sacrifice on the altar (Lev. ix. 23). In the last three instances the mode or form of the revelation of divine glory is distinctly specified. It appears over the cherubim (Ezek. x. 19, xi. 22); on the threshold of the house and on the mountain

[1] I am under obligation to my colleague, Dr. Briggs, for kindly furnishing me with a proof of the article כָּבוֹד from the new Hebrew Lexicon.

(Ezek. x. 4, xi. 23). The earth shined with it (Ezek. xliii. 2). None of these exhibitions answer to the definition of μορφὴ θεοῦ. They are mostly symbolical. Again, the glory of the Lord will be revealed in a march through the wilderness to the Holy Land (Is. xl. 5); it will be the "rearward" of Israel (Is. lviii. 8); the resting-place of the Messiah will be glory (Is. xi. 10). The impossibility of identifying such expressions with μορφὴ θεοῦ will be seen if we attempt to substitute this for δόξα. Shall we say "the heavens declare the form of God" (Ps. xix. 1); "the form of God shall dwell in the land" (Ps. lxxxv. 9); "the rest of the Messiah shall be the form of God" (Is. xi. 10)? These instances are fairly representative; and the Old Testament furnishes no others which, any more than these, warrant the identification of μορφὴ θεοῦ with δόξα.

In the New Testament the following may be specially noted: Jn. xvii. 5, 22, 24. In vs. 5, 24, Jesus speaks of his preincarnate glory which he laid aside in his incarnation. In vs. 22 he speaks of a glory which he had not relinquished, but had retained in his incarnation, and had imparted to his disciples. The two conceptions cannot be identical. The μορφὴ θεοῦ was laid aside, and could not be imparted (Jn. i. 14). Δόξα was something which Jesus possessed in the flesh, and which the disciples beheld. It could not be identical with μορφὴ θεοῦ (2 Cor. iii. 18). Εἰκὼν approximates more closely to μορφὴ θεοῦ than perhaps any other word in the New Testament. But δόξα here is not the same as εἰκών. The *image* of the Lord is attained by a process, through successive stages or grades of *glory*. (See Heinrici, *Comm.* ad loc.; 1 Cor. xi. 7.) Man is the image (εἰκὼν) *and* glory of God. The preincarnate Son of God was the effulgence of God's glory, *and* the very impress (χαρακτὴρ) of his substance (Heb. i. 3).

In short, it is apparent that δόξα is used with too large a range and variety of meaning to warrant its identification with an expression which is unique in the New Testament, and entirely wanting in the Old Testament, and which, if the definition given be correct, is strictly limited in its meaning.

A common error of the Greek Fathers, adopted by Calvin, Beza, and others, was the identification of μορφὴ with οὐσία, 'essence,' and φύσις, 'nature.' Μορφὴ is identified with οὐσία, not identical with it. It is the perfect expression of the essence, proceeding from the inmost depths of the perfect being, and into which that being spontaneously and perfectly unfolds, as light from fire. If the two were identical, the parting with the μορφὴ in the incarnation would have involved parting with the οὐσία. But Jesus did not surrender the divine essence in his incarnation, nor did he surrender the divine nature, which is the οὐσία clothed with its appropriate attributes. Μορφὴ expresses both οὐσία and φύσις, but neither is surrendered in the surrender of the μορφή.

The Greek Fathers and Augustine, followed by the Catholic and most of the Reformed expositors, held that vs. 6 referred to Jesus in his preincarnate state; while vs. 7 and 8 referred to the incarnate Saviour. According to this view, Christ exchanged the divine mode of existence for the human, not insisting for the time on holding fast to his divine majesty. The form of God was voluntarily exchanged for the form of a bondservant.

The majority of the Lutheran and rationalistic expositors, on the other hand, explained vs. 6 of the incarnate Son. According to this view, the form of God was retained by him in his incarnate state, and was displayed in his miracles and words of power. He retained the μορφὴ θεοῦ as his right, not regarding it an act of robbery when he claimed equality with God. Thus the statement was used to vindicate the divinity of our Lord in the flesh. This view shaped the rendering of King James' Bible.

But this is contrary to the entire structure and drift of the passage, the main point of which is Christ's example of humility in renouncing his divine dignity and becoming man. The emphasis is upon the humanity, not upon the deity, of our Lord. The prominent thought is "thought it not a thing to be grasped." Moreover, this interpretation utterly destroys the manifest antithesis of οὐχ ἁρπαγμὸν ἡγήσατο, etc., and ἑαυτὸν ἐκένωσεν, which is indicated by ἀλλὰ. It makes the writer say, he *maintained* the form of God, *but* emptied himself. It also weakens the sharp contrast between μορφὴ θεοῦ and μορφὴ δούλου. It would imply the contemporaneous existence of the same subject in two opposite forms, both having reference to the outward condition. (See Klöpper, *Comm.* ad loc.)

The doctrine of the preincarnate existence of Christ I assume. Statements like those of 1 Cor. i. 24, viii. 6, xi. 3, x. 3, 4; 2 Cor. viii. 9, show that Paul held a real and not a merely ideal preëxistence of the Son of God, — a unique position of the preincarnate Christ with God. The truth is well stated by Professor Bruce (*St. Paul's Conception of Christianity*, p. 330): "To make the conception of Christ's earthly experience as a humiliation complete, is it not necessary to view it as a whole, and regard it as resulting from a foregoing resolve on the part of Christ to enter into such a state? If so, then the necessary presupposition of the Pauline doctrine of redemption is the *preëxistence* of Christ, not merely in the foreknowledge of God, as the Jews conceived all important persons and things to preëxist, or in the form of an ideal in heaven answering to an imperfect earthly reality, in accordance with the Greek way of thinking, but as a moral personality capable of forming a conscious purpose." Similarly Weizsäcker (*Ap. Zeit.* p. 122), to whom Professor Bruce refers: "He had a personal existence before his human birth, and his earlier life was divine, and absolutely opposed to the dependent life of man upon earth. . . . Christ becomes man by a personal act. . . . Precisely because of this the conception is perfectly consistent with the notion of 'the second man' who comes from heaven. For the heavenly descent is equivalent to the thought that he was in the form of God, and Paul can therefore say without hesitation, that it was Jesus, the Christ, who first existed in the divine form and then humbled himself, just as he says of him that he was rich and voluntarily submitted to poverty. Had he not given his doctrine of Christ this backward extension, the human life of Christ would have become for him a sort of impersonal event, and Jesus a mere instrument. His doctrine of the preëxistence accordingly enables him to look upon Christ's work as a personal act, and to preserve the bond between him and humanity."

The phrase ἐν μορφῇ θεοῦ ὑπάρχων is then to be understood of Christ's preincarnate state. To say that he was ἐν μορφῇ θεοῦ is to say that he existed before his incarnation as essentially one with God, and that objectively, and not merely in God's self-consciousness as the not yet incarnate Son — the ideal man. (See Beyschlag, *Die Christologie des neuen Testaments*, and *Neutestamentliche Theologie*, 2 Aufl. vol. ii. p. 77 ff.; Pfleiderer, *Paulinismus*, 2 Aufl. p. 126; Bruce's discussion of Beyschlag's view, *Humiliation of Christ*, p. 431.)

Do ἐν μορφῇ θεοῦ ὑπάρχων and τὸ εἶναι ἴσα signify the same thing? — "No," it is said. Equality with God did not inhere in Christ's preincarnate being. He received it first at his exaltation and as a reward for his perfect obedience. Thus Dorner (*Christliche Glaubenslehre*, ii. p. 286 f.) says: "His manhood is raised to a full share in the divine majesty as a reward of its maintaining true obedience. He could not have been exalted if he had not exhibited a faultless development in a true human existence and obedience."

Along with this view goes an assumed antithesis between Christ and Adam. Dorner says: "While the first Adam grasped at equality with God, the second obtained exaltation to the divine majesty, since not only would he not assume the divine dignity, but, though himself elevated in dignity, humbled himself and became obedient even unto death." The parallel is developed by Ernesti (*Stud. u. Krit.* Hft. 4, p. 858, 1848). Adam would be God; Christ renounces his godlikeness. Adam suffered death as a doom; Christ voluntarily. Adam incurred the divine curse; Christ won the approval of God, and the reward of exaltation to equality with God.

The same view is held by my friend and colleague Dr. Briggs (*Messiah of the Apostles*, p. 180). He says: "It was indeed involved in his existing in the form of God that he should be equal in rank with God. From that point of view it might be said that he would not grasp after his own rank to which he was entitled as the Son of God; but it is probable that the apostle had in mind the antithesis between the first and the second Adam which is so characteristic of his theology. He is thinking of the sinful grasping of the first Adam after equality with God under the instigation of the serpent. As the second Adam, he will not grasp after equality with God, even though it is his birthright. He will receive it from the hands of God as a gift of love, after he has earned it by obedience, just as the first Adam ought to have done." Similarly Beyschlag, *N. T. Theol.* 2 Aufl. Bd. ii. p. 88.

Setting aside for the moment the question of the two Adams, I do not quite see the consistency of Dr. Briggs' first statement — that equality in rank with God was involved in Christ's existence in the form of God, and his last statement, that equality with God was something which Christ *earned*, and *received as a recompense* for his obedience. The inconsistency is not reconciled by the antithesis between the two Adams. But passing this, these statements can mean only that the status of the preincarnate Christ was inferior to that in which he was after his incarnation; that the being whom Paul describes as existing in the form of God was something less than the being whom God highly exalted. This is clearly stated by Beyschlag (*N. T. Theol.* ii. p. 86): "The subject of this passage is not Son of God as in the so-called Athanasian symbol, but one sharply distinguished from God. The *μορφὴ θεοῦ* in which he preëxisted is not a *μορφὴ τοῦ θεοῦ*, and the *ἴσα θεῷ εἶναι* is not an *ἴσα τῷ θεῷ εἶναι*. There remains between him and the one God who is the Father (vs. 11) so decided a difference that the incomparable glory which Christ won through his self-emptying and obedience unto death does not belong to him as his eternal, natural possession, but is given to him by God's free grace, and must redound only to the honor of the Father. Hence ἑαυτὸν ἐκένωσεν cannot signify a laying aside of his divine being, but only the laying aside of his mode of manifestation."

Such statements cannot be reconciled with passages like Col. i. 15-17. Speaking of the Epistle to the Colossians, Dr. Briggs justly says: "It unfolds the doctrine of the preëxistent Messiah beyond anything that we could be prepared to expect from our study of the other epistles. To the doctrine of the form of God in the Epistle to the Philippians, we have added the doctrine that the preëxistent Son of God was the mediator between God and the creature, in creation, in providence, and in redemption" (*Messiah of the Apostles*, p. 215). Add to this Jn. i. 1, 2, v. 21, vi., x. 18, and especially Heb. i. 2, 3. In this last passage we have a more technical and formal statement, after the manner of the Alexandrian school, and according to this statement the preëxistent Christ was the very impress of God's substance.

Beyschlag, as Philo (*De Somn.* i. 39, 41), insists on the distinction between ὁ θεός and θεός, claiming that this distinction is observed in Jn. i. 1. But in that passage, θεός, predicated of the λόγος, is used attributively, with a notion of kind, and is thus necessarily anarthrous. It excludes identity of person, but emphasises unity of essence and nature. Accordingly, what John says is, that the λόγος was with God, and that with no lower nature than God himself. Philo, on the contrary, claims that the anarthrous θεός describes the λόγος as of subordinate nature — "δεύτερος θεός."

Dorner cites Rom. i. 4 to show that Christ was constituted the Son of God *with power*, only after his resurrection. "Therefore, before this, he was not 'the Son of God with power,' though he was already the Son (*Chr. Glaubensl.* ii. p. 284). But this inference rests on a misinterpretation. Ἐν δυνάμει does not belong with υἱοῦ θεοῦ, but is adverbial and qualifies ὁρισθέντος. Paul's statement is that Christ was designated as Son of God in a powerful, impressive, efficient manner, by his resurrection from the dead as a work of divine power. So Sanday, Mey., Godet, Alf., Moule, Gifford. (Comp. 2 Cor. xiii. 4 and Eph. i. 19.)

Besides all this, how can equality with God be conferred or superinduced? The words are τὸ εἶναι ἴσα. It is a matter of essential *being*. Equality with God can belong only to essence. Equality of power or of rank can be conferred, but not equality of being.

As to the antithesis of the two Adams. It seems forced at the best, but is there any real antithesis? According to the narrative in Gen. iii., Satan declared that the eating of the fruit would confer a knowledge which would make the eaters as gods, knowing good and evil; and the woman saw that the tree was to be desired to make one wise. Nothing is said of a desire to be equal with God in the absolute and general sense. The temptation and the desire turned on forbidden knowledge. The words "as gods" are defined and limited by the words "knowing good and evil"; and it is nowhere asserted or hinted in Scripture that Adam desired equality with God in the comprehensive sense of that expression. Moreover, if Adam had proved obedient, his reward would not have been equality with God.

Yet something was obtained by Christ as the result of his incarnation and of his perfect obedience therein, which he did not possess before his incarnation, and which he could not have possessed without it. Equality with God he had as his birthright, but his Messianic lordship was something which could come only through his incarnation and its attendant humiliation; and it was this, and not equality with God, that he received in his exaltation. The διὸ of vs. 9 is not to be taken as if God bestowed exaltation as a reward for perfect obedience, but rather, as Meyer correctly says, as "the accession of the corresponding consequence." The sequence is logical rather than ethical. Out of the human life, death, and resurrection of Christ comes a type of sovereignty which could pertain to him only through his triumph over human sin (Heb. i. 3), through his identification with men as their brother. Messianic lordship could not pertain to his preincarnate state. As Messianic lord he could be inaugurated only after his human experience (Acts ii. 36). Messianic lordship is a matter of function, not of inherent power and majesty. The phrase "seated at the right hand of God" is Messianic, and expresses Christ's Messianic triumph, but not to the detriment of any essential dignity possessed before his incarnation. But the incarnation places him, in a new sense, in actual, kingly relation to the collective life of the universe. There cannot be the bowing of every knee and the confession of every tongue so long as Christ merely remains *being* in the form of God, — until he has made purification of sins, redeemed creation, and been manifested to earth, heaven, and hades as the Saviour of men.

Thus new elements enter into the life and sovereignty of the exalted Christ. He exists no less as Son of God, but now also as Son of Man, which he could be only through being born of woman and made in the likeness of men. The glory of God shines through the bodily form which he carried into heaven with him (Col. ii. 9), yet in him dwelleth all the fulness of the Godhead. He is what he was not before his incarnation, the Great High Priest. Having begun the high-priestly work in his death and sacrifice, he now carries it on in the heavenly places by his work of intervention (ἐντυγχάνειν, Heb. vii. 25) in the lives of those who believe in him. He is the minister of the resurrection-life to his redeemed, ever bringing to bear on them through the Spirit the divine forces which cause them to "walk in newness of life." Thus lordship won by conquest in incarnation is distinguished from inherent lordship. This is the lordship which Jesus preferred to that which was merely inherent in him as the equal of God, — lordship through self-renunciation, mastery through service.

And in this fact lies the answer to the much-discussed question, What is the name which God gave him at his exaltation? As the lordship is Messianic, as the Messianic lordship comes only through the human experience and victory, the name will unite the human experience and the Messianic dominion, — 'Jesus' the human name, 'Christ' the Messianic name. Not 'Lord,' for lordship was his inherent right and his prerogative before incarnation. Not Jesus alone, for that represents only the human experience of humiliation; but JESUS CHRIST — Christ the Messiah only as he was Jesus. Accordingly "Lord" in vs. 11 is defined by "Jesus Christ."

This whole statement in Phil. is, in a broad sense, parallel with the words in Heb. i. 3, and the two passages should be studied together. In both the preincarnate Son's conditions of being are set forth. To these Heb. adds a statement of the preincarnate *activity* of the Son. Φέρων is "bearing onward," not simply "upholding" or "sustaining"; for, as Westcott remarks, "the Son is not an Atlas sustaining the dead weight of the world." (See *Comm. on Heb.* ad loc. and the striking parallels cited.) The Son was persistently carrying on from eternal ages the universe of God towards its consummation. Incarnation and atonement were not a break in the history of humanity, nor in the eternal activity of God in Christ. They were in the line of the eternal purpose of God. The Lamb was "slain from the foundation of the world." In pursuance of this purpose the Divine Son assumed our humanity, purged our sins, and then "sat down on the right hand of the majesty on high."

In Phil. the parallel to this is found in the statement and detail of Christ's humiliation. In his human nature, in the form of a servant, in the likeness of men, in humbling himself and enduring the death of the cross, he is still bearing on all things, restoring humanity to the divine archetype by making purification of sins and inaugurating the High-Priestly function developed in Heb. In Phil. the mediatorial aspect is not treated, but both passages depict the exaltation which followed the humiliation.

Whether ἁρπαγμὸν is active or passive is treated in the note. If taken actively,—"an act of robbery," "a seizing,"—it expresses Christ's *assertion* of equality with God; that is to say, he did not think being equal with God an act of robbery, but claimed it as his right in his incarnate state. The awkwardness of regarding a *state* of being as an *act* of robbery needs no comment. If taken passively,—"a prize, a thing to be snatched or clutched,"—it expresses the *surrender* of the preincarnate state of majesty. He did not think equality with God a prize to be eagerly grasped (and held fast), but surrendered it, though it was his right.

Lightfoot's citations from the Greek Fathers show that they conceived the passage as carrying the idea of a surrender of preincarnate glory, and a condescension from a higher estate. (Note on "Different Interpretations of οὐχ ἁρπαγμὸν ἡγήσατο," *Comm.* p. 133.)

I am not convinced that Lightfoot's interpretation is wrong by the strictures of Mr. Beet in his *Commentary*, ad loc., and in the *Expositor*, 3d ser. vol. 5, p. 115, especially when I find him adopting Meyer's explanation. See below.

It may be observed that Lightfoot does not bring out the full force of his first quotation, from the Letter of the Gallican church (Euseb. *H. E.* v. 2), which lies in the exhibition of the martyrs' humility as shown in their refusal to accept the title of "witnesses," which they had earned by their sufferings. Thus, in refusing to insist upon their rightful claim, they imitated Christ, who refused to grasp at the majesty which was rightfully his. Also it should be observed that in Origen *on Romans* (Lat. v. § 2), *rapinam*, which is given for ἁρπαγμὸν, occurs in both the active and the passive sense, the latter in late Latin.

Meyer's explanation should be noticed. He paraphrases: "Jesus Christ, when he found himself in the heavenly mode of existence of divine glory, did not permit himself the thought of using his equality with God for the purpose of seizing possessions and honor for himself on earth."

He translates "Nicht als ein Rauben betrachtete er das gottgleiche Sein" (Not as a robbing did he regard the being equal with God), and then explains that he did not put being equal with God under the point of view of gaining booty, as if it (being equal with God) was, with respect to its expression in action, to consist in seizing what did not belong to him.

According to this, τὸ εἶναι ἴσα is not the object but the subject of the seizing. Christ did not regard equality with God as a *means* of grasping. This interpretation is adopted by Beet. It is an illustration of the excessive literalism which sometimes mars Meyer's splendid exegetical qualities. The interpretation turns on the endeavor to preserve the active force of ἁρπαγμὸς, which, in the very ragged condition of the evidence concerning that word, seems desperate. If this had been Paul's meaning, I can conceive of no mode of expression which he would have been less likely to choose. Moreover, the explanation misses Paul's point, which is to show the magnitude of the renunciation from the preincarnate and heavenly point of view, and not from the earthly and incarnate side. According to Meyer, Christ's self-renunciation consisted in his refusal to grasp at earthly possessions and honors by means of his equality with God. According to Paul, it consisted in his relinquishment of heavenly glory and majesty.

As regards ἑαυτὸν ἐκένωσεν, any attempt to commit Paul to a precise theological statement of the limitations of Christ's humanity involves the reader in a hopeless maze. The word ἐκένωσεν was evidently selected as a peculiarly strong expression of the entireness of Jesus' self-renunciation, and in order to throw the preincarnate glory and the incarnate humiliation into sharp contrast: to show that Christ utterly renounced and laid aside the majesty which he possessed in his original state. Its most satisfactory definition is found in the succeeding details which describe the incidents of Christ's humanity, and with these exegesis is compelled to stop. The word does not indicate a surrender of deity, nor a paralysis of deity, nor a change of personality, nor a break in the continuity of self-consciousness. Christ's consciousness of deity was not suspended during his earthly life. He knew that he came from God and went to God; that he had glory with the

Father before the world was, and would receive it back. But he was made in all things like unto his brethren. "He took to himself all that belongs to the perfection of man's being. He lived according to the conditions of man's life, and died under the circumstances of man's mortality" (Westcott).

III. 1–3. A WARNING AGAINST FALSE TEACHERS

As for the rest, my brethren, whatever your trials, past, present, or future, continue to rejoice in the Lord. I am not backward about writing to you concerning a matter of which I have spoken in former letters, but I am moved by my anxiety for your safety to refer to it again. Beware of those dogs; those evil workers; those whose boasted circumcision is no better than a physical mutilation without any spiritual significance. It is we Christians who are the true 'circumcision'; whose service is prompted by the Spirit of God; whose rejoicing is in Christ Jesus as the only source of true righteousness, and who do not trust the flesh.

It is claimed by many that Paul is here about to close the epistle, but that his attention is suddenly diverted, perhaps by some new reports of the doings of his Judaistic adversaries; and that he is thus drawn on to add to his letter what he had not originally intended. Nothing in the text warrants this conclusion. It is, of course, possible that fresh thoughts may have come to the apostle in the course of his writing; but, on the other hand, we are not forced to conclude that the main topics were not in his mind from the first. (See Introd. VII.)

1. τὸ λοιπόν: 'as to what remains.' It may mean 'finally,' as 2 Cor. xiii. 11; or 'henceforth,' as Mk. xiv. 41; 1 Cor. vii. 29; Heb. x. 13; 2 Tim. iv. 8; or 'for the rest,' 'besides,' 'as to what remains,' as 1 Thess. iv. 1; 2 Thess. iii. 1. The formula is common with Paul in cases where he attaches, in a somewhat loose way, even in the midst of an epistle, a new subject to that which he has been discussing. In 1 Thess. iv. 1 two entire chapters follow the phrase, and here the special subject introduced by it is followed by several others. If Paul had been intending to close his letter, it is likely that he would have added his thanks for the Philippians' remittance before he reached τὸ λοιπόν. The formula therefore merely introduces what follows. The preceding topic is closed, and he passes to another.

Ellic., Ead., Lightf., render 'finally,' but as an introduction to what remains. 'For the rest,' Kl., De W., Lips., Weizs., Beet.

χαίρετε ἐν κυρίῳ: 'rejoice in the Lord.' (Comp. i. 18, ii. 18, iv. 4, 10.)

Not as Lightf., 'farewell,' for which there is no sufficient ground. In class. the word is used as a salutation both at meeting and parting; but it does not occur in N.T. in the sense of 'farewell.' 2 Cor. xiii. 11 is more than doubtful.

The exhortation need not be specifically referred either to what precedes or to what follows. There has been a reason for encouraging them to rejoice in the face of their former trials, as there is a like reason in the prospect of coming trials of which he is about to speak. The summons to rejoice is general, in view of all trials, past, present, and future, as well as of the eternal consolations of the gospel.

ἐν κυρίῳ: Comp. i. 14, ii. 19, 24. The sphere or element of rejoicing.

Several of the older expositors found in ἐν κ. a contrast of the joy in God with the bitterness of the cross (Calv.); or with all worldly things (Theo., Mop., v. Lyra); or with works of the flesh and fleshly renown (Ans.); or with the Jewish errors treated in the following verses (Calov., Croc., Pisc.).

τὰ αὐτὰ γράφειν: The reference is probably to a former letter, or to former letters to the Philippians, which are lost. (See Lightf.'s excursus on "Lost Epistles to the Philippians," *Comm.* p. 138.) This has been inferred from Polyc. *ad Phil.* iii. (Comp. xiii., and see Lightf.'s *Ignatius*, iii. pp. 327, 348.) The question turns on Polyc.'s use of ἐπιστολαὶ, whether it means one letter or several.

Lightf. decides for the single letter, and collects in his excursus a large number of passages to show the use of the plu. for 'a letter.' Mey. thinks that the plu. in Polyc. indicates several letters, and affirms that doctrinal epistles, both in N.T. and the Apost. Fath., are always described in the sing. where only one letter is intended, and in the plu. where several are meant. There can be no doubt that the plu. is used of a single letter in individual cases; but the question of usage is not definitely enough settled to warrant a decision.

Our conclusion rests rather on the antecedent probability of lost letters. Considering Paul's connection with so many churches during at least twenty-five years, it is highly probable that he wrote more than thirteen letters, and some of them important. Intimations of such are found in 1 Cor. v. 9; 2. Cor. x. 10, 11; 2 Thess. ii. 15, iii. 17. If what have come down to us are his only epistles, we must suppose that he wrote several letters within a short time, while at long intervals he wrote nothing. (See Jowett, *Eps. of St. Paul*, 3d ed. i. p. 107.) Lightf. refers τὰ αὐτὰ to matter in this epistle concerning divisions or dissensions in the Philippian church; but intimations to that effect in i. 27, ii. 2, 3, 4, are too slight to warrant this inference. The reference is probably to the character and work of the Judaising Christians. To refer τὰ αὐτὰ to χαίρετε (Alf., Weiss) would be to make Paul say: 'It is not irksome for me to write to you to rejoice, but it is safe for you.'

ὀκνηρόν: 'irksome'; orig. 'sluggish,' 'slothful.' (See Mt. xxv. 26; Rom. xii. 11.) Frequent in LXX, in Prov.

ὑμῖν δὲ ἀσφαλές: 'and for you it is safe.' Ἀσφ. primarily 'steadfast,' 'stable'; thence 'trustworthy'; a thing *to be relied on* as profitable. Not as Luth., Erasm., with an active meaning, 'that which makes safe or confirms,' which is contrary to usage.

2. βλέπετε τοὺς κύνας: 'behold the dogs.' Βλέπετε, not 'beware of,' which would be βλέπ. ἀπὸ; but as 1 Cor. x. 18. A caution, however, is implied, 'look to'; 'look out for.' The article with κύν. indicates a well-known class. 'Dog' was a term of contempt and loathing with both Jews and Gentiles. The dog was an unclean animal according to the Levitical law. The price of a dog and the hire of a courtesan were placed in the same category, and an Israelite was forbidden to bring either into the house of God in fulfilment of a vow (Deut. xxiii. 18). Gentiles were termed 'dogs' by Jews (Mt. xv. 27). Comp. Apoc. xxii. 15, of those whose impurity excludes them from the heavenly city. In Hom. often of the audacious or shameless, especially women. The emphasis here is upon the impurity, the profane character of the false teachers contrasted with true Christians. There is no subordinate reference to shamelessness, greediness, snappishness, disorderly wandering or howling. So some earlier expositors, as Chr., Aug., Calov., Calv., Croc., etc.

τοὺς κακοὺς ἐργάτας: 'the evil workers.' The same persons regarded on the side of their activity and its moral quality; as proselytisers; as 'huckstering' (καπηλεύοντες) the word of God (2 Cor. ii. 17); as opposing the doctrine of justification by faith. (Comp. Mt. xxiii. 15; 2 Cor. xi. 3, 13.)

τὴν κατατομήν: 'the concision.' Not elsewhere in Bib. The word directs attention to the fact that these persons had no right to claim circumcision in the true sense. Unaccompanied by faith, love, and obedience, it was nothing more than physical mutilation. Thus they belonged in the category of those against whom the legal prohibition of mutilation was directed (Lev. xxi. 5). Comp. Paul's bitter sarcasm in Gal. v. 12.

Reasons have been given for not identifying the persons characterised here with those referred to in i. 15–17. (See note on i. 15.) The reference here is to Judaising Christians. In view of their habit of keeping an eye on the Pauline churches and of introducing their emissaries into them, it is not likely that they had overlooked Philippi; and it is quite probable that Paul had previously found it necessary to warn the church against their designs. Some fresh intelligence of their operations may have prompted him to repeat those cautions.

Against the reference to Jews it may be said that Paul's dealing with the Jews in 1 Thess. ii. 14–16 would lead us to expect something similar here if the parties had been Jews, since their proceedings against the Christians would probably have been marked by the open violence which they practised against the other Macedonian churches. Here Paul's warning is directed at the misleading of his converts by false teaching, which was quite according to the Judaising method. Moreover his expressions here are similar to those in 2 Cor. and Gal. as respects the motive, object, and methods of these agitators, and the way in which he meets them. That the Judaisers were referred to in those epistles is not questioned. Their object was the overthrow of Paul's form of Christian doctrine and the establishment of a Christianity in which the Mosaic law should continue in full force, especially in the matter of circumcision. The Messiah was regarded by them solely in his relation to the Jewish law. The attempt of Croc. to show that Paul here designates three classes, — κύνας, Libertine Christians or backsliders to Judaism; κακ. ἐργ., those who would combine Christianity with Gentile wisdom or Jewish superstition; κατατ., unbelieving Jews, — is one of the curiosities of exegesis. Weiss also thinks that three classes are intended: κύν., heathen; κακ. ἐργ., those mentioned in i. 15; κατατ., Jews.

3. ἡμεῖς γάρ ἐσμεν ἡ περιτομή: 'for *we* are the circumcision.' I call them κατατομή, and not περιτομή, for it is we who are the περιτομή. The contemptuous κατατομή suggests the first point of contrast between the Judaisers and the true Israel of God. The abstract περιτομή, 'circumcision,' stands for the concrete, 'the circumcised.' (See Rom. iv. 9; Gal. ii. 9; Eph. ii. 11, and the phrase οἱ ἐκ περιτομῆς, Acts x. 45, xi. 2.) We are the true circumcision as compared with them, for their circumcision is only outward, in the flesh, while the true circumcision is that of the heart. (See Rom. ii. 25–29; Eph. ii. 11; Col. ii. 11; comp. Lev. xxvi. 41; Deut. x. 16, xxx. 6; Jer. vi. 10, ix. 25, 26; Ezek. xliv. 7. See also Just. M. *Dial. Tr.* xii., xix., xliii.)

For this claim three reasons are given:

(1) οἱ πνεύματι θεοῦ λατρεύοντες: 'who serve by the spirit of God.' A.V. 'who worship God in the Spirit' follows TR, which reads θεῷ for θεοῦ.

πνεύματι: Instrumental dat. (See Rom. viii. 14; Gal. v. 5, 18.) Who serve under the impulse and direction of the divine Spirit. (Comp. Rom. ii. 29.)

λατρεύοντες: The verb originally means 'to serve for hire,' then simply 'to serve.' In N.T. both of ritual service, as Heb. viii. 5, ix. 9, x. 2, xiii. 10, and of worship or service generally, as Lk. i. 74; Rom. i. 9. Especially of the service rendered to God by Israelites as his peculiar people, as Acts xxvi. 7; λατρεία, Rom. ix. 4; Heb. ix. 1, 6. In LXX always of the service of God or of heathen divinities. A Jew would be scandalised by the application of this term to Christian service. It is purposely chosen with reference to ἡ περιτομή.

(2) καὶ καυχώμενοι ἐν Χριστῷ Ἰησοῦ: 'and boast in Christ Jesus.'

καυχώμενοι: See Rom. ii. 17; 1 Cor. i. 31; 2 Cor. x. 17; Gal. vi. 14.

ἐν Χριστῷ Ἰησοῦ: As the only source of true righteousness compared with the legal observance of the Jew.

(3) καὶ οὐκ ἐν σαρκὶ πεποιθότες: 'and do not trust in the flesh.' Not the same conception as the preceding (so Chr., Theoph., Calv., De W.), nor is it a more precise definition, to express the purport of καυχ. (Weiss). It indicates and repudiates the disposition out of which the false boasting of the Judaiser proceeds. For πεποιθ., see i. 14.

ἐν σαρκὶ: Comp. 2 Cor. xi. 18; Gal. vi. 13, 14. Σάρξ is the human nature without the divine Spirit; the state of man before or in contrast with his reception of the divine element whereby he becomes a new creature; the whole being of man as it exists and acts apart from the influence of the Spirit. It properly characterises, therefore, not merely the lower forms of sensual gratification, but all,—the highest developments of the life estranged from God, whether physical, intellectual, or æsthetic. So here it covers legal observances, circumcision, descent, ritual strictness, as they exist without the spirit of loyalty to God. (See *W. St.* on Rom. vii. 5.)

In illustration of the statement that Christians have no confidence in the flesh, he adduces his own case, showing what exceptional ancestral and ecclesiastical advantages as a Jew he renounced for Christ's sake.

4–7. *If any man may think himself warranted in trusting in the flesh, it is myself. For I was circumcised when eight days old, as a genuine Israelite. I was not a proselyte, but of direct Israelitish descent. I belonged to the honored tribe of Benjamin. I was a child of Hebrew ancestors who spoke the Hebrew tongue. As a member of the sect of the Pharisees, I was a strict legalist. I was zealous for my religion, even to the extent of persecuting Christians, and I was blameless in my legal righteousness. But all these advantages I counted as a loss, and renounced them for Christ's sake.*

4. καίπερ ἐγὼ ἔχων πεποίθησιν καὶ ἐν σαρκί: 'although having myself confidence in the flesh also.' It might be urged that Paul, in his conversion from Judaism, had renounced and contemned that which he did not himself possess, and of which he did not know the value. He anticipates this by saying that he has renounced advantages which he possessed in an eminent degree, and the value of which no one knew better than himself. This is

not urged as an attack upon the Judaisers, but only to show that he had already possessed all that upon which the Jews especially prided themselves. He puts himself for the moment at the Jewish point of view. If the true ground of confidence is the flesh, he has stronger ground than even his Judaising adversaries. (Comp. 2 Cor. xi. 21 ff.) The apparent awkwardness of construction is owing to the quick transition from the plu. *πεποιθότες* to a similar participial construction in the singular (*ἔχων*). The *ἐγὼ* of vs. 4 really lies in the *ἐσμεν* of vs. 3, since Paul reckons himself among the *ἡμεῖς*. He is separated by *ἐγὼ*. The sentence proceeds from *καίπερ ἐγὼ*, as if the previous clause had been, '*I* have no confidence in the flesh.'

καίπερ: Only here in Paul, and, as usual, with the participle. (Comp. Heb. v. 8, vii. 5, xii. 17.) It may be correctly rendered 'although' if it is remembered that that sense lies in the participle and not in *καίπερ*, which literally means 'even very much.'

ἔχων: Not to be rendered 'I might have,' as A.V. and R.V., a translation which grew out of the fear of the older interpreters of seeming to commit Paul to a declaration of his confidence in the flesh. Paul actually possessed these advantages, and, from the Jewish point of view, declares that he had confidence in them.

πεποίθησιν: 'confidence' or 'ground of confidence.' The noun only in Paul. For the phrase *πεποίθ. ἔχ.*, comp. 2 Cor. iii. 4.

καὶ: In the flesh '*also*.' As well as in Christ.

Not only have I ground of confidence, but I have more than they.

εἴ τις δοκεῖ ἄλλος πεποιθέναι ἐν σαρκί: 'If any one is disposed to think that he has ground of confidence in the flesh.' The indefinite *εἴ τις* is not introduced for the sake of policy, or in a conciliatory way, as if Paul were avoiding reference to any particular case, since this assumes a polemic bearing of the words. Nor does *δοκεῖ* imply that the advantage was only apparent (Chrys., Theoph.), or that they had only arrogated it to themselves (Thdrt.); for Paul uses *δοκεῖν* of himself. He merely says that he possessed advantages on which any Jew might have congratulated himself.

Δοκεῖ may be rendered 'seems'; so Vulg. *videtur;* comp. 1 Cor. xii. 22; 2 Cor. x. 9; Gal. ii. 9; or 'thinks,' as 1 Cor. iii. 18, viii. 2, x. 12. The latter is Paul's more common usage. So here, 'if any one is disposed to think.' (Comp. Mt. iii. 9; 1 Cor. xi. 16.)

ἐγὼ μᾶλλον: Supply *δοκῶ πεποιθέναι ἐν σαρκί*. 'I think that I have reason for confidence in the flesh in a higher degree than they.'

The grounds of this last, general statement are now given in the enumeration of Paul's advantages as a Jew, beginning with his inherited privileges. First is circumcision, the main point in a Jew's eyes, and that by which the whole nation was named.

5. περιτομῇ ὀκταήμερος: 'eight days old in circumcision.' Ὀκταήμερος not elsewhere in Bib. It denotes here not interval, but duration. 'I was eight days old when circumcised.' For the idiom, 'an eight-day one,' comp. τεταρταῖος, Jn. xi. 39; δευτεραῖοι, Acts xxviii. 13; and see Wetst. on Jn. xi. 39 for a long list of class. parallels. The dative is the dat. of reference. (See ii. 7; 1 Cor. xiv. 20, etc.; Win. xxxi. 6.) Paul was circumcised on the eighth day as a genuine Israelite (Gen. xvii. 12; Lev. xii. 3). An Ishmaelite was circumcised in his thirteenth year (Gen. xvii. 25).

He was not a proselyte, but of direct Israelitish descent: ἐκ γένους Ἰσραήλ, 'of the race of Israel.' (Comp. Rom. xi. 1.) He was descended from the patriarch Jacob, whose name of honor, bestowed by God himself (Gen. xxxii. 28), was the sacred name of the Jews as God's covenant people (Rom. ix. 4; 2 Cor. xi. 22; Eph. ii. 12), and was therefore the Jews' especial badge and title of honor. Their descent from Abraham they shared with the Ishmaelites; their descent from Abraham and Isaac, with the Edomites. The Israelite claimed descent from the patriarch, not as Jacob 'the supplanter,' but as Israel, 'wrestler with God.' (See Hos. xii. 3, 4.) Ἰσραήλ is the appositive genit., and is the name of the *race* (γένος), as Gal. i. 14; 2 Cor. xi. 26.

φυλῆς Βενιαμείν: Comp. Rom. xi. 1. Benjamin was the son of the beloved wife of Jacob (Gen. xxxv. 17, 18). The tribe of Benjamin gave Israel its first king (1 Sam. ix. 1, 2). The tribe was alone faithful to Judah at the separation under Rehoboam (1 K. xii. 21). After the return from exile, it formed with Judah the kernel of the new colony in Palestine (Ezra iv. 1). The tribe always held the post of honor in the army. Hence the battle-cry, 'After thee Benjamin!' (Jud. v. 14; Hos. v. 8). Of the twelve patriarchs, Benjamin only was born in the Land of Promise. The great national deliverance commemorated in the feast of Purim was due to Mordecai, a Benjamite. Paul's own name, Saul, was probably from the son of Kish, the Benjamite king.

But Paul's descent was not only from the choice race and tribe, but from parents of the pure Hebrew stock. There is a climax.

Ἑβραῖος ἐξ Ἑβραίων: 'a Hebrew sprung from Hebrews.' (Comp. 2 Cor. xi. 22.) The Greek Ἑβραῖος (Lat. *Hebraeus*) comes through the Aramaic vernacular of Palestine (*Hebrājā*). Greek and Roman writers, however, rarely used it instead of Ἰουδαῖος (*Judaeus*) which prevailed after the exile. In the O.T. 'Hebrew' was used habitually and consistently to denote the descendants of Abraham as designated by foreigners, or as applied by the Hebrews themselves when addressing foreigners, or when speaking of themselves in contrast with other nations. The name by which the Hebrew nation habitually called itself was 'Israel' or 'the Children of Israel.' In the N.T. Ἑβραῖος appears in Acts vi. 1, where the native Palestinian Jewish-Christians are distinguished from the Hellenists or Greek-speaking Jews. This distinction marks a difference of language. The O.T. does not know the word 'Hebrew' with reference to language. The old Hebrew is called 'the language of Canaan' (Is. xix. 18), indicating the close relationship of this Semitic tongue with that of the Canaanites, especially the Phœnicians. In the Apocr. and N.T. the term 'Hebrew' is used almost exclusively of the Aramaic vernacular. (See Jn. v. 2, xix. 13, 17, 20; Acts xxi. 40, xxii. 2, xxvi. 14.) Here the term expresses the difference of language. Though a Hellenist, Paul was trained in the use of the Hebrew tongue by Hebrew-speaking parents. Though born outside of the Holy Land, yet as a child of Hebrew ancestors, and 'the son of Pharisees' (Acts xxiii. 6), in speech and habits of life he remained allied to the people of Palestine. He might have been an Israelite and not a Hebrew speaker; but he emphasises the fact that he was both a true Israelite and one who used the language of his forefathers. He was trained under a Hebrew teacher at Jerusalem (Acts xxii. 3); he spoke Hebrew, *i.e.* Aramaic (Acts xxi. 40, xxii. 2); and he quotes often from the Hebrew Scriptures. (See Riehm. *Handw. des bibl. Alterthums*, sub "Eber" and "Hebräer"; Trench, *Syn.* xxxix.)

Similar expressions, denoting position or character as resting upon birth from parents of like position and character, are common in class. (See Aristoph. *Ran.* 730; Soph. *Elect.* 589; *Philoc.* 384; Eur. *Alc.* 677; Hdt. ii. 143, etc.)

These four specifications of inherited privilege are summed up by Paul in Gal. ii. 15. Matheson, *Spiritual Development of St. Paul*, remarks that a man trained under such influences must, on every side, have been repelled by the spectacle of the cross of Jesus. He was required to accept him precisely at the point where his national characteristics were assailed (pp. 36, 37).

He now passes to advantages of a distinctly personal character, relating to his theological and ecclesiastical position.

κατὰ νόμον Φαρισαῖος: 'as touching the law a Pharisee.' (Comp. Acts xxii. 3, xxiii. 6, xxvi. 5.)

νόμον: The Mosaic law, the standing authority of which was the principle on which the Judaisers insisted. This is confirmed by θρησκίας, Acts xxvi. 5; by the allusions here to concision and circumcision, and also by the fact that in all the words connected with νόμον in vs. 5, there is an immediate reference to the Jewish race and ideas. Moreover, δικαιοσ. τ. ἐν νόμ. corresponds with similar phrases in Rom. and Gal. where the Mosaic law is contemplated, as Gal. iii. 11, 12. It was the righteousness of the Mosaic system which Paul had abandoned for Christ.

These considerations do not seem to favor Lightf.'s explanation, "the Mosaic law regarded in the abstract as a principle of action, being coördinated with ζῆλος and δικαιοσύνην."

No sharp distinction can be fixed between νόμ. and ὁ νόμ. It is unquestionable that νόμ. is used of the Mosaic law as well as ὁ νόμ. If Paul sometimes uses νόμ. in a wider sense, — of law considered as a principle, with the stress upon the conception of law itself, rather than upon its historical and outward form, — the Mosaic law is habitually in the background of his thought as the great embodiment and representative of the conception.

Φαρισαῖος: Belonging to the party of the most orthodox defenders, observers, and expounders of the law. There may be a subtle irony in these words. Paul never ceased to reverence the law itself as the expression of God's holiness (Rom. ii. 13, 20, iii. 31, vii. 7, 12, 14, etc.); but the Pharisees' treatment of the law struck at its original dignity, since they made it void by the oral tradition with which they overlaid it. (See Mt. xv. 2, 3, 6; Mk. vii. 3, 5, 8, 9, 13; and comp. Jos. *Antiq.* xiii. 10, 6.) Paul then may mean, 'I kept the law with Pharisaic strictness, practically dishonoring it; observing the traditions rather than the law itself.' From this point of view comp. Gal. i. 14.

6. κατὰ ζῆλος διώκων τὴν ἐκκλησίαν: Ironical. 'I was so very zealous that I became a persecutor of the church of Christ.' Zeal for God, for his house, and for his law, was the highest praise of an O.T. saint. (See Num. xxv. 11, 13; 1 K. xix. 10, 14; Ps. lxix. [lxviii.] 9. Comp. Acts xxi. 20, xxii. 3; Rom. x. 2.) Thdrt. comments: οὐ γὰρ διὰ τὴν φιλοτιμίαν, οὐδὲ διὰ δόξαν κενήν, οὐδὲ φθόνῳ βαλλόμενος, ὡς Ἰουδαίων ἄρχοντες, ἀλλὰ τῷ ὑπὲρ τοῦ νόμου φλεγόμενος ζήλῳ, τὴν ἐκκλησίαν ἐπορθοῦν. — "Not because of ambition nor for empty renown, neither being smitten with envy like the rulers of the Jews, but being inflamed with zeal for the law, I persecuted the church."

διώκων: Used adjectively, parallel with ἄμεμπτος. Not as a substantive, as Mey., Weiss, Lips., which occurs with the article (Win. xlv. 7).

δικαιοσύνην τὴν ἐν νόμῳ: 'righteousness which is in the law.' Δικ. is used abstractly, and then concretely defined by τ. ἐν νόμ. 'As regards righteousness — I mean that which is in the law': which resides in the righteous law and consists in its strict observance. Δικαιοσύνη is used here in its objective sense of conformity to an external rule of righteousness. The righteousness is in (ἐν) the law, not in the man: in the man only as he conforms to the law. It is not regarded as an inward righteousness like the righteousness of faith. Comp. ἐκ νόμου (vs. 9), where the righteousness is treated as *proceeding from* the law. The reference need not be confined to the ceremonial law, for the law is a whole (Gal. iii. 10).

γενόμενος: 'having become': in the course of my pursuit of legal righteousness.

ἄμεμπτος: See on ii. 15. Not absolutely blameless, according to God's standard, but in human judgment. (Comp. Gal. i. 14.)

On Holsten's attempt to impugn the authenticity of the epistle by endeavoring to show in this statement a contradiction of Paul's teaching elsewhere that man is unable perfectly to keep the law, see Introd. vi. The blamelessness here asserted is according to human, Pharisaic standards.

7. ἀλλὰ ἅτινα ἦν μοι κέρδη: 'but such things as were gains to me.'

ἅτινα: instead of the simple ἅ, because of κέρδη: 'things which were of such a kind that they could be called κέρδη.' It presents a category of the things specified in vs. 5, 6. See for this usage Gal. iv. 24, v. 19; Phil. ii. 20; Col. ii. 23.

μοι: dative of advantage; not of judgment, 'in my estimation.'

κέρδη: 'gains,' taken separately; the profits of descent, of legal strictness, of zeal, etc., each attended with its own particular gain.

ταῦτα: defining and emphasising κέρδη.

ἥγημαι: 'I have counted': with deliberate judgment. (See on ii. 6.)

ζημίαν: 'a loss.' The several gains are massed in one loss. The word only in this epistle and Acts xxvii. 10, 21. See farther on ἐζημιώθην (vs. 8).

From his former experience he now turns to his present Christian ideal and his efforts to attain it.

8–14. *Since the hour of my conversion my estimate of the worthlessness of my legal righteousness and its profits has not changed. I continue to count them all but loss as compared with the surpassing worth of the knowledge of Christ Jesus my Lord. To me they are mere refuse, if I can but make Christ my own and may be found living in him, not having a righteousness of my own, which is of the law, but rather a righteousness which proceeds from God, which is based upon faith, and which becomes mine through faith in Christ: a righteousness which means such intimate and practical knowledge of Christ as that his risen life shall be a power in my life, and his sufferings shall be mine, even unto death; and that so, at last, if this may be, I may be raised from the dead as he was. I speak of my desire, not of my attainment, for I have not yet realised my ideal; but I am pressing on toward the attain-*

ment and fulfilment of that which Christ contemplated in my conversion. No, I have not yet attained; but one thing I do. Not encouraged to self-satisfaction or relaxation of effort by what is past, I stretch forward, like a racer to the goal, toward that high destiny to which God in Christ is ever summoning me from heaven.

8. ἀλλὰ μενοῦνγε καὶ ἡγοῦμαι: 'nay then I am indeed also counting.'

BDFGKL read μεν ουν; μενουνγε ℵ AP, 17, 37.

Μὲν confirms ἡγοῦμαι, and οὖν, strengthened by γε, recurs to ἥγημαι and carries it forward, thus guarding against a possible misunderstanding of the last statement. 'Nay then, if my ἥγημαι be thought to have been a mere impulsive *act* of breaking with the past, — I *am*, in truth, also *counting* all things as loss for Christ's sake.' His break with legal righteousness perpetuates itself. For μενοῦνγε see Rom. ix. 20, x. 18.

Πάντα corresponds with ἅτινα (vs. 7): all things which formed the ground of my false confidence.

διὰ τὸ ὑπερέχον τῆς γνώσεως Χριστοῦ Ἰησοῦ τοῦ κυρίου μου: 'for the surpassing worth of the knowledge of Christ Jesus my Lord.' This expands διὰ τὸν Χριστὸν, thus defining more clearly the motive of ἥγημαι ζημίαν. The ἥγημαι was caused by an overpowering impression of Christ; the ἡγοῦμαι by the knowledge of Christ. The ὃν in the next clause gathers additional force from γνώσεως. Τὸ ὑπ. τ. γνώσ. is not a hendiadys, 'the excellent knowledge,' as Vulg. 'eminentem scientiam.' The neuter participle with the article is more graphic than the noun ὑπεροχή. (See Blass, p. 151.) On substantivised neuters see Win. xxxiv. 2, and comp. Rom. ii. 4, viii. 3, ix. 22; 1 Cor. i. 25; Heb. vi. 17. Γνῶσις is used in its original, simple sense, as Rom. ii. 20; 1 Cor. i. 5, viii. 1. Not in the later, philosophic sense.

τοῦ κυρίου μου: κυρίου adds emphasis to τὸν Χριστὸν (vs. 7). For μου, with its sense of personal appropriation, comp. i. 3. The knowledge is surpassing because its subject is Lord, to be confessed and worshipped by the created universe (ii. 11). Christ, as the subject of this knowledge, is regarded with reference to all that he is or becomes to a believer. So Croc.: "Complectitur personam, officium et beneficium, quae separari non possunt."

The designations of Christ in the Epistles of the Captivity resemble those in the earlier letters. Ἰησοῦς alone occurs only in Eph. iv. 21; Phil. ii. 10. Χριστός and ὁ Χρ. are very frequent. The title κύριος added to the personal name occurs chiefly in the beginnings of the epistles, as Eph. i. 2; Philem. 3; Phil. i. 2; but Christ is commonly styled κύριος or ὁ κύριος simply, especially in the formula ἐν κυρίῳ. In Phil. ὁ κυρ. ἡμ. 'IX is not found. In Philem., which contains nearly all the formulas, the simple Χτός occurs only in vs. 6.

τὰ πάντα: collectively. (Comp. Rom. viii. 32, xi. 36; 1 Cor. viii. 6.) Accusative of reference. 'I became loser in respect of all things.'

ἐζημιώθην: 'I became loser.' The verb means 'to fine,' 'to amerce,' 'to mulct,' and is to be taken in its passive sense; not as middle or reflexive, 'I have made myself lose,' which is contrary to N.T. usage. (See Mt. xvi. 26; Lk. ix. 25; 1 Cor. iii. 15; 2 Cor. vii. 9; LXX; Ex. xxi. 22; Prov. xix. 19, xxii. 3.) The middle sense would ascribe ἐζημ. as an act to Paul himself, whereas the thought is that, having been grasped and possessed by Christ, his former possessions fell away. The aorist points to the definite period of his conversion. In that great crisis all his legal possessions were lost.

καὶ ἡγοῦμαι: continuous present. (See above.) It may be regarded as dependent on δι' ὃν (Mey., Ellic., Lightf.), or as a new point, and parallel with ἡγοῦμ. πάν. ζημ. (Weiss). The latter seems a little simpler, ἐζημ. having its motive in δι' ὃν, and ἵνα κερδ. being the motive of ἡγοῦμ. σκύβ., thus contrasting the gain with what he threw away as worthless. On the other explanation, ἵνα κερδ. adds a motive to δι' ὃν.

σκύβαλα: 'refuse.' Only here in N.T. (Comp. LXX; Sir. xxvii. 4.) Belonging wholly to later Gk., as Plut., Jos. The derivation cannot be certainly shown. Suidas says κυσιβαλόν; *i.e.* τὸ τοῖς κυσὶ βαλλόμενον, 'that which is thrown to the dogs.' More probably connected with σκώρ, 'stercus.' (See Curtius, *Gk. Etym.* i. 167 [Eng.].) It signifies either 'excrement' or 'the leavings of the table.' A strong expression from the man who could write Gal. i. 14. Some of the patristic interpreters were embarrassed by this passage because the apparent disparagement of the law was seized upon by Antinomians, and used in their own interest. Hence they tried to modify Paul's meaning by referring it to the *comparative* value of the law. The law was a light, but unnecessary after the sun had arisen. It was a ladder, useful to mount by, but useless after one had mounted. On the same line σκύβαλα was explained by the chaff, which is part of the ripening corn, but is thrown away in the threshing. (See Chr.)

Χριστὸν κερδήσω: Appropriate Christ and make him his own, with all of grace and glory that attaches to him. Paul's earnestness is shown in his reiteration: κέρδη, ζημίαν, ἐζημιώθην, πάντα, Χριστόν, etc.

He proceeds to show what is involved in winning Christ.

9. καὶ εὑρεθῶ ἐν αὐτῷ: For εὑρεθῶ, see on ii. 7. Often in the passive in the sense of 'to be seen, discovered, or proved to be.' (See Acts v. 39; Rom. vii. 10; 1 Cor. iv. 2; 2 Cor. xi. 12; Gal. ii. 17.) Here pointing to the recognition by others of Paul's

union with Christ. (Comp. Ign. *Eph.* xi.; *Trall.* xiii.) By some commentators it is referred to the last day, either wholly or in part (see Lightf.); but the entire line of thought refers to union with Christ in this life. The final result appears in vs. 11. Calv. wrongly makes εὑρεθῶ active, and explains that Paul had renounced all that he had in order that he might find it in Christ.

ἐν αὐτῷ: See on ἐν Χριστῷ Ἰησοῦ (i. 1). The same idea appears in i. 21; Gal. ii. 20: the state of identification with Christ's life as the principle of salvation; the immanence of that principle in the human life. Comp. also Jn. xiv. 20, xv. 2, 4, 5, 7, xvii. 21, 23. "The Christian," says Weiss, "exercises all the functions of his life in Christ. In him, or in fellowship with him, are rooted trust (Phil. ii. 19, 24), joy (Phil. iii. 1, iv. 4, 10), boldness (Philem. 8), Christian refreshment (Philem. 20). In him one speaks (Eph. iv. 17); executes his ministry (Col. iv. 17); entertains another (Phil. ii. 29); maintains unanimity with another (Phil. iv. 2); obeys another (Eph. vi. 1). In him one is strengthened, and can do all things (Eph. vi. 10; Phil. iv. 13)." —*Bib. Theol.* § 101. Christ, the personified revelation of the divine love, is the ruling principle of the human personal life, so that this life moves in Christ as in its own peculiar element. To be in Christ is to have the Spirit of Christ and to be one Spirit with him (Rom. viii. 9; 1 Cor. vi. 17). See note at the end of this chapter on Paul's conception of righteousness by faith.

μὴ ἔχων: Expressing the mode, not the condition of being in Christ.

ἐμὴν δικαιοσύνην: 'a righteousness of my own.' Not 'my own righteousness,' as A.V., for no such thing exists; but a righteousness which might be described as my own. 'My own righteousness' would be τὴν ἐμὴν δικ. (Comp. Rom. x. 3.)

τὴν ἐκ νόμου: Defining ἐμ. δικ. A righteousness which could be called 'mine' would be a righteousness 'proceeding from (ἐκ) the law.' He lays down a general proposition: Human righteousness is legal righteousness. It is contained in the law (vs. 6), and passes from the law to the man as the man obeys the law (Rom. x. 5). The man's righteousness is generated by its precepts.

διὰ πίστεως Χριστοῦ: 'through faith of (in) Christ.' Διὰ marks faith as the medium of attaining righteousness. (Comp. Rom. iii. 22; Gal. ii. 16; Eph. ii. 8.) For 'faith *of* Christ' = 'faith *in* Christ,' comp. Mk. xi. 22; Rom. iii. 22; 2 Cor. x. 5; Gal. ii. 16, iii. 22; 2 Thess. ii. 13; Jas. ii. 1.

τὴν ἐκ θεοῦ δικαιοσύνην ἐπὶ τῇ πίστει: 'the righteousness which is from God resting upon faith.' A further definition of τὴν διὰ πίσ. Χρ., describing its source and its basis. It proceeds from God, and is therefore in contrast with ἐμὴν δικ. The phrase is not synonymous with δικαιοσύνη θεοῦ (Rom. i. 17), which signifies righteousness which is God's; which resides in him as his attribute; not, as commonly explained, righteousness which is from God, and is bestowed by him upon man. Δικαιοσύνη θεοῦ is of course assumed in τ. ἐκ θε. δικ. The ideal and the source of righteousness are in God. God is the source of the atoning work of Christ which contemplates man's righteousness, and Christ is 'the image of his substance' (Heb. i. 3; see 2 Cor. v. 21, and Sanday on *Rom.* p. 162). As related to man, the righteousness of God rests upon (ἐπὶ) faith, *the* (τῇ) faith which each man exercises towards God in Jesus Christ. This is the only instance of the phrase ἐπὶ τῇ πίστει in N.T. It expresses διὰ πίστεως a little more definitely, and sets forth the only true basis of all human righteousness. It is, indeed, true that righteousness rests ultimately on God, and not on faith; but if that is an objection, the same would lie against δικ. ἐκ πίστ. (Rom. ix. 30, x. 6). Lightf., following Ril. and van Heng., renders ἐπὶ 'on condition of.' But Paul is here speaking rather of the essential character of this righteousness than of the terms on which it is received by men. It belongs to the nature of God's righteousness as imparted to man that it rests upon faith (Rom. iv. 5).

Lightf. refers to Acts iii. 16, though ἐπὶ there is a doubtful reading. WH. omit, with ℵ* B. Tisch., R.T., and Weiss retain.

Mey. supplies ἔχων, repeated after ἀλλὰ; 'having on the ground of faith righteousness through faith,' which is harsh and quite unnecessary. Equally awkward is the connection of ἐπὶ τῇ πίστει with εὑρεθῶ, as Weiss. Rather it is to be connected with δικαιοσύνην immediately preceding. The omission of the article before ἐπὶ τ. πίστ. has numerous precedents in cases where the whole expression represents one idea.

He goes on to show in what this righteousness by faith consists.

10. τοῦ γνῶναι αὐτὸν: 'that I may come to know him.' Taken up from the γνώσεως of vs. 8, and explaining it. Τοῦ γνῶναι is the infinitive of design, setting forth the end contemplated in the righteousness of faith. For this usage see Mt. xxiv. 45; Lk. ii. 24, 27; Acts xxvi. 18; 1 Cor. x. 13; Gal. iii. 10; and Burt. 397; Win. xliv. 4 *b*.

Lips. and Kl. coördinate τοῦ γν. with ἵνα εὑρεθῶ, as representing, not the purpose of being found in Christ, nor the object for which Paul possesses the righteousness of faith, but the *mode* in which he desires to be found in Christ. But the dependence on what immediately precedes is most natural. In τὸν Χτὸν κερδ. and εὑρεθῶ two elements are given which do not furnish a parallel to τοῦ γνῶναι, and Paul's habit is to join two parallel clauses of design with a double ἵνα. (See Rom. vii. 13; 2 Cor. ix. 3; Gal. iii. 14.) The difference, however, is not important. Calv., Grot., Beng., make τοῦ γν. dependent on τῇ πίστ., describing the power and the nature of faith. But this construction with πίστ. has no parallel in N.T. The change of construction from ἵνα in vs. 9 to the infin. of design is not uncommon in Paul. (See Rom. vi. 6; Col. i. 9, 10.)

For γνῶναι, see on i. 19. Paul's end is, indeed, εἰδέναι, the absolute knowledge; but he is here speaking rather of his *coming into* a knowledge of the riches of Christ in the *process* of his experience. See Lightf. on Gal. iv. 9; and comp. Jn. vii. 27; 1 Cor. ii. 11; Gal. iv. 8, 9; Eph. v. 5; 1 Jn. ii. 18, 29, iii. 1, 16, iv. 16. It should also be noted that, in N.T. Greek, γινώσκειν often implies a personal relation between the knower and the known, involving the influence of the object of knowledge upon the knower. (See Jn. ii. 24, 25; 1 Cor. ii. 8; 1 Jn. iv. 8.) In Jn. the relation itself is expressed by the verb (Jn. xvii. 3, 25; 1 Jn. ii. 3, 4, v. 20). Here, therefore, 'that I may come to know,' appropriating with the increase of knowledge.

The two following details are involved in personal knowledge of Christ:

καὶ τὴν δύναμιν τῆς ἀναστάσεως αὐτοῦ: 'and the power of his resurrection.' Καὶ is more than a simple connective. It introduces a definition and fuller explanation of αὐτὸν. Δύναμιν is not the power by which Christ was raised from the dead (Chr., Œc.), nor, as Theoph., "because to arise is great power"; nor Christ's power to raise up believers. Like the preceding expressions, it describes a subjective experience. It is the power of the risen Christ as it becomes a subject of practical knowledge and a power in Paul's inner life. It is thus within the same circle of thought as Rom. vi. 4–11. (Comp. Col. iii. 1 ff.) The resurrection is viewed, not only as something which Paul hopes to experience after death, nor as a historical experience of Christ which is a subject of grateful and inspiring remembrance, but as a present, continuously active force in his Christian development. The beginning of the life of faith is a moral resurrection, a rising with Christ (Rom. vi. 5; Col. iii. 1), inaugurating 'newness of life' (Rom. vi. 4),—life in the Spirit (Rom. vii. 6), a life essentially identical with the ζωὴ αἰώνιος and ἐπουράνιος of the glorified Jesus. Comp. Eph. i. 19, 20, ii. 5, 6; and see the very suggestive remarks of Pfleiderer, *Paulinismus*, ch. v. "The rising with Christ is put, not as an object of hope, but as belonging to the present, from the moment when 'the spirit of him that raised up Jesus from the dead' (Rom. viii. 11) takes up its abode in believers; so that the rising with Christ is so far a fact as that for them a new life is opened (2 Cor. v. 15; Gal. ii. 19). Thus, equipped with the death-overcoming, spiritual life-power of Christ, they enter upon a condition in which they are enabled to overcome the power of sin in their members, so that sin shall not have dominion over them (Rom. vi. 13, 14; Col. iii. 5)."—*Klöpper*. Thus the knowledge of the power of Christ's resurrection appears as an element of the righteousness of faith. This explains Paul's phrase 'justification of *life*' (Rom. v. 18). This knowledge includes the assurance of immortality.

καὶ κοινωνίαν παθημάτων αὐτοῦ: 'and the fellowship of his sufferings.'

DFGKLP την before κοιν.

Comp. 2 Cor. i. 5, iv. 10, 11; Gal. vi. 17; Col. i. 24; 1 Pet. iv. 13. A participation in the sufferings which Christ endured in his mortal life. (Comp. Heb. xii. 2, 3.) Such participation is involved in the knowledge of Christ. It is not merely ethical. It does not refer, except by implication, to the victorious power of suffering. Nor is a mere likeness to the sufferings of Christ intended. Like the knowledge of the power of the resurrection, the fellowship of the sufferings is involved in the mystical union with Christ, and is treated by Paul as a verification of this "at its hardest and most decisive point" (Weiss). Being in Christ involves fellowship with Christ at all points,—his obedient life, his spirit, his sufferings, his death, and his glory. The order of arrangement here is the true one. The fellowship of the sufferings follows the experience of the power of the resurrection. For the power of the resurrection appears in justification of life; and the new life in and with Christ puts its subject where Christ was,—in that attitude towards the world which engenders contradiction, reproach, and persecution. As Mey. truthfully observes: "The enthusiastic feeling of drinking the cup of Christ is not possible unless a man bears in his heart the mighty assurance of resurrection through the Lord." One who is not under the power of the resurrection will not share Christ's sufferings, because his moral attitude will not be such as to call out the assaults of the world. (Comp. Jn. vii. 7.) How this desire was fulfilled in Paul appears in the Acts, and in allusions in his letters. (See 1 Cor. iv. 10–13, xv. 31; 2 Cor. iv. 8–12; Gal. vi. 17.) Christ had said of him, 'I will show him how great things he must suffer for my name's sake' (Acts ix. 16).

συμμορφιζόμενος τῷ θανάτῳ αὐτοῦ: 'becoming conformed unto his death.'

ℵ^c D^c EKL συμμορφουμενος.
FG συνφορτειζομενος, 'being burdened together.'

The conception of fellowship with Christ's sufferings is further unfolded to its last point—even unto death. (Comp. ii. 8.) Συμμορφίζεσθαι not elsewhere in Bib. The adj. σύμμορφος occurs iii. 21; Rom. viii. 29. The participle is in apposition with the subject of τοῦ γνῶναι. (Comp. Eph. iv. 2; Col. i. 10.) Not middle, 'conforming myself to,' but passive. The conformity is not ethical, as Rom. vi. 3–11, but is a conformity with the sufferings of Christ's earthly life, even unto death. It does not necessarily indicate, as Mey., a distinct contemplation of Paul's martyrdom. (Comp. i. 25, 26, ii. 23, 24.) The thought is rather that of 1 Cor. xv. 31; 2 Cor. iv. 10. (Comp. Rom. viii. 17.) The suffering of this present time works together with all things for the good of those who love God (Rom. viii. 28); and such God ordained to be 'conformed [συμμόρφους] to the image of his Son' (Rom. viii. 29). The participle indicates the process of development.

11. εἴ πως καταντήσω εἰς τὴν ἐξανάστασιν τὴν ἐκ νεκρῶν: 'if possibly I may attain unto the resurrection from the dead.' The words connect themselves most naturally with συμμορφ. τῷ θαν. αὐ., according to Paul's habitual association of resurrection with death. Resurrection, physical or ethical, is attained only through death.

Lips., without assigning any reason, and Kl. for reasons which seem fanciful, connect with γνῶναι.

For εἴ πως see Acts xxvii. 12; Rom. i. 10, xi. 14. Much unnecessary difficulty has been made over the apparent uncertainty expressed in these words, and the fancied inconsistency with the certainty elsewhere expressed by Paul, as Rom. viii. 38, 39, v. 17, 18, 21; 2 Cor. v. 1 ff.; Phil. i. 22, 23. He elsewhere urges the necessity of caution against a possible lapse from faith (ii. 12; 1 Cor. x. 12; Gal. iii. 3, v. 4), and he takes the same caution to himself (1 Cor. ix. 27). His words here are an expression of humility and self-distrust, not of doubt. Weiss remarks that while, on the human side, the attainment of the goal may be regarded as doubtful, or at least conditioned upon humble self-estimate, on the side of the working of divine grace it appears certain.

καταντᾷν: Only in Paul and Acts. In Paul, of persons, 1 Cor. x. 11, xiv. 36; of ethical relations, Eph. iv. 13. In Acts always of places, except xxvi. 7.

καταντήσω is aor. subj., as καταλάβω (vs. 12). Εἰ with the subj. is rare in good class. prose, but occurs in LXX, and is common in later Greek. (See Burt. 253, 276.)

τὴν ἐξανάστασιν τὴν ἐκ νεκρῶν:

KL, Arm., Cop., read ἐξαν. των νεκρων. So TR.

Ἐξανάστασις occurs only here in Bib. The verb ἐξανιστάναι is found Mk. xii. 9; Lk. xx. 28; Acts xv. 5, but in neither of the passages of the rising of the dead. Why the compound word was selected instead of the simple ἀνάστασις, we cannot explain. Possibly, as Mey., in order to give greater vividness to the image; but this is far from satisfactory. Beng.'s explanation, that it is intended to mark the resurrection of believers as distinguished from that of Christ, is arbitrary and fanciful. Ἀνάστ. or ἐξανάστ. ἐκ is found only three times in N.T. (Lk. xx. 35; Acts iv. 2; 1 Pet. i. 3).

Lightf. says: "The general resurrection of the dead, whether good or bad, is ἡ ἀνάστ. τῶν νεκ. (*e.g.* 1 Cor. xv. 42); on the other hand, the resurrection of Christ and of those who rise with Christ is generally [ἡ] ἀνάστ.

[ἡ] ἐκ νεκ." This can hardly be borne out. See Rom. i. 4, ἀνάστ. νεκ., of Christ, — so Acts xxvi. 23; 1 Cor. xv. 42, 43, ἀνάστ. τ. νεκ., of a resurrection which is in incorruption, glory, and power; Acts xvii. 31, ἐκ νεκ., of Christ; vs. 32, ἀνάστ. νεκ. It is true that in every case where ἐκ occurs the reference is to the resurrection of the just, but three instances are not enough to build such a distinction upon.

The reference here is clearly to the resurrection of believers. The question of the resurrection of the wicked is irrelevant; and the idea of a reference to a spiritual resurrection while still in the body is entirely without support.

12. οὐχ ὅτι: See on iv. 11. Supply λέγω, 'I say not that.' (Comp. Jn. vi. 46; 2 Cor. i. 24, iii. 5; Phil. iv. 17; 2 Thess. iii. 9.)

ἤδη ἔλαβον: Ἤδη 'now,' marks the point of time at which all the past experience has arrived. Ἔλαβον covers Paul's entire past up to the time of writing. Its object is not expressed, but is all that is included in vs. 8–11.

Lightf. is wrong in insisting that the aorist points to a definite past epoch, and translating 'Not as though by my conversion I did at once attain.' The aorist is frequently used to express duration extending to the present. See Ellic. on 1 Thess. ii. 16, and comp. Lk. xiv. 18; Rom. iii. 2; Gal. v. 24; Eph. iii. 5; 1 Thess. ii. 16. See also Beet, *Expositor*, 1st ser. xi. p. 375, 6.

The variety of objects suggested for ἔλαβον is bewildering. A favorite one is βραβεῖον from vs. 14. So Chr., Œc., Theoph., Beng., Ellic., Mey., Ead., Beet, Ril. Meyer says that βραβεῖον is the bliss of Messiah's kingdom, and that ἔλαβον is to be explained of his having attained in ideal anticipation(!); Beet, "the full blessedness of the kingdom of Christ for which he must wait till the resurrection from the dead." But who could possibly have imagined that he *had* attained this? There is no reason for anticipating βραβεῖον.

ἤδη τετελείωμαι: 'am already made perfect.'

DFG add η ηδη δεδικαιωμαι.

Τετελ. explains ἔλαβον more definitely, or puts literally what ἔλ. had put figuratively. Ἔλ. regards the whole past as a completed act; τετ. the whole past gathered up in its relation to the present. The perfection referred to is moral and spiritual perfection. (Comp. Eph. iii. 17–19, iv. 13–16; Col. i. 28; and Ign. *Eph.* iii. Οὐ διατάσσομαι ὑμῖν, ὡς ὤν τι· εἰ γὰρ καὶ δέδεμαι ἐν τῷ ὀνόματι, οὔπω ἀπήρτισμαι ἐν Ἰησοῦ Χριστῷ: 'I do not command you as though I were somewhat, for even though I am in bonds for the Name's sake, I am not yet perfected in Jesus Christ.' Comp. *Philad.* v.) The verb is used by Paul only here, but is common in Heb.

διώκω δὲ: 'but I pursue,' or as A.V., 'follow after'; better than R.V., 'press on.' The eagerness of Paul to attain his ideal is emulated by that of some of the commentators to bring βραβεῖον up into this verse. There is no need of supplying it with διώκω, nor need διώκω be taken absolutely. Its object lies in ἐφ' ᾧ καὶ κατελήμφθην, etc., and is the same as that of ἔλαβον. The pursuit is no groping after something undefined, nor is it prosecuted with any feeling of doubt as to the attainment of its end. Though he had zealously pursued the 'law of righteousness' (Rom. ix. 31) as a son of Israel, he was now pursuing the righteousness of faith with even greater zeal, under a mightier impulse, and with a clearer view of his goal. It is doubtful whether the metaphor of the race comes in here (as Ellic., Mey., Alf., Ead.): κατελήμφθην does not suit it. Διώκειν is often used by Paul, without that reference, for striving after the blessings and virtues of the Christian life. (See Rom. ix. 30, 31, xii. 13, xiv. 19, 1 Cor. xiv. 1; 1 Thess. v. 15.) Instead of the idea of the race giving color to διώκω, it is quite as likely that διώκω suggested the metaphor in vs. 14. For διώκειν with καταλαμβάνειν, see Rom. ix. 30; LXX; Sir. xi. 10, xxvii. 8.

εἰ καὶ καταλάβω ἐφ' ᾧ καὶ κατελήμφθην: 'if I may also grasp that for which I was grasped.'

Tisch. omits καὶ before καταλάβω with ℵ* DFG, Syr., Cop., Arm., Goth., Æth. καὶ is found in ℵ^c ABDKLP, Syr.^p. So WH., R.T., Weiss.

καὶ: 'if I may not only pursue but *also* attain.' For εἰ καὶ, see on ii. 17. For the progression from διώκειν to καταλαμβάνειν, comp. Rom. ix. 30. From λαμβάνειν to καταλαμ., and from τρέχετε to καταλαμ., 1 Cor. ix. 24. Καταλαβεῖν is 'to overtake and seize.' (See Jn. i. 5, xii. 35; Rom. ix. 30; 1 Cor. ix. 24.)

ἐφ' ᾧ καὶ κατελήμφθην: The divine grace in Paul's conversion is the moving power of his Christian development. The fulfilment of the ideal contemplated by Christ when he transformed him from a persecutor to an apostle is the goal which invites him. He desires to grasp that for which he was grasped by Christ. The aorist marks the time of his conversion, which was literally a seizure. Not, however, as Chr. and Thdrt., that Paul is conceived as running to destruction and pursued and seized by Christ.

To view his conversion as a seizure is not to deny the work of previous influences upon his mind preparing the way for the crisis of the journey to Damascus. (See Pfleiderer, *Paulinismus*, *Einl.*; Bruce, *St. Paul's Conception of Christianity*, ch. ii.; Matheson, *Spiritual Development of St. Paul*, ch. ii., iii., — see especially pp. 46, 47.)

Ἐφ' ᾧ is relative to a suppressed antecedent, ἐκεῖνο, as Lk. v. 25, '*that* for which I was grasped.'

Weiss refers the relative to καταλάβω simply, and renders 'wherefore.' So Lightf. Others, as Chr., Thdrt., Mey., Lips., make ἐφ' ᾧ = ἐπὶ τουτῷ ὅτι, and render 'because,' taking καταλάβω absolutely. Calv., 'quemadmodum, just as.'

Καὶ refers to ἐφ' ᾧ, adding the purpose of his being grasped to the assertion of his effort to grasp: 'which I not only strive to grasp, but for which *also* I was grasped.'

The next two verses substantially repeat the assertions of vs. 12 — the disavowal of satisfaction with his attainment, and the declaration of his strenuous pursuit of his spiritual ideal.

13. ἐγὼ ἐμαυτὸν οὔπω λογίζομαι κατειληφέναι: 'I count not myself yet to have grasped.'

ουπω, WH. [], Tisch., R.T., with ℵ ADP, 17, 31, 47, 80, Cop., Syr.p, Æth.; BDFGKL, Vulg., Goth., Arm., read ου.

Both ἐγὼ and ἐμαυτὸν are emphatic, expressing strongly his own estimate of himself. (Comp. Lk. vii. 7; Jn. viii. 54; 1 Cor. iv. 3.) It is quite superfluous to introduce an implied comparison with the judgment of others, either of those who think too highly of him, or of those who think too highly of themselves. Such an estimate, in itself, is in strong contrast with self-righteousness and religious conceit.

λογίζομαι: 'I count' or 'reckon,' very often in Paul, and almost confined to his epistles. Only four times elsewhere in N.T. The idea of a process of reasoning always underlies it.

ἓν δέ: Supply ποιῶ, not λογίζομαι, as Mey., for ἓν refers to what follows, which is a matter of doing, not of reckoning.

Others supply φροντίζω, μεριμνῶ, διώκω, οἶδα, λέγω. Such ellipses of the verb are common in Paul; *e.g.* ii. 3, 5; Rom. iv. 9, v. 18; Gal. iii. 5; 2 Cor. vi. 13. (See Win. lxvi. 1 *b*.)

τὰ μὲν ὀπίσω: 'the things which are behind.' The portion of his *Christian* course already traversed. Not his experience as a persecutor of the church. With τὰ ὀπίσω, comp. τοῦ νῦν (i. 5); τὰ κατ' ἐμὲ (i. 12); τὰ περὶ ὑμῶν (i. 27, ii. 19, 20); τὰ περὶ ἐμέ (ii. 23). 'Οπίσω only here by Paul.

The metaphor of the race now first enters.

ἐπιλανθανόμενος: 'forgetting.' The word nowhere else in Paul; sparingly in Synop., Heb., and Jas.; often in LXX. No special emphasis attaches to the compound. In class. it occurs sometimes, but rarely, in the sense of 'forgetting *wilfully*' (Hdt. iii. 147, iv. 43). But so also does the simple verb (Hom. *Il.* ix. 537; Æsch. *Ag.* 39). Not to be understood as if Paul were ashamed of what lay behind him in his Christian career, or as if he did not emphasise it as exhibiting the grace of God. (See 1 Cor. iv. 11–16, xv. 10; 2 Cor. xi. 23–xii. 6.) Rather that he does not use the memory of what God has wrought in him and through him to encourage self-satisfaction and relaxation of effort. He is stimulated by the past to renewed energy in Christian self-development and in the building-up of Christ's church. (See 1 Cor. ix. 19–27.)

τοῖς δὲ ἔμπροσθεν: The higher attainments in the Christian life. Only here.

ἐπεκτεινόμενος: 'stretching forward.' A graphic word from the arena. The body of the racer is bent forward, his hand is outstretched towards the goal, and his eye is fastened upon it. "The eye outstrips and draws onward the hand, and the hand the foot" (Beng.). The metaphor is from the foot-race, not from the chariot-race. Lightf. observes that *not* looking back would be fatal to the charioteer. The word has passed into sporting language — 'the home-stretch.' Ἐπεκ., nowhere else in Bib. Ἐκτείνειν, often in Synop. with χείρ. (Comp. ἐκτένεια, Acts xxvi. 7; ἐκτενής, 1 Pet. iv. 8; ἐκτενῶς, Acts xii. 5; 1 Pet. i. 22.)

14. κατὰ σκοπὸν διώκω: 'I press on towards the mark.'

κατὰ: Bearing *down* upon. Σκοπὸν, only here in N.T. That on which one fixes his *look*. (Comp. σκοποῦντες, ii. 4.) In class. a mark for shooting at; also a moral or intellectual end (Plat. *Gorg*. 507 D; *Phileb*. 60 A). In LXX; Job xvi. 13; Lam. iii. 12, of an archer's mark. It is not used in a technical sense of an appliance of the race course, as R.V. 'goal.'

διώκω: "εὐφαντικώτατα δὲ τὸ διώκειν εἶπεν. Ὁ γὰρ διώκων οὐδὲν ἄλλο ὁρᾷ ἢ πρὸς ὃ σπεύδει, πάντα δὲ παρέρχεται, καὶ τὰ φίλτατα καὶ τὰ ἀναγκαιότατα." "Most appropriately did he say διώκειν; for he who pursues sees nothing but that towards which he is hastening, and passes by all things, the dearest and the most necessary" (Theoph.).

εἰς τὸ βραβεῖον: Βραβ., only here and 1 Cor. ix. 24. The kindred verbs, βραβεύειν, 'to be umpire,' and καταβραβεύειν, 'to be umpire against,' 'to defraud of a prize,' are peculiar to the Colossian letter. (See iii. 15, ii. 18.) βραβ. is not used technically of the prize in the games, the technical word being ἆθλον. Here the heavenly reward; the 'crown of righteousness' (1 Cor. ix. 24–27; 2 Tim. iv. 8; Apoc. ii. 10); a share in the glory of the exalted Christ (Rom. viii. 17; 2 Tim. ii. 10, 11). (Comp. 1 Thess. ii. 12; 1 Tim. vi. 12.)

τῆς ἄνω κλήσεως τοῦ θεοῦ ἐν Χριστῷ Ἰησοῦ: 'of the upward calling of God in Christ Jesus.'

The expression ἡ ἄνω κλῆσις is unique. The only analogous phrase in N.T. to βραβ. τ. ἄνω κλ. is ἐλπὶς τῆς κλήσεως (Eph. i. 18, iv. 4). The genitive of κλ. is the genitive of belonging. The prize is attached to the calling and involved in it.

Lips. and De W. make the genitive appositional: 'the prize which is the high calling.' This would identify the calling with the heavenly reward, and would leave βραβ. without definition.

Ἄνω means both 'above,' local, as Gal. iv. 26, and 'upwards,' as Jn. xi. 41; Heb. xii. 15. Here the latter. Comp. the striking parall. in Philo, *De Plant. Noe.* § 6. The whole passage is full of movement, onward and upward. (Comp. Col. iii. 2.)

Most comms., however, make ἄνω = ἐπουράνιος, describing the *quality* of the calling as heavenly. (Comp. Heb. iii. 1.) Mey. and Weiss say, 'because it issues from God in heaven.' Why not then ἄνωθεν?

κλήσεως: The *act* of calling. Not that to which he is called (De W., Lips.). The word does not lose its active sense in N.T. It may include the original call of God to Paul, but it is not to be limited to that. God is continually summoning men upward in various ways. Nor does the expression suggest God as the judge of the contest, summoning the runners to the race (so some earlier comms. as Wolf, Rosenm., am E., Hoel., van Heng.). The genitive is that of the subject, that which offers the prize. God, in calling men upward, calls them to a heavenly reward. The prize is the object of 'the hope of the calling' (Eph. i. 18).

τοῦ θεοῦ ἐν Χριστῷ Ἰησοῦ: Connect with κλήσεως. The calling is 'of God,' because God is its author, and 'in Christ Jesus' as the sphere or element in which it is issued and prosecuted. For the expression 'called in Christ Jesus,' comp. 1 Cor. vii. 22; 1 Pet. v. 10.

Mey. and Weiss connect with διώκω; but the position is against this.

15–21. *Let us, therefore, who, by our profession, are committed to this high Christian ideal of perfection, cherish this spirit of humble dissatisfaction with past attainments and of earnest striving after all that is involved in our heavenward calling. And if, in any particular, your ideal of the possibilities of Christian attainment and of your proper attitude towards these differs from that which I have held up to you, God will correct this by future revelations; but only on the condition that you act up to the ideal which you already have, and follow the rule which it imposes. Brethren, unite in imitating me, and carefully observe those whose conduct resembles mine. For there are many, of whom I have told you often, and now tell you, even weeping, that their conduct marks them as the enemies of the cross of Christ. The end of such is destruction. Their god is their belly. Their minds are set upon earthly things. They glory in that which is their shame. We, on the other hand, are citizens of a commonwealth which is in heaven, whence we await the appearing of the Lord Jesus Christ as Saviour; and when he shall appear, he will, by that power which enables him to subject all things to himself, refashion this body* *which belongs to our mortal state of humiliation, and fashion it after the likeness of that body which belongs to him in his heavenly glory.*

The exhortation of vs. 15, 16 shows the effect of the strong emotion which pervades the preceding passage. The general sense is clear, and becomes embarrassing only when the attempt is made to adjust all its parts and their connection according to rigid rhetorical rules. The apostle has just held up his own lofty ideal of Christian character. He has disclaimed the having attained it, because its transcendent greatness will not allow him to be satisfied with past attainments, and only stimulates him to more strenuous effort. In this attitude of humility and aspiring exertion, he exhorts his readers to imitate him. At the same time, he recognises the possibility that their ideal of Christian perfection may differ from his own in some particulars, and be lower than his own, in which case God will correct the defect by future revelations. But the condition of such revelations is, that they practically carry out their own ideals, such as they are, and live strictly according to the rule of conduct which they impose.

15. *ὅσοι οὖν τέλειοι, τοῦτο φρονῶμεν*: 'Let as many of us therefore as are perfect be thus minded.' Paul here includes himself among the *τέλειοι*, although in vs. 12 he has said *οὐχ ἤδη τετελείωμαι*. Evidently the two expressions are not used in the same sense. In vs. 12 he is speaking of *absolute* perfection, such as would relieve him of the necessity of further striving. In *τέλειοι* he is speaking of *relative* perfection. (Comp. Mt. v. 48.) Τέλειος has two senses in the N.T.: 1. 'full-grown,' 'mature,' in contrast with childish ignorance and weakness, as 1 Cor. ii. 6, xiv. 20; Heb. v. 14. 2. Absolutely, as Mt. v. 48; Jas. i. 4, iii. 2. Yet, in this absolute usage, there is a distinction which is illustrated in Mt. v. 48. As used there of the absolute perfection of God, it cannot be used of the perfection which is enjoined by Jesus upon men. That perfection is relative. Similarly here, the ideal condition is ascribed to those who are, by their profession, committed to it as their own ideal, just as *ἅγιοι* is used of those who are, though not absolutely holy, yet consecrated to the holy God. As Rilliet remarks, "The word meaning what ought to be is taken by concession to mean what is, evidently with the intention of attaching the reality to the ideal, and of recalling to believers the obligations involved in the title." Τέλειοι here is, therefore, a general designation of the Christian condition in all its aspects, not, as

Lips., with reference only to Christian knowledge. It is the same, practically, as πνευματικοί (1 Cor. iii. 1; Gal. vi. 1). It does not imply any special contrast, as with weaker brethren, Judaisers, indifferentists, etc., nor is there any reason for attributing to it an ironical sense, as Lightf., who compares 1 Cor. viii. 1.

Alf., Mey., Lightf., Ead., Beet, explain τέλειοι as 'mature,' 'advanced in Christian experience.'

τοῦτο φρονῶμεν: For φρον., see on i. 7. A more delicate quality is given to the exhortation by Paul's associating himself with his readers. (Comp. Rom. v. 1.)

The *immediate* reference of τοῦτο is to vs. 13, 14. Let us beware of thinking that our attainment is such as to make further striving unnecessary. 'Let us rather cherish that humble self-estimate which shall stimulate us to press toward the mark for the prize of our heavenward calling.' Nevertheless we cannot entirely separate these two verses from the whole representation of the Christian ideal from vs. 7. To have such an estimate of the greatness of the future as to forget the past, to have such a sense of the magnitude of the prize as to be constantly dissatisfied with former attainments and to be ever pressing on to something higher, to have such an ideal of Christ as to make one constantly feel his own littleness and insufficiency, — implies knowing Christ, being found in Christ, the casting aside of human righteousness, and such knowledge of the eternal possibilities of life in Christ as can be obtained only through mystical union with him.

καὶ εἴ τι ἑτέρως φρονεῖτε: Εἰ with the indicative implies a case which is quite supposable. Ἑτέρως, only here in N.T. 'Otherwise' than what? The point of comparison must not be too rigidly fixed at any detail of the context, such as the humble self-estimate and the earnest striving, or the great fundamental elements of Christian life, such as having the righteousness of faith, or being found in Christ; for ἑτέρως would express too feebly differences on points so vital, and Paul would have met such with something more than the promise of further revelations. The reference is loose, and concerns minor points in the characteristics of the τέλειοι generally considered. It was entirely possible that many of his readers, although having a genuine faith in Christ, and fully accepting the doctrine of justification by faith, might not have apprehended his profound views of mystical union, or have had the same clear ideas as himself concerning certain practical applications of doctrine; even that they might not have felt the impulse to higher spiritual attainment in its full stringency, and might have been inclined to regard his conduct and sentiments in certain particulars as exaggerated. Such facts are familiar to every Christian pastor. In the first Corinthian letter Paul insists on the unity of the body of Christ and the sin and danger of breaking it. Yet there were those in that church, many of them, no doubt, sincere and earnest believers, who did not grasp the application of this truth to the question of eating idol-meats. The force of φρονεῖτε should be carefully noted. It has been shown (ch. i. 7) that φρονεῖν signifies the general disposition of mind rather than the specific act of thought; and its use here shows that the apostle is not dealing specially, if at all, with differences of opinion, but rather with dispositions which underlie the spiritual life. The differences concern form, point of emphasis, extent of application, rather than substance or subject-matter.

Lightf. explains, 'if progress be your rule, though you are *at fault* on any subject, God will reveal this also to you'; translating ἑτέρως 'amiss.' So Ril. and Lum. There is classical precedent for this meaning, but it is entirely unknown in N.T.

καὶ τοῦτο: 'this also'; in addition to what God has already revealed. Τοῦτο refers to τι; 'this,' whatever it be, in which you may be otherwise minded. Not, 'shall reveal that you are wrong, and that I am right' (Œc., Calv., Grot.), nor 'shall show whether you are right or I' (Ew.), nor identical with the preceding τοῦτο (Beng.).

ἀποκαλύψει: Ἀποκαλύπτειν is to *unveil* something that is hidden, thus giving light and knowledge. (See Gal. i. 16, iii. 23; Eph. iii. 5.) Hence, of God's giving to his servants insight into divine truth (Mt. xi. 25, 27, xvi. 17; 1 Cor. ii. 10, xiv. 30. See Westcott, *Introd. to the Study of the Gospels*, p. 9; Trench, *Syn.* xciv.). Paul here means a revelation by the indwelling Spirit of God (comp. 1 Cor. ii. 10–16), either directly or through apostolic teaching, experience, or other means.

16. πλὴν: 'nevertheless'; 'notwithstanding.' (Comp. i. 18.) Though there may be things concerning which you need further revelation, 'nevertheless,' the condition of your receiving this is your walking according to your present attainment of light and knowledge.

εἰς ὃ: 'whereunto'; to whatever divinely revealed knowledge. Thus ὃ carries on the thought of ἀποκαλύψει. You need further revelation, nevertheless, walk according to such revelation as you have received. Notice the καὶ before τοῦτο (vs. 15), implying previous revelation.

ἐφθάσαμεν: 'we have attained.' The verb means, primarily, 'to come before,' 'to anticipate,' as 1 Thess. iv. 15. In N.T. it mostly loses the sense of anticipation, and signifies simply 'to come' or 'arrive at,' though occasionally with a sense of suddenness or surprise, as Mt. xii. 28; 1 Thess. ii. 16.

τῷ αὐτῷ στοιχεῖν: 'by that same walk.' That same knowledge already revealed. For the dative of the norm or standard, see Acts xv. 1; Gal. v. 16, 25, vi. 16; Win. xxxi. 6 *b*.

Στοιχεῖν from στοίχος, 'a row.' Hence 'to walk *in line*.' (Comp. Acts xxi. 24; Gal. vi. 16.) 'To march in battle-order' (Xen. *Cyr.* vi. 3, 34). Comp. συνστοιχεῖ (Gal. iv. 25), 'answereth to;' *i.e.* belongs to the same row or column with. Hence the letters of the alphabet were called στοιχεία, and also the elements or parts of a system. (See Gal. iv. 3, 9; Col. ii. 8; 2 Pet. iii. 10.)

The infin. here for the imperat., as Rom. xii. 15.

TR. after στοιχειν adds κανονι το αυτο φρονειν with ℵ[c] KLP, Syr.[utr]; this was inserted from Gal. vi. 16; DEFG, 31, 37, 80, It., Vulg., Goth., Arm., read το αυτο φρονειν τω αυτω στοιχειν; D[c] E, Vulg., Goth., Arm., add κανονι.

Alf., Mey., Dw., refer εἰς ὃ to the *grade* of moral and spiritual progress already attained. But this involves an awkwardness in the correlation of εἰς ὃ and τῷ αὐτῷ. Εἰς ὃ in that case would imply a *common* point of attainment which it is impossible to determine, and which does not agree with ἑτέρως φρονεῖτε. Lightf. explains τῷ αὐτῷ as the rule of faith opposed to works, and thinks that the words were added as a parting caution against 'the dogs,' 'the concision,' etc. He renders, 'let us walk by the same rule whereunto we attained.' But the rule is not the point of attainment, but only the way to it. Kl. explains ἐφ' ὃ of a *potential* attainment in the possession of the law of righteousness which Israel had not attained in its pursuit (Rom. ix. 30). This norm, in virtue of which they are new creatures, is the rule by which they are to walk. This seems forced.

17. Στοιχεῖν marks an advance of thought, from the principle and spirit of Christian life (φρονῶμεν) to its practice (περιπατεῖν). The following clause is awkwardly constructed, and lends itself to different interpretations.

Συνμιμηταί μου γίνεσθε, etc.: Render, 'Brethren, be ye unitedly imitators of me, and carefully observe those who walk as ye have us for an example.' The exhortation consists of two parts: 1. Unite in imitating me. 2. Observe those whose conduct resembles mine. Thus οὕτω and καθὼς are correlative, 'who walk *so*, *as* ye have,' etc. The awkwardness is in ἔχετε where we should expect ἔχουσι: 'observe those who walk as *they* have us,' etc. The phrase, however, is compressed, and means 'walk as you do who have me for an example.'

ἡμᾶς: Paul and his associates, as Timothy, Epaphroditus, and others known to the Philippians. Paul, in speaking of himself, occasionally uses the plural for the singular, as in 2 Cor. i. 23, 24, xi. 21; but the instances are not as numerous as is sometimes supposed. (See Lightf. on 1 Thess. ii. 4.)

Mey., Weiss, Ellic., render 'Be imitators *with others* (σὺν) who imitate me (viz. those described in the next clause), and mark those who walk *in this way* (οὕτω absol. and not correl. with καθὼς): *inasmuch as* (καθὼς) ye have *us* (*i.e.* both myself and those who thus walk) as an example.' This relieves the awkwardness of ἔχετε, but: 1. It lays unnecessary emphasis on Paul's calling attention to his own example. 2. It shifts σὺν from its emphatic position in an independent clause to the next clause, from which it is separated by καὶ and another verb. 3. It makes οὕτω περιπ. refer to συνμιμ. γίν., in which, indeed, it may be implied; but by the other construction it is directly and naturally related to what follows by περιπ. of vs. 18.

συνμιμηταί μου: Σὺν signifies the union of the subjects of γίνεσθε: 'be *unitedly* imitators of me.' Not as Beng., 'be imitators along with me in imitating Christ.' There is no reference to Christ in the context. Συνμιμ. only here in Bib. No self-conceit is implied in μοῦ. (Comp. 1 Cor. iv. 16, xi. 1; 1 Thess. i. 6; 2 Thess. iii. 7, 9.)

σκοπεῖτε: See on ii. 4, and comp. Rom. xvi. 17; 2 Cor. iv. 18.

τοὺς περιπατοῦντας: Paul often uses περιπατεῖν to describe conduct. (See Rom. vi. 4, viii. 1; 1 Cor. iii. 3; Gal. v. 16; Eph. ii. 2.) Never in the literal sense. In the Synop., on the other hand, it never occurs in the metaphorical sense, and but once in Acts (xxi. 21). The metaphorical sense appears in John, especially in the Epistles. (See Jn. (Ev.) viii. 12, xii. 35; 1 Jn. i. 6, 7, ii. 6, 11, etc.)

τύπον: Frequent in Paul; as Rom. v. 14, vi. 17; 1 Cor. x. 6, 11; 1 Thess. i. 7. Originally 'the impression left by a stroke' (τύπτειν). (See Jn. xx. 25.) Generally, 'image,' 'form,' always with a statement of the object which it represents. Hence 'pattern,' 'example.'

The exhortation is enforced by the contrast presented by those who follow a different example.

18. πολλοὶ: Precisely who are meant cannot be determined. According to most of the earlier expositors, the Judaisers described in vs. 2. So Lips. Some later authorities, as Weiss and Ril., the heathen. The majority of modern comms., antinomian Libertines of Epicurean tendencies: nominal Christians of immoral life. So Lightf., Mey., Kl., De W., Ellic., Alf., Beet.

Weiss (*Am. Journ. of Theol.* April, 1897, p. 391) is very severe upon this explanation. He reasons that it is impossible to conceive of such nominal Christians in the beloved Philippian church, and identifies the πολλοὶ with the κύνες of vs. 2, who, according to him, are the heathen. He cites Apoc. xxii. 15 for κύνες, and in his latest commentary, 2 Pet. ii. 22. But the latter passage is distinctly of apostate Christians.

περιπατοῦσιν: 'conduct themselves'; 'behave,' as vs. 17. It is unnecessary to supply a qualifying word, as κακῶς.

πολλάκις ἔλεγον: When he was at Philippi, or possibly in former letters. (See on vs. 1.)

νῦν: Contrasted with πολλ. ἔλ.

κλαίων: This deep emotion would more probably be excited by recreant Christians than by heathen whose sensuality and worldliness were familiar to the Apostle. He would be most sorrowfully affected by the reproach and injury to the church wrought by professing Christians, and by their own unhappy and perilous condition.

τοὺς ἐχθροὺς : In apposition with the preceding relative *οὓς*. (See Win. lix. 7.) The article marks the class which they represent.

τοῦ σταυροῦ τοῦ Χριστοῦ : Comp. Gal. vi. 12. *Σταυρὸς* is the usual N.T. word for Christ's cross. In Acts v. 30, x. 39, both quotations, *ξύλον* occurs; also in 1 Pet. ii. 24. Paul uses *ξύλον* in quotation, Gal. iii. 13, and in his speech at Pisidian Antioch as reported in Acts xiii. 29. (Comp. Ign. *Smyr.* i.; *Trall.* xi.) Different surmises (for they are little more) have been offered as to the particular point at which Paul conceives this enmity to be directed, such as the preaching of the law against the cross (Theo. Mop., Thdrt.); the hatred of the cross through fear of persecution (Grot., Beng.); the hatred of the gospel because the cross is its central truth (Calv., Weiss); hatred of the cross through reluctance to crucify self or to suffer with Christ (Chr., Mey.). Such limitations of the Apostle's thought are uncalled for. Enmity to the cross might include any or all of these particulars. Assuredly the title 'enemies of the cross' was justly applied to such as are described in vs. 19.

These enemies are more specifically described as to their character and destiny. Their destiny is significantly treated first.

19. *ὧν τὸ τέλος ἀπώλεια* : 'whose end is destruction.'

Τὸ marks the definiteness of the point to which their conduct tends. Τέλος is more than mere termination. Rather consummation; the point into which the whole series of transgressions finally gathers itself up. (Comp. Rom. vi. 21; 2 Cor. xi. 15; Heb. vi. 8.) Ἀπώλεια occurs in N.T. both in the physical and in the moral sense. For the former see Mt. xxvi. 8; Acts viii. 20. The latter is the more common, and Paul always uses it thus.

ὧν ὁ θεὸς ἡ κοιλία : Comp. Rom. xvi. 18; 2 Pet. ii. 13. The rare word *κοιλιοδαίμων*, 'one who makes a god of his belly,' occurs in the Κόλακες of the comic poet Eupolis, and in Athenæus. (Comp. Eurip. *Cyclops*, 335.) Xen. *Mem.* i. 6, 8, ii. 1, 2, has *δουλεύειν γαστρί*, 'to be the slave of the belly'; and Alciphro, ii. 4, *γαστρομαντεύομαι*, 'to divine by the belly.' The contrast appears in Rom. xiv. 17. The suggestion of Lips. (so Theo. Mop.) that the reference may be to Jewish laws about meats, is fanciful.

καὶ ἡ δόξα ἐν τῇ αἰσχύνῃ αὐτῶν : That in which they glory is their disgrace. Their so-called liberty is bondage to slavish lusts. For *δόξα*, see on i. 11. With *ἐν* supply *ἔστι*; 'consists in.' Beng., Mich., Storr, with Lips., refer *αἰσχύνῃ* to 'the concision' (vs. 2), and explain '*pudenda*.'

οἱ τὰ ἐπίγεια φρονοῦντες : 'who mind earthly things.' Their general disposition and moral tendency are worldly. (See on i. 7.) This is the root of their depravity. A contrast is suggested, probably intended, with τοῦτο φρονῶμεν, vs. 15. (Comp. Col. iii. 2.)

The change of construction to the nominative οἱ φρονοῦντες is variously explained. Win. xxix. 2, takes οἱ φρον. as a disconnected nominative with an exclamatory force. So De W., Lightf. Mey. and Hack. refer it to the logical subject of what precedes. Ellic. and Alf. regard it as a return to the primary construction, πολλοὶ περιπατοῦσιν. Of these explanations Win. is the least probable. The two others have grammatical precedent, but it is better to place the construction in the category of those instances which are not uncommon in N.T. and in class., where the nominative is introduced in a kind of apposition with what precedes. This is especially frequent in Apoc. (See Mk. vii. 19; Acts x. 37; Apoc. i. 5, vii. 4, xx. 2; Blass, § 31, 6; Jelf, 477.)

Τὰ ἐπίγ. φρον. is the basis of a new contrast. Their character and conduct mark them as belonging to this world; but we are citizens of a heavenly commonwealth.

20. ἡμῶν: Emphatic as contrasted with οἱ τὰ ἐπίγ. φρον. (vs. 19).

γὰρ: As in Gal. iii. 10, v. 5, confirming the statement concerning the one party by showing the opposite course or character of the other. The connection is with ἐπίγ. φρον. Their course is the opposite of ours; *for*, while they mind earthly things, our mind is set upon the interests of the heavenly commonwealth to which we belong. The repetition of φρονεῖν as marking the general moral tendency or disposition is noticeable.

τὸ πολίτευμα: 'commonwealth.' (Comp. πολιτεύεσθε, i. 27, note.)

No sharp distinction can be drawn between πολίτευμα and πολιτεία. Arist. makes πολίτευμα the concrete of πολιτεία, 'the government' as the expression of citizenship (Pol. iii. 6, 1, iii. 7, 2), and also identifies the two (Pol. iii. 13, 8, iv. 6, 8). He defines πολιτεία as 'commonwealth' (Pol. iii. 7, 3, iv. 8, 1, iv. 4, 19). In 2 Macc. iv. 11, viii. 17, πολιτεία is 'government'; in xiii. 14, apparently, 'state' or 'commonwealth.' Lightf. gives only two meanings of πολίτευμα, 'the state,' and 'the functions of citizens.' But it also means 'an act of administration'; 'a measure of government'; and 'a form of government.' In the absence of any permanent distinction, the rendering 'citizenship' (R.V. 'commonwealth' in marg.) is justifiable. The rendering of the A.V., 'conversation,' is founded on the original sense of that word, 'conduct or behaviour in intercourse with society.'

ὑπάρχει: 'is.' (See on ii. 6.) Due emphasis must be laid on the use of the present tense. The believer *now is*, in this present world, a citizen of the heavenly commonwealth. The πολίτευμα is not, therefore, as Mey., to be explained as Messiah's kingdom which has not yet appeared, and of which Christians are citizens only in an ideal or proleptic sense which is to be completely realised at the *parousia*. While it is true that the full realisation of the heavenly commonwealth will come with the *parousia*, it is no less true that those who are in Christ, whose 'life is hid with Christ in God' (Col. iii. 3), for whom 'to live is Christ' (Phil. i.

21), who are 'crucified with Christ' and live their present life by faith in him (Gal. ii. 20), are *now* members of the heavenly commonwealth, and live and act under its laws. Their allegiance is rendered to it. They receive their impulses to action and conduct from it. Their connection with it is the basis of their life of 'righteousness and peace and joy in the Holy Ghost' (Rom. xiv. 17), as distinguished from the life of belly-worship and worldliness. They *are* 'fellow-citizens with the saints and of the household of God (Eph. ii. 19). The commonwealth of believers *is* an actual fact on earth, because it is one with 'the Jerusalem that is above' (Gal. iv. 26). Comp. *Ep. to Diognetus*, 5, which describes Christians: ἐπὶ γῆς διατρίβουσιν ἀλλ' ἐν οὐρανῷ πολιτεύονται; apparently a reminiscence of this passage. See also Plat. *Repub.* 592, and the remarkable parall., Philo, *De Confus.* i. 416.

The consummation of this citizenship, however, is yet to come. As members of the heavenly commonwealth they are still pressing on in obedience to the upward call (vs. 14). Hence they are in an attitude of expectation.

ἐξ οὗ: 'whence': from heaven. Not from the πολίτευμα as Beng., Lips. The phrase is adverbial. (See Win. xxi. 3.)

Καὶ marks the correspondence of the expectation with the fact of the πολίτ. ἐν οὐρ.

ἀπεκδεχόμεθα: 'we await.' (Comp. 1 Thess. i. 10.) The word occurs but twice outside of Paul's letters (Heb. ix. 28; 1 Pet. iii. 20; comp. Rom. viii. 19, 23, 25; Gal. v. 5). It denotes *earnest* expectation. (See on ἀποκαραδοκία [i. 20].) Used habitually in N.T. with reference to the future manifestation of the glory of Christ or of his followers.

σωτῆρα: 'as Saviour.' Without the article, and predicative. Notice the emphatic position. The Lord is also to come as Judge; but they come not into judgment (Jn. iii. 18, v. 24). Among the privileges of Christians described in Heb. xii. 22–24, is that of drawing near to the Judge who is God of all. It is in the capacity of Saviour that they await him — the same capacity in which they have already received and known him. They look for him to complete their salvation, and therewith to deliver them from the sufferings which they have shared with him, and from the infirmities and limitations of the flesh. (Comp. Rom. viii. 19 ff.; 2 Cor. v. 4.)

To await him as Saviour from ἀπώλεια (Weiss) is quite out of place in a Christian's expectation of his Redeemer. Σωτήρ is found often in 2 Pet. and in the Pastorals. In the other Pauline epistles only Eph. v. 23. In six cases in the Pastorals and one in Jude, it is applied to God.

κύριον: See on ii. 11. Answering to the idea of πολίτευμα.

The special aspect in which the expected Saviour is viewed is that of a transformer, changing the mortal body of the believer into the likeness of his own glorified body.

21. ὃς μετασχηματίσει: 'who shall refashion.' For the verb see 1 Cor. iv. 6; 2 Cor. xi. 13–15. (See on ii. 8, and comp. ἀλλαγησόμεθα [1 Cor. xv. 51].) The verb signifies the change of the outward fashion (σχῆμα), the sensible vesture in which the human spirit is clothed. See Just. M. *Dial. Try.* i., where σχῆμα is used of the philosopher's dress.

The Jews looked merely for the restoration of the present body. Paul's idea includes an organic connection with the present body, but not its resuscitation. The new body is not identical with the present body. There is a change of σχῆμα, but not a destruction of personal identity. "There is a real connection or some correlation between the present and the future embodiment, but not identity of substance. The life, the principle of life, the individuality of it, shall remain unbroken, but 'the matter of life,' as the physiologists say, shall be changed" (Newman Smyth, *Old Faiths in New Light*, p. 364). Paul's conception is developed under the figure of the seed-corn in 1 Cor. xv.

τὸ σῶμα τῆς ταπεινώσεως ἡμῶν: 'the body of our humiliation.' Not as A.V. 'vile body.' To construe the phrase as a hendiadys is grammatically wrong (see on iii. 8), and the apostle is far from characterising the body which Christ honored by his tenancy as base in itself. Such a sense, moreover, would lend countenance to the Stoic contempt for the body. The meaning is, the body in which our mortal state of humiliation is clothed. This body is called 'the body of our humiliation,' primarily in order to emphasise the contrast between it and the glorified body of the Lord, but also with a subordinate reference to its weakness, its subjection to vanity, corruption, and death, — its sufferings, and the hindrances which it offers to Christian striving and spiritual attainment. (Comp. Rom. viii. 20–24.)

There may possibly be an implied contrast of the glory of the transformed body with that glory of the sensualists which is their shame (Ellic., Mey., Weiss), but this must not be pressed. Nor do I find in the expression the hortative element which Ellic. thinks that he detects, and likewise Kl., who says it is an exhortation to preserve their bodies as temples of the Holy Ghost.

σύμμορφον: '*that it may be* conformed.'

TR. adds εις το γενεσθαι αυτο with D$^{b \text{ and } c}$ EKLP, Syr.^{utr}. Probably supplied to meet the apparent difficulty of the appositional accusative.

The adjective denoting the effect of the transformation is added appositionally instead of forming an independent sentence with εἰς τὸ γενέσθαι αὐτό. (Comp. Mt. xii. 13; 1 Thess. iii. 13; and see Win. lxvi. 3 *g*.) As μετασχ. denoted change of outward fashion, σύμμορφ. denotes conformation to what is essential, permanent, and characteristic in a body which is the appropriate investiture of Christ's glorified condition — a 'spiritual body': a conformity which is inward and thorough, and not merely superficial. On the union of Christians with the spiritual life of Christ which belongs to the heavenly world (Rom. vi. 5), rests their hope that they shall be saved in his life and conformed to its heavenly investiture. (See Rom. v. 9, 10, viii. 10, 11.)

σώματι τῆς δόξης αὐτοῦ: 'to the body of his glory.' Not as A.V. 'glorious body,' by hendiadys, which dilutes and weakens the conception. See on vs. 8, and for other misapplications of the figure hendiadys, comp. A.V. Rom. viii. 21, 'glorious liberty'; 2 Cor. iv. 4, 'glorious gospel'; Eph. i. 19, 'mighty power'; 1 Pet. i. 14, 'obedient children.' The resurrection in the N.T. is habitually conceived in connection with corporeity, but a corporeity in keeping with the heavenly life. (See Weiss, *Bib. Theol.* Eng. §§ 19, 34.) The phrase 'body of his glory' signifies the body in which he is clothed in his glorified state, and which is the proper investiture of his heavenly glory; the form in which his perfect spiritual being is manifest. This glory is peculiarly and originally the glory of the incorruptible God, and therefore belongs to an embodiment which retains no trace of earthly materiality or corruption, but is altogether informed and determined by the higher vital principle (πνεῦμα) and is its appropriate organ (σῶμα πνευματικόν, 1 Cor. xv. 44). Accordingly this glorified body is no longer in antithesis to the πνεῦμα. It is the investiture which the πνεῦμα forms for itself, and which perfectly reveals it. In the resurrection, through which, as completed by the ascension, Christ received this body, he became wholly πνευματικός — a πνεῦμα ζωοποιοῦν (1 Cor. xv. 45), and therefore is called τὸ πνεῦμα (2 Cor. iii. 17). A foreshadowing of this appeared in his bodily manifestation between the resurrection and the ascension. His body appeared as πνευματικόν though not in its full manifestation as the σῶμα τῆς δόξης αὐτοῦ. (See Newman Smyth, *Old Faiths in New Light*, p. 358; Westcott, *Gospel of the Resurrection*, ch. ii. p. 19–21; J. Oswald Dykes, *Expositor*, 1st ser. iii. p. 161; Mey. on 1 Cor. xv. 45.)

The change into the body of Christ's glory is the consummation of the believer's life in him. (Comp. vs. 9–11.) The entire passage (vs. 9–21) is a complete statement of the Pauline doctrine of salvation:

1. The beginning, the intermediate stages, and the sum of all are Christ (vs. 9).

2. Justification by faith and mystical union with Christ form one conception — righteousness of God by faith and being found in Christ (vs. 9).

3. This conception is carried out on the line of mystical union with Christ: to know him, the power of his resurrection, and the fellowship of his sufferings, being made conformable to his death. Notice the repetition of *αὐτοῦ*, keeping Christ continually before the eye (vs. 10).

4. The life in Christ is marked by earnest striving to realise the ends for which the believer was grasped by Christ. He follows the beckoning of God which ever summons him heavenward, in order that he may at last win the heavenly prize (12–16).

5. Vital communion with Christ constitutes him a member of a heavenly commonwealth. To this his allegiance is rendered; by its laws his life is regulated; its members are his brethren. As a citizen of this commonwealth he eagerly awaits its consummation in the final triumph and eternal establishment of the Messianic kingdom (vs. 20).

6. Therefore, living in the power of Christ's resurrection, he awaits in hope the actual resurrection from the dead, wherein the saving power of Christ will be displayed in the change of the mortal bodies of all believers into the likeness of Christ's glorified body, and which will inaugurate the absolute and eternal dominion of the commonwealth of God (vs. 21).

The warrant for this confident expectation is the divine power of Christ to subject all things to himself.

κατὰ τὴν ἐνέργειαν τοῦ δύνασθαι αὐτὸν: 'according to the working whereby he is able'; or, more literally, 'according to the energy of his ability.'

κατὰ: The change is 'in accordance with' or 'appropriate to' Christ's power of universal subjection. The statement both as to the change itself and the power which effects it, is in accordance with 1 Cor. vi. 14, xv. 53, 55; Eph. i. 19.

Ἐνέργεια occurs only in Paul. It is power in exercise; "potentia in actu exserens" (Calv.), and is used in N.T. only of superhuman power. (See Col. i. 29, ii. 12; 2 Thess. ii. 9.) It is the active energy in which *δύναμις* displays itself. (Comp. Eph. iii. 7, and see on *ὁ ἐνεργῶν*, ii. 13.) The power or virtue which was in Christ when the woman touched the hem of his garment (Mk. v. 30; Lk. viii. 46) was *δύναμις*. In the healing of the woman it became *ἐνέργεια*.

καὶ: 'also' or 'even,' marking the measure of the power. Able not only to transform the body but *also* to subject all things to himself.

ὑπόταξαι: Originally 'to arrange' or 'marshal under.' Often simply 'to subject.' (See 1 Cor. xv. 27, 28; Eph. i. 22; Heb. ii. 8; Jas. iv. 7.)

τὰ πάντα: 'all things,' collectively, as vs. 8.

PAUL'S CONCEPTION OF RIGHTEOUSNESS BY FAITH.

M. Ménégoz, in his treatise *Le Péché et la Rédemption*, says that Phil. iii. 8–10 contains the most precise statement of the Pauline doctrine of justification by faith. Without assenting to his view that Christ was justified by his own death and resurrection, I agree with him as to the importance of the statement contained in these verses. It does not contradict any previous utterance of Paul, nor does it present any new feature; but it combines and exhibits as a single conception what are commonly regarded as two distinct elements of the righteousness of faith. These two elements are assumed to be separately treated in the Epistle to the Romans. They are, the initial, objective, judicial act of declaring righteous, whereby a believer is placed in a state of reconciliation with God, and the establishment, through faith, of a vital union with Christ; or, to put the matter more briefly, the righteousness of faith viewed as objective justification and as subjective sanctification. I say 'regarded' and 'assumed,' because, both on the ground of this passage and of the Epistle to the Romans, I do not regard this separation as justifiable. For I think that these two elements are inseparably united in the Apostle's conception of righteousness by faith. The distinction between justification and sanctification I regard as largely technical. They represent, it is true, respectively, the initiation and the consummation of the work of salvation; but Paul uses ἁγιασμός both of the *state* and of the *process* of sanctification; and that word, in Rom. vi. 19, is associated with the 'walk in newness of life' rather than with the consummation of subjection to righteousness. Having become servants of righteousness, the readers stand committed to an *economy* of sanctification, in which they are to 'perfect holiness in the fear of the Lord' (2 Cor. vii. 1. See Sanday on Rom. vi. 19). The point is well stated by Liddon in his *Analysis of Romans*, pp. 17, 18: "The δικαιοσύνη which God gives includes these two elements, — acquittal of the guilt of sin, or justification in the narrower sense of the word, and the communication of a new moral life, 'that the ordinance of the law might be fulfilled in us' (Rom. viii. 4). These two sides of the gift of δικαιοσύνη can only be separated in thought: in fact they are inseparable. . . . The true righteousness is one, not two or more. The maxim 'justitia alia justificationis, sanctificationis alia' is not Paul's. Paul knows nothing of an external righteousness which is reckoned without being given to man; and the righteousness which faith receives is not external only, but internal; not imputed only, but imparted to the believer. Justification and sanctification may be distinguished by the student as are the arterial and nervous systems in the human body; but in the living body they are coincident and inseparable."

I think that, so far as justification is a judicial act following upon repentance and faith, it is regarded by Paul as the initial stage of a condition of actual inward righteousness, which is to develop itself in the believer's experience as fruit from seed. (Comp. Lips. *Hand-Com. Ep. to Rom.* Einl. p. 82.) Hence I differ from Professor Bruce (*St. Paul's Conception of Christianity*, p. 158 ff., Amer. ed.), who claims that the two aspects of justification are separately treated by Paul in Romans. He says: "He does not refer to the subjective aspect of faith as a renewing power till he has finished his exposition of the doctrine of justification. He takes up faith's function in establishing a vital union with Christ in the sixth chapter. . . . Does not this amount to the exclusion of faith's sanctifying function from the grounds of justification?" I think not. For, as Professor Bruce admits, Paul already alludes to the subjective aspect of justification in the opening of the fifth chapter. Being justified, we have peace with God, joy in hope of glory, in tribulation, and in God himself. But, what is more to the point, Paul, in the third and fourth chapters, does not treat of the *operation* of justification. His main point is the *essential quality* of justification, as being by faith and not by works of the law. When he does take up the operation of justification in ch. vi., he treats the two aspects in combination. He does not confine himself to what follows justification. He begins with the death to sin. With Christ we die to sin; we are raised up with him unto a walk in newness of life. Union with him by the likeness of his death implies union with him by the likeness of his resurrection. Our old man was crucified with him, that the body of sin might be done away, that so we should no longer be in bondage to sin. "But if we died with Christ, we believe that we shall also live with him (here, not only hereafter); knowing that Christ, being raised from the dead, dieth no more; death no more hath dominion over him. For the death that he died, he died unto sin once for all: but the life that he liveth, he liveth unto God. Even so reckon ye also yourselves to be dead unto sin, but alive unto God in Christ Jesus." Comp. "be found in him" (Phil. iii. 9).

(1) In our passage Paul represents the righteousness of faith as a *real* righteousness in the believer. It is not founded upon human merit; it is not a righteousness of legal obedience. It proceeds from God and comes to man through faith in Christ (vs. 9). It is not perfect (vs. 12–14). None the less it is an actual righteousness in the man. Justification contemplates rightness — right living, feeling, and thinking. Faith is not a substitute for this rightness. It is its generative principle; its informing

quality. God's plan of salvation is not intended to effect, by a mere legal adjustment, something which cannot be an actual fact. It is not true that God practically gives up the possibility of righteous men, and merely allows the perfect righteousness of Jesus Christ to stand for it. God's intent is to make men personally righteous. Paul does not teach, nor is it anywhere taught in Scripture, that the requirement of personal righteousness is fulfilled for man by some one else, and that man has only to accept this substitute by faith. Rather Paul declares explicitly that God predestined his children 'to be conformed to the image of his Son' (Rom. viii. 29).

I shall not enter upon the discussion of the meaning of δικαιοῦν, since the question does not turn upon that. It may be conceded that the *dominant* sense of that word is forensic, 'to declare or pronounce righteous.' That that sense can be vindicated in every instance, I very much doubt. (See E. P. Gould on "Paul's Use of δικαιοῦν," *Amer. Journ. of Theol.* vol. i. No. 1, and W. A. Stevens in vol. i. No. 2.) But, that question apart, it should be noted that the sense of a declared or imputed righteousness, if it belong to δικαιοσύνη at all, is peculiar to Paul. Elsewhere it has the meaning of personal rightness, or righteous quality. In the LXX it occurs in nine instances as the translation of חֶסֶד, 'kindness'; while צְדָקָה, 'justice,' usually translated by δικαιοσύνη, is, in nine cases, rendered by ἐλεημοσύνη, and three times by ἔλεος. In Mt. vi. 1, the TR, with the later uncials and most cursives, read ἐλεημοσύνην for δικαιοσύνην; while א[a] gives δόσιν. (See Hatch, *Essays in Biblical Greek*, p. 49 ff.)

(2) This conception of a real righteousness in the believer is opposed to the familiar dogmatic explanation that δικαιοσύνη πίστεως is not a personal but an imputed quality. According to this, the righteousness is not in the man, but in Christ; and Christ's righteousness is imputed, or reckoned, or set down to his account through his faith. This imputation works no subjective change in the man. It is merely placing to his account the righteousness of another. He is, though not actually righteous, judicially declared to be righteous. Thus Dr. Hodge (*Syst. Theol.* iii. p. 144 ff.): The imputation of the righteousness of Christ to a believer for his justification "does not and cannot mean that the righteousness of Christ is infused into the believer, or in any way so imparted to him as to change or constitute his moral character. Imputation never changes the inward, subjective state of the person to whom the imputation is made. . . . When righteousness is imputed to the believer, he does not thereby become subjectively righteous." Thus justification, having its foundation in the imputation of Christ's righteousness, is only a declarative act whereby a man is pronounced righteous without any actual righteousness in him answering to the declaration, but solely on

the ground of another's righteousness, which, in some inexplicable way, is transferred to his credit. This is simply a legal fiction which reflects upon the truthfulness of God. God declares a man righteous when he is not righteous. "To Paul," says Sabatier, "the word of God is always creative and full of power. It always produces an actual effect. In declaring a man justified, therefore, it actually and directly creates in him a new beginning of righteousness" (*Apostle Paul*, Eng. Trans. p. 300).

(3) This is clearly not the conception expressed in this passage. The righteousness of faith which Paul here desires for himself is a winning Christ and a being in Christ. This righteousness is first described generally as knowing Christ, and then, more specifically, as knowing the power of his resurrection and the fellowship of his sufferings, and being made conformable unto his death; that is to say, the righteousness of God by faith is a being and dwelling in Christ in such wise as that his resurrection, his sufferings, his death, become actual parts of Paul's experience and active forces in it. Christ is not merely apprehended as an object of trust. He is not merely known as an objective personality. The believer is taken up into his life; and his life in turn possesses the believer, and becomes his informing principle and prime motor. (See Gal. ii. 20.)

In short, the conception of the righteousness of faith here presented is not that of an external righteousness made over to the believer by a legal declaration, but that of a righteousness which is a real fact in the man, springing from union with the personal Christ. In this mystical union the life and power of Christ are transfused into the believer's life, so that, in a sense, the personality of Christ becomes his; so that he can say, 'for me to live is Christ,' and 'not I live but Christ liveth in me.' The old man, the natural *ego*, is crucified with Christ; the new man is raised up, and, in the power of Christ's risen life, walks in newness of life, in fellowship with the Father and with his Son Jesus Christ. All the righteousness which inheres in that perfect personality becomes potentially his from the moment that faith puts him into living connection with it. All the experience of Christ's life becomes a fact and a power in his experience. Did Christ die to sin? He also dies to sin. Was Christ justified from sin by death? So likewise is he. Did Christ rise from the dead? He rises from the death of sin, besides sharing finally in Christ's physical resurrection. The knowledge of Christ's death and resurrection is not merely an insight into the historical meaning of those facts. Did Christ suffer? The heavenly nature which he receives from Christ insures for him, as it did for Christ, the contradiction of sinners against himself. Was Christ perfected through suffering? He attains perfection by the same road. Does Christ live unto God? He is alive unto God through Jesus Christ, and all the powers of that divine life descend upon him and work in him to conform him to the image of the Son of God.

Says Calvin (*Inst.* iii. 1): "First, it is to be held that, so long as Christ is outside of us and we are separated from him, whatever he has suffered and done for the salvation of the human race is useless and without significance to us. Therefore, in order that he may communicate to us what he has received from the Father, he must become ours and dwell in us. Hence he is called our 'head,' and 'the first-born among many brethren'; while we in turn are said to be ingrafted into him and to put him on, because whatever he possesses is nothing to us until we coalesce into one with him." And again (xi. 10): "Christ, having become ours, makes us partakers of the gifts with which he is endowed. *We do not therefore view him as outside of us, so that his righteousness is imputed to us;* but because we put on himself and are ingrafted into his body, he has deigned to make us one with himself. Therefore we boast that we have his righteousness." So, too, Luther (*Werke*, Erlang. Ausg. 37, 441): "Christ is God's grace, mercy, wisdom, strength, comfort, and blessedness. I say not as some, *causaliter;* that is, that he gives righteousness, and remains without. For in that case righteousness is dead, nay, it is never given. Christ is there *himself*, like the light and heat of the fire, which are not where the sun and the fire are not."

(4) This passage presents a conception of faith different from that implied in the imputative theory. According to that, faith is merely a medium by which the man is put into contact with something outside of himself — "a mere hand," as Professor Bruce puts it, "to lay hold of an external righteousness." According to Paul's teaching here, an ethical quality inheres in faith. Faith is a moral energy. It "*works* by love" (Gal. v. 6). This accords with Heb. xi., where faith is exhibited as the generator of moral heroism. Righteousness, as already observed, is effected in a believer by the transfusion into him of Christ's life and character, not by Christ's righteousness being placed to his account. To assume the latter is to fall back from the gospel upon the law. Paul says, "not having a righteousness of my own which is of the law"; but if the righteousness of faith is legally and forensically imputed, it *is* of the law. Righteousness has its roots in personal relation to God. Sin is more than bad conduct. Bad conduct is only the result of personal separation and estrangement from the Father, God. The terrible significance of sin lies in the break between a human life and its divine source; and the attainment of righteousness is possible only through the reëstablishment of the original birth-relation, as Christ declared in the words, "Ye must be born anew." The mere genealogical fact of sonship must be translated into a living, personal relation. This is possible only through faith. A handbook of laws will not effect it. Rules will

not establish personal relations. Precepts will not put a son's heart into a man. He will not love to order, nor obey because he is bidden, nor trust because a trustworthy object is commended to him, nor be meek and merciful because it is right to be so. Being righteous is not a matter of assent to a proposition. It is a matter of surrender to a person. Such surrender comes about only through faith, because only faith has in it that element which draws personalities, lives, hearts together. Therefore faith does not count *instead* of righteousness. It counts as *making for* (εἰς) righteousness; with a view to righteousness; as tending to righteousness, just as the corn of wheat counts for the full corn in the ear. Therein is its value. It is counted for what it is, not for what it is not. It is the prime agent in righteousness. The righteousness which is of God becomes in man the righteousness of faith, because in faith, which inaugurates the vital union of the man with Christ, which constitutes personal and not mere legal relation, lie enfolded all the possibilities of righteousness. Faith is presumptive righteousness. It is the native element in which righteousness evolves itself. Righteousness is begun, continued, and perfected in the exercise of the faith which holds the life in living contact with the personal source of holiness; in the trust and self-surrender which make possible the inpouring and appropriation of all heavenly forces. "With the heart man believeth unto righteousness" (Rom. x. 10). In Christ the believer *becomes* the righteousness of God (2 Cor. v. 21). "Faith is that temper of sympathetic and immediate response to another's will which belongs to a recognised relation of vital communion. It is the spirit of confident surrender which can only be justified by an inner identification of life. Faith is the power by which the conscious life attaches itself to God; it is an apprehensive motion of the living spirit by which it intensifies its touch on God; it is an instinct of surrender by which it gives itself up to the fuller handling of God; it is an affection of the will by which it presses up against God, and drinks in divine vitality with quickened receptivity" (Henry Scott Holland, in *Lux Mundi*, pp. 17, 18). There is no true faith in Christ without the indwelling of Christ. Paul makes the latter the criterion of the former (2 Cor. xiii. 5).

Pfleiderer's treatment of this subject is interesting and suggestive. (See *Paulinismus*, ch. iv.)

IV. 1–9. VARIOUS EXHORTATIONS TO UNITY, JOY, FORBEARANCE, TRUSTFULNESS, PRAYER, ATTENTION TO ALL VIRTUES, AND THE PRACTICE OF ALL THAT THEY HAVE LEARNED FROM PAUL; WITH ASSURANCES OF THE PRESENCE, GUARDIANSHIP, AND PEACE OF GOD

In view of this glorious future, do you, my brethren beloved, continue steadfast in the Lord. I learn that Euodia and Syntyche are at variance. I beseech them to be reconciled; and I entreat you, Synzygus, who are justly so named, to use your influence to this end; for those women were my helpers in the gospel work, along with Clement and other faithful laborers. Rejoice in the Lord, always. I repeat it, rejoice. Let all men see your forbearing spirit; and in no case be anxious, for the Lord is at hand. Commit every matter to God in prayer, and pray always with thankful hearts; and God's peace which, better than any human device, can lift you above doubt and fear, shall guard your hearts and thoughts in Christ Jesus. Finally, my brethren, take account of everything that is venerable, just, pure, lovely, and of good report — in short, of whatever virtue there is, and of whatever praise attaches to it. Practise what you have learned from me, and the God of peace shall be with you.

1. ὥστε: 'so that'; 'accordingly.' (Comp. Mt. xii. 12; Rom. vii. 4, 12; 1 Cor. xv. 58; Phil. ii. 12.) Connected immediately with iii. 20, 21; but through those verses with the whole of ch. iii., since in heavenly citizenship are gathered up all the characteristics which Paul in that chapter has commended to his readers. This verse may therefore be regarded as the proper conclusion of ch. iii.

ἐπιπόθητοι: 'longed for.' A hint of the pain caused by his separation from them. Only here in N.T. (Comp. Clem. *ad Cor.* lxv.) The verb ἐπιποθεῖν occurs mostly in Paul. (See Rom. i. 11; 2 Cor. v. 2; Phil. i. 8, ii. 26.) Ἐπιποθία only in Rom. xv. 23. Ἐπιπόθησις, 2 Cor. vii. 7, 11. (See on i. 8.)

χαρὰ καὶ στεφανός μου: 'my joy and crown.' (Comp. 1 Thess. ii. 19.) Χαρὰ by metonymy for the subject of joy. Στεφανός in class. mostly of the woven crown — the chaplet awarded to the victor in the games; a wreath of wild olive, green parsley, bay, or pine; or the garland placed on the head of a guest at a banquet.

(See *Athen.* xv. p. 685; Aristoph. *Ach.* 636; Plat. *Symp.* 212.) So mostly in N.T., though στεφανός occurs with χρυσοῦν (Apoc. xiv. 14). The kingly crown is διάδημα, found only in Apoc. The distinction is not strictly observed in Hellenistic Greek. (See Trench, *Syn.* xxiii.) Neither χαρὰ nor στεφανός applied to the Philippians is to be referred to the future, as Calv., Alf. They express Paul's sense of joy and honor in the Christian fidelity of his readers. (Comp. Sir. i. 11, xxv. 6.)

οὕτως στήκετε: 'so stand fast.' 'So,' as I have exhorted you, and as becomes citizens of the heavenly commonwealth. Not, 'so as ye do stand,' as Beng., Calv. For στήκετε see on i. 27. The particle ὥστε with the imperative retains its consecutive force, but instead of a *fact* consequent upon what precedes, there is a consequent exhortation.

ἐν κυρίῳ: With the exception of Apoc. xiv. 13 only in Paul, who uses it more than forty times. See on ἐν Χριστῷ Ἰησοῦ (i. 1). Denoting the sphere or element in which steadfastness is to be exhibited. (Comp. 1 Thess. iii. 8.)

ἀγαπητοί: repeated with affectionate emphasis.

B, 17, Cop., Syr.^{sch}, add μου.

Two prominent women in the church are urged to become reconciled to each other.

2. Εὐοδίαν — Συντύχην: 'Euodia — Syntyche.' Not 'Euodias,' as A.V. Both are female names; see αὐταῖς (vs. 3). Both occur in inscriptions, and there are no instances of masculine forms. The activity of the Macedonian women in coöperating with Paul appears from Acts xvii. 4, 12.

I am a little doubtful, however, as to Lightfoot's view that a higher social influence was assigned to the female sex in Macedonia than was common among the civilised nations of antiquity. I fail to find any notice of this elsewhere. Lightf.'s inference is drawn wholly from inscriptions which do not appear to be decisive. For example, all the inscriptions which he cites to show that monuments in honor of women were erected by public bodies, distinctly indicate Roman influence. The names are Roman, and perpetuate the memory of different Roman *gentes*, a point which would naturally be emphasised in a Roman *colonia* distant from the mother city. His assertion, moreover, that the active zeal of Macedonian women is without a parallel in the apostle's history elsewhere, seems open to question in the light of the closing salutations of the Epistle to the Romans. Klöpper thinks that the names Euodia and Syntyche represent two women in each of whose houses a separate congregation assembled, the one Jewish-Christian and the other Gentile-Christian. Lipsius thinks this possible. For some of the fanciful interpretations of these two names, see Introd. vi. Theo. Mop. mentions a story he had heard to the effect that they were a married pair, the latter name being Syntyches, and that the husband was the converted jailer of Philippi. The climax is reached by Hitzig (*Krit. paulin. Br.* 5 ff.), who affirms that Euodia and Syntyche were reproductions of the patriarchs Asher and Gad; their sex having been changed in the transition from one language to the other; and that they represent the Greek and the Roman elements in the church.

παρακαλῶ: 'I exhort.' See on παράκλησις (ii. 1). The repetition of the word emphasises the separate exhortation to each.

τὸ αὐτὸ φρονεῖν: 'to be of the same mind.' (See on ii. 2.)

ἐν κυρίῳ: With τ. αὐ. φρον. In that accord of which the Lord is the bond: each individually in Christ, and each therefore at one with the other.

3. ναὶ: 'yea.' The reading καὶ has almost no support. (Comp. Mt. xv. 27; Rom. iii. 29; Philem. 20.) The preceding exhortation is enforced by introducing a third party. 'I have urged Euodia and Syntyche to live in harmony; *yes*, and I entreat you also,' etc.

ἐρωτῶ καὶ σέ: 'I beseech thee also.' Ἐρωτᾷν originally 'to question,' as Lk. xxii. 68; Jn. ix. 21. Only in that sense in class. The meaning 'to entreat' belongs to later Greek. Thus rendered, it usually signifies to ask a *person;* not to ask a *thing* of a person; and to ask a person *to do;* rarely *to give*. See Trench, *Syn*. xl.; but his distinction between ἐρωτᾷν and αἰτεῖν does not hold. (See Ezra Abbot, *The Authorship of the Fourth Gospel and Other Critical Essays*.)

γνήσιε Σύνζυγε: 'Synzygus, who art rightly so named.' The A.V. 'yoke-fellow,' gives the correct sense of the proper name, and γνήσιε marks the person addressed as one to whom the name is justly applied. (See on γνησίως, ii. 20. Comp. ἑτεροζυγοῦντες, 2 Cor. vi. 14.) It is true that this proper name has no confirmation from inscriptions; but such descriptive or punning names are very common, as Onesimus, Chrestus, Chresimus, Onesiphorus, Symphorus, etc.

The attempts to identify the person referred to are numerous, and the best are only guesses. Clem. Alex., Paul's own wife; Chr., the husband or brother of Euodia or Syntyche; Lightf., Epaphroditus. But it is improbable that Paul would have written thus in a letter of which Epaph. was the bearer. Others, Timothy or Silas; Ellic. and De W., the chief bishop at Philippi. Wiesel., Christ; ναί introducing a prayer.

συλλαμβάνου αὐταῖς: 'help those (women).' Lit. 'take hold with.' Assist them in reconciling their differences. (Comp. Lk. v. 7.)

Lips., following Chr. and Theoph., explains the verb in a general sense: 'interest yourself in them.' Grot. refers it to their support as widows.

αἵτινες: 'inasmuch as they.' See on ἅτινα (iii. 7). Not as A.V. 'who.' The double relative classifies them among Paul's helpers, and gives a reason why Synzygus should promote their reconciliation.

συνηθλησάν μοι: 'they labored with me.' The verb only here and i. 27, on which see note. It indicates an activity attended with danger and suffering. (Comp. 1 Thess. ii. 2.)

ἐν τῷ εὐαγγελίῳ: the sphere of their labors. (Comp. Rom. i. 9; 1 Thess. iii. 2.)

μετὰ καὶ Κλήμεντος: Construe with *συνηθ*. 'Who labored with me in the gospel along with Clement and others.' The position of *καὶ* between the preposition and the noun is unusual, and shows that the force of the preposition extends over the whole clause.

Lightf. takes *μετὰ Κλήμ.* with *συλλαμβ.* According to this, Paul calls upon Clement and the rest whose names are in the book of life to help the women. But the relative clause *ὧν τὰ ὀνόμ.*, etc., associates itself more naturally with *συνηθ.* Paul gives this confidential commission to one person, and not to an indefinite number.

Philippi was probably the scene of the labors referred to, since Paul speaks of them as familiarly known. Clement appears to have been a Philippian Christian who assisted in the foundation of the church at Philippi. This is suggested by *τῶν λοιπῶν*.

The attempt to identify him with Clement of Rome, which originated with Origen (*In Joann.* i. 29), is generally abandoned. (See Lightf. *Comm.* p. 168 ff.; Langen, *Geschichte der Römischen Kirche*, Bd. i. S. 84; Möller, *Kirchengeschichte*, i. 89; Salmon's art. "Clemens Romanus" in Smith and Wace, *Dict. Chn. Biog.*)

συνεργῶν: Comp. ii. 25. Only once in N.T. outside of Paul's letters. (See 3 Jn. 8.)

ὧν τὰ ὀνόματα ἐν βίβλῳ ζωῆς: 'whose names are in the book of life.' Supply *ἐστί*, not *εἴη*, 'may they be,' as Beng., who says, "they seem to have been already dead, for we generally follow such with wishes of that sort." The names are in the book of life, though not mentioned in the apostle's letter. The expression *βίβλος* or *βιβλίον τῆς ζωῆς* in N.T. is peculiar to Apoc. This is the only exception, and the only case in which *ζωῆς* occurs without the article. (See Apoc. iii. 5, xiii. 8, xvii. 8, xx. 12, 15, xxi. 7, xxii. 19.) It is an O.T. metaphor, drawn from the civil list or register in which the names of citizens were entered. The earliest reference to it is Ex. xxxii. 32. (Comp. Is. iv. 3; Ezek. xiii. 9; Dan. xii. 1.) To be enrolled in the book of life is to be divinely accredited as a member of God's commonwealth (comp. Lk. x. 20), so that the expression falls in with *τὸ πολίτευμα ἐν οὐρανοῖς* (iii. 20). To be blotted out from the book of life (Ex. xxxii. 32, 33; Ps. lxix. 28) is to be disfranchised, cut off from fellowship with the living God and with his kingdom. The phrase was also in use by Rabbinical writers. (See Wetst.) Thus in the Targum on Ezek. xiii. 9: "In the book of eternal life which has been written for the just of the house of Israel, they shall not be written." Any reference to the doctrine of predestination is entirely out of place. Flacius, cit. by Mey., justly observes that it is not *fatalis quaedam electio* which is pointed to, but that they are described as written in the book of life because possessing the true righteousness which is of Christ.

Exhortations to the Church at Large

4. χαίρετε: 'rejoice'; the keynote of the epistle. Not 'farewell.' (See on iii. 1.)

πάντοτε: With a look at the future no less than at the present, and at the possibility of future trials. Only as their life shall be ἐν κυρίῳ will they have true joy.

πάλιν ἐρῶ: 'again I will say it.' As if he had considered all the possibilities of sorrow. 'In spite of them all, I will repeat it — rejoice.'

Not as Beng., joining πάντοτε with the second χαίρετε, 'again I will say, always rejoice.'

5. τὸ ἐπιεικὲς ὑμῶν: 'your forbearance.' From εἰκός, 'reasonable'; hence, 'not unduly rigorous.' Aristot. *Nich. Eth.* v. 10, contrasts it with ἀκριβοδίκαιος, 'severely judging.' The idea is, 'do not make a rigorous and obstinate stand for what is your just due.' Comp. Ign. *Eph.* x., ἀδελφοὶ αὐτῶν εὑρεθῶμεν τῇ ἐπιεικείᾳ: 'Let us show ourselves their brothers by our forbearance.'

Ἐπιεικής in N.T., 1 Tim. iii. 3; Tit. iii. 2, where it is joined with ἄμαχος; 1 Pet. ii. 18; Jas. iii. 17, with ἀγαθὸς and εὐπειθής. Ἐπιείκεια, Acts xxiv. 4; 2 Cor. x. 1; the latter with πραΰτης. LXX, ἐπιεικής, Ps. lxxxvi. (lxxxv.) 5: ἐπιείκεια, Sap. ii. 19; 2 Macc. ii. 22; 3 Macc. iii. 15. Ἐπιεικῶς, not in N.T., 1 Sam. xii. 22; 2 K. vi. 3; 2 Macc. ix. 27. The neuter adjective with the article = the abstract noun ἐπιείκεια. (Comp. τὸ χρηστὸν, Rom. ii. 4; τὸ μωρὸν, 1 Cor. i. 25.)

Mey. remarks that the disposition of Christian joyfulness must elevate men quite as much above strict insistence on their rights and claims as above solicitude.

πᾶσιν ἀνθρώποις: Not to your fellow-Christians only.

ὁ κύριος ἐγγύς: 'the Lord is near.' For κύριος, see on ii. 11. In the Gospels usually 'God.' In Paul mostly 'Christ,' and more commonly with the article (Win. xix. 1). The phrase expresses the general expectation of the speedy second coming of Christ. Comp. Μαρὰν ἀθά (1 Cor. xvi. 22), 'the Lord will come,' or 'the Lord is here.' See also Rom. xiii. 12; Jas. v. 8. Ἐγγύς, of time. The connection of thought may be either with what precedes, or with what follows; *i.e.* the near approach of Christ may be regarded as a motive to either forbearance or restfulness of spirit. Most modern expositors connect with the former, but the thought proceeds upon the line of the latter. Apart from this fact there is nothing to prevent our connecting ὁ κύρ. ἐγ. with both, as Alf.

and Ellic. 'Be forbearing; the Lord is at hand who will right all wrongs and give to each his due. Be not anxious. The Lord is at hand. Why be concerned about what is so soon to pass away? The Lord's coming will deliver you from all earthly care.' (Comp. 1 Cor. vii. 29–31.)

Some of the earlier interpreters, taking ἐγγύς in a local sense, explain of the perpetual nearness of Christ; as Mt. xxviii. 20 (Aug.). Others, taking κύριος = 'God,' of the helpful presence of God's providence; as Ps. xxxiv. 18, cxix. 151, cxlv. 18 (am E., Calov., Ril.). But this does not accord with the Pauline usage of κύριος.

6. μηδὲν μεριμνᾶτε: 'in nothing be anxious.' Μεριμνᾷν occurs most frequently in the Gospels. In Paul only here and 1 Cor. From the root μερ or μαρ, which appears in the Homeric μερμηρίζειν, 'to be anxious,' 'to debate anxiously.' The verb may mean either 'to be full of anxiety,' or 'to ponder or brood over.' In N.T. usage it does not always involve the idea of worry or anxiety. See, for inst., 1 Cor. vii. 32, xii. 25; Phil. ii. 20. In other cases that idea is emphasised, as here, Mt. xiii. 22; Lk. x. 41. (See Prellwitz, *Etymol. Wörterb. d. griech. Sprache*, sub μέριμνα; Schmidt, *Synon.* 86, 3; *W. St.* on Mt. vi. 25.) The exhortation is pertinent always to those who live the life of faith (1 Pet. v. 7), and acquired additional force from the expectation of the speedy coming of the Lord.

ἐν παντὶ: 'in everything.' Antithesis to μηδὲν. The formula is found only in Paul. Not 'on every occasion,' supplying καιρῷ (see Eph. vi. 18), nor, as Ril., including the idea of time; nor, as Vulg., 'in omni oratione et obsecratione,' construing παντὶ with προσ. κ. δεήσ. Prayer is to include all our interests, small and great. Nothing is too great for God's power; nothing too small for his fatherly care.

τῇ προσευχῇ καὶ τῇ δεήσει: 'by prayer and supplication.' *The* (or *your*) prayer and *the* supplication appropriate to each case. In N.T. the two words are joined only by Paul. (See Eph. vi. 18; 1 Tim. ii. 1, v. 5; LXX; Ps. vi. 10, lv. [liv.] 2.) For the distinction, see on i. 4. The dative is instrumental.

μετὰ εὐχαριστίας: 'with thanksgiving.' The thanksgiving is to go with the prayer, *in everything* (comp. Col. iii. 17); for although the Christian may not recognise a particular ground of thanksgiving on the special occasion of his prayer, he has always the remembrance of past favors and the consciousness of present blessings, and the knowledge that all things are working together for good for him (Rom. viii. 28). This more comprehensive application of εὐχαριστία may explain the absence of the article, which appears with both προσευχῇ and δεήσει, and which Paul uses with εὐχαρ. in only two instances (1 Cor. xiv. 16; 2 Cor. iv. 15), where the reason is evident. Rilliet observes that the Christian, "being, as it were, suspended between blessings received and blessings hoped for, should always give thanks and always ask. Remembrance and supplication are the two necessary elements of every Christian prayer." Thanksgiving expresses, not only the spirit of gratitude, but the spirit of submission, which excludes anxiety, because it recognises in the will of God the sum of its desires. So Calv., "Dei voluntas votorum nostrorum summa est." Paul lays great stress upon the duty of thanksgiving. (See Rom. i. 21, xiv. 6; 2 Cor. i. 11, iv. 15, ix. 11, 12; Eph. v. 20; Col. i. 3; 2 Thess. i. 3.)

τὰ αἰτήματα ὑμῶν: 'your requests.' Only here; Lk. xxiii. 24; 1 Jn. v. 15. According to its termination, αἴτημα is 'a thing requested,' and so in all the N.T. instances. Vulg. 'petitiones.'

In class. it sometimes has the sense of αἴτησις, 'the act of requesting,' which does not occur in N.T., as Plato, *Repub.* viii. 566 B. On the other hand, αἴτησις is found in the sense of αἴτημα, as Hdt. vii. 32; LXX; 3 K. ii. 16, 20.

γνωριζέσθω: 'be declared' or 'made known.' (See on i. 22.) As if God did not know them. (Comp. Mt. vi. 8.)

πρὸς τὸν θεόν: Not merely '*to* God,' but implying intercourse with God, as well as the idea of direction. (See on ii. 30; and comp. Mt. xiii. 56; Mk. vi. 3, ix. 16; Jn. i. 1; 1 Cor. xvi. 6.)

7. καὶ: Consecutive; 'and so.'

ἡ εἰρήνη τοῦ θεοῦ: 'the peace of God.' Only here in N.T. Comp. ὁ θεὸς τῆς εἰρήνης (vs. 9). Not the objective peace *with* God, wrought by justification (Rom. v. 1 [Chr., Theoph., Aug.]); nor the *favor* of God (Grot.); nor peace with one another (Thdrt., Lips.), since mutual peace cannot dissipate anxiety; but the inward peace of the soul which comes from God, and is grounded in God's presence and promise. It is the fruit of believing prayer; "the companion of joy" (Beng.). Of course such peace implies and involves the peace of reconciliation with God. In the hearts of those who are reconciled to God through faith in Christ, the peace of Christ rules (Col. iii. 15). As members of the heavenly commonwealth (iii. 20), they are in a kingdom which is "righteousness and peace and joy" (Rom. xiv. 17). "The God of hope," to whom their expectation is directed, fills them "with all joy and peace in believing" (Rom. xv. 13). They are not disquieted because they know that "all things are working together for good to them that love God" (Rom. viii. 28).

ἡ ὑπερέχουσα πάντα νοῦν: 'which surpasseth every thought (of man).' For ὑπερέχειν, 'to rise above,' 'overtop,' 'surpass,' see ii. 3, iii. 8. The verb is not common in N.T. Only four times in Paul, and once in 1 Pet. ii. 13. Paul has been enjoining the duty of prayer under all circumstances as a safeguard against anxiety. Hence this assurance that the peace of God surpasses every human thought or device as a means of insuring tranquillity of heart. The processes and combinations of human reasoning result only in continued doubt and anxiety. Mere reason cannot find a way out of perplexity. The mysterious dealings of God present problems which it cannot solve, and which only multiply its doubts and questionings. Within the sphere of God's peace all these are dismissed, and the spirit rests in the Lord, even where it cannot understand. A different and widely-accepted explanation is that of the Greek expositors: that the peace of God is so great and wonderful that it transcends the power of the human mind to understand it. So Ellic., Ril., Alf., Ead. Aug. and Theoph. add that even the angels cannot comprehend it. But this thought has no special relevancy here, while the other explanation is in entire harmony with the context. Comp. also 1 Cor. ii. 9–16.

Νοῦς is the reflective intelligence; in Paul, mostly as related to ethical and spiritual matters. It is the organ of the natural moral consciousness and knowledge of God (Rom. i. 20, 28, vii. 23). It is related to πνεῦμα as the faculty to the efficient power. Until renewed by the divine πνεῦμα, it cannot exercise right moral judgment (Rom. xii. 2); and although it may theoretically approve what is good, it cannot conform the practice of the life to its theory (Rom. vii. 25). It is this which is incapable of dealing with the painful and menacing facts of life in such a way as to afford rest.

φρουρήσει: 'shall guard.' A promise, not a prayer, 'may the peace of God guard,' as the Greek Fathers (Chr., however, says it may mean either), some of the older expositors, and Vulg. 'custodiat.' The word, which is a military term, in the N.T. is almost confined to Paul. (See 1 Pet. i. 5.) The metaphor is beautiful — the peace of God as a sentinel mounting guard over a believer's heart. It suggests Tennyson's familiar lines:

> "Love is and was my King and Lord,
> And will be, though as yet I keep
> Within his court on earth, and sleep
> Encompassed by his faithful guard,
> And hear at times a sentinel
> Who moves about from place to place,
> And whispers to the worlds of space,
> In the deep night, that all is well."

All limitations of the promise, such as guarding from the power of Satan, from spiritual enemies, from evil thoughts, etc. are arbitrary. The promise is general, covering all conceivable occasions for fear or anxiety. "He teaches us the certain result of our prayers. He does not, indeed, promise that God will deliver us in this life entirely from calamities and straits, since he may have the best reasons for leaving us in this struggle of faith and patience with a view to his and our greater glory at the appearing of Christ; but he does promise us that which is greater and more desirable than all the good things of this life — the peace of God" (Schlichting).

τὰς καρδίας ὑμῶν καὶ τὰ νοήματα ὑμῶν: 'your hearts and your thoughts.' Καρδία in the sense of the physical organ is not used in N.T. It is the centre of willing, feeling, and thinking. Never, like ψυχή, to denote the individual subject of personal life, so as to be exchanged with the personal pronoun; nor as πνεῦμα, of the divine principle of life in man. Like our 'heart,' it denotes the seat of feeling, as contrasted with intelligence (Rom. ix. 2, x. 1; 2 Cor. ii. 4, vi. 11; Phil. i. 7). But not this only. It is also the seat of mental action — intelligence (Rom. i. 21; Eph. i. 18), and of moral choice (1 Cor. vii. 37; 2 Cor. ix. 7). It gives impulse and character to action (Rom. vi. 17; Eph. vi. 5). It is the seat of the divine Spirit (Rom. v. 5; 2 Cor. i. 22; Gal. iv. 6), and the sphere of his operation in directing, comforting, establishing, etc. (Col. iii. 15; 1 Thess. iii. 13; 2 Thess. ii. 17, iii. 5). It is the seat of faith (Rom. x. 9), and of divine love (Rom. v. 5), and is the organ of spiritual praise (Col. iii. 16).

νοήματα, only in Paul. Things which issue from the καρδία; thoughts, acts of the will. Hence, of Satan's 'devices' (2 Cor. ii. 11). (See 2 Cor. iii. 14, iv. 4, x. 5, xi. 3.) The two nouns are emphatically separated by the article and the personal pronoun attached to each.

Calv.'s distinction between καρδ. and νο. as 'affections' and 'intelligence' is unpauline. Neither are they to be taken as synonymous, nor as a popular and summary description of the spiritual life (De W.).

ἐν Χριστῷ Ἰησοῦ: As so often, the sphere in which divine protection will be exercised. This divine peace is assigned as guardian only to those who are in Christ (iii. 9).

Some, as De W., Ril., Kl., Weiss, explain: 'Shall keep your hearts *in union with* Christ.' So Theoph., ὥστε μὴ ἐκπεσεῖν αὐτοῦ ἀλλὰ μᾶλλον μένειν ἐν αὐτῷ.

8. τὸ λοιπόν: 'finally.' (See on iii. 1.) Introducing the conclusion of the letter. No reference to iii. 1, by way of resuming after a long digression; nor does it introduce what remains for *them* to do in addition to God's protecting care (De W.), since there is no indication of an antithesis. It prefaces an exhortation parallel with vs. 4–6, containing a summary of duties, to which is added a promise of the presence of the God of peace. The exhortation is not to the cultivation of distinct virtues as such (so Luth., Calv., Beza, Beng.), but each virtue represents general righteousness of life viewed on a particular side, the different sides being successively introduced by the repeated ὅσα, and summed up by the twofold εἴ τις.

ἀληθῆ: 'true.' God is the norm of truth. That is true in thought, word, or deed, which answers to the nature of God as revealed in the moral ideals of the gospel of his Son, who manifests him, and who can therefore say, 'I am the truth' (Jn. xiv. 6). Not to be limited to truth in speaking, as Thdrt., Beng.

σεμνά: 'reverend' or 'venerable.' Exhibiting a dignity which grows out of moral elevation, and which thus invites reverence. In class. an epithet of the gods. 'Venerable' is the best rendering, if divested of its conventional implication of age. Matthew Arnold (*God and the Bible*, Pref. xxii.) renders 'nobly serious,' as opposed to κοῦφος, 'lacking intellectual seriousness.'

With the exception of this passage, σεμνὸς occurs only in the Pastorals, and the kindred σεμνότης only there. (See 1 Tim. ii. 2, iii. 4, 8, 11; Tit. ii. 2, 7.) In LXX, of the name of God (2 Macc. viii. 15); of divine laws (2 Macc. vi. 28); of the Sabbath (2 Macc. vi. 11); of the words of wisdom (Prov. viii. 6); of the words of the pure (Prov. xv. 26).

δίκαια: 'just.' In the broadest sense, not merely in relation to men, but according to the divine standard, satisfying all obligations to God, to their neighbor, and to themselves. (Comp. Rom. ii. 13.)

ἅγνα: 'pure.' Always with a moral sense. So ἁγνότης (2 Cor. vi. 6). Not to be limited here to freedom from sins of the flesh: it covers purity in all departments of the life, motives as well as acts. In class. ἁγνός is 'pure,' 'chaste,' in relation to life (as of female purity, purity from blood-guilt), or to religious observances, as of sacrifices. (See Schmidt, *Synon.* 181, 11.) Both ἁγνός and ἅγιος mean pure in the sense of 'sinless.' The radical difference between them is, that ἅγιος is 'holy,' as being set apart and devoted; ἁγνός, as absolutely undefiled. Christ is both ἅγιος and ἁγνός. See on ἁγίοις, i. 1. In 1 Jn. iii. 3, ἁγνός is applied to Christ, and ἁγνίζειν to the imitation of his purity. In 2 Cor. xi. 2, of virgin purity. (Comp. Clem. *ad Cor.* xxi.) In 1 Tim. v. 22, of moral spotlessness. In Jas. iii. 17, as characterising heavenly wisdom. Ἁγνῶς (Phil. i. 17), of preaching the gospel with unmixed motives. Ἁγνίζειν, which in LXX is used only of ceremonial purification, has that meaning in four of the seven instances in N.T. (Jn. xi. 55; Acts xxi. 24, 26, xxiv. 18). In the others (Jas. iv. 8; 1 Pet. i. 22; 1 Jn. iii. 3), of purifying the heart and soul. Neither ἁγνός, ἁγνότης, nor ἁγνῶς occur in the Gospels.

Ἁγνός and all the kindred words which appear in N.T. are found in LXX. Ἅγνισμα (Num. xix. 9), not in N.T. For ἁγνιασμός (Num. viii. 7), the correct reading is ἁγνισμός. In LXX ἁγνός is used of the oracles of God, of the fear of God, of prayers, of the heart, of works, of fire, of a virgin, of a man free from cowardice, and of the soul. (See Ps. xii. [xi.] 6, xix. [xviii.] 10; Prov. xix. 13, xx. 9, xi. 8; 2 Macc. xiii. 8; 4 Macc. v. 37, xviii. 7, 8, 23.)

The two following qualities appeal to the affectionate or admiring recognition of others.

προσφιλῆ: 'lovely,' 'amiable.' Whatever calls forth love. Only here in N.T. In LXX in a passive sense (Sir. iv. 7, xx. 13).

εὔφημα: 'fair-sounding.' A.V. and R.V. 'of good report.' 'Gracious,' R.V. marg. is vague. Not merely having a fair sound to the popular ear, "vox et praeterea nihil," but fair-sounding, as implying essential worthiness.

In class. of words or sounds of good omen. Hence *εὔφημος*, 'abstaining from inauspicious words'; 'keeping a holy silence.' (See Æsch. *Ag.* 1247; Soph. *O. C.* 132.)

A comprehensive exhortation follows, covering all possible virtues.

εἴ τις: 'if there be any': whatever there is. For the form of expression, comp. ii. 1; Rom. xiii. 9; Eph. iv. 29. Not 'whatever other.'

ἀρετὴ: 'virtue'; moral excellence. In class. it has no special moral significance, but denotes excellence of any kind — bravery, rank, excellence of land or of animals. It is possibly for this reason that Paul has no fondness for the word, and uses it only here. Elsewhere in N.T. only by Peter, who uses it of God (1 Pet. ii. 9; 2 Pet. i. 3), and enjoins it as a Christian quality (2 Pet. i. 5). It is found in LXX; of God, Hab. iii. 3 = *δόξα*; Is. xlii. 8, 12, plu., in connection with *δόξα*, and xliii. 21, signifying God's attributes of power, wisdom, etc.; Zech. vi. 13, of him whose name is 'the Branch,' and who shall receive *ἀρετὴν*, *i.e.* the attributes of sovereignty; Esth. (interpol.) xiv. 10, of the pretended attributes of the vain; Sap. iv. 1, of moral excellence in men.

Lightf.'s explanation is ingenious and suggestive. 'Whatever value may reside in your old heathen conception of virtue'; as if he were anxious to omit no possible ground of appeal.

ἔπαινος: 'praise.' If there is any praise that follows the practice of virtue, as the praise of love (1 Cor. xiii.). Not 'that which is praiseworthy' (Weiss).

ταῦτα λογίζεσθε: 'these things take into account.' 'Reckon' with them. "Horum rationem habete" (Beng.). It is an appeal to an independent moral judgment, to thoughtfully estimate the value of these things. Not = *φρονεῖν*, as De W. 'Think on these things' (A.V., R.V.) is a feeble and partial rendering.

He now brings the scheme of duties more clearly before them, and at the same time reminds them, by appealing to his own previous instructions and example, that he is making no new demands upon them. "Facit transitionem a generalibus ad Paulina" (Beng.).

9. ἃ καὶ: 'those things which also.' Those things which are true, venerable, etc., which *also* ye learned of me.

Others coördinate the four καὶs: 'those things which ye have as well learned as received; as well heard as seen' (Vulg., Calv., Beza, Lightf.).

The four verbs form two pairs: ἐμάθετε and παρελάβετε referring to what they had learned by teaching; ἠκούσατε and εἴδετε, by example.

ἐμάθετε . . . παρελάβετε: 'learned' . . . 'received.' The meanings do not differ greatly, except that παρελ. adds, to the simple notion of learning, that of what was communicated or transmitted.

Kl. ἐμάθ. by personal instruction; παρελ. as oral or epistolary traditions obtained from him or transmitted by his delegates. Mey. renders παρελ. 'accepted'; but that sense is rare in Paul. 1 Cor. xv. 1 is doubtful. 1 Cor. xi. 23, xv. 3; Gal. i. 12; 2 Thess. iii. 6, signify simple reception. (See Lightf. on Gal. i. 12; Col. ii. 6; 1 Thess. ii. 13.)

ἠκούσατε καὶ εἴδετε: 'heard and saw.' In their personal intercourse with him. Not through preaching (Calv.), which has already been expressed. Lightf. and others explain ἠκ. of what they heard when he was absent. But all the other verbs refer to the time of his presence at Philippi.

Ἐν ἐμοι properly belongs to ἠκ. and εἴδ., but is loosely taken with all four verbs. Ἐμάθ. and παρελ., strictly, would require παρ' ἐμοῦ.

πράσσετε: 'do,' or 'practise.' A distinction between πράσσειν and ποιεῖν is recognisable in some cases; πράσσειν, 'practise,' marking activity in its progress, and ποιεῖν in its accomplishment or product. The distinction, however, is not uniformly maintained, and must not be pressed. (See Schmidt, *Synon.* 23, and Trench, *Syn.* xcvi.)

καὶ: Consecutive, as vs. 7; 'and so.'

ὁ θεὸς τῆς εἰρήνης: 'the God of peace.' Who is the source and giver of peace. The phrase only in Paul and Heb. (See Rom. xv. 33, xvi. 20; 1 Thess. v. 23; Heb. xiii. 20.) Peace, in the N.T. sense, is not mere calm or tranquillity. All true calm and restfulness are conceived as based upon reconciliation with God. Christian peace implies the cessation of enmity between God and man (Rom. viii. 7); the complete harmony of the divine and the human wills; the rest of faith in divine love and wisdom (Is. xxvi. 3). God is 'the God of peace' only to those who are at one with him. God's peace is not sentimental, but moral. Hence the God of peace is the *sanctifier* of the entire personality (1 Thess. v. 23). Accordingly 'peace' is habitually used in connection with the Messianic salvation, both in the Old and the New Testaments. The Messiah himself will be 'peace' (Mic. v. 5). Peace is associated with righteousness as a Messianic blessing (Ps. lxxii. 7, lxxxv. 10). Peace, founded in reconciliation with God, is the theme of the gospel (Acts x. 36); the gospel is 'the gospel of peace' (Eph. ii. 17, vi. 15; Rom. x. 15); Christ is 'the Lord of peace' (2 Thess. iii. 16), and bestows peace (Jn. xiv. 27, xvi. 33). "It is through God, as the author and giver of peace, that man is able to find the harmony which he seeks in the conflicting elements of his own nature, in his relations with the world, and in his relations to God himself" (Westcott, on Heb. xiii. 20).

He now returns thanks for the gift which the Philippian church has sent him by Epaphroditus, and praises their past and present generosity.

10–20. *I greatly rejoice in the Lord because of your kind thought for me as shown in your gift; a thought which you have indeed entertained all along, but have had no opportunity to carry out. I do not speak as though I had been in want; for I have learned the secret of being self-sufficient in my condition; not that I am sufficient of myself, but I can do all things in Him that strengtheneth me. It was a beautiful thing for you thus to put yourselves in fellowship with my affliction; but this is not the first time; for in the very beginning, as I was leaving Macedonia, you were the only church that contributed to my necessities, sending supplies to me more than once in Thessalonica. But my chief interest is not in the gift itself, but in the spiritual blessing which your acts of ministry will bring to you. Nevertheless my need is fully met by this gift which Epaphroditus brought from you — this sacrifice of sweet odor, acceptable to God. And as you have ministered to my need, so God will supply every need of yours, with such bounteousness as befits his riches in glory in Christ Jesus. To him, our God and Father, be glory forever. My salutations to all the members of your church. The brethren who are with me send you greeting, and all the members of the Roman church, especially those of Cæsar's household. The grace of the Lord Jesus Christ be with your spirit.*

10. ἐχάρην δὲ ἐν κυρίῳ: 'but I rejoice in the Lord.' Again the keynote of the epistle is struck. (See i. 18, ii. 17, 18, 28, iii. 1, iv. 4; comp. Polyc. *ad Phil.* i.) 'Εχάρ.: epistolary aorist.

ἐν κυρίῳ: The gift, its motive, and the apostle's joy in it, were all within the sphere of life in Christ. The gift has its distinctive and choicest character for him as proceeding from their mutual fellowship in Christ. Thus Chr., οὐ κοσμικῶς ἐχάρην, φησὶν, οὐδὲ βιωτικῶς: "I rejoice, he says, not in a worldly fashion, nor as over a matter of common life."

μεγάλως: 'greatly.' Only here in N.T. (See LXX; 1 Chron. xxix. 9; Neh. xii. 43.) Notice the emphatic position.

ἤδη ποτὲ: 'now at length.' Only here and Rom. i. 10. Ἤδη marks a present as related to a past during which something has been in process of completion which is now completed, or something has been expected which is now realised. Ποτὲ indicates indefinitely the interval of delay. With ἤδη the writer puts himself at the point where the interval indicated by ποτὲ terminates.

Others, as Weiss, render 'already once'; which would be a mere reference to something past and now repeated. This is precluded by the connection, and especially by the latter part of vs. 10.

ἀνεθάλετε τὸ ὑπὲρ ἐμοῦ φρονεῖν: 'ye have revived your thought for me.' Ἀνεθ. is transitive, and τὸ ὑπ. ἐμ. φρ. is accusative of the object. You caused your thought for me to sprout and bloom afresh, like a tree putting out fresh shoots after the winter. So Weiss, Lips., Lightf., De W.

Others, as Mey., Kl., Ellic., Alf., Beet, regard the verb as intransitive. In that case either τὸ ὑπ. ἐμ. must be taken as accus. of the obj. after φρον., 'ye revived to think of that which concerned me,' which is awkward and improbable; or τὸ φρ. ὑπ. ἐμ. must be taken as the accus. of reference, 'ye revived as regarded the thinking concerning me.' According to this the following clause would mean, 'ye took thought concerning the taking thought for me.' The only serious objection urged against the transitive sense of ἀνεθ. is that it seems to make the revival of interest dependent on the will of the Philippians, and thus implies a reproach. But this is straining a point. Paul simply says: 'I rejoice that, when the opportunity permitted, you directed your thought towards me and sent me a gift which circumstances had prevented your doing before.' That no reproach is implied is evident from the following words. Ἀναθάλλειν only here in N.T. In LXX, transitively, Ezek. xvii. 24; Sir. i. 18, xi. 22, l. 10.

ἐφ ᾧ: 'wherein,' or 'with reference to which'; namely, the matter of my welfare. Ὑπὲρ (ἐμοῦ) emphasises the personal interest; ἐπὶ merely marks a reference to the matter in question.

καὶ: Besides your ἀναθάλλειν at the favorable opportunity, you were '*also*' concerned all the time until the opportunity occurred.

ἐφρονεῖτε: imperfect tense: 'ye were all along taking thought.' Every possible suggestion of reproach is removed by this.

ἠκαιρεῖσθε δέ: 'but ye were lacking (all the while you were thus taking thought) opportunity.' The verb (only here in Bib.) refers to the circumstances which had prevented them from sooner sending their gift; either lack of means, or want of facilities for transmitting the contribution, etc.

There is a possibility of their misunderstanding his expression of joy to mean merely satisfaction at the relief of his personal needs. He will guard this.

11. *οὐχ ὅτι*: 'not to say that,' or 'I do not say that.' A distinctively N.T. formula. (See Jn. vi. 46, vii. 22; 2 Cor. i. 24, iii. 5.) In class. 'not only'; or, when not followed by a second clause, 'although.'

καθ' ὑστέρησιν λέγω: 'I speak according to want'; *i.e.* 'as if I were in a state of want.' Lightf. aptly, 'in language dictated by want.' Comp. *κατ' ἐριθίαν, κατὰ κενοδοξίαν*, ii. 3. Ὑστέρησις, only here and Mk. xii. 44. He does not deny the want itself, but the want as the motive and measure of his joy.

ἐγὼ γὰρ ἔμαθον: 'for I have learned.' The aorist for the perfect. See on *ἔλαβον*, iii. 12 (Burt. 46, 55). The tuition has extended over his whole experience up to the present. Ἐγὼ emphasises his personal relation to the matter of want. '*I*, so far as *my* being affected by want.'

ἐν οἷς εἰμὶ: 'in the state in which I am.' Not as A.V. and R.V., 'in whatever state I am,' but in all the circumstances of the present. For *εἶναι* or *γίνεσθαι ἐν*, see Mk. v. 25; Lk. xxii. 42; 1 Cor. xv. 17; 1 Thess. ii. 6, v. 4.

αὐτάρκης: 'self-sufficing.' Only here in N.T.; LXX; Sir. xl. 18; *αὐτάρκεια*, 2 Cor. ix. 8; 1 Tim. vi. 6. Αὐτάρκεια is an inward self-sufficing, as opposed to the lack or the desire of outward things. Comp. Plat. *Tim.* 33 D, *ἡγήσατο γὰρ αὐτὸ ὁ ξυνθεὶς αὔταρκες ὂν ἄμεινον ἔσεσθαι μᾶλλον ἢ προσδεὲς ἄλλων*: "For the Creator conceived that a being which was self-sufficient would be far more excellent than one which lacked anything." It was a favorite Stoic word. See on *πολιτεύεσθε*, i. 27. It expressed the doctrine of that sect that man should be sufficient unto himself for all things, and able, by the power of his own will, to resist the force of circumstances. Comp. Seneca, *De Vita Beata*, 6, addressed to Gallio: "Beatus est praesentibus, qualiacunque sunt, contentus." A list of interesting paralls. in Wetst. Paul is not self-sufficient in the Stoic sense, but through the power of a new self — the power of Christ in him. (Comp. 2 Cor. iii. 5.)

He proceeds to explain *ἐν οἷς . . . αὐτάρκης* in detail. The *ἔμαθον* is developed by *οἶδα* and *μεμύημαι*.

12. *οἶδα*: 'I know,' as the result of having learned. (See on i. 19, 25.)

καὶ ταπεινοῦσθαι: 'also how to be abased.' Καὶ connects *ταπ.* with the preceding more general statement, *ἐμ. . . . αὐτάρ. εἶν.* Ταπεινοῦσθαι: 'to be brought low,' with special reference to the abasement caused by want. Not in the spiritual sense, which is all but universal in N.T. The usual antithesis of ταπεινοῦν is ὑψοῦν. (See 2 Cor. xi. 7; Phil. ii. 8, 9; 1 Pet. v. 6.) Here the antithesis is περισσεύειν, contrasting abundance with the want implied in ταπ.

οἶδα καὶ περισσεύειν: 'and I know how to abound.' Οἶδα is repeated for emphasis. Περισ., 'to be abundantly furnished.' Not 'to have superfluity,' as Calv. Paul says, 'I know how to be abased and not crushed; to be in abundance and not exalted.' (Comp. 2 Cor. iv. 8, 9.)

ἐν παντὶ καὶ ἐν πᾶσιν: 'in everything and in all things.' In all relations and circumstances. In every particular circumstance, and in all circumstances generally. "In Allem und Jedem." (Comp. 2 Cor. xi. 6.) For ἐν πᾶσιν, comp. Col. i. 18, iii. 11; 1 Tim. iii. 11; Heb. xiii. 18. Paul more commonly uses ἐν παντὶ. Both adjectives are neuter, after the analogy of οἷς (vs. 11).

Such interpretations of ἐν παντὶ as 'ubique' (Vulg., Calv., Beza); or reference to time (Chr.); or, taking παντὶ as neuter, and πᾶσιν as masculine (Luth., Beng.), are fanciful.

μεμύημαι: 'I have been initiated.' R.V., 'I have learned the secret.' In class., mostly in the passive, of initiation into the Greek mysteries, as the Eleusinian. (See Hdt. ii. 51; Plat. *Gorg.* 497 C; Aristoph. *Plut.* 846; *Ran.* 158.) In a similar sense, LXX; 3 Macc. ii. 30. The kindred word μυστήριον is common in Paul of the great truths hidden from eternity in the divine counsels, and revealed to believers (Eph. iii. 3, 4, 9; Col. i. 26, ii. 2, etc.). Comp. Ign. *Eph.* xii., Παύλου συμμύσται τοῦ ἡγιασμένου: "associates in the mysteries with Paul who has been sanctified." Connect ἐν παν. κ. ἐν πᾶσ. adverbially with μεμύ., while the infinitives depend on μεμύ. Thus: 'In everything and in all things I have been instructed to be full,' etc.

Others, as De W., Lips., Ellic., while connecting ἐν παν. κ. ἐν πᾶσ. with μεμύ. as above, make the following infinitives simply explicative; while that in which Paul has been instructed is represented by ἐν παντὶ, etc. The objection urged against this is that μυεῖσθαι appears to be habitually construed, either with the accusative of the thing, the dative, or, rarely, with the infinitive; though there is one instance of its construction with a preposition, κατὰ (3 Macc. ii. 30). This objection is not formidable, and is relieved by our rendering.

χορτάζεσθαι: 'to be full.' The verb, primarily, of the feeding and fattening of animals in a stall. Comp. Apoc. xix. 21, of feeding birds of prey with the flesh of God's enemies. In Synop., of satisfying the hunger of the multitude (Mt. xiv. 20 and paralls.). In Mt. v. 6; Lk. vi. 21, of satisfying spiritual hunger.

ὑστερεῖσθαι: 'to suffer need.' From ὕστερος, 'behind.' The phrase 'to fall behind' is popularly used of one in straitened circumstances, or in debt. It is applied in N.T. to material deficiency (Lk. xv. 14; Jn. ii. 3); and to moral and spiritual shortcoming (Rom. iii. 23; 1 Cor. viii. 8; Heb. xii. 15). The middle voice (not pass. as Thay.) indicates the *feeling* of the pressure of want, as Lk. xv. 14; Rom. iii. 23; 2 Cor. xi. 8. The mere *fact* of want is expressed by the active voice, as Mt. xix. 20; Jn. ii. 3. In 2 Cor. xii. 11, Paul says that he was in no respect *behind* the 'extra super' apostles; οὐδὲν ὑστέρησα, expressing the *fact* of his equality, not his *sense* of it.

See some good remarks of Canon T. S. Evans on 1 Cor. i. 7 (*Expositor*, 2d Ser. iii. p. 6); also Gifford, in *Speaker's Comm.*, on Rom. iii. 23.

13. πάντα ἰσχύω: 'I can do all things.' Not only all the things just mentioned, but everything.

Ἰσχύειν and the kindred words ἰσχὺς, ἰσχυρὸς, are not of frequent occurrence in Paul. The meanings of ἰσχὺς and δύναμις (see ἐνδυναμοῦντι) often run together, as do those of δύναμις and ἐνέργεια. (See on iii. 21.) The general distinction, however, is that ἰσχὺς is indwelling power put forth or embodied, either aggressively, or as an obstacle to resistance; physical power organised, or working under individual direction. An army and a fortress are both ἰσχυρὸς. The power inhering in the magistrate, which is put forth in laws or judicial decisions, is ἰσχὺς, and makes the edicts ἰσχυρὰ, 'valid,' and hard to resist. Δύναμις is rather the indwelling power or virtue which comes to manifestation in ἰσχὺς. (See Schmidt, *Synon.* 148, 3, 4, 5.) For the accus. with ἰσχύειν, comp. Gal. v. 6.

ἐν τῷ ἐνδυναμοῦντί με: 'in him that strengtheneth me,' or, more literally, 'infuses strength into me.' The ἐνδυν. appears in the ἰσχύω.

Χριστω is added by ℵ[c] DFGKLP.

ἐν: Not 'through,' but 'in'; for he is *in* Christ (iii. 9). Ἐνδυναμοῦν, mostly in Paul. (See Rom. iv. 20; Eph. vi. 10; 1 Tim. i. 12.) With the thought here, comp. 2 Cor. xii. 9; 1 Tim. i. 12; 2 Tim. ii. 1, iv. 17; and Ign. *Smyr.* iv., πάντα ὑπομένω, αὐτοῦ με ἐνδυναμοῦντος τοῦ τελείου ἀνθρώπου: "I endure all things, seeing that he himself enableth me who is perfect man." Any possible misunderstanding of αὐτάρκης (vs. 11) is corrected by these words.

He guards against a possible inference from his words that he lightly esteems their gift, or thinks it superfluous. Not, as Chr., Œc., and Theoph., very strangely, that he feared lest his apparent contempt for the gift might dissuade them from similar acts in the future. It is characteristic that there is no formal expression of thanks beyond his recognition and commendation of the moral and spiritual significance of the act, in which he virtually acknowledges the benefit to himself. The best thanks he can give them is to recognise their fidelity to the principle of Christian love, and to see in their gift an expression of that principle. On the other hand, there is no attempt to conceal the fact that he was in real affliction (θλίψει), and that their act relieved it; and only the most perverted and shallow exegesis, such as Holsten's, can read into his words an expression of indifference to the love displayed by the church, and describe them as "thankless thanks," or see in them a contradiction of 1 Thess. ii. 9.

14. πλὴν: 'nevertheless.' (See on i. 18, iii. 16.) 'Nevertheless, do not think that, because I am thus independent of earthly contingencies, I lightly prize your gift.'

καλῶς ἐποιήσατε: 'ye did nobly.' Positive and generous praise: not a mere acknowledgment that they had simply done their duty. It was a beautiful deed, true to the gospel ideal of καλὸς. For the phrase καλῶς ποιεῖν, see Mk. vii. 37; Lk. vi. 27; 1 Cor. vii. 37.

συνκοινωνήσαντές μου τῇ θλίψει: 'that ye made common cause with my affliction'; 'went shares with' (Lightf. on Gal. vi. 6). The A.V. 'communicate' is correct, if 'communicate' is understood in its older sense of 'share,' as Ben Jonson, "thousands that communicate our loss." (Comp. Rom. xii. 13.) The verb occurs only in Eph. v. 11; Apoc. xviii. 4. The participle, as the complement of ἐποι., specifies the act in which the καλ. ἐποι. was exhibited. For the construction, comp. Acts v. 42; 2 Thess. iii. 13; Win. xlv. 4. The dative θλίψει expresses that with which common cause was made.

Their gift is not the first and only one which he has received. It is a repetition of former acts of the same kind, a new outgrowth from his long and affectionate relations with them. He might justly expect and could honorably accept help from those who had been the first to minister to his necessities, and who had so often repeated their ministry. The idea of a *quasi*-apology for his reproach of the Philippians, because his former relations with them had justified his disappointment in not receiving earlier supplies (Chr., Œc., Theoph.), is utterly without foundation, since no reproach had been uttered or implied. There is no specific praise of their earlier gifts, but the καλ. ἐποι. is confirmed by the fact that the last gift was a continued manifestation of the same spirit that had marked them from the beginning.

Baur's inference from 2 Cor. xi. 9, that the Philippians had been accustomed to send him a regular annual contribution which had now for some time been intermitted, requires no notice.

15. οἴδατε δὲ καὶ ὑμεῖς Φιλιππήσιοι: 'and ye also, Philippians, know.' Δὲ passes on to the mention of former acts of liberality, or perhaps marks the contrast between the expression of his own judgment (vs. 14) and the appeal to their knowledge. Καὶ marks the comparison of the Philippians with the apostle himself. 'Ye as well as I.' Not, as Calv., 'ye as well as other witnesses whom I might cite.' It is quite unnecessary to assume, as Hofn. and Weiss, any special sensitiveness of Paul in alluding to his relations with other churches, which causes him to appeal to the knowledge of the Philippians.

Φιλιππήσιοι: Paul is not accustomed thus to address his readers by name. (See 2 Cor. vi. 11; Gal. iii. 1.) The address is not intended to point a contrast with other churches, but expresses earnestness and affectionate remembrance.

ὅτι: 'that.' Habitual construction with οἶδα. (See i. 19, 25; 1 Cor. iii. 16; Gal. iv. 13, etc.) Not 'because,' as Hofn., whose explanation, 'ye know that ye have done well because this is not the first time that you have sent me similar gifts,' needs no comment. (See Mey. ad loc.)

ἐν ἀρχῇ τοῦ εὐαγγελίου: 'in the beginning of the gospel.' The reference is clearly shown by the succeeding words to be to the first preaching of the gospel in Macedonia, about ten years before the composition of this letter. It is equivalent to 'when the gospel was first proclaimed among you.' He alludes, no doubt, to money supplied before or at his departure from Macedonia (Acts xvii. 14).

Some, as Lightf., De W., Weiss, refer to the contribution given at Corinth (2 Cor. xi. 9), in which case ἐξῆλθον must be rendered as pluperf. This, of course, is grammatically defensible. Lightf. says that as the entrance into Macedonia was one of the two most important stages in Paul's missionary life, he speaks of his labors in Macedonia as the *beginning* of the gospel, though his missionary career was now half run. "The faith of Christ had, as it were, made a fresh start" (*Biblical Essays*: "The Churches of Macedonia"). This is fanciful. (See Ramsay, *St. Paul, the Traveller*, etc. p. 199.)

Explanations which assume to fix the exact points of correspondence between Paul's statements here and the narrative in Acts must needs be tentative and indecisive. No doubt the different parts of the N.T., in some cases, exhibit "undesigned coincidences"; but in many other cases the coincidences are imperfect, or are altogether wanting. It is most unlikely that all the contributions of the Philippians to Paul were accurately chronicled by Luke. That Paul in vs. 16 mentions a contribution earlier than that noted in vs. 15 presents no difficulty. Having said that the Philippians were the very first to assist him on his departure from Macedonia, he emphasises that readiness by going back to a still earlier instance. 'Not only on my departure, but even before I departed you were mindful of my necessities.'

Μακεδονίας: In Paul's later letters he always prefers to mention provinces rather than cities in connection with his own travels, and does so in cases where a definite city might have been as properly referred to. (See Rom. xvi. 5; 1 Cor. xvi. 15; 2 Cor. ii. 13, vii. 5, viii. 1, ix. 2, and Weizs. *Apost. Zeit.* p. 195.)

μοι . . . ἐκοινώνησεν: 'became partner with me,' or 'entered into partnership with me.' See on συνκοιν., vs. 14. Comp. Ril., "ne se mit en rapport avec moi." For the construction with dat. of the person, see Gal. vi. 6, and Ellic.'s note there.

εἰς λόγον δόσεως καὶ λήμψεως: 'as to an account of giving and receiving.' The matter is expressed in a mercantile metaphor. He means that the question of money given and received did not enter into his relations with any other church. The Philippians, by their contributions, had 'opened an account' with him.

Others, as Ril. and Lightf., dismiss the metaphor and render εἰς λόγον 'as regards,' or 'with reference to.' This has classical but not N.T. precedent. (See Thuc. iii. 46; Dem. *De Falsa Leg.* 385; Hdt. iii. 99, vii. 9.) But the recurrence of λόγον in vs. 17, where the metaphor is unmistakable, seems to point to the other explanation.

For ἐκοιν. εἰς comp. κοιν. εἰς (i. 5), and see Win. xxx. 8 *a*. Ἐκοιν. εἰς λόγ. forms one idea. For λόγος, in the sense of 'account' or 'reckoning,' see Mt. xii. 36; Lk. xvi. 2; Rom. xiv. 12; and comp. Ign. *Philad.* xi., εἰς λόγον τιμῆς, "as a mark of honor"; *Smyr.* x., οἳ ἐπηκολούθησάν μοι εἰς λόγον θεοῦ, "who followed me in the cause of God."

Δόσ. καὶ λήμψ., in the sense of credit and debt, occurs in LXX, Sir. xli. 19, xlii. 7. (Comp. Arist. *Eth. Nic.* ii. 7, 4; Plat. *Repub.* 332 A.) Δόσις in N.T. only here and Jas. i. 17. The giving by the Philippians and the receiving by Paul form the two sides of the account. Chr., Theoph., Œc., Aug., followed by Calv., Weiss, Lips., and others, explain of an exchange: Paul giving spiritual gifts to the Philippians, and receiving their material gifts. This is possible, but seems far-fetched.

εἰ μὴ ὑμεῖς μόνοι: 'but ye only.' (Comp. 1 Cor. ix. 6–18; 2 Cor. xi. 7–10; 1 Thess. ii. 9.) In all those cases he is speaking of rightful remuneration for apostolic service, and not, as here, of free offerings.

16. ὅτι: 'for,' or 'since,' justifying the statement of vs. 15. Not 'that,' as Ril., Weiss, connecting with οἴδατε.

καὶ ἐν Θεσσαλονίκῃ: 'even in Thessalonica.' A Macedonian city, near Philippi, where a church was founded by Paul before his departure into Achaia (Acts xvii. 1–9); yet the contribution came from Philippi, and not from Thessalonica, and that while he was actually *in* Thessalonica. Ἐν cannot be explained as 'to.'

καὶ ἅπαξ καὶ δὶς: 'not merely once, but twice.' (Comp. 1 Thess. ii. 18.)

εἰς τὴν χρείαν: 'with reference to the (then) present need.' Εἰς, as in i. 5; 2 Cor. ii. 12. Τὴν with a possessive sense, 'my,' or *the* particular need of the time. For χρείαν, comp. ii. 25.

They are not, however, to understand him as implying that he desired their gifts principally for his own relief or enrichment. He prizes their gift chiefly because their sending it will be fruitful in blessing to them. In vs. 11 he disclaimed the sense of want. Here he disclaims the desire for the gift in itself considered.

17. οὐχ ὅτι: See on vs. 11.

ἐπιζητῶ: Used by Paul only here and Rom. xi. 7. The continuous present, 'I am seeking,' characterising his habitual attitude. Ἐπὶ marks the direction, not the intensity of the action. See on ἐπιποθῶ, i. 8.

τὸ δόμα: 'the gift.' In Paul only here and Eph. iv. 8. Not the particular gift which they had sent, but the gift as related to his characteristic attitude, and which might be in question in any similar case.

ἀλλὰ ἐπιζητῶ: The verb is repeated in order to emphasise the contrary statement. (Comp. the repetitions in vs. 2, 12.)

τὸν καρπὸν: 'the fruit.' (See on i. 11.) The recompense which the gift will bring to the givers. (Comp. 2 Cor. ix. 6.)

τὸν πλεονάζοντα: 'that increaseth' or 'aboundeth.' The verb, which is often used by Paul, signifies large abundance. Paul does not use it transitively, exc. 1 Thess. iii. 12, though it is so found in LXX, as Num. xxvi. 54; Ps. l. (xlix.) 19; lxxi. (lxx.) 21; 1 Macc. iv. 35. In class. mostly, 'to superabound.' It is associated with ὑπεραυξάνειν in 2 Thess. i. 3 (see Lightf. ad loc.), and with περισσεύειν in 1 Thess. iii. 12. The phrase πλεον. εἰς is unique, since πλεον. habitually stands alone. In 2 Thess. i. 3, εἰς goes with ἀγάπη. For this reason, some, as De W., connect with ἐπιζητῶ: 'I seek, with a view to your advantage, fruit which aboundeth,' etc. But this is against the natural order of the sentence, since τὸν πλεον. εἰς λόγ. ὑμ. forms one idea in contrast with ἐπιζ. τ. δόμ.; and, as Mey. justly remarks, the preposition is not determined by the word in itself, but by its logical reference.

λόγον: 'account' or 'reckoning,' as vs. 15. The idea of 'interest' (τόκος), as Kl., is, perhaps, not exactly legitimate, though it suits the metaphor in πλεον. εἰς λόγ., and καρπὸς is used in class. of profit from material things, as flocks, honey, wool, etc. Mey.'s objection that this sense is unsuited to δόμα is of little weight, since the δόμα might be figuratively regarded as an investment. It is arbitrary to limit the meaning to the future reward (Mey., Alf., Ellic.). The present participle may, indeed, signify, 'which is rolling up a recompense to be awarded in the day of Christ'; but it may equally point to the blessing which is continually accruing to faithful ministry in the richer development of Christian character. (Comp. Rom. vi. 21, 22.) Every act of Christian ministry develops and enriches him who performs it. (Comp.

Acts xx. 35.) Aug., distinguishing between the gift as such and the gift as the offering of a Christian spirit, says that a mere gift might be brought by a raven, as to Elijah.

18. ἀπέχω δὲ πάντα: 'and I have all things.' Δὲ is not adversative, but connective, introducing an additional reason for οὐχ ἐπιζητῶ τὸ δόμα, 'I do not seek the gift but the fruit; and as to my need, I have all that I could need.'

Otherwise Ellic., De W., Ead., Weiss, Alf., Vulg., who take δὲ as adversative. So Alf. "*But*, notwithstanding that the gift is not that which I desire, I have received it, and am sufficiently supplied by it." This seems feeble and superfluous after the strong adversative ἀλλὰ.

ἀπέχω: 'I have to the full.' Nothing remains for me to desire. Ἀπὸ marks correspondence; *i.e.* "of the contents to the capacity; of the possession to the desire" (Lightf.). (See Win. xl. 46.) So Mt. vi. 2. "They have their reward in full." There is nothing more for them to receive. (Comp. Lk. vi. 24.) Not a formal acknowledgment of the gift, omitted in vs. 17 (Chr., Œc., Theoph.).

καὶ περισσεύω: 'and abound.' Not only is my need met, but I have more than I could desire. On περισσεύειν see Lightf. on 1 Thess. iii. 12.

πεπλήρωμαι: 'I am filled.' Hardly the completion of a climax (Ellic.), since fulness is not an advance on περισσ. It rather introduces the following clause, which is an explanatory comment upon what precedes.

δεξάμενος: Explanatory of πεπλ. 'I am filled, now that I have received.'

παρὰ Ἐπαφροδίτου: See on ii. 25.

τὰ παρ' ὑμῶν: 'the things sent from you' (through him). Παρὰ emphasises the idea of transmission, and marks the connection between the giver and the receiver, more than ἀπὸ, which merely points to the source. (See Win. xlvii.; Lightf. on Gal. i. 12; Schmidt, *Synon.* 107, 18.)

ὀσμὴν εὐωδίας: 'an odor of a sweet smell.' Their offering of love is described as a sweet-smelling sacrifice. The expression is common in O.T. to describe a sacrifice acceptable to God. (See Gen. viii. 21; Lev. i. 9, 13, 17. Comp. 2 Cor. ii. 15, 16; Eph. v. 2.) Ὀσμὴν is in apposition with τὰ παρ' ὑμῶν; εὐωδίας is genit. of quality. Ὀσμὴ is more general than εὐωδία, denoting an odor of any kind, pleasing or otherwise.

θυσίαν: 'a sacrifice.' Not the act of sacrifice, but the thing sacrificed. (See on ii. 17.) Here in the same sense as Rom. xii. 1.

δεκτήν: 'acceptable.' Rare in N.T., and only here by Paul, 2 Cor. vi. 2 being a quotation. (See LXX; Lev. i. 3, 4, xix. 5, xxii. 19.)

εὐάρεστον: 'well-pleasing,' as Rom. xii. 1. In N.T. only in

Paul and Heb. (See Rom. xiv. 18; 2 Cor. v. 9; Eph. v. 10; Heb. xiii. 21; LXX; Sap. iv. 10, ix. 10.)

τῷ θεῷ: Connect with both ὀσμ. εὐωδ. and θυσ.

19. ὁ δὲ θεός μου πληρώσει πᾶσαν χρείαν ὑμῶν: 'and my God shall fulfil every need of yours.' *My* God who has made you his instruments in fulfilling my need (πεπλήρωμαι, vs. 18) will fulfil every need of yours. The δὲ is not adversative, 'but' (Beng., De W., A.V.), which would seem to emphasise the loss incurred in sacrifice by setting over against it the promise of the divine supply. It rather adds this statement to the preceding; and this statement expresses God's practical approval of the Philippians' offering, and not their compensation by him. (Comp. 2 Cor. ix. 8–11.)

κατὰ τὸ πλοῦτος αὐτοῦ: 'according to his riches.' The measure or standard of the supply; the infinite possibility, according to which the πληρώσει will be dispensed.

ἐν δόξῃ: 'in glory.' The mode or manner of the fulfilment, 'gloriously'; in such wise that his glory will be manifested. Construe with πληρώσει, not with πλοῦτος (as Grot., Rhw., Heinr., A.V., R.V.), 'riches in glory,' which is contrary to N.T. usage, since δόξα with πλοῦτος is invariably in the genitive. See, *e.g.*, τὸν πλοῦτον τῆς δόξης αὐτοῦ (Rom. ix. 23); and comp. Eph. i. 18, iii. 16; Col. i. 27. Ἐν δόξῃ is always used in connection with a verb (see 2 Cor. iii. 8, 11; Col. iii. 4), and so are all similar phrases, as ἐν ἀληθείᾳ, ἐν δυνάμει, ἐν δόλῳ, ἐν ἐξουσίᾳ, ἐν ἀδικίᾳ, ἐν ἀγάπῃ, etc. There is not in the N.T. a phrase like πλοῦτος ἐν δόξῃ. Comp. πληρώσῃ ἐν δυνάμει (2 Thess. i. 11).

Mey. makes ἐν instrumental, though dependent on πληρώσει, 'with glory,' or 'in that he gives them glory,' and characterises the explanation given above as "indefinite and peculiarly affected," in which he is followed by Alf., who calls it "weak and flat in the extreme." Nevertheless it is adopted by Thay., Lips., De W., Calv., Ead., Weiss, Kl. Comp. Rom. i. 4, where ἐν δυνάμει is adverbial with ὁρισθέντος, and 2 Cor. iii. 7, 8, 11. Mey.'s explanation is shaped by his persistent reference to the *parousia*, which narrows his interpretation of πλεονάζοντα in vs. 17. He cannot conceive how Paul, with his view of the *parousia* as imminent, could promise, *on this side of it*, a glorious recompense. So Lightf. 'by placing you in glory.' But πληρώσει is not to be limited to the future reward. It includes, with that, all that supply which God so richly imparts in this life to those who are in Christ. (See Jn. i. 16; 1 Cor. i. 5; Eph. iii. 16–20; Col. ii. 10.)

ἐν Χριστῷ Ἰησοῦ: Not to be connected with δόξῃ, but with πληρώσει, as the domain in which alone the πληρώσει can take place.

The dignity and tact with which Paul treats this delicate subject have been remarked by all expositors from the Fathers down. Lightf. has justly observed that Paul had given to the Philippians "the surest pledge of confidence which could be given by a high-minded and sensitive man, to whom it was of the highest importance, for the sake of the great cause which he had advocated, to avoid the slightest breath of suspicion, and whose motives nevertheless were narrowly scanned and unscrupulously misrepresented. He had placed himself under pecuniary obligations to them." With his tone of manly independence and self-respect, mingles his grateful recognition of their care for him and a delicate consideration for their feelings. He will not doubt that they have never ceased to remember him, and have never relaxed their eagerness to minister to him, although circumstances have prevented their ministry. Yet he values their gift principally as an expression of the spirit of Christ in them, and as an evidence of their Christian proficiency. He can give their generosity no higher praise, no higher mark of appreciation and gratitude, than to say that it was a sacrifice of sweet odor to God. He is not raised above human suffering. Their gift was timely and welcome; yet if it had not come, he was independent of human contingencies. They have not only given him money, but they have given him Christian love and sympathy and ministry — fruit of his apostolic work.

The promise just uttered, by its wonderful range and richness, calls forth an ascription of praise.

20. *τῷ δὲ θεῷ καὶ πατρὶ ἡμῶν*: 'to our God and Father'; the God who will supply every need out of his fatherly bounty. For the formula, see Gal. i. 4; 1 Thess. i. 3, iii. 11, 13. Ἡμῶν probably belongs to both nouns, since the article is unnecessary with *θεῷ*, and is apparently prefixed in order to bind both nouns with the pronoun. On the other hand, Ellic. suggests that, as *πατρὶ* expresses a relative idea and *θεὸς* an absolute one, the defining genitive may be intended for *πατρὶ* only. (See Ellic. and Lightf. on Gal. i. 4.)

εἰς τοὺς αἰῶνας τῶν αἰώνων: 'to the ages of the ages.' Forever. For the formula, see Gal. i. 5; 1 Tim. i. 17; 2 Tim. iv. 18; 1 Pet. iv. 11, and often in Apoc. LXX habitually in the singular; *εἰς τὸν αἰῶνα τοῦ αἰῶνος* (Ps. lxxxix. 29 [lxxxviii. 30], cxi. [cx.] 3, 10); *εἰς τοὺς αἰῶνας*, omitting *τῶν αἰώνων* (Ps. lxi. 4 [lx. 5], lxxvii. [lxxvi.] 8; 2 Chron. vi. 2). For similar doxologies in Paul's letters, see Rom. xi. 36; Gal. i. 5; Eph. iii. 21; 1 Tim. i. 17. Paul has *εἰς τοὺς αἰῶνας* (Rom. i. 25, ix. 5, xi. 36); *εἰς τὸν αἰῶνα* (1 Cor. viii. 13; 2 Cor. ix. 9); *εἰς πάσας τὰς γενεὰς τοῦ αἰῶνος τῶν αἰώνων* (Eph. iii. 21). Αἰὼν is a long space of time; an age; a cycle. In the doxology the whole period of duration is conceived as a succession of cycles.

CLOSING SALUTATIONS

21. πάντα ἅγιον: 'every saint'; individually. Comp. πᾶσιν τοῖς ἁγίοις (i. 1); πάντας ἀδελφούς (1 Thess. v. 26); ἀλλήλους (Rom. xvi. 16; 1 Cor. xvi. 20; 2 Cor. xiii. 12). The salutation is probably addressed through the superintendents of the church (i. 1), into whose hands the letter would be delivered, and who would read it publicly. For ἅγιον, see on i. 1.

ἐν Χριστῷ Ἰησοῦ: May be construed either with ἀσπάσασθε or with ἅγιον. The matter is unimportant. Ἀσπάζεσθαι with ἐν Χτῷ does not occur in N.T.; with ἐν Κυρίῳ, 1 Cor. xvi. 19. Ἅγιος with ἐν Χτῷ Ἰ., i. 1. The passages commonly cited from the closing salutations of Rom. are not decisive. The evidence is rather in favor of ἅγιον. It is true that ἅγ. implies ἐν Χ. Ἰ.; but the same reason may possibly apply here which is given by Chr. for the phrase in i. 1; namely, that he speaks of them as 'saints,' in the Christian as distinguished from the O.T. sense.

οἱ σὺν ἐμοὶ ἀδελφοί: 'the brethren who are with me.' The circle of Paul's immediate colleagues or more intimate friends. The apparent disagreement of these words with ii. 20 cannot be considered until we can explain the latter passage, which, with our present knowledge, seems hopeless. In any case, Paul would not withhold the name 'brethren' even from such as are described there. Probably there were equally unworthy members of the Philippian church, yet he addresses the whole body by that title (i. 12, iii. 1, iv. 1, 8). See, for a different view, Weiss in *Amer. Jour. Theol.*, April, 1897, p. 391.

22. πάντες οἱ ἅγιοι: The church-members in Rome generally, as distinguished from the smaller circle just named.

μάλιστα δὲ οἱ ἐκ τῆς Καίσαρος οἰκίας: 'especially they that are of Cæsar's household.' Οἰκία does not signify members of the imperial family, but the whole *ménage* of the imperial residence — slaves, freedmen, household servants, and other dependants, possibly some of high rank. Freedmen, and even slaves, were often entrusted with high and confidential positions in the palace. The imperial establishment was enormous, and the offices and duties were minutely divided and subdivided. (See R. Lanciani's *Ancient Rome in the Light of Recent Excavations*, p. 128 ff.) Many Christians were doubtless numbered among these retainers. Some have thought that οἰκία included the prætorian guard, members of which might have come from Macedonia; for though the prætorians were originally of Italian birth, they were drawn, later, from Macedonia, Noricum, and Spain, as well as from Italy. But this is improbable. I cannot do better than to refer the reader to Lightf.'s dissertation on "Cæsar's Household," *Comm.* p. 171, to which may be added Professor Sanday on *Rom.* Introd. p. xciv., and notes on Ch. xvi., p. 422 ff. Lightf. argues, fairly I think, that, assuming the earlier date of the Philippian letter (see Introd. v.), the members of Cæsar's household who sent their salutations to Philippi were earlier converts who did not owe their knowledge of the gospel to Paul's preaching at Rome; that Paul assumes the acquaintance of the Philippians with these, and that therefore we must look for them among the names in the closing salutations of the Roman Epistle, composed some three years before this letter.

Why *μάλιστα*, cannot be explained. It may imply some previous acquaintance of these persons with the Philippians.

23. *ἡ χάρις τοῦ κυρίου Ἰησοῦ Χριστοῦ μετὰ τοῦ πνεύματος ὑμῶν*: 'the grace of the Lord Jesus Christ be with your spirit.' So Philem. 25; Gal. vi. 18.

For *μετα του πνευματος*, TR reads *μετα παντων* with ℵ[c] KL, Syr.[utr].
ℵ ADKLP, Vulg., Cop., Syr.[utr], Arm., Æth., add *αμην*, which is omitted by WH., Tisch., Weiss, with BFG, 47, Sah.

THE EPISTLE OF ST. PAUL TO PHILEMON

THE EPISTLE OF ST. PAUL TO PHILEMON

INTRODUCTION

PHILEMON was a citizen of Colossæ. Onesimus, his slave, is described in the Epistle to the Colossians as "one of you" (iv. 9); while in the letter to Philemon, written and sent at the same time, the return of Onesimus to his master is announced (10, 12, 17).

The opinion of Wieseler (*Chron. des Apost. Zeital.*), that both Philemon and Archippus belonged to Laodicæa, and that the epistle was therefore sent to that place, is entitled to no weight. He assumes that the Epistle to Philemon was identical with the Epistle to Laodicæa (Col. iv. 16. See note on vs. 2). Equally unimportant is the view of Holtzn. (*Einl.* 246), which places Philemon and his household at Ephesus.

That Philemon had been converted to Christianity through Paul's ministry, appears from vs. 19. The conversion of the Colossians is probably to be connected with the apostle's long residence at Ephesus, from which city his influence seems to have extended very widely. (See Acts xix. 26, and comp. the salutation to the Corinthian church from "the churches in Asia," 1 Cor. xvi. 19.) We do not hear of his visiting the neighboring cities, but people from these came to Ephesus to listen to his teachings (Acts xix. 9, 10), since the relations were very close between that city and the cities of the Lycus. (See Lightf. *Introd. to Colossians*, p. 31.)

From this epistle it appears that Philemon was active and prominent in Christian work at Colossæ, and very helpful in his ministries to his fellow-Christians (vs. 5, 7). His house was a meeting-place for a Christian congregation, and the apostle's relations with him were intimate and affectionate (vs. 2, 13, 17, 22).

The traditions which represent him as a presbyter, bishop, or deacon, are valueless. In the *Menaea*[1] of Nov. 22, he is commemorated as a "holy apostle." (See Lightf. *Ign.* ii. p. 535.)

Onesimus, Philemon's slave, had run away from him, and had possibly robbed him. (See on vs. 18.) He had found his way to Rome, and had there met Paul. Perhaps, in former days, he had accompanied his master in his visits to Ephesus, and had seen the apostle there. Through Paul's influence he became a Christian (vs. 10), and devoted himself to the service of the Lord's prisoner. Paul had conceived a strong personal affection for him (vs. 10–13, 16, 17, comp. Col. iv. 9), and would gladly have kept him with himself; but was unwilling to do so without Philemon's consent (vs. 14). Moreover, Onesimus, by his flight, had deprived his master of his services, if he had not also robbed him of property; and therefore, as a Christian, was bound to make restitution. Accordingly, as Tychicus was about to go to Colossæ and Laodicæa bearing letters from Paul, the apostle placed Onesimus in his charge, and sent by him this letter to Philemon, in which he related the slave's faithful ministries to himself, commended his Christian fidelity and zeal, entreated his master to receive him kindly, and offered himself as surety for whatever loss Philemon had suffered by him.

All that is known of Onesimus is that he was a slave, and a Phrygian slave, which latter fact would mark him in common estimation as of poor quality.

Suidas gives the proverb: Φρὺξ ἀνὴρ πληγεὶς ἄμεινον καὶ διακονέστερος, 'a Phrygian is the better and the more serviceable for a beating.' It is quoted by Cicero (*Pro Flacco*, 27. See Wallon, *Histoire de l'Esclavage dans l'Antiquité*, ii. p. 61, 62).

The martyrologies make him bishop of Ephesus (see Ign. *Eph.* i.) and of Berœa in Macedonia, and represent him as laboring for the gospel in Spain, and suffering martyrdom at Rome.

His name appears in the *Menaea* of Feb. 15, where he is called a slave of Philemon, a Roman man, to whom the holy Apostle Paul writes. It is further said that he was arraigned before Tertullus, the prefect of the

[1] *Menaea*, from μήν, 'a month': corresponding, in the Greek Church, to the Roman Breviary, and containing for each holiday and feast of the year the appointed prayers and hymns, together with short lives of the saints and martyrs.

country, sent to Puteoli, and put to death by having his legs broken. The *Roman Acts*, 10, speak of him as perfected by martyrdom in the great city of the Romans.

The letter was included in the collection of Marcion, and is named in the Muratorian Canon in connection with the Pastoral Epistles. The supposed references in Ignatius (*Eph.* ii.; *Mag.* xii.; *Polyc.* vi.) are vague. In *Eph.* ii. the name Onesimus occurs in connection with the verb ὀναίμην, and the reference is inferred from a similar play on the name, Philem. 20. (See Westcott, *Canon of the N.T.*, p. 48.) It is found in the Syriac and Old Latin versions, and is ascribed to Paul by Origen (*Hom. in Jer.* 19; *Comm. in Mt.* tract. 33, 34.) Tertullian is the first who distinctly notices it. He says: "This epistle alone has had an advantage from its brevity; for by that it has escaped the falsifying touch of Marcion. Nevertheless, I wonder that when he receives one epistle to one man, he should reject two to Timothy, and one to Titus which treat of the government of the church" (*Adv. Marc.* v. 42). Eusebius (*H. E.* iii. 25) puts it among the ὁμολογούμενα. Jerome, in his preface to his commentary on the epistle, refers to those who hold that it was not written by Paul, or if by him, not under inspiration, because it contained nothing to edify. These also alleged that it was rejected by most of the ancients because it was a letter of commendation and not of instruction, containing allusions to everyday matters. Jerome replies that all St. Paul's letters contain allusions to such matters, and that this letter would never have been received by all the churches of the world if it had not been Paul's. Similar testimony is given by Chrysostom, who, like Jerome, had to defend the letter against the charge of being on a subject beneath the apostle's notice.

The only serious attack upon the epistle in modern times is that of Baur, who intimates that he rejects it with reluctance, and exposes himself by so doing to the charge of hypercriticism. "This letter," he says, "is distinguished by the private nature of its contents; it has nothing of those commonplaces, those general doctrines void of originality, those repetitions of familiar things which are so frequent in the supposed writings of the apostle. It deals with a concrete fact, a practical detail of ordinary life. . . . What objection can criticism make to these pleasant and charming lines, inspired by the purest Christian feeling, and against which suspicion has never been breathed?" (*Paulus*). Rejecting Ephesians, Philippians, and Colossians, he is compelled to reject Philemon along with them. The diction is unpauline. Words and expressions occur which are either not found at all in Paul's epistles, or only in those which Baur rejects. The epistle exhibits a peculiar conjunction of circumstances in the flight of Onesimus and his meeting St. Paul at Rome, which savors of romance. The letter is the embryo of a Christian romance like the *Clementine Recognitions*, intended to illustrate the idea that what man loses in time in this world he regains forever in Christianity; or that every believer finds himself again in each of his brethren.

Holtzmann is inclined to receive the epistle, but thinks that the passage 4–6 shows the hand of the author of the Ephesian letter.

Weizsäcker (*Apost. Zeital.* p. 545) and Pfleiderer (*Paulinismus*, p. 44) hold that the play on the name Onesimus proves the letter to be allegorical (see note on vs. 11).

Steck thinks that he has discovered the germ of the letter in two epistles of the younger Pliny.

It is needless to waste time over these. They are mostly fancies. The external testimony and the general consensus of critics of nearly all schools are corroborated by the thoroughly Pauline style and diction, and by the exhibition of those personal traits with which the greater epistles have made us familiar. The letter, as already remarked, was written and sent at the same time with that to the Colossians. Its authenticity goes to establish that of the longer epistle. "In fact," remarks Sabatier, "this short letter to Philemon is so intensely original, so entirely innocent of dogmatic preoccupation, and Paul's mind has left its impress so clearly and indelibly upon it, that it can only be set aside by an act of sheer violence. Linked from the first with the Colossian and Ephesian Epistles, it is virtually Paul's own signature appended as their guarantee to accompany them through the centuries" (*The Apostle Paul*, Hellier's trans.).

The general belief from ancient times has been that this, with the Colossian and Ephesian letters, was composed at Rome; but the opinion which assigns their composition to Cæsarea has had some strong advocates, among whom may be named Reuss,

Schenkel, Weiss, Holtzmann, Hilgenfeld, Hausrath, and Meyer. The principal arguments are the following:

1. It is more natural and probable that the slave should have fled from Colossæ to Cæsarea, than that he should have undertaken a long sea voyage to Rome.

On the contrary, it is more natural and probable that Onesimus should have gone to Rome as quickly as possible, both because it was farther away from Colossæ, and because there would be much less chance of detection in the vast city and population of the metropolis.

2. According to Phil. ii. 24, Paul intended, if liberated, to go directly to Macedonia; whereas, according to Philem. 22, he proposed to go to Colossæ. On this, see note on Philem. 22.

3. The absence from the Colossian Epistle of any mention of the earthquake by which the cities of the Lycus had been visited. According to Tacitus, an earthquake overthrew Laodicæa in the year 60 A.D., the last year of Paul's imprisonment at Cæsarea. According to Eusebius (*Chron.* Ol. 210), the date is four years later, and Laodicæa, Hierapolis, and Colossæ are named as having suffered. Assuming that Tacitus and Eusebius refer to the same event, and that Tacitus' date is correct, the omission of reference in the letter written at Cæsarea is explained by the fact that the letter preceded the event. But if the letter was written during the latter part of the Roman imprisonment, the omission of all reference to such an event is incredible. (See Weiss, *Einl.* § 24; Lightf. *Colossians*, Introd. p. 37; Hort, *Romans and Ephesians*, p. 105.)

It is possible to found a valid argument upon an earthquake; but in this case the tremors of the earthquake pervade the argument. Nothing more indecisive can be imagined than this process of reasoning. The argument *e silentio* is always suspicious, and, in this instance, proves absolutely nothing. Assuming all the premises to be definitely settled, it does not follow that the apostle must have referred to the earthquake. But the premises are not settled. Which is right, Tacitus or Eusebius? Supposing Eusebius to be right, the Roman, as well as the Cæsarean captivity, might have preceded the earthquake. If St. Paul arrived in Rome in 56 (see Introd. to Philippians, iv.), his imprisonment was over before the dates assigned by both Tacitus and Eusebius. What is the date of Paul's departure from Cæsarea? What are the exact dates of the Epistles of the Captivity? Do Tacitus and Eusebius refer to the same event? Both Lightf. and Hort quote Herzberg's supposition that the two notices refer to two different earthquakes, and that, since Tacitus mentions Laodicæa only, the first one did not extend to Colossæ.

It may be added that the plans of the apostle, as indicated in both Philippians and Philemon, agree better with the hypothesis of the Roman captivity. In Cæsarea all his plans would have pointed to Rome. Moreover, his situation in Rome, if we may judge from the account in Acts, afforded the slave much greater facilities for intercourse with him than he could have had in Cæsarea.

This letter cannot be appreciated without some knowledge of the institution of slavery among the Romans, and its effect upon both the slave and the master. Abundant information on this subject is furnished by the elaborate work of Wallon (*Histoire de l'Esclavage dans l'Antiquité*, 2d ed. 1879), by the Roman jurists and the Roman codes, and by the comedians and satirists. The excursus on the slaves, in Becker's *Gallus*, trans. by Metcalfe, will also be found very useful, and ch. ii. and iv. of Lecky's *History of European Morals* will repay reading.

Slavery grew with the growth of the Roman state until it changed the economic basis of society, doing away with free labor, and transferring nearly all industries to the hands of slaves. The exact numbers of the slave population of the Empire cannot be determined; but they were enormous. Tacitus speaks of the city of Rome being frightened at their increase (*Ann.* xiv. 45); and Petronius (37) declared his belief that not a tenth part of the slaves knew their own masters. (See Wallon, Liv. ii. ch. iii.) Most of them were employed on the country estates, but hundreds were kept in the family residences in the cities, where every kind of work was deputed to them. In the imperial household, and in the houses of nobles and of wealthy citizens, the minute subdivisions of labor, and the number of particular functions to each of which a slave or a corps of slaves was assigned, excite our laughter. (See note on Phil. iv. 22.) Some of these functions required intelligence and culture. The *familia* or slave-household included not only field-laborers and household drudges, but architects, sculptors, painters, poets, musicians, librarians, physicians, readers who beguiled the hours at the bath or at the table, — ministers, in short, to all forms of cultivated taste, no less than to common necessities.

On slaves as physicians, see Lanciani, *Ancient Rome*, etc. p. 71 ff.

But, no matter what his particular function, the slave, in the eye of the law, was a chattel, a thing, inventoried with oxen and wagons (Varro, *De Re Rust.* i. 17, 1). He could be given, let, sold, exchanged, or seized for debt. His person and his life were absolutely in the power of his master. Every one will recall the familiar passage of Juvenal (vi. 28), in which a dissolute woman of fashion orders the crucifixion of a slave, and refuses to give any reason save her own pleasure. "Hoc volo, sic jubeo, sit pro ratione voluntas." The slave had no right of marriage. He was allowed concubinage (*contubernium*), and such alliances were regulated by the master. The master's caprice in the matter of punishment was unlimited. Sometimes the culprit was degraded from the house to the field or the workshop, and was often compelled to work in chains (Ter. *Phorm.* ii. 1, 17; Juv. viii. 180). Sometimes he was scourged, sometimes branded on the forehead, or forced to carry the *furca*, a frame shaped like a V, and placed over the back of the neck on the shoulders, the hands being bound to the thighs. He might be crucified or thrown to wild beasts, or to voracious fish.

The moral effects of such an institution upon both slave and master it would not be difficult to predict, and they meet the student in every phase of Roman life, — domestic, social, and political. There was, first, the fearfully significant fact that a whole vast section of the population was legally deprived of the first element of manhood, — self-respect. No moral consideration could be expected to appeal to a chattel to prevent his seeking his own interest or pleasure by any means, however bad. He gave himself up to his own worst passions, and ministered, for his own gain, to the worst passions of his master, all the more as he stood higher in the scale of intelligence, and acquired thereby a certain influence and power. Knowledge and culture furnished him for subtler and deeper villainy. His sense of power and his love of intrigue were gratified when he came, as he often did, between members of the same family, making of one a dupe, and of the other an accomplice, an ally, and sometimes a slave. Every circumstance of his life was adapted to foster in him viciousness, low cunning, falsehood, and treachery.

On the master the effect was that which always follows the possession of absolute authority without legal or moral restraint. It encouraged a tyrannical and ferocious spirit. It was demoralising even to the best and the most kindly disposed. It made beasts of the naturally licentious and cruel. It corrupted the family life. The inevitable and familiar contact of childhood and youth with the swarm of household slaves could have but one result, fatal alike to personal virtue and to domestic union.

It is true there was another side. Affectionate relations between master and slave were not uncommon. The younger Pliny expressed his deep sorrow for the death of some of his slaves (*Ep.* viii. 16). Instances of heroic devotion on the part of slaves are on record. The slave had a right to whatever he might save out of his allowance of food and clothing, and with it he sometimes purchased his freedom (Ter. *Phorm.* i. 1, 9). There were frequent cases of manumission. Although the slave's marriage was not recognised, it was not customary forcibly to separate him from his companion. Yet, after the best has been said, these were exceptions which proved the rule. Confronting them are the pictures of Terence, Plautus, Petronius, Tacitus, Juvenal, and Persius. It was the institution that was demoralising. Its evil possibilities were inherent, and any one of a hundred causes might bring them into full play. Wallon remarks that "for public depravity to reach its utmost depths of licentiousness, there needed to be a being with the passions and attractions of a man, yet stripped by public opinion of all the moral obligations of a human being, all whose wildest excesses were lawful provided they were commanded by a master."

The evil created and carried in itself its own retribution. Every wrong is expensive; and it is the unvarying testimony of history that the price of slavery is paid, both materially and morally, to the last penny, and with compound interest, by the masters. The price was not discounted by emancipation. Emancipation might change the political standing of the slave, but it did not change the slave. Rome had trained her later generation of freemen as slaves, and she reaped what she had sown. The emancipated slave carried into his free condition the antecedents, the habits, the spirit, the moral quality of a slave. The time came when the majority of the free population were either freedmen or descended from slaves. Tacitus tells of their insolence and insubordination (*Ann.* xii. 26, 27). The slave-taint crept into the offices of state. Labor was stigmatised and its avenues were barred to the free poor. Almost every sphere of industry was occupied by slaves, and the free poor became literally paupers, dependent upon the imperial doles of bread.

The attitude of the great Christian apostle towards this institution is, naturally, a subject of much interest; and this epistle, which represents that attitude in a practical issue, has therefore figured in most discussions on the moral aspect of slavery. These discussions have developed two errors, against which it is important to guard. On the one hand, the epistle has been regarded as committing St. Paul to the concession of the abstract rightfulness and of the divine sanction of slavery. On the other hand, it has been claimed that the epistle represents him as the enemy and the condemner of slavery, and as working with a conscious intent for its abolition by the deep and slow process of fostering Christian sentiment. Neither of these views expresses the whole truth of the case.

It is more than questionable whether St. Paul had grasped the postulate of the modern Christian consciousness that no man has the right to own another. He had been familiar with slavery all his life, both in his Hebrew and in his Gentile associations. Hebrew law, it is true, afforded the slave more protection than Greek or Roman law, and insured his ultimate manumission; none the less, the Hebrew law assumed the right to own human beings. The tendency is much too common to estimate the leaders of the primitive church in the light of nineteenth-century ideas, and to attribute to a sentiment which was only beginning to take shape, the maturity and definiteness which are behind its appeal to us, and which are the growth of centuries. It is safe to say that St. Paul was a good way removed from the point of view of the modern abolitionist. If he had distinctly regarded the institution of slavery as wrong, *per se*, there is every reason for believing that he would have spoken out as plainly as he did concerning fornication; whereas there is not a word to that effect nor a hint of such an opinion in his epistles. In this epistle, and wherever he alludes to the subject, the institution of slavery is recognised and accepted as an established fact with which he does not quarrel, as a condition which has its own opportunities for Christian service and its own obligations which the Christian profession enforces. In 1 Cor. vii. 21 ff. he advises the bondsman to use and improve his condition for the service of God, and to abide in it, even though he may have the opportunity of becoming free.[1]

In Eph. vi. 5–8 and Col. iii. 22, 23 he enjoins the obedience of slaves to their masters as a Christian duty. They are to serve their masters as servants of God.

Hence it is, I think, a mistake to regard Paul's silence concerning the iniquity of the institution as caused by the obvious hopelessness of eradicating a long-established, deeply rooted, social factor. I cannot agree with the view so graphically presented by Dr. Matheson (*Spiritual Development of St. Paul*, ch. xiii.), that Paul recognised Onesimus' right to freedom, but refrained from exhorting him to claim his right, because his connivance at Onesimus' flight would have been the signal for a servile insurrection and consequent anarchy. It is equally a mistake to say that he consciously addressed himself to the task of abolishing slavery by urging those aspects of the gospel which, in their practical application, he knew would eventually undermine it. It is not likely that he saw the way to its destruction at all.

On the other hand, this by no means commits the apostle to the indorsement of the abstract rightfulness of slavery. It is only to say that if that question presented itself to his own mind, he did not raise it. The same thing, for that matter, may be said of Christ, and of God in the administration of the Old-Testament economy. The fact is familiar that God temporarily recognised, tolerated, and even legalised certain institutions and practices, as polygamy, for instance, which New-Testament morality condemns, which he purposed ultimately to abolish, and which Christ does abolish.

Paul knew and appreciated the actual abuses and the evil possi-

---

[1] My view of this disputed passage differs from that of Bishop Lightfoot and Canon Evans. (See Lightf. *Introd. to Philemon*, p. 390, and Evans, *Speaker's Comm.* ad loc.)

bilities of slavery: yet it is quite possible that he may not have looked beyond such an operation of gospel principles as might rid the institution of its abuses without destroying it. What we see is, that he addressed himself to the regulation, and not to the destruction, of existing relations. He does see that the slave is more than a chattel (Philem. 10–12, 16). The Christian bondservant is the Lord's freedman (1 Cor. vii. 22). The difference between bond and free lapses in Christ with the difference between uncircumcision and circumcision, between Greek and Jew, between male and female (1 Cor. xii. 13; Gal. iii. 28). He does see that the Christian master has a duty to the slave no less than a right over him, and on this duty he insists (Eph. vi. 9; Col. iv. 1; Philem. 8–12, 15, 17).

The slave, too, was quick to perceive this, and discerned in Christianity his only prospect of betterment. It is true that Plato and Aristotle, Zeno, Epicurus, and Seneca had insisted on the duty of humanity to slaves. Seneca urged that the accident of position does not affect the real dignity of man; that freedom and slavery reside in virtue and vice rather than in outward condition, and that a good man should abstain from even the feeling of contempt for his slaves (*De Benef.* iii. 18–28; *De Vita Beata*, xxiv.; *Ep.* xlvii.). Truthful and noble sentiments these, but they did not reach far beyond the cultivated classes; they did little or nothing to engender moral aspiration in the slave, and their comparatively superficial and limited influence is shown by the condition of the slave during the prevalence of Stoicism. The slave sought his refuge where such sentiments were enforced by love rather than by philosophy; where they healingly touched those "accidents of position" and those "outward conditions," of which philosophy declared him independent, but from which, with their accompanying wrongs and cruelties and degradations, he could not extricate himself; and hence the fact that the early church was so largely recruited from the ranks of slaves.

Whatever may have been the range of Paul's outlook, the policy which he pursued vindicated itself in the subsequent history of slavery. The principles of the gospel not only curtailed its abuses, but destroyed the thing itself; for it could not exist without its abuses. To destroy its abuses was to destroy it. It survived for centuries, but the Roman codes showed more and more the impress of Christian sentiment. The official manumission of slaves became common as an act of piety or of gratitude to God; and sepulchral paintings often represent the master standing before the Good Shepherd with a band of slaves liberated at his death, pleading for him at the last judgment. Each new ruler enacted some measure which facilitated emancipation. "No one can carefully study the long series of laws, from Constantine to the tenth century, in regard to slavery, without clearly seeing the effect of Christianity. It is true that the unjust institution still survived, and some of its cruel features remained; but all through this period the new spirit of humanity is seen struggling against it, even in legislation, which is always the last to feel a new moral power in society. The very language of the acts speaks of the inspiration of the Christian faith; and the idea which lay at the bottom of the reforms, the value of each individual, and his equality to all others in the sight of God, was essentially Christian. But laws are often far behind the practices of a community. The foundation-idea of Christ's principles compelled his followers to recognise the slave as equal with the master. They sat side by side in church, and partook of the communion together. By the civil law, a master killing his slave accidentally by excessive punishment was not punished, but in the church he was excluded from communion. The chastity of the slave was strictly guarded by the church. Slave priests were free. The festivals of religion — the Sundays, fast-days, and days of joy — were early connected in the church with the emancipation of those in servitude. The consoling words of Christ, repeated from mouth to mouth, and the hope which now dawned on the world through him, became the especial comfort of that great multitude of unhappy persons, — the Roman bondsmen. The Christian teachers and clergymen became known as 'the brothers of the slave,' and the slaves themselves were called 'the freedmen of Christ'" (Charles L. Brace, *Gesta Christi*).

Tributes to the beauty, delicacy, and tact of the Epistle to Philemon come from representatives of all schools, from Luther and Calvin to Renan, Baur, and von Soden. A number of these have been collected by Lightfoot (Introd. p. 383 ff.). The letter has been compared with one addressed by the younger Pliny to a friend on a somewhat similar occasion. "Yet," to quote Bishop

Lightfoot, "if purity of diction be excepted, there will hardly be any difference of opinion in awarding the palm to the Christian apostle. As an expression of simple dignity, of refined courtesy, of large sympathy, and of warm personal affection, the Epistle to Philemon stands unrivalled. And its preëminence is the more remarkable because in style it is exceptionally loose. It owes nothing to the graces of rhetoric; its effect is due solely to the spirit of the writer." "We delight to meet with it," says Sabatier, "on our toilsome road, and to rest awhile with Paul from his great controversies and fatiguing labors in this refreshing oasis which Christian friendship offered to him. We are accustomed to conceive of the apostle as always armed for warfare, sheathed in logic, and bristling with arguments. It is delightful to find him at his ease, and for a moment able to unbend, engaged in this friendly intercourse, so full of freedom and even playfulness."

TEXT

See Introduction to Philippians

COMMENTARIES

PATRISTIC

Chrysostom, Theodore of Mopsuestia, Theodoret, Œcumenius, Theophylact. (See under Commentaries on Philippians.)

SIXTEENTH AND SEVENTEENTH CENTURIES

L. DANÆUS or DANÆU:	1579	SC. GENTILIS:	1618
R. ROLLOCK:	1598	T. TAYLOR:	1659
D. DYKE:	1618	J. H. HUMMEL:	1670

MODERN

AUG. KOCH: 1846.

J. C. WIESINGER: 1850. Trans. by Fulton: 1851. Rev. and notes, A. C. Kendrick, 1858.

H. EWALD: 1857.

J. J. VAN OOSTERZEE: *Lange's Bibelwerk.* Schaff's ed. Notes by Hackett, 1869.

LD. BP. OF DERRY: *Speaker's Comm.*

HUGUES OLTRAMARE: *Commentaire sur les Épitres de S. Paul aux Colossiens aux Éphésiens et à Philémon.* 1891. Good and scholarly, but adds nothing of special value to former commentaries.

H. VON SODEN: *Hand-Commentar.* Bd. iii. Valuable. See Comms. on Philippians, Lipsius.

For Bengel, Calvin, Alford, Meyer, Lightfoot, Beet, De Wette, Ellicott, Lumby, Dwight, Hackett, see under Commentaries on Philippians.

TO PHILEMON

THE SALUTATION

1–3. *Paul a prisoner of Christ Jesus, and Timothy the brother, to Philemon our beloved and fellow-laborer, and to Apphia our sister, and to Archippus our fellow-soldier, and to the church which assembles in thy house: Grace be unto you, and peace from God our Father, and from the Lord Jesus Christ.*

1. δέσμιος Χριστοῦ Ἰησοῦ : 'a prisoner of Christ Jesus.' (Comp. Eph. iii. 1.) In fetters because of his labors as an apostle of Christ. These words, at once awakening special interest and compassion, prepare the way for the apostle's request. The title 'apostle' is laid aside as not befitting a private and friendly letter.

Τιμόθεος : The name of Timothy is associated with that of Paul in 2 Cor., Phil., Col., 1 and 2 Thess. Here each has a separate designation. Comp. Phil. i. 1, where they are joined under the common title δοῦλοι Χτοῦ Ἰησοῦ. When Paul names others with himself in the address, it is usually because of the relations of those named to the church addressed. The mention of Timothy here may be owing to personal relations between him and Philemon; so that the appeal would be the stronger by the addition of Timothy's name. Timothy appears to have been with Paul during a great part of his three years' residence in Ephesus. He may have become acquainted with Philemon there.

ὁ ἀδελφὸς : Thus also are designated Quartus, Rom. xvi. 23; Sosthenes, 1 Cor. i. 1; Apollos, 1 Cor. xvi. 12. Timothy is not called an apostle. (See 2 Cor. i. 1; Col. i. 1.) Although Paul does not confine the name of apostle to the twelve (see Rom. xvi. 7; 1 Cor. ix. 5, 6), the having been an eyewitness of the risen Christ was an indispensable condition of the apostolate; and Timothy was a late convert, residing at Lystra, far distant from the scene of Christ's personal ministry. (See Lightf. on "The Name and Office of an Apostle," *Comm. on Galatians*, p. 92.)

Φιλήμονι : See Introduction.

τῷ ἀγαπητῷ καὶ συνεργῷ ἡμῶν: 'our beloved and fellow-laborer.' (Comp. Acts xv. 25.) Theoph. says: εἰ ἀγαπητός, δώσει τὴν χάριν, εἰ συνεργός, οὐ καθέξει τὸν δοῦλον ἀλλὰ πάλιν ἀποστελεῖ πρὸς ὑπηρεσίαν τοῦ κηρύγματος. "If beloved, he will grant the favor; if a fellow-worker, he will not retain the slave, but will send him forth again for the service of preaching."

Weizsäcker's statement (*Apost. Zeit.* p. 333) that ἀγαπητός applied by Paul to individuals indicates that they were his own converts, needs more evidence than is furnished by Rom. xvi. 5, 8, 9, 12.

συνεργὸς: Only in Paul and 3 Jn. 8. (See Rom. xvi. 3, 9, 21; Phil. ii. 25; Col. iv. 11, etc.)

ἡμῶν: Of myself and Timothy.

2. καὶ Ἀπφίᾳ τῇ ἀδελφῇ: 'and to Apphia our sister.'

DKL, Syr.[sch], Syr.[p], add αγαπητῃ.

Ἀπφία is a Phrygian name. Not the same as Ἀππίου (Acts xxviii. 15). She is commonly supposed to have been Philemon's wife, which is the more probable because the case of the slave was a household matter. "Uxori ad quam nonnihil pertinebat negotium Onesimi" (Beng.). Unless especially related to Philemon, her name would naturally have stood after the one which follows.

ἀδελφῇ: In the Christian sense.

Ἀρχίππῳ: Possibly a son of Philemon. He is mentioned Col. iv. 17 with a special admonition to fulfil the ministry (διακονίαν) which he received in the Lord; from which it may be inferred that he was an office-bearer in the church. A reason for addressing him in this letter, even if he was not a member of Philemon's household, might lie in the fact that Onesimus was to be received into the church in which Archippus exercised his ministry.

Different speculations have made him a bishop, a deacon, a presbyter, and an evangelist. Opinions differ as to whether his ministry was at Colossæ or at the neighboring city of Laodicæa, since his name occurs in the epistle to Colossæ, immediately, it is said, after the salutations to the Laodicæans. On the other hand, Wieseler (*Chronol. des Apost. Zeital.*) argues that if Archippus had been a Colossian it is not easy to see why Paul in vs. 17 makes him to be admonished by others. We do not know the motive of the exhortation. It does not immediately follow the salutations to the Laodicæans. If Archippus had not resided at Colossæ, Paul would probably have caused a salutation to be sent to him as well as to Nymphas. It is very strange that Paul should have conveyed this admonition to Archippus through a strange church, more especially when he had written at the same time to Archippus in this letter, addressing him jointly with Philemon. That the admonition to Archippus in Col. implies a rebuke (Lightf.) is not certain. (Comp. Acts xii. 25.)

συστρατιώτῃ: 'fellow-soldier.' Only here and Phil. ii. 25; but comp. 2 Tim. ii. 3. The veteran apostle salutes his younger friend as a fellow-campaigner in the gospel warfare. It is unnecessary to search for any particular crisis or contest in church affairs in which they were associated. The figure may have been suggested by Paul's military associations in Rome.

τῇ κατ' οἶκον σου ἐκκλησίᾳ : 'to the church in thy house.' The assembly of believers which met at Philemon's house. In large cities there would be several such assemblies, since no one house could accommodate the whole body, and besides, a large assembly of the whole church would have awakened the suspicion of the Roman authorities. (Comp. Acts xii. 12; Rom. xvi. 5; 1 Cor. xvi. 19; Col. iv. 15, and see note at the end of the chapter.) Ἐκκλησία was originally a secular word: 'an assembly of citizens *called out*.' So Acts xix. 39; LXX; 1 Kings viii. 65. Used of the congregation of Israel (Acts vii. 38). The Jewish assembly is more commonly styled συναγωγή, as Acts xiii. 43. Ἐκκλησία denotes the Christian community in the midst of Israel (Acts v. 11, viii. 1, xii. 1, xiv. 23, 27). Συναγωγή, however, is used of a Christian assembly (Jas. ii. 2). Both in the Old and New Testament ἐκκλησία implies a community based upon a special religious idea, and established in a special way. The word is also used in N.T. of a single church or assembly, or of a church confined to a particular place, as the church in the house of Prisca and Aquila (Rom. xvi. 5), or of Philemon as here; the church at Corinth, Jerusalem, etc. In these assemblies in private houses messages and letters from the apostles were announced or read. It is perhaps to the address of this letter to a congregational circle, as well as to an individual correspondent, that we are indebted for its preservation. Paul must have written many such private letters. The character of the address emphasises the importance of the subject of the letter as one affecting both the household circle and the church.

3. χάρις ὑμῖν, etc.: See on Phil. i. 2.

4–7. *Because I hear of the love and faith which you have towards the Lord Jesus and to all the saints, I thank God whenever I make mention of you in my prayers; praying that in your full knowledge of every spiritual blessing which we as Christians possess, your faith may prove itself for the glory of Christ in the communication of its fruits to others. For on hearing from you, I had much joy and comfort on account of your love, because of the refreshment which the hearts of the saints have received from you, my brother.*

4. εὐχαριστῶ, etc.: 'I thank my God always when I make mention of you in my prayers.' (See on Phil. i. 3.) Thus πάντοτε is connected with εὐχαρ. (Comp. Rom. i. 8–10; 1 Cor. i. 4; Col. i.

3, 4.) The construction probably accords with Col. i. 3, 4, since there is a close correspondence of the phraseology, and the two letters were written at the same time. Ποιούμενος defines πάντοτε. (See on Phil. i. 4.)

Ellic. differs from most of the modern commentators by connecting πάντοτε with ποιούμενος.

All that the apostle had heard of Philemon caused him to add thanksgiving to his prayers. "Notandum quod pro quo gratias agit, pro eodem simul precatur. Nunquam enim tanta est vel perfectissimis gratulandi materia, quamdiu in hoc mundo vivunt, quin precibus indigeant, ut det illis Deus non tantum perseverare usque ad finem, sed in dies proficere. Haec enim laus quam mox Philemoni tribuit, breviter complectitur totam Christiani hominis perfectionem" (Calv.).

ἐπὶ τῶν προσευχῶν μου: 'when engaged in offering my prayers.' Ἐπὶ blends the temporal with the local force. For προσευχή, prayer in general, see on Phil. iv. 6. Any special petition would be δέησις, which is implied in μνείαν.

5. *ἀκούων*: 'because I hear,' through Epaphras (Col. i. 7, 8, iv. 12), or possibly from Onesimus himself.

Ἀκούων indicates the cause of εὐχαριστῶ; not the motive of the intercession, as De W., which would leave εὐχ. without a cause assigned for it; while the 'mention' of Philemon did not require that a motive should be assigned.

σου τὴν ἀγάπην καὶ τὴν πίστιν ἣν ἔχεις πρὸς τὸν κύριον Ἰησοῦν καὶ εἰς πάντας τοὺς ἁγίους: 'thy love and faith which thou hast towards the Lord Jesus and to all the saints.'

εις τ. κυρ. εις παντ. ACD*, 17, 137, WH.
προς τ. κυρ. ℵ DFGKLP, Syr.p, Tisch., R.T., Weiss.

Love and faith are both exercised towards the Lord Jesus, and by a hasty and compressed construction, due to the momentum of the previous part of the clause, the saints also are made the objects of both love and faith, instead of his writing, 'the love and the faith which thou hast towards the Lord Jesus, and the love which thou hast to all the saints.' (Comp. Col. i. 4.) Faith works by love, and love exercised towards the saints is a work of faith. In the next clause he speaks of a 'communication' of faith to others. Lumby very aptly says: "The love was displayed towards the Christian congregation, the faith towards the Lord Jesus Christ; but they are so knit together where they truly exist that St. Paul speaks of them both as exhibited alike towards Christ and towards his people."

A parallel is furnished by Eph. i. 15, if ἀγάπην is omitted from the text with AB, WH., R.T. Tisch. retains. See WH., ad loc., *Gk. Test.*, "Notes on Select Readings." (Comp. Tit. iii. 15.) Mey., Win. (l. 2), Beet, render πίστιν 'fidelity' or 'faithfulness,' a sense which is found in N.T. though rarely (see Rom. iii. 3; 1 Tim. v. 12; Tit. ii. 10), and which is habitual in LXX. (See Lightf. *Comm. on Gal.* p. 152, and Hatch, *Essays in Bib. Gk.* p. 83 ff.). But (1) πίστις with ἀγάπη never occurs in this sense in N.T. (See 1 Cor. xiii. 13; Gal. v. 6; 1 Thess. i. 3, v. 8; 1 Tim. i. 14, vi. 11; 2 Tim. ii. 22.) This is not affected by the fact that ἀγάπην here precedes πίστιν. (See Eph. vi. 23.) Gal. v. 22 and 1 Tim. iv. 12 are not in point. In those passages the words occur in enumerations; and in Gal. v. 22 ἀγάπη is entirely detached from πίστις. (2) Ἔχειν πίστιν in N.T. never means 'to have fidelity.' The phrase occurs eleven times, and always means 'to have faith.' A very common explanation is by the rhetorical *chiasmus* or cross-reference, by which ἀγάπην is referred to τοὺς ἁγίους, and πίστιν to Κυρ. Ἰησ. But the examples of *chiasmus* commonly cited, even from the class., illustrate mainly the mere *arrangement* of the words, as where the adjective and the noun are in inverse order in two successive clauses. (See Jelf, *Gram.* 904, 3; Farrar, on the rhetoric of St. Paul, *Life and Work*, i. 626.) Besides, the ἣν ἔχεις connects πίστιν with the entire clause πρὸς τ. κυρ. . . . ἁγίους. The position of σου indicates that it belongs to both ἀγάπ. and πίσ. Comp. the different arrangement in Col. i. 4.

πρὸς τὸν κύριον: Πρὸς nowhere else with πίστις as directed at Christ. Of faith 'towards' God, 1 Thess. i. 8. Comp. πεποίθησιν πρὸς τὸν θεὸν (2 Cor. iii. 4). Ἀγάπη commonly with εἰς in Paul. (See Rom. v. 8; 2 Cor. ii. 8; Col. i. 4; 1 Thess. iii. 12; 2 Thess. i. 3; but comp. 2 Cor. viii. 7; 1 Cor. xvi. 24.) The use of different prepositions is not to be accounted for on the ground of Paul's fondness for varying the prepositions without designing to express a different relation (Mey.). Paul does, indeed, often use different prepositions in one clause and with reference to one subject in order to define the conception more accurately (Rom. iii. 30, xi. 36; Gal. i. 1, ii. 16; Col. i. 14); but it is too much to say that no different relation is intended.

See Holtzn. *Pastoralbr.* p. 101; Winer, xlvii.; Deissmann, *Die neutest. Formel 'in Christo Jesu,'* pp. 5, 6.

Bearing in mind that τὴν ἀγάπ. and τὴν πίστ. are so closely related in this passage (see above, and Oltr. ad loc.), πρὸς may be taken in the sense indicated in the notes on Phil. ii. 30, iv. 6, as expressing, not the mere direction of faith and love towards Christ (Lightf., Ellic., Alf.), but the relation of loving and believing intercourse with him; while εἰς indicates the direct practical bearing of faith and love on the Christian brethren.

πρὸς in class. occurs frequently of all sorts of personal intercourse. (See Hom. *Od.* xiv. 331, xix. 288; Thucyd. ii. 59, iv. 15, vii. 82; Hdt. i. 61.) It occurs with φιλία, εὔνοια, ἀπιστία, and with πίστις in the sense of 'a pledge' (Thucyd. iv. 51; Xen. *Cyr.* iii. 1, 39).

6. ὅπως ἡ κοινωνία τῆς πίστεώς σου ἐνεργὴς γένηται: 'that the communication of thy faith may become (or prove itself) effectual.' The thought grows directly out of εἰς πάντ. τ. ἁγ., and ὅπως expresses the purpose of the intercession, μνεί. ποιούμ. etc., in vs. 4. (Comp. Mt. ii. 23, vi. 2, 16; Acts ix. 17; 1 Cor. i. 29; 2 Thess. i. 12.) He prays that the love and faith which so greatly aid and comfort all the saints may likewise communicate their blessing to Onesimus, though he does not mention his name. Notice the general similarity of structure between this passage and Eph. i. 16, 17; Phil. i. 3 ff.; Col. i. 3 ff. — a prayer after the thanksgiving, followed by a final particle introducing a clause. Alf. and Oltr. take ὅπως with εὐχαριστῶ. Κοιν. τ. πίστ. signifies 'the communication of thy faith' to others, Onesimus among them: your faith imparting its virtue through your deeds of love. Κοινωνία is used as in Rom. xv. 26; 2 Cor. viii. 4, ix. 13; Heb. xiii. 16.

Mey. connects ὅπως with ἣν ἔχεις, and explains κοινωνία as the fellowship entered into by the saints with Philemon's Christian fidelity. Thus, 'the faith which thou hast in order that the fellowship of the saints with it may not be a mere idle sympathy, but may express itself in action.' Oltr., the communion established by faith between Paul and Philemon. Beng., 'the faith which thou hast and exercisest in common with us.' Lightf., apparently taking πίστεως as genit. of possession or source, 'your charitable deeds which spring from your faith.'

Ἐνεργὴς: 'effectual,' only twice by Paul. (See 1 Cor. xvi. 9, and comp. Heb. iv. 12.) Effectual by reason of the fruit which follows. The Vulg. 'evidens' is probably from a reading ἐναργής.

ἐν ἐπιγνώσει: 'in the full knowledge.' For ἐπιγ., see on Phil. i. 9. The subject of the ἐπιγ. is Philemon. The apostle prays that, working in the sphere of full knowledge, the communication of Philemon's faith may prove itself effective. In other words, the knowledge of every good thing — gospel truth, the principles of Christian fraternity and ministry, the ends of Christian striving, the supplies furnished by the divine Spirit — is the element in which Philemon's faith will develop to the greatest advantage of others, including Onesimus. The larger his knowledge of such good things, the more will he be moved to deal kindly and Christianly. He will recognise through this knowledge the rightness of Paul's request, and will not allow his resentment towards Onesimus to prevent his recognising the good which the knowledge of Christ has developed in him.

Mey., Ellic., Beet, Calv., refer ἐπίγνωσις to the knowledge possessed by others. Thus, Mey., "That whoever enters into participation of the same (fellowship) may make this partaking, through knowledge of every Christian blessing, effective for Christ." This is determined by his explanation of κοιν. πίστ. See above.

The prayer for ἐπίγνωσις is characteristic of this group of epistles. (See Eph. i. 17; Phil. i. 9; Col. i. 9, 10, ii. 2, and comp. Rom. xii. 2; Eph. iv. 13; Tit. i. 1.) For this use of ἐν, marking the sphere or element in which something takes place, see 2 Cor. i. 6; Col. i. 29.

παντὸς ἀγαθοῦ τοῦ ἐν ὑμῖν: 'of every good thing that is in you,' as Christians. Every spiritual gift which you possess. (Comp. Eph. i. 3, 17.)

του after αγαθου, ℵ DF[gr] GKLP; Tisch., WH. [], Weiss, R.T.; AC, 17, om. του.

υμιν, ℵ FGP, 17, 31, 37, 47, 80, 137, Vulg., Cop., Syr.[sch et p], Tisch., Weiss, R.T.

For υμιν ACDKL, WH., read ημιν.

εἰς Χριστόν: 'unto Christ.' Connect with ἐνεργ. γέν. Unto Christ's glory — the advancement of his cause. Compare εἰς τὸ εὐαγγέλιον (Phil. i. 5). "That ultimate reference to Christ which is the life of all true Christian work, and alone renders communication energetic" (Bp. of Derry). "Bonum nobis exhibitum redundare debet in Christum" (Beng.). Not = ἐν Χριστῷ.

Ιησουν added by ℵ[c] DFGKLP, Vulg., Syr.[p], Arm.
Text, WH., Tisch., R.T., Weiss.

7. χαρὰν γὰρ πολλὴν ἔσχον: 'for I had much joy.'

A few secondary uncials and some Fath. read χαριν.
DCKL, Syr.[utr], εχομεν for εσχον.

Γὰρ gives the reason for the thanksgiving in vs. 4, 5, and this verse takes up the two points of the thanksgiving, — the love and the ministry to the brethren.

Ellic., De W., v. Sod., Alf., connect with the prayer just preceding. Beet with both the thanksgiving and the prayer.

Ἔσχον: 'I had,' when I received the report. Comp. ἀκούων (vs. 5).

ὅτι: 'because.' Explaining more particularly the ἐπὶ τ. ἀγ. σου.

τὰ σπλάγχνα: 'the hearts.' (See on Phil. i. 8.)

τῶν ἁγίων: See on Phil. i. 1.

ἀναπέπαυται: 'have been refreshed.' Ἀναπαύειν, originally 'to cause to cease' as pain or sorrow. Hence 'to relieve' or 'refresh.' (See Mt. xi. 28, xxvi. 45; Mk. vi. 31; 1 Cor. xvi. 18; 2 Cor. vii. 13.) In Attic prose it is almost a technical expression for the resting of soldiers. Its dominant idea is refreshment in contrast with weariness from toil. (See Schmidt, *Synon.* 25, 2.) Lightf. says it expresses a *temporary* relief, as the simple παυέσθαι expresses a final cessation. This needs qualifying. The compound does express a temporary relief. Ἀνάπαυσις frequently in LXX of the rest of the Sabbath. So Mk. vi. 31, of the temporary retirement of the disciples. But, on the other hand, the refreshment promised by Christ to the weary (Mt. xi. 28, 29) is not a mere temporary relief, and the word is used of the rest of the blessed dead, Apoc. xiv. 13.

Often in Ign. in the phrase ἀναπαύειν με (αὐτοὺς) κατὰ πάντα (*Eph.* ii.; *Smyr.* ix., x., xii.; *Trall.* xii.; *Mag.* xv.; *Rom.* x.).

ἀδελφέ: Not 'brother indeed,' but a simple expression of affection. (Comp. Gal. vi. 18.)

8–20. *Wherefore, although my relations to you would warrant me in enjoining on you that which is fitting, yet, for love's sake, I prefer to ask it of you as a favor; being such as I am, Paul, an old man, and a prisoner for the gospel's sake. I entreat you, therefore, on behalf of my son Onesimus, who has been converted through my instrumentality during my imprisonment. Once indeed he was not what his name implies, but was useless to you. Now, however, he is profitable both to you and to myself. I send him back to you, dear though he is to me. I had indeed a mind to keep him with me in order that he might minister to me in my imprisonment as you yourself would gladly have done; but I was unwilling to do anything without your concurrence, for I desired that your service to me should be voluntary and not of necessity. And then it occurred to me that God had allowed him to be thus separated from you for a time, in order that he might come back to you a better servant and a Christian brother besides. Such a brother he is to me; how much more to you his rightful master. I ask you then, in view of our mutual fellowship, to receive him as you would me; and if he has wronged you in any way, or is in your debt, put that to my account. This is my promise to repay it, signed with my own hand; though I might intimate that it is you who are my debtor for your very self; since it was through me that you became a Christian. Receive Onesimus then, and thus render me a personal favor, affording me joy and refreshment in Christ.*

8. διό: 'wherefore': because I am thus comforted by you. Connect with παρακαλῶ, vs. 9, and not with the participial clause.

πολλὴν ἐν Χριστῷ παρρησίαν ἔχων: 'though I have much boldness in Christ.' Boldness growing out of their Christian relations. Their personal intimacy, St. Paul's apostolic office, and Philemon's obligation to him for his conversion (vs. 19), would warrant the apostle, if so disposed, in laying his commands upon Philemon in the matter of receiving Onesimus.

v. Soden thinks that no allusion to apostolic authority is intended, because the apostolic title is omitted in the introduction. But this does not necessarily follow. Even though the title is omitted, there is no reason why Paul should not allude to his apostolic authority.

For παρρησίαν, see on Phil. i. 20. Ἐπιτάσσειν, 'to enjoin' or 'command,' is used rather of commanding which attaches to a definite office and relates to permanent obligations under the office, than of special injunctions for particular occasions (ἐπιτέλλειν. See Schmidt, *Synon.* 8, 10).

τὸ ἀνῆκον: 'that which is fitting.' (See Eph. v. 4; Col. iii. 18; LXX; 1 Macc. x. 40, xi. 35; 2 Macc. xiv. 8.) The primary meaning of the verb is 'to have come up to' or 'arrived at,' as to have attained a standard of measurement or weight, or to have reached a height. Hence, to have come to one so as to have become his; to pertain to or belong to him. Comp. Hdt. vi. 109: καὶ κῶς ἐς σέ τι τούτων ἀνήκει τῶν πραγμάτων τὸ κῦρος ἔχειν: 'and how it comes to thee to have, in some sort, authority over these things.'

9. διὰ τὴν ἀγάπην: 'for love's sake.' Love in its widest sense, as the characteristic virtue of all Christians. Not to be limited to the affection between Paul and Philemon.

μᾶλλον: 'rather' than command thee. The object of comparison is omitted. (See on Phil. i. 12.) Paul desires to obtain for love's sake and by asking, what he might have obtained by authority. Comp. the opening and close of Pliny's letter to a friend on a similar occasion: "Vereor ne videar non rogare sed cogere" (*Ep.* ix.).

τοιοῦτος ὢν, ὡς Παῦλος πρεσβύτης νυνὶ δὲ καὶ δέσμιος Χριστοῦ Ἰησοῦ παρακαλῶ: 'being such (as I am), as Paul the aged and now also a prisoner of Jesus Christ, I beseech thee.' Paul would say: I might justly enjoin thee, but, for love's sake, I rather beseech thee. This general statement of his attitude stands by itself, and forms a complete sentence. He then goes on to define. I do not speak as an apostle, but simply in my personal capacity. Being such as I am, — Paul, an old man, a prisoner of Christ, — I beseech thee, etc. Thus a period is placed after παρακαλῶ, vs. 9. Τοιοῦτος is Paul's general description of himself, which is farther defined with the three particulars, — Paul, aged, a prisoner. Accordingly τοιοῦτος points forward to these details.

There is much difference among interpreters as to the connection. The points in question are:

(1) Whether τοιοῦτος ὢν is to be connected with ὡς Παῦλος or separated from it.

(2) Whether τοιοῦτος ὢν begins a new sentence or is connected with the preceding παρακαλῶ, *i.e.* whether a period or a comma shall be placed after παρακ. (vs. 9).

(3) Whether the thought in τοι. ὢν refers back to Paul's attitude as a suppliant (διὰ τ. ἀγ. μᾶλ. παρακ.), or to his claim as an apostle (παρρησ. ἔχ. ἐπιτ.), or points forward to his attitude as merely Paul, an old man and a prisoner.

As to (1), Lightf., Dw., Beet, R.V., make τοιοῦ. and ὡς correlative: 'such an one as Paul.' But τοιοῦτος can be defined only by a following adjective, or by οἷος, ὅς, ὅσος, or ὥστε with the infin. Never by ὡς. Τοιοῦτος followed by ὡς occurs nowhere in N.T., and Lightf. has not established the correlation by the single citation from Plat. (*Symp.* 181 E) and another from Alexis. Besides it is doubtful whether the reference to *Symp.* is in point; for τὸ τοιοῦτον may be taken absolutely there, and need not be correlated with ὥσπερ. (See Jelf, 655.) This absolute use of τοιοῦτος is well established. (See Hom. *Il.* vii. 42; Soph. *Aj.* 1298; *Philoct.* 1049; Plat. *Repub.* 429 B.) Moreover, the rule which makes τοιοῦτος refer to what precedes, while τοιόσδε refers to what follows, is often reversed (Jelf, 655). Professor Sophocles says: "Unless the Greek be irregular, τοιοῦτος and ὡς cannot be reciprocal terms."

(2) Period after παρακαλῶ (vs. 9), by Ellic., Mey., Alf., De W., v. Sod., Oltr. Comma after παρακαλῶ, and τοι. ὢν the continuation of the preceding clause (Lightf., Dw.). 'I beseech thee, being such an one as Paul,' etc. In that case the παρακ. of vs. 10 is resumptive.

(3) τοιοῦτος ὢν is referred to Paul's attitude as a suppliant by Mey., v. Sod., Ellic., Alf.

Παῦλος, πρεσβύτης, δέσμιος: Apparently three details of τοιοῦ. are intended. Some, however, take Παῦλ. and πρεσβ. as one conception (Luth., Calv., De W., Ellic., Oltr.).

πρεσβύτης: 'an aged man.' His precise age cannot be determined. He is called νεανίας at the time of the martyrdom of Stephen (Acts vii. 58); and if, at the time of writing this letter he were sixty or even fifty years old, there would be no impropriety in his calling himself πρεσβύτης. The term is wholly relative. He might have aged prematurely under his numerous hardships. According to Hippocrates, a man was called πρεσβύτης from forty-nine to fifty-six; after that, γέρων.

Lightf. conjectures that the reading is πρεσβευτής, 'an ambassador,' in accordance with Eph. vi. 20; and that that should be the meaning even if πρεσβύτης is retained. So WH. The two forms are certainly interchanged in LXX. (See 2 Chron. xxxii. 31; 1 Macc. xiii. 21, xiv. 21, 22; 2 Macc. xi. 34.) Both in Eph. vi. 20, and 2 Cor. v. 20, πρεσβεύειν is used in connection with public relations. "Ambassador" does not seem quite appropriate to a private letter, and does not suit Paul's attitude of entreaty. The suggestion of public relations is rather in δέσμιος 'I. X.

νυνὶ δὲ καὶ: 'now,' at the time of my writing this; καὶ: 'besides,' in addition to my age.

δέσμιος Ἰησοῦ Χριστοῦ: Comp. vs. 1; Eph. iii. 1; iv. 1; 2 Tim. 1, 8. Not 'a prisoner belonging to Christ,' nor 'for Christ's sake,' διὰ Χριστὸν δεδεμένος (Chr.), but one whom Christ has brought into captivity. (See Win. xxx. 2.)

Lightf., in accordance with his explanation of πρεσβύτης, thinks that the genit. 'I. X. belongs to both πρεσβ. and δέσμ.

10. τοῦ ἐμοῦ τέκνου: An affectionate designation of Onesimus. The slight hesitation in mentioning the name of the slave, and the delay in coming to the point of the letter, are noticeable. Τέκνον in a similar sense, a spiritual child, 1 Cor. iv. 14, 17; Gal. iv. 19 (τεκνία); 1 Tim. i. 2, 18; 2 Tim. ii. 1.

ὃν ἐγέννησα : Of whose conversion I was the instrument. The appeal in the thought of his won child is heightened by ἐμοῦ, and by the fact that he is the spiritual child of his captivity. For this figurative use of γεννᾷν, comp. 1 Cor. iv. 15. Thayer, *Lex.*, cites *Sanhedr.* fol. 19, 2, of one who brings others to his own way of life. "If one teaches the son of his neighbor the law, the Scripture reckons this the same as though he had begotten him."

ἐν τοῖς δεσμοῖς : 'in my bonds.'

μου added by ℵ^c CDKLP, Syr.^utr, Cop., Arm., Æth.

'Ονήσιμον : 'profitable' (ὀνίνημι). A common name among slaves, like many others expressing utility, as Chresimus, Chrestus, Onesiphorus, Symphorus, Carpus. (See Lightf.'s *Introd. to Philem.* sec. 4.) Accordingly, Weizsäcker's statement that the allegorical character of the epistle is apparent from this name has no relevancy whatever (*Apost. Zeital.* p. 545). 'Ονήσιμον is accus. by attraction after ἐγένν.

11. ἄχρηστον : 'useless,' 'unserviceable.' Titmann (*Syn.*) says that to the idea of uselessness it adds that of harmfulness, while ἀχρεῖος means simply that of which there is no need. (See Schmidt, *Synon.* 166, 6.) It is not, however, probable that the idea of harmfulness is implied in connection with a possible robbery of his master by Onesimus. (See on vs. 18.)

Ἄχρηστος only here in N.T., LXX, Hos. viii. 8; Sap. ii. 11, iii. 11; Sir. xvi. 1, xxvii. 19; 2 Macc. vii. 5.

νυνὶ δε : 'but now,' that he has become a Christian disciple. Νυνὶ δε, mostly and very often in Paul. (See Rom. vi. 22, vii. 6, 17, xv. 23, 25; 1 Cor. v. 11, etc.)

σοὶ καὶ ἐμοὶ εὔχρηστον : 'profitable to thee and to me.' Formerly useless to *thee*, when he was thy worthless, runaway slave, and before *I* had known him. Now profitable to us both. The nice use of the personal pronouns and the assumption of a joint interest in Onesimus are very charming. (Comp. Rom. xvi. 13; 1 Cor. xvi. 18; Phil. ii. 27.)

ℵ* F^gr G, 17, 31, 47, 67, Syr.^sch, Æth., add και before σοι. So Tisch., Weiss.
και om. by ACDKLP, Syr.^p, Arm., WH., R.T.

εὔχρηστον occurs only here, 2 Tim. ii. 21, iv. 11. Profitable to Philemon in the new and higher character of his service as a Christian, as described (Eph. vi. 5 ff.; Col. iii. 22 ff.). Profitable to Paul as an evidence of his successful apostolic labor (καρπὸς ἔργου, Phil. i. 22), and therefore a cause of joy and encouragement. There may also be a reference to Onesimus' kindly ministries to himself in his imprisonment (vs. 13).

12. ὃν ἀνέπεμψά σοι αὐτόν, τοῦτ' ἔστιν τὰ ἐμὰ σπλάγχνα: 'whom I send back to thee in his own person, that is my very heart.' Αὐτόν thus emphasises ὅν, and prepares the way for τὰ ἐμὰ σπλ.

Lightf. punctuates ἀνέπ. σοι. Αὐτόν, τουτέστιν τὰ ἐμὰ σπλ., ὃν ἐγὼ, etc., thus beginning a new sentence with αὐτὸν as depending on the idea of προσλαβοῦ (vs. 17). Such a "dislocation" is hardly conceivable, even in Paul's writing.

Ἀνέπεμψα is the epistolary aorist, by which the writer puts himself at the point of time when the correspondent is reading his letter. (See Acts xxiii. 30; Phil. ii. 28; Win. xl. 2; and note on ἔγραψα, vs. 19.) For τὰ ἐμὰ σπλάγχνα, see on Phil. i. 8, ii. i. Pesh. renders 'my son.' Wetst. cites Artemidorus, Ὀνειροκριτικά (i. 46) οἱ παῖδες σπλάγχνα λέγονται; also *Id.* 35, v. 57, and Philo, *De Joseph.* 5 (ii. 45). In Latin poetry and post-Augustine prose *viscera* is used in the same sense. (See Ov. *Met.* vi. 651, viii. 478, x. 465; Q. Curt. iv. 14, 22.) So Chr. and Thdrt. But this does not agree with Paul's usage elsewhere. (See 2 Cor. vi. 12, vii. 15; Phil. i. 8, ii. 1; Col. iii. 12.) Besides, it would be tautological after ὃν ἐγέννησα.

13. ὃν ἐγὼ ἐβουλόμην πρὸς ἐμαυτὸν κατέχειν: 'whom I was minded to keep with myself.' The expression of an actual thought and desire entertained by Paul; ἐβουλόμην indicating deliberation with an accompanying inclination. I was inclined to keep him, and was turning over the matter in my mind. See on τὸ θέλειν, Phil. ii. 13.

Lightf. prefers the conditional sense of the imperfect, 'I could have wished,' referring it to a suppressed conditional clause, 'if circumstances had favored.' This is a well-known use of the imperf. (See Acts xxv. 22; Rom. ix. 3; Gal. iv. 20; and Lightf. *On Revis. of N.T.*, under "Faults of Grammar.") But no such conditional clause is implied; for Paul does not intimate that the fulfilment of his wish was impossible, and that therefore he did not cherish it, but only that, though he entertained the wish, he refrained from acting upon it until he should have learned Philemon's pleasure in the matter (vs. 14).

πρὸς ἐμαυτὸν: 'with myself.' See on πρὸς, vs. 5; and Phil. iv. 6.

κατέχειν: For the verb, see Lk. iv. 42, viii. 15; Rom. i. 18; 1 Thess. v. 21.

ἵνα ὑπὲρ σοῦ μοι διακονῇ: 'that he might serve me on thy behalf.' A delicate justification of ἐβουλόμην, and full of tact. The ὑπὲρ σου is exquisite, assuming that his friend would delight in rendering him, through the slave, the service which he could not personally perform. Ὑπὲρ is not for ἀντὶ, 'instead of,' or 'in thy place' (Thdrt., Œc., Calv., De W., Bleek, van Oos.), but has its usual N.T. sense, 'on behalf of,' or 'for thy sake.' The expression thus gains in delicacy. Onesimus is more than a mere substitute for Philemon. In these words the relation of master and slave disappears for the moment. Both are servants for Christ's sake in the discharge of a ministry congenial to both. The suggestion is already conveyed by εὔχρηστον that Onesimus, in becoming a Christian disciple, has passed into a new and higher sphere of service, in which he and his master are on common ground. At the same time, there is a hint that Onesimus, even as a slave, is rendering better service to the master whom he has wronged, in thus serving Philemon's friend and teacher; serving no longer as a menial, but in hearty sympathy with his master.

ἐν τοῖς δεσμοῖς τοῦ εὐαγγελίου: 'in the bonds of the gospel'; of which the gospel is the cause; in my imprisonment which has resulted from the preaching of the gospel. Thus a hint is added of his need of such service as that of Onesimus, which has the force of an appeal, as in vs. 9, 10. (Comp. Eph. iv. 1, vi. 20, and Ign. *Trall.* xii.: παρακαλεῖ ὑμᾶς τὰ δεσμά μου, ἃ ἕνεκεν Ἰησοῦ Χριστοῦ περιφέρω: "my bonds exhort you which I wear for the sake of Jesus Christ." See also *Eph.* xi: *Magn.* i.).

14. χωρὶς δὲ τῆς σῆς γνώμης: 'but without thy judgment.' 'But,' though I had the inclination. Χωρὶς, 'apart from,' in N.T. almost entirely supplements ἄνευ, 'without,' which occurs only three times, and not in Paul. (See Ellic. on Eph. ii. 12.) Γνώμης, not frequent in N.T. Primarily 'a means of knowing' (γινώσκειν): the organ by which one knows. Hence mind and its operations, thought, judgment, opinion. (See Acts xx. 3; 1 Cor. i. 10, vii. 25; 2 Cor. viii. 10; Apoc. xvii. 13, 17.) 'Mind' or 'judgment' is the meaning throughout the N.T. Paul was unwilling to take any steps without having Philemon's judgment as to what was right in the case.

ἠθέλησα: 'I determined.' Comp. the aor. with the imperf. ἐβουλόμην. I was deliberating and came to the decision.

ἵνα μὴ ὡς κατὰ ἀνάγκην τὸ ἀγαθόν σου ᾖ: 'in order that thy benefit might not be as of necessity'; the benefit, namely, which Philemon would confer by allowing Onesimus to remain with Paul. Ἀγαθόν not in the sense of 'morally good,' but 'kindly,' 'beneficent.' (Comp. Rom. v. 7, vii. 12; 1 Thess. iii. 6; Tit. ii. 5; 1 Pet. ii. 18, and see Lightf. *Notes on Eps. of St. P. from Unpublished Commentaries*, pp. 45, 286, 303.)

The point made by Mey., Ellic., Beet, Alf., that τὸ ἀγαθὸν is general — the category under which falls the special ἀγαθὸν of Onesimus' remaining — seems to be an over-refinement. The special reference to πρὸς ἐμαυτὸν κατέχειν (vs. 13) is not affected by the fact that Paul did not intend to keep Onesimus (Mey.). His intention was in abeyance for a time. He actually wished to keep him, and debated with himself whether he should not keep him, but he did not resolve to keep him. In that case Philemon would have served Paul, and Paul would have received a benefit from him without consulting him, which was what he did not wish.

ὡς κατὰ ἀνάγκην: 'as of necessity'; 'compulsion-wise' (Ellic.). Ὡς, seeming as, wearing the appearance of. Introduced because

Paul is satisfied that his retaining Onesimus would have been agreeable to Philemon; but he would not have it *appear* as if Philemon's permission was constrained. Κατ. ἀνάγ., not = ἐξ ἀνάγκης (as Oltr.), which marks the origin of the action, but indicating that the action is performed according to a certain rule or model. (See Ellic. on Tit. iii. 5.) This particular phrase only here in N.T., but see κατὰ νόμον, φύσιν, ἀλήθειαν, σάρκα, πνεῦμα, ἐρίθειαν. LXX, only 2 Macc. xv. 2.

κατὰ ἑκούσιον: 'of free will'; 'according to what is voluntary.' Ἑκούσιος only here in N.T. (See LXX, Num. xv. 3.) For the same antithesis see 1 Pet. v. 2.

15. Another reason for not detaining Onesimus. Paul might thus have crossed the purpose of divine Providence. The consideration is modestly introduced with τάχα as the suggestion of a possibility, and not as assuming acquaintance with God's designs. It might be that God allowed the slave to leave you in order that he might become a Christian disciple; and if I should retain him, you would not have him back in your household as a Christian brother. Philemon's attention is thus turned from his individual wrongs to the providential economy which has made these wrongs work for good.

Γὰρ explains the additional motive of ἠθέλησα. Τάχα is found only here and Rom. v. 7.

ἐχωρίσθη: 'he was parted (from thee).' The word is chosen with rare tact. He does not say 'he ran away,' which might excite Philemon's anger; but 'he was separated,' and, by the use of the passive, he puts Onesimus' flight into relation with the ordering of Providence. See Chrysostom's comparison with the case of Joseph, who says, "God did send me before you" (Gen. xlv. 5).

πρὸς ὥραν: 'for a season.' Indefinite. (Comp. 2 Cor. vii. 8; Gal. ii. 5; 1 Thess. ii. 17.) Whatever the period of separation, it was but 'an hour' as compared with its lasting consequences.

ἵνα . . . ἀπέχῃς: 'that thou mightest have him.' The compound verb denotes the completeness of the possession. (See on Phil. iv. 18.) The bond between the master and the slave would no longer be that of ownership by purchase which death would dissolve, but their common relation to Christ which made them brethren, now and evermore.

Lightf. explains ἀπέχῃς 'receive *back*.' If this is correct, it is the only instance in N.T., though ἀπὸ has this meaning in composition with διδόναι, καθιστάναι, καταλλάσσειν, and λαμβάνειν. (See Mt. xii. 13; Mk. iii. 5; Lk. iv. 20, ix. 42, xix. 8.)

16. οὐκέτι ὡς δοῦλον: 'no longer as a slave.' Ὡς denotes the subjective conception of Onesimus' relation to his master, without reference to the external relation; *i.e.* Paul does not say that

Philemon is to receive Onesimus freed, and no longer a slave, which would be δοῦλον simply, but that, whether he shall remain a slave or not, he will no longer be regarded *as* a slave, but as a brother beloved. The relation between the master and the slave is transformed. The slave, even without ceasing to be a slave, is on a different and higher footing with his master. Both are in Christ. (See 1 Cor. vii. 20–24; Col. iii. 11.) The relation is conceived absolutely, without special reference to Philemon's view of it.

ὑπὲρ δοῦλον: 'above a slave'; 'more than a slave.' For this sense of ὑπὲρ, see Mt. x. 24, 37; Acts xxvi. 13; Win. xlix.

ἀδελφὸν ἀγαπητόν: Explaining ὑπὲρ δοῦλον.

μαλίστα ἐμοί: 'especially to me' whose spiritual child he is.

πόσῳ δὲ μᾶλλον σοὶ: 'but how much more to thee.' Because he is your property. There is a hint that the property relation involves more than mere ownership and receiving of service. Ownership should be a basis for Christian fraternity and its mutual ministries.

καὶ ἐν σαρκὶ καὶ ἐν κυρίῳ: 'both in the flesh and in the Lord.' Explaining πόσῳ μᾶλλον. In the mere external relation (ἐν σαρκὶ) Onesimus will be a better servant; in the spiritual relation (ἐν κυρίῳ) he will be on a higher footing, and will have acquired a new value as a Christian brother.

The main point of the letter is at last reached, backed by an appeal to Philemon's fellowship with Paul. Paul has sent Onesimus back (vs. 11). He prays Philemon to give him a kindly reception.

17. εἰ οὖν με ἔχεις κοινωνόν: 'if therefore thou regardest me as a partner.' Οὖν sums up the considerations just urged, and resumes the request foreshadowed in vs. 11, 12. For ἔχεις comp. Luke xiv. 18; Phil. ii. 29. Κοινωνόν: The noun and its kindred verbs are used in N.T. almost exclusively of ethical and spiritual relations. Even when applied to pecuniary contributions, they imply Christian fellowship as the basis of the liberality. Comp., however, Lk. v. 10; Heb. ii. 14. Here a partner in Christian faith, so that the refusal of Paul's request would be inconsistent with such a relation. Surely not as Beng. "that what is thine may be mine, and mine thine."

προσλαβοῦ αὐτὸν ὡς ἐμέ: 'receive him as myself.' Take him unto thee. Admit him to Christian fellowship. Ὡς ἐμέ. Comp. τὰ ἐμὰ σπλάγχνα (vs. 12).

He guards against certain possible hindrances to Onesimus' favorable reception.

18. εἰ δέ τι ἠδίκησεν σε ἢ ὀφείλει: 'if he hath in aught wronged thee or is in thy debt.' Another exhibition of the apostle's tact in dealing with a delicate subject. Besides running away, Onesimus had possibly robbed his master. He had at least deprived him of his services by his flight. Paul states the case hypothetically, and puts the offence as a debt.

τοῦτο ἐμοὶ ἐλλόγα: 'place this to my account.' He will be responsible for the amount.

Ἐλλόγα, only here and Rom. v. 13. Not in class., though occurring in one or two inscriptions. It does not occur in LXX.

The reading ελλογει has very scanty support.

19. ἐγὼ Παῦλος ἔγραψα τῇ ἐμῇ χειρί: 'I, Paul, write it with my own hand.' Paul's promissory note. Ἔγραψα is the epistolary aorist. (Comp. 1 Pet. v. 12; 1 Jn. ii. 14, 21, 26.) It would appear that Paul wrote these and at least the two following words with his own hand. How much more he may have written, whether the entire letter, or all the verses from 19 to the end, is purely a matter of speculation.

Lightf. says that this incidental mention of his autograph, occurring where it does, shows that he wrote the whole letter with his own hand instead of employing an amanuensis as usual. So De W. and Alf., and Ellic. and Oltr. think it not improbable. (See Lightf. and Ellic. on Gal. vi. 11.)

ἐγὼ ἀποτίσω: 'I will repay it.' Probably without any serious expectation that Philemon would demand payment; but yet not as a mere graceful pleasantry (as v. Sod., Mey., Oltr.). Oltr. imagines how Philemon must have laughed at such a promise from a man who had not a penny in the world. But why? Paul on his anticipated release from prison might have found means to pay if payment should be demanded, just as he found means to live in prison or to earn the money by his own labor as he had done more than once.

ἵνα μὴ λέγω σοι: 'not to say to thee.' (Comp. 2 Cor. ix. 4.) A sort of elliptical construction in which the writer delicately protests against saying something which he nevertheless does say. Similar phrases are οὐχ ὅτι (Phil. iv. 11); οὐχ οἷον ὅτι (Rom. ix. 6). In many such cases the phrase becomes stereotyped, and the connection with a suppressed thought is not consciously present to the writer. The thought completely expressed would be: 'I agree to assume the obligation *in order to avoid* mentioning your great personal debt to me.'

ὅτι καὶ σεαυτόν μοι προσοφείλεις: 'that thou owest me also thine own self besides.' You owe to me your conversion. The καὶ 'also,' and πρὸς (προσοφ.) 'in addition to' are correlated. You are my debtor not only to the amount for which I here become responsible, but *also* for your own self *in addition to that.* Even if you remit the debt, you will still owe me yourself. Προσοφείλειν only here in N.T.

20. ναί, ἀδελφέ: 'yea, brother.' Ναί is a particle of confirmation. See on Phil. iv. 3, and comp. Matt. xv. 27; Rom. iii. 29; Apoc. xiv. 13. It confirms the request in vs. 17.

ἐγώ σου ὀναίμην ἐν κυρίῳ: 'let me have profit from thee in the Lord.' The ἐγώ is emphatic. Receive *him*, and so may *I* be profited. I ask for him as a favor to myself. This emphasis delicately points to Onesimus, and the allusion is strengthened by the play on his name in ὀναίμην. Ὀνίνασθαι 'to have profit or advantage.' Only here in N.T. It is common in class. with the genitive of that from which profit accrues. See Hom. *Il.* xvi. 31; *Od.* xix. 68; Eurip. *Med.* 1025, 1348: Aristoph. *Thesm.* 469. Also Ign. *Polyc.* i. vi; *Mag.* ii. xii; *Eph.* ii.

ἐν κυρίῳ: Not material advantage, but advantage accruing from their both being in Christ, and from the act as a Christian act.

ἀνάπαυσόν: see on vs. 7.

μου τὰ σπλάγχνα: 'my heart.' Not a designation of Onesimus. (Comp. vs. 12.)

21, 22. *Being assured of your obedient spirit, I write to you, knowing that you will do even more than I ask. While you thus receive Onesimus, be ready to receive me also, and prepare a lodging for me, since I hope that, in answer to your prayers, I may soon be permitted to visit you.*

21. πεποιθὼς τῇ ὑπακοῇ σου: 'having confidence in thine obedience.' Not recurring to the note of authority in vs. 8, but meaning his obedience to the claims of Christian duty as they shall appeal to his conscience.

ἔγραψά σοι: 'I write to thee.' See on vs. 19.

ὑπὲρ ἃ λέγω: 'above what I say.' For ὑπέρ, see on vs. 16. It is not certain that he alludes to the manumission of Onesimus (De W., Oltr., Reuss, Godet), though this may possibly be implied. The expression is general. My confidence in your love and obedience assures me that you will more than fulfil my request.

22. ἅμα δὲ: 'but withal.' At the same time with your kindly reception of Onesimus. For ἅμα see Acts xxiv. 26, xxvii. 40; Col. iv. 3; 1 Tim. v. 13.

ἑτοίμαζέ μοι ξενίαν: 'prepare me a lodging,' or 'entertainment.' Indicating his hope of speedy liberation as expressed in Phil. ii. 24. According to Phil. ii. 24, Paul proposed to go to Macedonia in the event of his liberation; whereas here he expresses a wish to go immediately to Colossæ. (See Weiss, *Einl.* § 24.) But between writing the two letters, he might have found reason to change his mind; or he might take Philippi on his way from Rome to Colossæ, since Philippi was on the great high-road between Europe and Asia. (See Hort, *The Romans and the Ephesians*, pp. 103, 104.)

ξενίαν: Only here and Acts xxviii. 23. Suid. and Hesych. define 'an inn, καταγώγιον, κατάλυμα.' Ξενισθῶμεν, however, Acts xxi. 16, is used of entertainment in a private house. The primary meaning of ξενία is 'hospitality,' 'friendly entertainment or reception.' Ἐλθεῖν ἐπὶ ξενίαν is 'to come seeking entertainment' (Pind. *N.* 49); ἐπὶ ξενίαν καλεῖν is 'to invite as a guest' (Dem. 81, 20). Comp. *Clem. Hom.* xii. 2, προάξωσιν τὰς ξενίας ἑτοιμάζοντες. The phrase here may therefore mean, 'prepare to entertain me.'

διὰ τῶν προσευχῶν ὑμῶν: Comp. Phil. i. 19.

χαρισθήσομαι: 'I shall be granted' or 'given.' As a favor by God, and perhaps with a friendly assumption that his coming will be regarded by them as a favor. I shall be graciously restored to you who desire my safety, and who will welcome my restoration. (See Acts iii. 14, xxvii. 24.)

SALUTATIONS

23. All the persons saluted are named in the salutations of Col. except Jesus Justus.

Ἐπαφρᾶς: Paul's delegate to the Colossians (Col. i. 7). A Colossian, and not to be identified with Epaphroditus of Phil. ii. 25, on which see note.

Μάρκος: Probably John Mark, the son of Mary (Acts xii. 12, 25, xv. 37). Called ὁ ἀνεψιὸς Βαρνάβα (Col. iv. 10). The first mention of him since the separation twelve years before (Acts xv. 39) occurs in Col. and Philem. (Comp. 2 Tim. iv. 11 with the account of the separation.) He is commended to the church at Colossæ (Col. iv. 10). In 1 Pet. v. 13 he sends salutation to Asia, and appears to be there some years after the date of Col. and Philem. (2 Tim. iv. 11).

Ἀρίσταρχος: A Thessalonian who started with Paul on his voyage to Rome (Acts xxvii. 2). On his leaving Paul at Myra, see Introd. V. In Col. iv. 10, 11, he is mentioned with Mark and Jesus Justus as being of the circumcision. He appears at Ephesus as Paul's companion (Acts xix. 29), and as accompanying the apostle on his return from Greece through Macedonia to Troas (Acts xx. 4).

Δημᾶς: Contraction of Δημήτριος. Probably a Thessalonian (Col. iv. 14, comp. 2 Tim. iv. 10.)

Λουκᾶς: The evangelist. His connection with Paul first appears Acts xvi. 10, where he accompanies the apostle to Macedonia.

He remained at Philippi after Paul's departure, and was there seven years later, when Paul visited the city (Acts xx. 5, 6). He accompanied the apostle to Jerusalem (Acts xxi. 15), after which we lose sight of him until he appears at Cæsarea (Acts xxvii. 2), whence he accompanies Paul to Rome.

Note on "The Church that is in Thy House" (vs. 2)

The basilica did not appear until the third century. The oldest witnesses for special church buildings are Clem. Alex. *Strom.* vii. c. 5, and Hippol. *Fragm.* ed. Lagarde, p. 149. Both witnesses represent the beginning of the third century, about 202 A.D., and are older than the commonly cited passages in Tert. *Adv. Valent.* c. 3 (205–8 A.D.).

The liberty of assembling was due to the fact that in the Roman Empire Christians at this time passed as a Jewish sect. The Jews were allowed to assemble under the special exemptions granted by Julius Cæsar and Augustus, which declared their communities legally authorised, and gave them the right to establish societies in all places (Joseph. *Antiq.* xiv. 10, 8). They thus availed themselves of the widely spread institution of *collegia* or *sodalitates* which had prevailed in the empire from a very early period. Numerous clubs or confraternities existed, composed either of the members of different trades, of the servants of a particular household, or of the worshippers of a particular deity. A special object of these clubs was to provide decent burial for their members. A fund was raised by contribution, from which burial expenses were defrayed, and also the expenses of the annual feasts held on the birthdays of the deceased. (See *Antiochene Acts of Martyrdom of Ignatius*, vii.; Pliny's *Letter to Trajan*; Tert. *Apol.* 39.) For the celebration of these feasts special buildings were erected called *scholae*. Sometimes a columbarium was purchased by a club for its own use.

This right of forming *collegia* was at first freely granted to all parties under the republic, but began to be restricted before the close of the republican period. (See Cicero, *Orat. in L. Calp. Pison.* c. 4; and Livy's account of the extirpation of the Bacchanalian rites, xxxix. 8.)

Julius Cæsar suppressed all but the most ancient *collegia* (Suet. *Julius*, 42), and his decrees were confirmed by Augustus (Suet. *Augustus*, 32). From the operation of these edicts, however, the Jews were exempted. They had only to refrain from meeting in a single general association. They were allowed the free exercise of their worship, and government by the chiefs of their synagogues. It was easy for the Christians to take advantage of the general misconception which confounded them with the Jews, and to hold their assemblies. At a later period, when they became more distinct, and their ordinary assemblies were forbidden, they availed themselves of those exceptions to the Julian and Augustan edicts which allowed the existence of benefit-clubs among the poor for funeral purposes, and permitted them to meet once a week. This exception became important under Hadrian (A.D. 117–138).

See Edwin Hatch, *Organization of the Early Christian Churches;* E. Loening, *Gemeindeverfassung;* W. M. Ramsay, *The Church in the Roman Empire*, etc.; J. S. Northcote and W. R. Brownlow, *Roma Sotteranea*, 2d ed.; R. Lanciani, *Ancient Rome in the Light of Recent Excavations*, p. 128; and *Pagan and Christian Rome*, p. 117; De Rossi, *Roma Sotteranea*, i. p. 209.

INDEX OF SUBJECTS

INDEX OF GREEK WORDS

References to Philemon are denoted by P.